PROJECT MANAGEMENT

Tools and Trade-Offs

PROJECT MANAGEMENT

Tools and Trade-Offs

TED KLASTORIN

University of Washington

www.wiley.com/college/klastorin

Acquisitions Editor   *Beth Lang Golub*
Editorial Assistant   *Ailsa Manny*
Media Editor   *Allie Keim*
Marketing Manager   *Gitti Lindner*
Managing Editor   *Lari Bishop*
Associate Production Manager   *Kelly Tavares*
Production Editor   *Sarah Wolfman-Robichaud*
Illustration Editors   *Jennifer Fisher and Kris Pauls*
Cover Design   *Jennifer Fisher*
Cover Image   © Chad J. Shaffer/Stock Illustration Source/Images.com.

This book was set in Times by Leyh Publishing LLP. It was printed by RR Donnelly–Willard. The cover was printed by Phoenix Color Corp.

This book is printed on acid-free paper. ∞

USA ISBN: 0-471-41384-4
WIE ISBN: 0-471-45186-X

Printed in the United States of America

10 9 8 7 6 5 4 3 2 1

To Susan, Rachel, and Anna,
whose presence are my blessings.

BRIEF CONTENTS

CONTENTS

PREFACE

For most of my professional career, I have had a great interest in the area of project management (PM), but became intensely interested in this area almost nineteen years ago when I started working with Microsoft Corporation to design the original version of their PM software, Microsoft Project. At the same time, I began working on several projects as a manager and consultant. As I continued working in the PM area, I became increasingly frustrated by a "disconnect" that I saw between the tools that have been developed to assist project managers and the complex problems and issues faced by real-world project managers. As a result, I started developing materials that I felt would deal with the complex issues and trade-offs faced by most project managers and would illustrate how and when PM tools might be helpful to managers dealing with these issues.

To test these materials, I developed an MBA elective course in project management at the University of Washington and began to refine the course materials with the help of colleagues, students, and practitioners. Given the increasing emphasis in most university curricula on spreadsheet modeling, we based many of these materials on spreadsheet templates. The materials that proved successful in our educational experiments form the basis of this book. In addition, I have included many new concepts that are being explored both by academics and practitioners, and related these ideas (such as Goldratt's concept of a critical chain) to previous approaches. Finally, I have tried to include many new ideas reported in recent research; much of this work has been invisible to practicing managers but has significant implications and needs to be brought into classrooms, executive programs, and conference rooms.

It has been very gratifying to see how well this course has succeeded; it is now one of the most popular elective courses in the MBA program at the UW Business School. In addition, we offer a PM elective in our undergraduate program, as well as a required PM course in our Technology Management MBA (TMMBA) program and our new MSIS (Master of Science in Information Systems) program. Other PM-related courses at the University of Washington are offered in Construction Management (Architecture), Industrial Engineering, Health Services Management (School of Public Health & Community Medicine), Technical Communications, and Forest Resources. It is evident that this is an area of significant and increasing importance. I hope that this book and related materials encourage and assist other instructors to develop and teach their own PM courses.

In writing this book, my goal is to describe the underlying foundations on which most project management decisions are made and relate this foundation to practitioners' needs and goals. The book presents the fundamental concepts of project management in a concise fashion with an emphasis on the difficult trade-offs that must be made by most project managers. In addition, it emphasizes the "disconnect" between the commercially available methodologies and tools and the uncertain, risky projects that project managers have to manage in the real world. This link between theory and practice is illustrated in a variety of ways, including case studies, games, and study problems. In addition, I have tried

- to present the fundamental concepts of project management in a concise fashion with an emphasis on the difficult trade-offs that must be made by most project managers,
- to describe the tools and methodologies that have been developed to assist project managers using spreadsheet models and templates,
- to show how these tools and methodologies can be extended to deal with more realistic problems, and
- to integrate current research into PM educational materials.

The book uses spreadsheets to explain many PM concepts and methodologies. Most students today are familiar with spreadsheets and can easily relate to their use and application. I have tried to include all models that have important applications or present valuable insights for students and practitioners. These models are described analytically using both basic algebraic notation as well as spreadsheets. All spreadsheet models were created using Microsoft Excel 2001 and are included on the CD-ROM accompanying this book. I hope that these spreadsheet models will allow students to explore PM issues that are not addressed by commercial PM software (e.g., the time-cost trade-off problem).

I have tried to relate the material in the book to other business and engineering courses; for example, there is material on budgeting (relating to managerial accounting), the impact of organization design on project success (relating to organizational theory), project teams (courses in organizational behavior), project scheduling (relating to operations management courses), new product development (relating to marketing courses), and considerable material throughout the book on software project management (relating to courses in information systems). As such, the subject matter should relate to students in a variety of areas, including information systems, marketing, industrial engineering, and operations management students, among others.

There has been a great deal of recent research that is relevant to project managers but doesn't appear in most PM textbooks. For this reason, I have included much of this material into the text, including project taxonomies, recent work done on the effects of uncertainty on subcontracting and bidding, work on material management and purchasing in projects, work on software project management, and current research on risk management.

Finally, I have included a number of new cases, games, and study problems that have proven helpful in illustrating some of the complex issues faced by project managers. Included among these is the New Product Development Game, an interactive board game that I developed (with Chris Sandvig) and have used in numerous classes and executive programs. The game is especially useful for relating the concepts of project management to the problems of new product development in a high-tech environment (the game is based on the development of a hand-held marine radar unit). This game can be played in one class session or used as a case study.

This book is intended for use in undergraduate and graduate project management elective courses at most universities and colleges. In addition, it is expected that the book will serve as a general reference text and could be used in executive programs.

This book is written so that it can be used with a minimum number of prerequisites (I assume that the reader has had some basic exposure to linear and integer programming, understands basic concepts of probability and statistics, and is familiar with basic spreadsheets).

Finally, I welcome your comments and suggestions. I want to create a text that will provide a substantive and meaningful project management course that will motivate all stakeholders to consider issues beyond a superficial level. Any assistance that you can provide in this regard will be sincerely appreciated (and acknowledged). I can be contacted by e-mail at tedk@u.washington.edu.

ORGANIZATION OF THE TEXT

The book is organized somewhat differently than most other PM textbooks; for example, the issue of random task durations is discussed throughout most of the book (and not simply discussed in one chapter). In doing so, we can address the issue of a possible "disconnect" between most PM software (that assumes everything is deterministic) and real-world projects (that are subject to randomness in both time and cost). The text initially discusses an overview of project management and PM's importance in today's economic environment. Chapter 2 discusses the issues of project initiation and selection and presents a number of tools (including options theory) for evaluating project proposals. Chapter 2 also introduces project planning, including work breakdown structures and time and cost estimation. Chapter 3 discusses organizational and behavioral issues, including several issues relating to the formation and supervision of project teams. Chapter 4 presents the basics of the critical path method (CPM) and shows how they relate to managing project schedules. Chapter 5 extends the CPM to deal with costs (e.g., cash flows, time-cost trade-offs). The issue of randomness is further discussed in Chapter 6, including a discussion of the Classic PERT model and current methods (e.g., Monte Carlo simulation) for avoiding the pitfalls associated with that methodology. Chapter 7 is devoted to risk management, the task that occupies much of a project manager's time and effort. Chapter 8 discusses resource leveling and resource allocation, both when resource requirements are deterministic and when such requirements are uncertain. Chapter 9 deals with monitoring and control systems, and the final chapter (Chapter 10) deals with the management of multiple projects.

TEACHING SUGGESTIONS

This book is intended to provide a concise overview of most PM tools and fundamental concepts. In addition to the cases and study problems that are included in the text, I generally use a number of (field) case studies. I have tried to select cases that both reinforce the trade-offs discussed in the book and bring real-world complications and behavioral aspects into the classroom. Most of the case studies I have used are offered by Harvard Business School Publishing or the European Case Clearing House. In addition, I have found that careful selection of outside speakers can reinforce many of the concepts emphasized in the book and give students who have not been directly involved in managing a complex project a good sense of the difficulties and issues involved in managing messy real-world projects.

SOFTWARE ACCOMPANYING THE TEXT

The CD-ROM that accompanies the text includes the following resources for students:

- **Microsoft Project 2002:** A student version of the popular project management software package.
- **@Risk:** An add-in to Microsoft Project 2002 that increases the functionality of MS Project by letting the user easily construct powerful Monte-Carlo simulations.
- **PowerPoint slides:** A PowerPoint presentation with over 200 slides prepared by the author supports the material in the text.
- **Spreadsheet Templates:** Excel spreadsheets/templates for all models discussed in the text.

SUPPLEMENTARY MATERIALS

The following supplementary material is provided for adopting instructors on the text's companion Web site (www.wiley.com/college/klastorin):

- **PowerPoint slides:** A PowerPoint presentation with over 200 slides prepared by the author supports the material in the text.
- **Instructor's Manual/Solutions Guide:** Solutions for all homework problems and suggested teaching guides for case studies.

ACKNOWLEDGEMENTS

No text or work such as this is ever completed by one person, and this book is no exception; this is truly the joint contribution of many people over many years (although any errors or omissions are mine alone). I have learned much from my colleagues at the University of Washington, with special thanks to Professor Karen Brown. I owe great debts to my doctoral students over the years, including Professors Avy Shtub (Technion Israel Institute of Technology), Chris Sandvig (Western Washington University), Prabhu Aggarwal (College of William and Mary), Mark Cutler (Northwest Airlines), Weiyu Tsai (University of Utah), and Gary Mitchell. I am also grateful for the many suggestions and comments from Professors Phil Lederer (University of Rochester), Marty Wilson (University of Minnesota), Genaro Gutierrez (University of Texas), Charles Franz (University of Missouri), Frank Cesario (Keller School of Management), David Overbye (Keller School of Management), William Sherrard (San Diego State University), Richard Sheng (DeVry Institute of Technology), Karol Pelc (Michigan Technological University), Richard Peschke (Moorhead State University), Steve Robinson (University of Idaho), Jeffrey Reed (Marian College of Fond du Lac), Michael Poli (Wesley Howe School of Technology Management), Michael Ensby (Clarkson University), Raja Balakrishnan (Clemson University), Michael Vincenti (Central Connecticut State University), William Ibbs (University of California at Berkeley), and John Gleason (Creighton University). As mentioned previously, I have learned a great deal and developed enormous respect for those managers who are "on the line" managing complex projects with real costs and real risks; two of the best are Steve Levy (Microsoft) and Brian Cline (Boeing Corporation). Many of my MBA students over the years have served as guinea pigs with this material; I am especially grateful to Jack Eisenhower and Robert Barrick for their contributions to this book. For all other students who offered many helpful suggestions and comments, I sincerely and collectively thank them.

In addition, I am deeply grateful to the assistance and support from folks at John Wiley & Sons; if it weren't for Beth Golub, editor *par excellence,* I would probably be using this book as an example of a project that never got finished (or started for that matter). The assistance of Gitti Lindner and Ailsa Manny at John Wiley, and Michele Chancellor and Lari Bishop at Leyh Publishing has been most helpful and most appreciated. I would also like to thank Christianne Thillen for her valued suggestions. And last, but never least, my family truly created a project team that provided support and motivation that can never be adequately acknowledged.

ABOUT THE AUTHOR

Ted Klastorin is the Burlington Northern/Burlington Resources Professor of Operations Management in the Department of Management Science (School of Business), Adjunct Professor in the Department of Health Services (School of Public Health and Community Medicine), and Adjunct Professor of Industrial Engineering (College of Engineering) at the University of Washington–Seattle. He holds a B.S. degree from Carnegie-Mellon University (1969) and a Ph.D. from the University of Texas at Austin (1973).

Professor Klastorin is a senior research fellow at the IC^2 Institute, The University of Texas–Austin. He previously taught at the Babcock Graduate School of Management, Wake Forest University (Winston-Salem, North Carolina), as well as the University of Washington and the University of Texas. At the UW, he was the founding chair of the Management Science Department and a co-founder of the PEMM Program (Program in Engineering and Manufacturing Management)—a joint program of the College of Engineering and the School of Business.

Professor Klastorin's research interests include project management and supply chain management issues in manufacturing and service organizations. His current research projects include the study of uncertain disruptive events (e.g., strikes) on project planning and coordination issues in decentralized supply chains. His recent articles have appeared in *IIE Transactions, Journal of Applied Psychology, Management Science* and the *Wisconsin Law Review*.

Professor Klastorin has consulted with numerous organizations, including Boeing, Starbucks, Fluke Corp, and Microsoft (where he has assisted with the design of Microsoft Project). He is a member of INFORMS (Institute for Operations Research and the Management Sciences), IIE (Institute of Industrial Engineers), and POMS (Production and Operations Management Society), and serves on the editorial boards of *Manufacturing & Service Operations Management (M&SOM)* and *IIE Transactions*.

CHAPTER 1

INTRODUCTION TO PROJECT MANAGEMENT

What is behind the rapidly increasing demand for project management software, consultants, books, and training? Why are so many people focusing on project management today? What can project management offer that other management methodologies cannot?

The reasons for the rapidly increasing focus on project management (PM) are evident from a careful examination of the current business landscape. Perhaps most important, project management is synonymous with change management. Organizations that want to change their focus or direction increasingly recognize that implementing real change requires the introduction of new products, processes, or programs in a timely and cost-effective manner.

Rapid change has become an essential survival requirement for most organizations today. As product life cycles continue to decrease, new products and services must be developed and implemented as quickly and efficiently as possible. In addition, products are becoming obsolete at an increasing rate. Griffin and Page (1993) report that as much as 50 percent of a typical firm's revenues comes from products that were introduced in the last five years—compared to an estimate of 33 percent in the 1980s and 20 percent in the 1970s (Takeuchi and Nonaka, 1986). Shorter product life cycles require that the selection and development of new products be managed in a cost-effective manner that maximizes the chances of commercial success. In some industries, managers have considerably less than five years to develop, produce, and market new products. For example, Yang (2000) points out that the communications industry is subject to the 4–3–3 rule: four months to develop a new product, three months to make money from it, and three months to get it off the shelf. Consultants at McKinsey & Co. estimated that a typical firm's gross profit potential for a new product is reduced by approximately 12 percent if the product is introduced three months late, and 25 percent if five months late (Vesey, 1992). Yang stated the case for new product development very succinctly: "Time to market means life or death, and anything that can tip the scale in your favor is precious." Increasing numbers of managers are recognizing that effective project management can provide a significant part of that advantage.

The nature of projects has changed in the past decade as well. Project management has been used since the time of the Egyptian pyramids almost five thousand years ago. While we don't know if the Egyptian pyramids were completed on schedule and within budget, we do know that organizations today routinely conduct projects in complex global environments that make coordination and communication much more difficult than when the Egyptians were building five thousand years ago. Many of these projects, especially information technology (IT) projects, represent significant investments to an organization such that project failure can mean organizational demise. Project managers must use methods that will maximize the probability that these projects will be successful.

Given the increasing importance of managing complex projects, it is disturbing to see the high number of projects that fail to meet their basic goals. In a survey of twenty-three thousand application projects, the Standish Group reported that only 26 percent of the projects in 1998 were completely successful, while 46 percent of the projects were "challenged" (that is, completed but over budget and/or time with fewer functions than originally designed) and 28 percent were considered to be failures (Standish Group, 1999). According the Standish Group, these failed projects cost almost $75 billion in 1998.

The statistics reported by the Standish Group are disturbingly consistent with other studies. Bounds (1998) reported that only 26 percent of IT projects were completed on time and within budget. Yeo (1999) reported that approximately 31 percent of the two hundred thousand software development projects undertaken by U.S. companies in 1999 were canceled or abandoned before completion, representing a loss of almost $62 million. Yeo also reported that only 13 percent of IT system projects were considered successful by sponsoring managers, while only 16.2 percent of software development projects were completed on time and within budget.

Additional examples illustrate the importance of PM success and the high costs of PM failure. On the success side, BC Hydro recently completed a power plant replacement project in British Columbia, Canada on time and 21 percent under budget by using professional PM techniques. Effective PM not only saved BC Hydro millions of dollars but also demonstrated how these "techniques ensure that projects succeed technically, environmentally, and socially" (Water Power, 2000). In Germany, archaeologists have found that PM tools offer an effective way to manage the exploration and excavation of archaeological sites (Walker, 1996). In another success story, Taco Bell managers described how they completely rebuilt a Taco Bell restaurant that had been destroyed by fire. The managers were able to dramatically reduce the normal time for this project from sixty days to forty-eight hours by carefully applying PM techniques in fifteen-minute time increments (Industrial Engineering, 1992). These examples indicate what PM can accomplish when there is thorough planning, skillful implementation, and good luck.

Conversely, there have been many notable project failures. The computerized baggage-handling system at the Denver International Airport delayed the opening of the airport for more than a year and added $85 million to the original budget. The project to build a tunnel under the English Channel cost £3 billion more than its original estimate and took two years longer than planned. Even Mickey Mouse has been unable to escape the difficulties imposed by managing complex projects, as many of Disney's frustrated customers would testify (see the accompanying article).

Given this recent history of project experience, professional project management offers a methodology that has been carefully defined, refined, and successfully applied over the past fifty years. Project management is a well-developed system that can help organizations meet their goals in a timely fashion. As a result, project management has become an essential part of high-technology management, a critical element of electronic commerce, and an important part of the globalization movement that has transformed the world economy in the past ten years. Given the size and scope of all projects undertaken annually, it is clear why project management has become a major focus of global business and government. In fact, project management itself is now estimated to be an $850 million industry that is expected to grow by as much as 20 percent annually (Bounds, 1998).

This book introduces the basic concepts of project management in order to give managers a clear understanding of the tools and trade-offs that complex projects require. Throughout the book, we focus on the problems faced by managers who must complete complex projects. In this first chapter, we consider the following issues:

- What is project management, and how does it differ from other forms of management (e.g., program management)?
- What is a project?
- How do you define project success and failure?

- What are some notable examples of project success and failure, and what lessons can be learned from these case studies?
- How do IT projects differ from other projects?
- What is a PM life cycle?
- What are some common life-cycle models?
- How can you consider project risk?
- What is the history of project management?
- What is the nature of PM software?

WHAT DEFINES A PROJECT?

What is a project, and how does it differ from a program? According to the Project Management Institute (2000), a project is a "temporary endeavor undertaken to create a unique product or service." Alternatively, a project can be viewed as a well-defined set of tasks or activities that must all be completed in order to meet the project's goals. Typically, we assume that these tasks or activities that constitute a project are defined such that:

- Each task may be started or stopped independently of each other (within a given sequence), and
- Tasks are ordered such that they must be performed in a technological sequence (e.g., you must build the walls of a house before the roof).

In addition, we usually assume that once tasks are started, they cannot be preempted (i.e., stopped) and must be continued until completed.

Several implications follow from this definition. First, projects have a well-defined life span between the time when the first task is started and the last task is completed (although, in reality, it is sometimes difficult to tell when a project is fully completed). Since projects consist of specific, well-defined tasks, there are usually specific goals allocated to the project; these goals usually include quality and design specifications as well as cost and schedule goals. In general, these goals are oriented toward the project's targeted customer, which may differ from an organization's typical customer base (e.g., a project that is designed for a specific client).

In addition, projects have several other unique characteristics. Projects are generally characterized by the use of multifunctional project teams. In fact, the current widespread

DELAYED OPENINGS ARE A FACT OF LIFE IN THE FOODSERVICE, HOSPITALITY INDUSTRY

Disney's shipbuilder was six months late in delivering its new cruise ships, and thousands of customers who had purchased tickets were stranded. Even with that experience, their second ship was also delivered well after the published schedules. Universal Studios in Orlando, Florida, had been building a new restaurant and entertainment complex for more than two years. They advertised a December opening, only to announce in late November that it would be two or three months late.

Even when facilities do open close to schedule, they are rarely finished completely and are often missing key components. Why do those things happen? With all of the sophisticated computers and project management software, why aren't projects completed on schedule?

Source: F. Frable, *Nation's Restaurant News* (12 April 1999).

use of multifunctional teams in most organizations is an outgrowth of early PM practice. The benefit from using project teams is now widely recognized, although it is less clear how to organize and manage these teams.

Given that projects must be completed in a finite time, resources are usually not acquired for specific projects but are drawn from other parts of the organization. An exception occurs when organizations hire part-time employees for a specific project, or subcontract part (or all) of the project. Nevertheless, it remains that projects must generally fit into the overall portfolio of experience and knowledge available in an organization.

All types of organizations undertake projects, including public and private organizations, as well as profit and nonprofit organizations (and individuals); for an interesting example, see the accompanying article by Janofsky "From Politics to Pies: New Life for Former Arizona Governor." Examples of projects include:

- Great pyramid built by King Cheops (Egypt)
- Finding a job after college graduation
- End-of-the-month closing of accounting records
- Installing and debugging a new computer system
- Planning and launching a new product
- Running a campaign for political office
- Maintenance and repair projects
- Trying to get tickets to a World Series baseball game

The definition of a project helps to differentiate projects from programs—the latter being ongoing operations that continue indefinitely and are larger in scope and duration than most projects. Unlike program managers, project managers strive to put themselves out of business as quickly as possible. It should be noted, however, that project management can be (and often is) applied to programs that are often composed of multiple projects. For example, consider an aircraft assembly line. In one sense, this line can be viewed as a continuous assembly process. However, in another sense, each aircraft can also be viewed as a separate project, with PM techniques applied to each aircraft on the line. This relationship between projects and continuous-flow production processes will be explored in more detail in later chapters.

Not All Projects Are the Same

Throughout much of this book, generic projects are discussed. Projects, however, are obviously not the same; a project to develop a complex new software product is quite different from, say, a road construction project. In the former case, the project design and scope may be difficult to clearly define, the external environment is rapidly changing, and the IT staff developing the software is usually involved with many other activities and projects. In contrast, most construction projects proceed in isolation from other projects; while there are many uncertain factors, of course, most would agree that a road construction project is more likely to meet its goals than most software development projects. In addition, it is far easier to measure progress on a construction project where progress (or lack thereof) is quite visible than on an IT project that typically proceeds from 0 to 90 percent completion in the final minutes of the project.

A number of researchers (including Yap and Souder, 1994; Brown and Eisenhardt; 1997; and Eisenhardt and Tabrizi, 1995; among others) have studied project types and argued that different project types require different organizational structures as well as strategies and management styles. For example, a highly centralized and hierarchical organization with limited communication may be very effective with road construction projects but would probably not fare well when developing a technologically complex new product in a highly uncertain environment.

Based on studies of engineering-based new product (or process or service) development projects, Shenhar (2001) suggested that projects can be classified by two dimensions: complexity and uncertainty. As indicated in Figure 1.1, one dimension indicates the relative degree of technological uncertainty/risk in a project, ranging from low-tech projects that use well-established and stable technologies (e.g., construction projects) to super-high-tech projects that require the development of new technologies during the course of the project itself (e.g., the Apollo moon landing project). Along this continuum, Shenhar defined medium-tech projects and high-tech projects. Medium-tech projects extend a stable technology in new directions (e.g., product upgrades); these types of projects are the most typical industrial projects. A high-tech project, on the other hand, represents a project that may be applying a new technology for the first time.

The second dimension used to define the taxonomy in Figure 1.1 is project complexity or system scope. According to Shenhar, a project with limited complexity is "a subsystem performing a well-defined function within a larger system, or it can be an independent stand-alone product that performs a single function of a limited scale." Shenhar refers to these types of projects as **assembly projects.** On the other end of the complexity spectrum are **array projects,** geographically dispersed projects that require the integration of many sophisticated subsystems; an example is the implementation of an ERP (Enterprise Resource Planning) system at a large multinational firm. Between the high and low complexity are **systems projects;** these types of projects require the development of numerous subsystems that, in turn, will define a functioning product (or process or service). Shenhar's taxonomy is represented in Figure 1.1.

FIGURE 1.1
Shenhar's Taxonomy of
Project Types

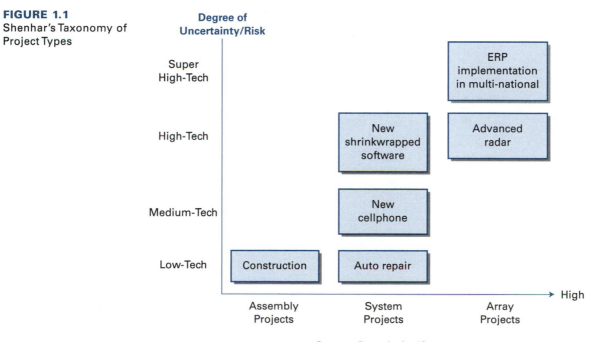

Throughout this book, it is useful to keep Shenhar's taxonomy in mind. Not surprisingly, Shenhar found that a project's location in his taxonomy has significant implications for organizational design, communication and control systems, resource planning and scheduling, extent of testing, and the need for prototype building. As project scope and complexity increase, for example, projects require more formal planning and control and communication systems; organizations associated with these types of projects tend to be larger, more formal, and more bureaucratic. These implications are further discussed in Chapter 3.

An alternative taxonomy for development project types was suggested by Wheelwright and Clark (1992) who also classified projects on two dimensions: the degree of product change, and the degree of manufacturing process change. Using this two-dimensional classification scheme, the authors identified various project types that require different resource levels and management styles. For example, in the area of low product and process change, they identified *derivative projects* as projects that make relatively minor enhancements to existing products. According to Wheelwright and Clark, derivative projects produce incremental change in the product and/or the process (e.g., a change in packaging, a new feature, or improved quality). *Platform projects* make significant changes in the product and/or process but avoid the major changes that occur with *breakthrough projects*. The former projects result in significant product and/or process improvements based on developed and proven technologies (examples include the Apple iMac computer and some new car models); breakthrough projects represent radically new products and/or processes (examples include the NASA space shuttle and the development of cell phones). Breakthrough projects typically result in the development of new markets; breakthrough projects have a high degree of risk and complexity. The taxonomy suggested by Wheelwright and Clark is indicated in Figure 1.2.

FIGURE 1.2
Project Taxonomy Suggested by Wheelwright and Clark

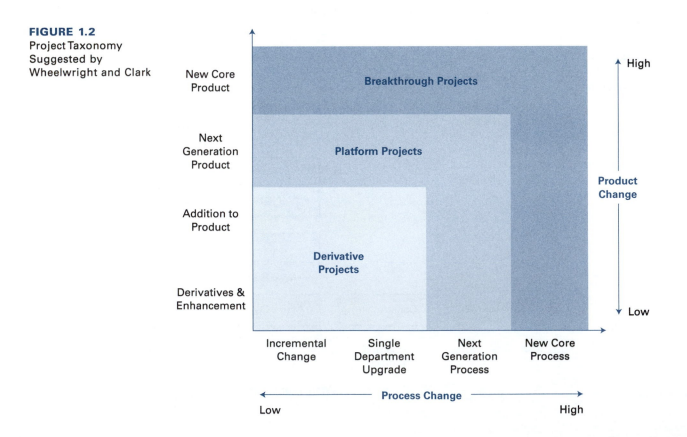

FROM POLITICS TO PIES: NEW LIFE FOR FORMER ARIZONA GOVERNOR

PHOENIX, April 4—It was not so many years ago that Fife Symington considered his proudest achievement the fiscal well-being of Arizona. As governor through much of the 1990s, he presided over tax reductions, income growth, and surging capital investments, a stewardship that made him a rising star in the Republican Party.

These days, Mr. Symington's main sources of professional pride include a tangy cheesecake laced with mascarpone, a Florentine frozen meringue filled with amaretto cream and a coffee-flavored chocolate cake known as the Governor, his signature dessert, which promises "low tax, high taste."

While some former politicians slide easily into lives as lawyers, lobbyists, and corporate executives, Mr. Symington is that rare public servant who has become a pastry chef. On most mornings, he toils away at Franco's Italian Caffè, a new restaurant here, creating desserts that the owner-manager, Franco Fazzuoli, insists are every bit as popular as the appetizers, entrees, and brick-oven pizzas that Mr. Fazzuoli favored as a restaurateur in lower Manhattan—he owned Ponte Vecchio, Cent'Anni and Zinno—before moving west.

"You have to keep track of a lot of things," he said the other day. "There is always a critical path to getting a menu or a meal together, and there's a lot of pressure. But there's also something about working with a wonderful group of people in the kitchen. Some would hate it. I think it's magic."

Source: Michael Janofsky, "From Politics to Pies: New Life for Former Arizona Governor," *New York Times*, 6 April 2003.

MEASURES OF PROJECT SUCCESS/FAILURE

Since most projects have clearly defined cost and schedule goals, we typically judge a project's success by whether the project was completed within its budgeted amount and before its due date. However, such a judgment may be naive in the sense that most projects have many goals in addition to the budget and schedule goals. For example, did the project meet its specifications? Was the final product successful in the marketplace? Did the project succeed in increasing long-term market share, revenues, profits, etc.? Did the project add to the organization's learning that would give future projects a greater chance to succeed?

For example, consider the development of the movie *Titanic,* which was finally released in 1997 after several years of development. When the movie was finally released, it was significantly delayed behind its original schedule and $90 million over its original budget of $110 million (an 82 percent cost overrun). However, the movie clearly succeeded in the marketplace, winning numerous awards (including the best picture of 1997) as well as becoming the first movie in history to gross over $1 billion in revenues. Was this project a success or a failure?

In some cases, projects may fail even though they are completed on time and within budget, as occurred with the Mars Lander project (see accompanying article). Even though the Mars probe crashed while trying to land, the project was a not complete failure in the sense that it generated new knowledge that may provide NASA a greater chance of succeeding on future missions. In other cases, projects may be undertaken as "loss leaders"; that is, an organization may knowingly undertake a project at a loss in order to gain a competitive edge when bidding on future contracts for similar projects, or to exert competitive pressure on a rival in a specific market.

Even when cost and schedule are the primary goals of a project, these goals may be difficult or even unrealistic to achieve, especially when set by senior managers who are not directly involved in a project's planning process. According to Frable (1999),

"…meeting outrageously short schedules seems to have become a badge of honor among certain owners and project managers…" It is little wonder that the PM consulting firm, Robbins-Gioia Inc., reported that 44 percent of all project managers have cost overruns ranging between 10 and 40 percent, and only 16 percent of managers consistently meet their scheduled due dates. In another study (*The Economist*, 2000), it was reported that "about 85 percent of all public-sector IT projects are deemed to be failures." The authors add "that does not mean they are total disasters, but that they usually take longer to implement, cost more and deliver less than was planned."

In a study examining project performance and organizational issues, Might and Fischer (1985) defined *six measures of project success:*

1. **Overall:** What is the overall perception of project success?

2. **Cost:** Is the final cost over or under the initial budget?

3. **Schedule:** Is the final completion time over or under the initial schedule?

4. **Technical goal 1:** What is the overall perception of the technical performance of the project compared to the initial specifications?

5. **Technical goal 2:** What is the overall perception of the technical performance of the project compared to other projects in the organization?

6. **Technical goal 3:** What is the overall perception of the technical performance of the project compared to the problems encountered during the project?

Might and Fischer also considered the possible correlation between these measures—is a project that meets its initial technical specifications more likely to be viewed as successful with respect to the second and third technical goals? In their survey of 103 development projects, Might and Fischer reported a positive correlation (0.68) between the cost and schedule goals, implying that projects that are delayed are more likely to have cost overruns. However, some of the other correlations indicate that managers often face a trade-off between technical goals on one hand and cost and schedule goals on the other. The correlation coefficients reported by Might and Fisher among the six measures of project success are given in Figure 1.3.

Four of these six measures are mostly subjective (only the cost and schedule goals have some objective basis), thus emphasizing the importance of meeting expectations to achieve project success.

Why do so many projects fail to meet expectations? A study by Hughes (1986) provides insight into some of the causes of project failure; according to Hughes, there are three main factors:

- A lack of understanding of PM tools and an overreliance on PM software

FIGURE 1.3
Correlations Among Measures of Project Success

	Overall Project Success	Cost	Schedule	Technical Goal 1	Technical Goal 2	Technical Goal 3
Overall Project Success	1	0.55	0.54	0.68	0.42	0.37
Cost		1	0.68	0.3	0.32	0.41
Schedule			1	0.36	0.29	0.4
Technical Goal 1				1	0.55	0.2
Technical Goal 2					1	0.28
Technical Goal 3						1

Source: R. Might and W. Fischer, 1985.

- Communication problems
- Failure to adequately adjust for changes that occur during the course of a project

In addition, Hughes notes that many managers lose sight of the project by focusing on PM software and managing the precedence network instead of the project. Hughes's observation, which has also been noted by others (including this author), is one of the reasons why this book does not emphasize PM software (although it is certainly mentioned) but focuses on basic concepts and trade-offs that project managers have to understand in order to successfully complete a project.

Hughes also observes that many project managers fail to reward those actions by project employees that contribute the most to meeting a project's most important goals. While it may be difficult to determine the relative benefit of individual actions, Hughes notes that such rewards can pay significant dividends.

Communication is clearly a major factor contributing to projects' outcomes; Michalski (2000) observes in her study of biotechnology projects that "good communication is the key to successful project management." Hughes states that projects fail when there are too many people involved, making communication difficult, but that no project has ever failed for having too few people. Failure also results when managers do not effectively communicate the project goals to other stakeholders and focus on unimportant project details. In this respect, the development of information technology is making communication issues easier to resolve; the Internet, fax machines, and even cellular telephones are helping to facilitate communication among project managers and teams, clients, and contractors (Schmidt, 2000; Bagli, C., 2000). Communication and coordination issues are further discussed in Chapter 3.

Finally, Hughes points out that managers fail to adjust for changes that always occur during the life of a project. To successfully manage a project, a manager must explicitly incorporate all changes into updated plans, budgets, and schedules and communicate these changes to all stakeholders associated with the project.

Hughes's conclusions are remarkably consistent with the findings of other authors. Examining numerous PM case studies, Pinto and Slevin (1987) identified nine factors that were critical to the success of many projects:

- Clearly defined goals
- Competent project manager
- Top management support
- Competent PM team members
- Sufficient resource allocation
- Adequate communication channels
- Control mechanisms
- Feedback capabilities
- Responsiveness to clients

While Pinto and Slevin did not indicate the relative importance of these factors, it appears from various other studies that having clearly defined goals, top management support, adequate communication, and an effective feedback and control mechanism are essential factors. Having these factors does not guarantee project success, but it is quite clear that *not* having these factors increases the likelihood of project failure significantly.

Many of the factors related to project success and failure are interrelated; that is, improving one factor will frequently improve others. For example, consider the use of PM software that offers the direct benefit of assisting with project scheduling, budgeting, and

Considered to be one of the finest baseball parks built in recent years, Safeco Field cost a total of $350 million—almost $100 million more than its original budget. Some officials charge that the cost overruns were the result of mismanagement and slack oversight.

control. In this case, these software packages can also improve communication among project stakeholders, especially Web-based PM software that also adds a critical feedback and control mechanism.

Information Technology Project Outcomes

Information technology (IT) projects have a high failure rate due to the enormous risks associated with these projects. After studying many IT projects, Flowers (1994) concluded that any IT project is a failure if:

- "the system as a whole does not operate as expected and its overall performance is sub-optimal";
- "…on implementation, it does not perform as originally intended or if it is so user-hostile that it is rejected by users and is under-utilized";
- "…The cost of the development exceeds any benefits the system may bring throughout its useful life"; and
- "…due to problems with the complexity of the system, or the management of the project, the IS development is abandoned before it is completed."

An examination of the effort by the Health Care Financing Administration (HCFA; the organization that administers the U.S. Medicare plan) to develop an IT system to administer Medicare claims sheds additional light on the causes of IT project failures (see appendix at the end of this chapter). Friel (2000) recently described the ill-fated effort by HCFA to develop a Medicare transaction system that was finally abandoned after six years of development and $50 million in costs. After studying the HCFA project failure, Friel concluded that the following lessons could be learned from the HCFA case:

- Set realistic milestones.
- Know what you want before you ask for it.
- Avoid mission creep.
- Have an investment review process.
- Manage expectations.
- Reduce risk as much as possible.

Friel points out that HCFA had given the primary contractor three years to submit a final product with little or no interim monitoring. This failure to define proper milestones and monitor the contractor's progress was a major factor in this project's failure. Likewise, Friel mentions that HCFA managers never fully understood their current systems and what they wanted their new system to do (no clearly identified goals). Due to this lack of understanding, HCFA managers made numerous changes in the specifications of the new system, causing significant delays and cost increases. Related to this lack of understanding, HCFA continuously added new requirements to the project as its managers learned more about the workings of their system.

Communication was also a problem. According to Friel, HCFA "promised the moon but delivered far less." The complexity of the system and the number of people involved clearly added to HCFA's communication problems. Finally, HCFA failed to implement effective incentives and controls for its contractors; Friel points out that HCFA has now moved to performance-based contracting for IT projects with appropriate milestones and incentives.

Many IT projects are undertaken without a clear statement of purpose or vision, as illustrated by the HCFA project. Furthermore, when such a statement does exist, it is frequently not communicated to the rest of the project team or organization. A second, and related, theme that appears common to many IT projects is a failure to set realistic goals. Not surprisingly, this often results when senior managers fail to adequately include project managers and team members in all phases of the planning process. The lack of effective communication appears to be a significant ingredient in most IT project failures.

Finally, the failure of many IT projects can be traced to factors that are exogenous to the organization. Technology continues to change at a rapid pace, as Gordon Moore's 1965 predictions continue to hold: every eighteen months, processor speeds and memory capacity appear to double for the same cost. The implication is clear. For an IT project that spans more than a year, the technology is most likely obsolete by the time the project is completed—assuming that the project is completed on time.

When to "Pull the Plug" on a Project

Related to the issue of project success and failure is the issue of knowing when to pull the plug on an ongoing project. Prematurely terminating a project means that there must exist an effective control and monitoring system as well as metrics that indicate when the project has reached a point where it can no longer be efficiently salvaged. Clearly, this is a difficult and challenging decision in most organizations where managers and workers are committed to successfully completing a project.

COOL YOUR JETS, NASA, TWO REVIEW PANELS URGE

Recent failures in two Mars missions suggest that NASA is pushing too hard to do more with less money and jeopardizing success by paying inadequate attention to risks, two review panels said today.... In its second report to the agency, the board that examined the failure of the Mars Climate Orbiter mission last year said lessons learned from that mishap and other failures with the quicker, cheaper approach indicated that there might have been too much emphasis on cutting costs and doing missions quickly. "The success of 'faster, better, cheaper' is tempered by the fact that some projects and programs have put too much emphasis on cost and schedule reduction," said the panel, the Mars Climate Orbiter Mishap Investigation Board, a group of NASA experts let by Arthur G. Stephenson, director of the Marshall Space Flight Center in Alabama.

Source: W. Leary, *New York Times*, 14 March 2000.

Losing sight of a project's goals can drive a project to failure.

THE FAR SIDE By GARY LARSON

"Say ... wait just a dang minute, here. ... We forgot the cattle!"

Staw and Ross (1987) discuss this issue in more detail, pointing out that it often benefits an organization to design a project in modular form. In this way, the organization may be able to realize some gain from a project that is prematurely terminated. Staw and Ross cite the Deep Tunnel project in Chicago several years ago as an example of such a project. In that case, the project (to upgrade the city's sewer system) was designed to provide benefit to the city only when completed in its entirety. When the project was delayed due to cost overruns, Chicago had nothing to show for its efforts and considerable expense.

When changing market forces make it clear that a project cannot succeed, management must terminate the project prematurely. This is especially critical with IT projects due to the rapidly changing nature of the underlying technology.

It is understandable that most managers are reluctant to prematurely terminate a project as individual careers and egos become tied to projects. The fallacy of sunk costs frequently plays a role as well (e.g., how can we terminate a project when we have already invested millions of dollars in it?). The result is that we typically continue projects well beyond the point of "no return" (or "negative" return).

To avoid this problem, managers must carefully monitor and control projects. In the planning phase, it is critical to define—and later enforce—milestones where a project will be terminated if necessary. This is discussed in more detail in Chapter 8, which deals with the issues of monitoring and control.

PROJECT LIFE CYCLE

There are numerous ways to view a project's life cycle. One interpretation is given in Figure 1.4, which defines four phases:

1. Formulation and selection
2. Planning
3. Scheduling and control
4. Implementation and project termination

In the first phase (formulation and selection), the managers define (and refine) the project and its scope and consider the impact of the project on the strategic plan of the

FIGURE 1.4
Project Life Cycle

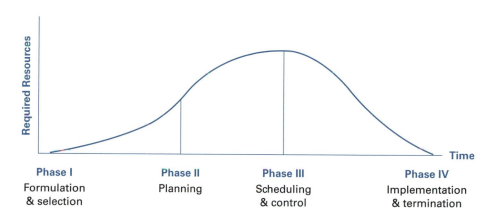

| Phase I | Phase II | Phase III | Phase IV |
| Formulation & selection | Planning | Scheduling & control | Implementation & termination |

organization. Assuming that the project is selected for further development, managers then proceed with more detailed planning in the second phase. In this phase, they define the specific tasks that will constitute the project and estimate the resources (workers, materials, etc.) that will be needed to successfully complete the project. As part of the planning phase, managers decide which tasks will be subcontracted and define RFBs (requests for bids) for these tasks. The planning phase is critical; it is this phase that defines the **6P Rule** of project management:

Prior **P**lanning **P**recludes **P**oor **P**roject **P**erformance

The work on the project is most intense during the third phase; as indicated in Figure 1.4, the resources assigned to the project peak during this phase. Finally, the project is implemented and handed off to the users in the fourth phase (e.g., this is the stage when a new building is occupied by the users or a new component is inserted into an assembly process).

In the second chapter, this view of a project's life cycle is discussed in more detail, as well as project initiation and selection, and the project planning phase. The relationship among the planning, scheduling, and control functions is indicated in Figure 1.5.

As indicated in Figure 1.5, the project team determines a baseline forecast in the project planning phase that serves as a benchmark for future performance. The team then monitors the deviations from this benchmark plan as the project is implemented. The problem of controlling the project becomes one of determining if these variances are the result of random fluctuations or represent a structural problem that must be addressed by the project team. When the latter occurs, the project team must take appropriate actions to bring the performance of the project back on track.

PROJECT MANAGEMENT TRADE-OFFS

Project management can be viewed as a series of trade-offs among multiple goals; managers must decide which goals are most important and which goals can be relaxed in order to achieve overall success for the organization. For example, in many new product development projects, time-to-market (e.g., schedule) is the most important goal while the budget goal may be a lesser consideration. In other projects, when the budget is of greater concern, managers may have to revise the design and specifications of the project in order to complete the project on time and within a given budget. Managers of the organization must also consider trade-offs among the portfolio of ongoing and future projects as well

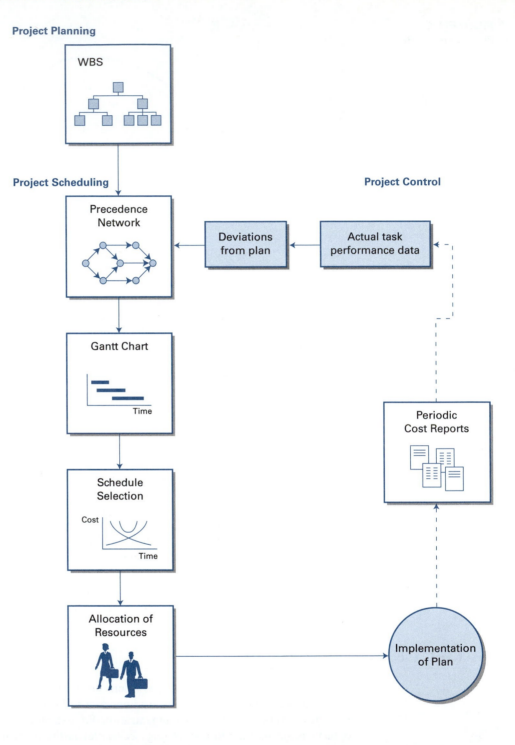

FIGURE 1.5
Relationship between
Project Planning,
Scheduling, and Control

as the rapidly changing technological environment. All of these factors determine the relative importance of each project and the level of resources that can be allocated.

These trade-offs can be visualized by viewing a project as a cube in which each axis represents a major project goal: *cost, time,* and *scope*—with *quality* as the fourth dimension. The relationship among these dimensions is represented in Figure 1.6.

FIGURE 1.6
Project Time, Cost, and
Design Trade-offs

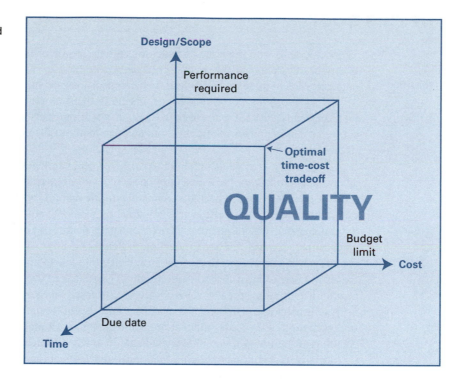

Many experienced project managers know that they can realistically achieve one (or perhaps two) of these goals in most situations. Since the goal of quality is the least visible and most difficult to measure, it frequently suffers in many projects. When scope is held constant, it is understandable why cost and schedule targets are often not met.

In the project planning stage, managers frequently assume that one or more goals are constant (e.g., scope) and optimize the remaining goals (e.g., the time-cost trade-off). This occurs in many bidding situations; that is, the design is considered fixed and an RFB is issued by a client. The bidder, given a fixed design, can compete only on the basis of time and cost (quality is rarely considered explicitly in these trade-offs). However, an increasing number of organizations are recognizing the need to make trade-offs among all four dimensions simultaneously. To accomplish this, they are using multifunctional project teams (e.g., design-build teams), involving the contractor in the design process as well as in the cost and schedule determination. Japanese companies, as well as some U.S. companies, have used this approach with considerable success.

Beck and Cleal (1999) have gone further and suggested that organizations issue "optional scope" contracts; such a contract would require that a supplier meets specified time, cost, and quality goals but is free to change the scope of the project itself. In this way, a contractor who experiences unexpected problems could change the scope of the project but would still be required to meet the stated time, cost, and quality goals. Beck and Clarl argue that a supplier with such a contract would still have an incentive to complete a reasonable design in the hope of getting additional contracts. They argue that such contracts could be effective if the term of such contracts is kept short and there is clear method to measure the quality of the project.[*]

---

[*] Some might argue that contract workers hired by many firms today represent a de facto "optional scope" contract.

SCOPE OF THIS BOOK

This book deals with the issue of trade-offs among these four dimensions and the tools and techniques that are available to assist managers who have to make these decisions. A better understanding of these trade-offs leads to better decisions and improved project management.

In addition, the book emphasizes the tools that are available to project managers, including most PM software packages. While these products are widely used, they have significant limitations in their ability to analyze many of the complex trade-offs required in most projects.

To provide a more general framework for analyzing PM trade-offs, a number of spreadsheet models are presented throughout the book. The reader should keep in mind that most of the PM software packages available on the market today are little more than specialized spreadsheet models; everything done by most PM software products can be done by a spreadsheet (although not as quickly or easily, perhaps). For small problems, however, spreadsheet models offer a great deal more flexibility. For example, project managers can use the optimization feature of most spreadsheet models to analyze trade-offs (something that is not part of most PM software products) or they can use the random-number generator built into most spreadsheet software to construct Monte-Carlo simulation models to analyze project risk. The use of spreadsheet models will hopefully give the reader a better understanding of the trade-offs that project managers must make as well as a better understanding of the PM software that is available to assist with these trade-offs.

Finally, it should be explicitly mentioned that project management, like management in general, is quintessentially an experiential activity. It is like learning to ride a bicycle—difficult, if not impossible, to learn from any book. However, it is the author's hope that this book will sensitize project managers to the issues they must consider while managing complex projects. By focusing on PM trade-offs and problems, project managers will gain a better understanding of the factors that result in various project outcomes (both good and bad) and, in doing so, will be better able to deal effectively with these factors.

MANAGING PROJECT RISKS

A critical part of managing any project is defining and analyzing risks associated with that project. Project risk is defined by two elements: (1) the probability of some adverse event or outcome, and (2) the severity or cost of that event or outcome. The probability of most events is influenced by both exogenous and endogenous factors; for example, bad weather (an exogenous factor) or bad management (an endogenous factor) can equally delay the completion of a project. In either case, the costs to the organization may be the same (delay costs, loss of customer goodwill, etc.); unlike bad weather, however, bad management can often be avoided.

This example illustrates another important factor in risk management. After analyzing possible adverse events, the project manager has two choices. Namely, she can take some preventive action before starting the project to reduce the likelihood of the adverse event or its consequence, or she can plan a contingency action if such an adverse event should occur. In the case of bad weather, the project manager might add coverings or shelters to a construction project (for example); this preventive action would increase the cost of the project but would mitigate the negative impact if the weather became inclement. Alternatively, the manager might plan to add additional workers to the project if the weather caused schedule delays. This contingency plan would be implemented only if the negative event (bad weather) actually occurred.

There are numerous sources of uncertainty in all projects, including random variations in component performance, inaccurate or incomplete data, and an inability to accurately forecast due to a lack of data, experience, or foresight. To reduce overall project risk, most organizations use several approaches, including selecting a portfolio of projects to minimize risk in the same way that an investor would diversify a stock portfolio. Subcontracting a part (or all) of the project is another way to mitigate project risk; the type of contract written with a subcontractor has significant implications for how the risk is allocated among project stakeholders.

Project managers should also recognize that the reverse side of risk is potential gain. Risks open new opportunities for organizations to expand their product line, improve their services, and improve their knowledge base. Typically, the larger the risk, the greater the potential return. The issue is not to control risk, but to manage it.

Finally, it should be noted that most PM software programs do not account for risk directly. By using the spreadsheet models in this book, however, project managers can learn to analyze risk as part of a project plan. The topics of risk analysis and risk management are further discussed in Chapter 7.

HISTORY OF PROJECT MANAGEMENT

Project managers have been working since the beginning of history. In fact, some theologians might say that the first project manager built the heavens and earth in six days (with one additional day as a buffer for unexpected contingencies). Many projects—such as the Egyptian pyramids of El Giza (2590 B.C.), the Colossus of Rhodes (292 B.C.–A.D. 654), and the Houston Astrodome (1965)—provide examples of effective management of massive construction projects. Two other projects, however, have probably had the greatest impact on the development and practice of project management methodologies (Fondahl, 1987).

In the late 1950s, engineers for the DuPont Corporation were concerned about the maintenance downtime at their Louisville, Kentucky plant, which had become a bottleneck in their neoprene production process. To avoid building an additional plant, DuPont executives hired the Catalytic Construction Company to study the Louisville plant and suggest ways to reduce the maintenance downtime. The study, which indicated that a significant reduction in the number of maintenance hours at the Louisville plant was possible, was based on a new methodology that has become known as the critical path method (CPM). As a result of this study, the engineers predicted that production at the Louisville plant could be increased to a level such that the plant would no longer be a bottleneck and a second plant would not be needed.

At approximately the same time, the consulting firm of Booze, Allen, and Hamilton was developing a new PM system for the Polaris Fleet Ballistic Missile program in the U.S. Navy's Special Projects Office. The Polaris missile, the first intercontinental ballistic missile that could be launched from an underwater submarine, represented the largest (and one of the riskiest) research and development efforts undertaken to date. Given the uncertainty involved with the project, the managers wanted a methodology that would not only incorporate uncertainty into their planning but also allow them to estimate probabilities for important milestones (for example, if the propulsion system proceeds as planned, what is the probability that we can test-launch a missile by a given date?). The methodology that was developed to assist with the management of this project became known as PERT (Program Evaluation and Review Technique) and explicitly introduced uncertainty into the project scheduling and allocation process. The basic concepts of PERT, as well as its shortcomings and advantages and related tools, are discussed in more detail in Chapter 6.

The DuPont study and the potential benefits from the new techniques of CPM and PERT were reported in *Business Week* (1959) and *Fortune* (1962) articles. In 1963, Levy et al. (1963) published an influential primer on CPM in the *Harvard Business Review*.

Following the publication of these articles, both CPM and PERT became widely adopted by both public and private organizations, and evolved into PM systems that were adopted by many organizations (some willingly and some not). These methodologies form the basis for most PM systems in use today.

While the terms CPM and PERT are frequently used interchangeably, this book uses these acronyms as they were originally defined. Specifically, CPM refers to the case when task durations and other parameters are deterministic and known with complete certainty, while the PERT model assumes that task durations are random variables that can be described by an appropriate probability distribution. It is important to note that the vast majority of commercial PM software programs today are based on the CPM model (even though many of these programs use the term PERT in their documentation and/or title).

PROJECT MANAGEMENT SOFTWARE

PM software packages are widespread today and available in a wide variety of price ranges. Most of the programs fall into two categories: low-end programs that are designed for a single user to run on a personal computer, and higher-end programs that are designed to network a group of computers. It appears that the current trend is toward the latter type of program; given the importance of effective communication in successful project management, it is critical to have a mechanism that allows all project stakeholders to share data and information on a real-time basis.

As noted earlier, most of the commercial PM software packages are based on the critical path method (CPM); that is, all parameters such as task durations are assumed to be known and constant. Most software packages are useful for drawing Gantt charts (bar charts), precedence networks, and resource-leveling histograms, as well as performing basic calculations and providing other diagrams and calculations for planning and control. Throughout this book, most—if not all—of the functions built into the most popular PM software products are demonstrated by providing spreadsheet templates that mirror these functions. The reader should then be able to take the examples provided in this book and implement this material into the PM software of her choice (e.g., Microsoft Project provided on the CD-ROM that accompanies this book).

In addition to PM software, there are an increasing number of "add-ons" that enhance the functionality of PM products. For example, some programs are available that will allow the user to include Monte Carlo simulations in the PM software. In this way, uncertainty can be directly included in the project planning phase and sensitivity analyses can be performed. Again, the functionality of these add-ons will be demonstrated using spreadsheet templates.

PROJECT MANAGEMENT INSTITUTE

The Project Management Institute (PMI) is a nonprofit professional organization dedicated to promoting project management. Founded in 1969, PMI has grown to an international organization that currently has over seventy thousand members. PMI sponsors seminars and workshops, as well as a certification process covering their twelve-area "body of knowledge" (PMBOK®). PMI has done much to further the idea that project management requires a set of skills and a body of knowledge that are unique to managing projects. More information about PMI can be found at the organization's Web site at www.pmi.org.

PROJECT MANAGEMENT MATURITY MODELS

Recognizing that project management is an advanced process that is more than tools and software, some researchers have developed methodologies for assessing an organization's level of PM competency. The motivation behind these methodologies is that organizations will improve their PM capabilities if they accurately assess their current PM competencies and have guidelines for improving. Many of these models were based on extensive empirical research that serves as a database for best practices as well as guidelines for improvement processes.

Much of the early work in this area was developed by researchers at the Software Engineering Institute (SEI) at Carnegie-Mellon University to improve software development processes; the SEI Capability Maturity Model (predecessor to most other PM maturity models) consists of six capability levels:

- Incomplete
- Performed
- Managed
- Defined
- Quantitatively managed
- Optimized

Many other PM maturity models have been built on the SEI framework. For more information on PM maturity models, see Kerzner (2001) as well as the Web sites for SEI and the Project Management Institute (PMI).

APPENDIX 1A. MEDICARE TRANSACTIONS: A $50 MILLION LESSON IN PROJECT MANAGEMENT

The Health Care Financing Administration, the agency that administers Medicare, spent six years, from 1991 to 1997, and at least $50 million developing the Medicare Transaction system. Today, HCFA's eighty-two-page strategic plan for information technology over the next five years makes no mention of the ill-fated system, instead only making oblique references to the errors of "earlier HCFA IT investment efforts." HCFA Chief Information Officer Gary Christoph, who was hired after MTS development was canceled, says the agency is moving on.

"Some of the concepts in MTS were really good concepts. Where we fell down was the implementation," Christoph says. "When you're growing up, you first learn to crawl, then walk, then run, then ride a bicycle. You don't just jump into a Ferrari."

The history of HCFA's computer problems is typical of federal agencies: Congress creates numerous programs over the years under the agency's domain. The agency builds a new information system for each new program, using various programming languages, platforms, and contractors for each. The systems tend to be proprietary (making it hard to make updates or get them to share information) and written in languages popular in the 1950s and 1960s, such as COBOL.

Then, sometime in the 1980s, it dawns on the agency that its systems are becoming unmanageable. So it decides to build one large, integrated system to handle all the agency's programs—a solution expected to reap huge cost savings over time (after a significant up-front investment, of course). Overseeing one system is obviously less expensive than managing multiple systems. Technology managers picture that glorious day about five years down the road when they will cut the ribbon, unsheathe the new system, and bask in the applause of the agency administrator, doting members of Congress, and cheering taxpayers.

But you know what happens instead.

In HCFA's case, the agency issued a request for proposals for its mega-system on September 17, 1992. Even before the call for bidders hit the street, the Health and Human

Services Department inspector general recommended that HCFA pause and "follow a more strategically oriented approach to streamlining, consolidating and integrating Medicare claims processing."

Four months after the request for proposals went out, the inspector general suggested that HCFA needed to more clearly define exactly what the agency wanted the Medicare Transaction System to do. The IG also recommended that the HCFA make sure contractors understood that Medicare is a constantly changing program that needs flexible, adaptable software. In response, HCFA established eleven work groups to examine various aspects of Medicare processing and provide information to the contractor. Later, the number of work groups would be expanded to twenty-four.

In the meantime, HCFA awarded GTE Government Services the MTS contract in January 1994. In April 1994, HCFA hired Intermetrics Inc., a small company in Virginia now known as AverStar, to independently monitor the contract's progress.

"This new system will bring to reality a new era of customer service and convenience for Medicare beneficiaries," beamed HHS Secretary Donna Shalala in a January 1994 press release. "It uses state-of-the-art technology to replace the forms and the hassles that have characterized Medicare in the past." The system would be completed by late 1998, the release said.

GTE began planning its strategy to help HCFA combine into one system Medicare's fourteen systems at sixty sites operated by more than seventy contractors, while the work groups tried to make sense of the agency's systems architecture.

The danger signs were all around. In December 1994, the inspector general again warned HCFA that it wasn't giving GTE enough information to help the contractor plan for the complexities of Medicare processing. The following year, HCFA assured the IG that it had begun providing ample information to GTE. The system was on track for full implementation by September 1999, HCFA said.

In November 1995, the General Accounting Office highlighted several concerns it had with MTS in a report to the House Government Reform Committee, including unclear contract requirements, a tight schedule, and a lack of reliable cost-benefit information.

Then-HCFA Administrator Bruce Vladeck responded: "We are well aware that this is a high-risk venture. We are conducting the project with a keen appreciation of the need to manage the risks involved." In mid-1996, Intermetrics warned HCFA and GTE that the MTS development schedule had too many overlapping milestones, but that warning went unheeded, an Intermetrics official would testify at a House hearing in May 1997.

A month before that hearing, HCFA ordered GTE to stop work for ninety days on all but one of the segments of MTS to evaluate the reasons for the project's increasing cost overruns and missed deadlines.

By May 1997, GAO was more adamant that MTS was in big trouble. HCFA had not planned the project's schedule well enough, did not have performance measures to gauge progress, and had failed to use "cost-benefit analyses and other tools to continually track and assess whether funds spent on MTS will contribute to a return on this investment," GAO said. In addition, the projected costs of MTS had mushroomed from $151 million to $1 billion. GAO estimated that HCFA had spent $80 million on the project so far, though HCFA says the total spent on MTS was $50 million. In response, HCFA, GTE, and even Intermetrics vowed that MTS would be completed, albeit probably not until 2000. Three months later, HCFA cancelled its contract with GTE.

"We had one major mistake in the life of (the MTS) experience, and that was probably having too much confidence in the ability of the contractor to deliver," former administrator Vladeck says. Until mid-1998, HCFA continued to work on reducing the number of systems it relied on. Then it suspended all modernization efforts to make sure that fifty million lines of software code were free of potential Y2K glitches.

HCFA didn't come out of the MTS project completely empty-handed. The agency did cut down the number of contractors and sites managing Medicare processing systems, and integrated its fourteen systems into six. In addition, the project gave agency officials a better understanding of how their systems, which are controlled primarily by contractors, operate.

"HCFA came out of (MTS) with a much clearer short- to medium-term strategy for managing claims processing," Vladeck says.

In fact, Vladeck says MTS probably still could have been salvaged after GTE's failure, except for two factors. First, Congress and the Clinton administration failed to consider many of the benefits that would justify the cost of an expensive single, integrated system, including better fraud detection and improvements in processing efficiency. Second, the project fell victim to the still-prevalent notion, first championed by former Office of Management and Budget Director Franklin Raines, that single "big-bang" procurements just don't work.

The project failed to realize the vision espoused by Shalala in 1994. There is no single system for Medicare processing. According to HCFA's new five-year information technology plan, its current systems still "clearly reflect business and system design philosophies of an era when, for example, claims processing was largely a paper-handling function … despite operating on newer equipment."

Source: B. Friel, "Medicare Transactions: A $50 Million Lesson in Project Management," *Government Executive* (April 2000).

STUDY PROBLEMS

1. How would you benefit from an application of PM techniques in a project you may have been involved with? Consider how you would define the specific tasks and their respective durations in this "project." What were the goals of the project? What constraints were imposed on the project managers?

2. Consider the formation of a project team. What characteristics do you feel members of the team should have? Should the team consist of members with similar training and background, or should team members have different skills and backgrounds? How should a project team operate? Who should have ultimate responsibility for the team's performance?

3. Consider the relationship between a project team and the functional parts of an organization. Who should have responsibility for approving specific tasks? If an engineering task goes beyond its proposed duration and budget, who is responsible—the director of engineering or the project manager? In general, how do you think a company that is functionally organized should deal with projects?

4. Suppose that your company has over a dozen projects to choose from—but can select only a limited few. What criteria would you suggest for ranking the projects? How would you ultimately decide which projects to select?

5. Investigate PM maturity models. Using one of the self-assessment tools available on the World Wide Web, estimate the PM capability level of your organization. How do you think that you can best improve the PM competencies of your organization?

REFERENCES

Bagli, C. "Digitally Speaking, Builders Remain on the Ground Floor," *New York Times*, 13 December 2000, 4.

Beck, K. and D. Cleal. "Optional Scope Contracts," (1999), URL: www.xprogramming.com/ftp/Optional +scope+contracts.pdf.

"Better Plans Come From Study of Anatomy of an Engineering Job," *Business Week*, 21 March 1959, 60–66.

Boehm, G. A.W. "Helping the Executive to Make Up His Mind," *Fortune*, April 1962, 127.

Bounds, G. "The Last Word on Project Management," *IIE Solutions* (November 1998).

Brown, S.L., and K.M. Eisenhardt. "The Art of Continuous Change: Linking Complexity Theory and Time-paced Evolution in Relentlessly Shifting Organizations," *Administrative Science Quarterly* 42 (1997): 1–34.

Eisenhardt, K.M. and B.N. Tabrizi. "Accelerating Adaptive Processes: Product Innovation in the Global Computer Industry," *Administrative Science Quarterly* 40 (1995): 84–110.

Frable, F. "Delayed Openings Are a Fact of Life in the Foodservice, Hospitality Industry," *Nation's Restaurant News* (12 April 1999): 18.

Friel, B. "Medicare Transactions: A $50 Million Lesson in Project Management," *Government Executive*, National Journal (April 2000): 68.

Griffin, A. and A. Page. "An Failure," *Management* 9, no. 1 (1993): 291–308.

Hughes, M.W. "Why Projects Fail: The Effects of Ignoring the Obvious," *Industrial Engineering* (April 1986): 14–18.

Kahneman, D.P., P. Slovic, and A. Tversky. "Judgment Under Uncertainty: Heuristics and Biases," Cambridge, U.K.: Cambridge University Press, 1982.

Kerzner, H. *Strategic Planning for Project Management Using a Project Management Maturity Model.* New York: John Wiley and Sons, Inc., 2001.

Levy, F., G.L. Thompson, and J.D. Wiest. "The ABC's of the Critical Path Method," *Harvard Business Review* (September–October 1963): 98–108.

A Guide to the Project Management Body of Knowledge (PMBOK® Guide). Newton Square, Pa.: Project Management Institute (PMI), 2000.

Might, R.J. and W.A. Fischer. "The Role of Structural Factors in Determining Project Management Success," *IEEE Transactions on Engineering Management* EM-32, no. 2, May, 1985.

Pinto, J. and D. Slevin. "Critical Factors in Successful Project Implementation," *IEEE Transactions on Engineering Management* EM-34, no. 1, (1 Feb 1987): 22–27.

"Riot-Ravaged Taco Bell Rebuilt in 48 Hours Using Project Planning Software," *Industrial Engineering* (September 1992): 18.

Shenhar, A. "One Size Does Not Fit All Projects: Exploring Classical Contingency Domains," *Management Science* 47, no. 3 (March 2001): 394–414.

"Stave Falls Wins Project of the Year Award," *Water Power and Dam Construction.* Wilmington Publishing Ltd. (31 July 2000): 3.

Staw, B. and J. Ross. "Knowing When to Pull the Plug," *Harvard Business Review*, (March–April, 1987): 68–74.

Schmidt, E. "Regional Construction Industry Is Going Through a Communications Revolution," *New York Construction* 48, no. 8 (March 2000): 59.

Shenhar, A. J. "One Size Does Not Fit All Projects: Exploring Classical Contingency Domains," *Management Science* 47, no. 3 (March, 2001): 394–414.

P. Slovic, and A. Tversky, *Judgment under Uncertainty: Heuristics and Biases.* Cambridge, UK: Cambridge University Press, 1982.

Standish Group, 1999. URL: www.standishgroup.com/.

Takeuchi, H. and I. Nonaka. "The New New Product Development Game," *Harvard Business Review* (January–February 1986).

A. Vazsonyi, "L'Histoire de Grandeur et de la Decadence de la Methode PERT," *Management Science* 16, no. 8 (April 1970): B449–455.

Walker. R. "Dig This: Building Boom Exposes E. Germans' Pre-Communist Past," *Christian Science Monitor* (12 August 1996): 6

Wheelwright, S. C. and K. B. Clark. "Creating Project Plans to Focus," *Harvard Business Review* (March–April, 1992): 70–82.

Yap, C.M. and W.E. Souder. "Factors Influencing New Product Success and Failure in Small Entrepreneurial High-Technology Electronics Firms," *Journal of Product Innovation Management* 11 (1994): 418–432.

Yang, S. "CSOC's Shorten Design Cycles," *Copyright Electronics News* (15 May 2000): 22.

Youker, R. "A New Look at the WBS: Project Breakdown Structures (PBS)," *Project Management Journal* (1989): 54–59.

PROJECT INITIATION, SELECTION, AND PLANNING

As indicated in the first chapter, projects generally have four phases: initiation and selection, planning, scheduling and control, and implementation (including termination and evaluation). These phases frequently overlap and, in fact, more accurately exist along the continuum indicated in Figure 1.1. This chapter focuses on the first two phases, project initiation and selection, and project planning, in more detail. These two phases are critical parts of project management since they directly address the issues of "doing the right things, and doing them right."

With respect to the project initiation and selection, we discuss

- How to initiate new projects
- Methods for evaluating project proposals
- Project selection as a portfolio problem
- Why project managers should have an "options" mind-set

Once an organization has started to seriously consider a new project, the proposal moves into the planning phase, during which managers further define the project specifications, user requirements, and organizational constraints. A primary goal of the project planning effort is to define the individual work packages or tasks that constitute the project. This is usually accomplished by developing a work breakdown structure (WBS) that defines specific work packages (tasks) as well as estimates of their costs and durations. This chapter will also cover the impact of learning, uncertainty, and risk, as well as numerous factors on the duration and cost estimation process.

As an organization continues the planning process, managers must design a detailed time and resource plan. Specifically, the project's baseline schedule and budget serves as a benchmark for much of the remaining project, and is frequently used to judge the ultimate success or failure of the project. Finally, we must specify the processes that will be used to monitor and control the project when it gets started. The issues of scheduling and monitoring/control are discussed in more detail in Chapters 4 and 8, respectively.

This chapter will also discuss the issue of subcontracting; specifically: How do managers decide which part(s) of a project should be subcontracted? How many subcontractors should be used? What is the role of a subcontractor in the planning phase? And what trade-offs do managers have to make when considering the possible use of subcontractors?

This chapter concludes with a case study, Christopher Columbus, Inc. This case deals with the relationship between goal definition and resource requirements, and illustrates how a project plan should be used to develop a proposal and bid in response to an RFP (request for proposal).

PROJECT INITIATION AND SELECTION

Project definition and selection are arguably the most important decisions faced by an organization. As noted by Cooper et al. (2000), an organization can succeed only by "doing projects right, and doing the right projects." An organization must have a project portfolio that is consistent with the overall goals and strategy of the organization while providing desired diversification, maintaining adequate cash flows, and not exceeding resource constraints. Managers should focus not only on the overall set of projects and the dynamic evolution of this portfolio over time (i.e., which projects are added, which are terminated, etc.) but also on the relationships between these projects—not on individual projects.

Projects are initiated to realize process, program, or organizational improvements that will improve existing conditions and exploit new opportunities. Many organizations use a project initiation form or other internal process to encourage workers to propose new projects that can benefit the organization. Some projects result from critical factors or competitive necessity (for example, the development of a Web site for customers and/or investors or other projects resulting from technological changes). Other projects may be initiated to maintain or expand market share. In many cases, customers or suppliers dictate new products or processes.

In general, projects can be initiated in a top-down (e.g., the boss wants it) or bottom-up (e.g., workers see the need) fashion. For any proposed project, however, the following information may be requested from those who have suggested the project. While this list is not intended to be comprehensive, it does represent a compilation the author has observed at numerous successful companies. Some project initiation forms use a checksheet (e.g., a list of yes or no questions), while others simply request information on the following topics:

- Project name
- Proposed project manager, division, or department
- Brief problem description that the project will address
- Benefits of the project
- Estimated time and cost of project
- Whether subcontractors will be used or work will be done by in-house personnel
- Impact on workforce safety
- Impact on energy requirements
- Impact on customers

The accompanying cartoon provides an example of project selection from the top down.

If managers decide to consider a project further, numerous numerical metrics are frequently used, including the payback period and net present value (NPV)/discounted cash flow (DCF). Alternatively, some organizations use a scoring or ranking approach whereby each proposal is rated over some range based on a series of questions. Typically, these ranking approaches include questions addressing qualitative factors as well as quantifiable factors (e.g., what is the proposed project's relationship with the organization's overall mission and strategic goals?).

These measures are useful for evaluating the potential value and profitability of a project and are therefore usually used in the earlier stages of the project selection and planning process. The numerical measures described in the following section represent some of the most commonly used metrics. All of these measures are dependent on accurate forecasts of future cash flows; as the quality of these forecasts is reduced, so is the usefulness of these measures.

Numerical Measures

Numerical measures are frequently used to assist with project selection. While these measures are often criticized (for example, they are based on forecasted values that are subject to great uncertainty), they can provide a better understanding of the explicit costs and benefits of any proposed project. Most organizations use these measures in conjunction with other judgments to validate their decisions to undertake or not undertake a proposed project.

Payback Period

Payback period is the number of time periods (e.g., years) needed to recover the cost of the project. For example, assume that a bank can install a new ATM at a cost of $90,000; with this new ATM, the bank can reduce its number of bank tellers by one. Assuming that bank tellers are paid approximately $30,000 per year, the payback period is defined as $90,000/$30,000 = 3 years; that is, it will take three years before the bank can recover the initial cost of ATM. In general, the payback period is defined as:

$$\text{Payback Period (yrs)} = \frac{\text{Estimated Project Cost}}{\text{Annual Savings (or increase in revenues)}}$$

We can extend this measure by considering the operating costs of the ATM, which were estimated at $4,000/year. The annual savings realized by the bank then becomes $30,000 − $4,000 = $26,000, resulting in a payback period approximately equal to 3.5 years.

The payback period measure suffers from numerous shortcomings. It ignores the time value of money including interest rates and inflation. To illustrate the limitations of this measure, consider the following two projects A and B:

> **Project A:** Cost = $75,000   Return: $25,000 for 4 years
> **Project B:** Cost = $75,000   Return: $15,000 for 8 years

The payback period for Project A is ($75,000/$25,000) = 3 years; the payback period for Project B is ($75,000/$15,000) = 5 years. Based on payback period, an organization might rank Project A higher than Project B, even though Project B will ultimately return $120,000; Project A will return only $100,000. Despite these limitations, payback period remains a popular measure; it is relatively easy to calculate and explain, and it may be useful for an organization that is concerned with short-run cash flows and profitability.

Net Present Value (NPV) or Discounted Cash Flow (DCF)

The discounted cash flow (DCF) over the estimated life of the project (also known as the deterministic discounted cash flow) based on the fundamental assumption that a dollar today is worth more than a dollar tomorrow. Net present value (NPV) is probably the most widely used measure that includes the time value of money.

Given an interest or discount rate (also referred to as the hurdle rate or cutoff rate), we can calculate the discounted stream of future costs and benefits. Let r denote the discount rate and F_t denote the forecasted cash flow in period t (that is, F_t represents the estimated benefits minus the costs in time period t), then the NPV or DCF of a project is defined as:

$$\text{Net Present Value (NPV)} = \sum_{t=0}^{T} \frac{F_t}{(1+r)^t}$$

where T denotes the estimated life of the project. For example, consider a project that has an expected life of six years. If we assume that the annual discount rate, r, is equal to 20 percent and we will incur an estimated cost of $750 in the first year, then the discounted cash flow in the first year ($t = 1$) is:

$$\frac{F_1}{(1+r)^1} = \frac{-\$750}{(1.20)} = -\$625$$

Given the forecasted costs and benefits for all six years, the calculations to find the NPV are indicated in Figure 2.1. Year 0 represents the present time; note that net benefits of this proposed project are not positive until year 2, when the project starts to generate revenues and the costs associated with the project have decreased to $550.

Summing the discounted values in the last column, we find that the NPV is equal to $2,912. Since the NPV is positive, we would consider this project although there are many reasons why an organization might consider a project with a negative NPV (e.g., to open up a new market or to block a competitor) or reject a project with a positive NPV. When managers are considering multiple projects, they can use NPV to rank alternative proposals.

While NPV has fewer limitations than the payback period measure, it has also been widely criticized (Faulkner, 1996; Cooper et al., 2000; Hodder and Riggs, 1985). First, it ignores the risk of a project (or uncertainty that is treated as risk) since our calculations assume that the forecasted cash flows are known with certainty. A related problem is caused by the human bias that is part of the estimation process (or, as one manager stated, "What numbers do you want to see?"). A second problem is the failure to explicitly consider the effects of inflation when estimating the discount rate r, especially in long-term projects. Third, NPV ignores interactions with other projects and programs in the organization since it treats each project proposal individually. This is an important point; NPV may not be an effective measure when an organization is considering a portfolio of projects that compete for the same resources. For example, a project with the small positive

FIGURE 2.1
NPV Calculations
Illustrated

Year	Benefits	Costs	Benefits – Costs	Discounted Benefits – Costs	
0	$ —	$ 1,000	$ (1,000)	$(1,000)	
1	$ —	$ 750	$ (750)	$ (625)	
2	$ 1,500	$ 550	$ 950	$ 660	
3	$ 2,000	$ 250	$ 1,750	$ 1,013	$\leftarrow \dfrac{1750}{(1.2)^3}$
4	$ 2,500	$ 150	$ 2,350	$ 1,133	
5	$ 2,500	$ 150	$ 2,350	$ 944	
6	$ 2,500	$ 150	$ 2,350	$ 787	

NPV that uses slack resources might be more attractive than a project with a larger NPV that requires new facilities or workers. For this reason, organizations must be concerned about their portfolio of projects as opposed to a single project. A fourth criticism is a result of the assumption that a single discount rate is used for the entire project. As a project evolves over time, the risk of the project is likely to be reduced and, accordingly, the discount rate as well. The following sections include a discussion of some of these criticisms further and show ways that they can be mitigated.

Internal Rate of Return (IRR)

Internal rate of return (IRR) is the discount rate that results in an NPV equal to zero. Given the uncertainties associated with estimating the discount rate and future cash flows, the IRR simply finds the value of r that results in an NPV equal to zero. Generally, those projects with a larger IRR are ranked higher than those with a lower IRR. In addition, the IRR is usually compared to the cost of capital for an organization; that is, under most conditions, a project should promise a higher return than the organization has to pay for the capital needed to fund the project.

The IRR measure suffers from many of the same limitations of the NPV: It assumes forecasted cash flows are reasonably accurate and certain, it is subject to the same estimation bias that plagues the forecasts needed to compute the NPV measure, etc. An additional problem with this approach is that often there is not a single value of r that satisfies the equation NPV = 0.

For example, assume that a project is expected to take 2 years (that is, $T = 2$). Finding the IRR requires solving the quadratic equation:

$$F_0 + \frac{F_1}{(1+r)} + \frac{F_2}{(1+r)^2} = 0$$

Assume that the proposed project will require an initial outlay of $100 but will return $40 (benefits minus costs) at the end of the first year and $75 in net benefits at the end of the second year. Finding the IRR requires solving the following equation for r:

$$-100 + \frac{40}{(1+r)} + \frac{75}{(1+r)^2} = 0$$

which becomes:

$$r^2 + 1.6r - .15 = 0$$

Solving this quadratic equation, we find that r can equal either 0.089 or −1.689 (both values set NPV equal to zero). While we can ignore the negative value of r in this case and assume that the IRR is equal to 8.9 percent, it becomes more difficult when there are many time periods that may result in multiple positive values of r. When this occurs, it is unclear how these multiple values should be interpreted or which value of r should be adopted.

Expected Commercial Value (ECV)

Expected commercial value (ECV) is the expected NPV of the project, adjusted by the probabilities of various alternatives. ECV-type measures extend the concept of net present value (NPV) to explicitly consider the fact that most projects consist of multiple stages (e.g., design, marketing, testing, and implementation). For example, consider a proposed new product development project with two alternative design options. ECV explicitly considers the probabilities that various outcomes will occur as a result of the design option that is selected, and it uses these probabilities to compute an expected NPV. ECV also allows managers to use different hurdle or discount rates at different stages of the project—thereby responding to one of the criticisms directed at the use of NPV/DCF. For these reasons, ECV-type measures are gaining increasing visibility and use.

ECV is based on the concept of a decision tree that is a logical framework for evaluating sequential decisions and outcomes. Such a decision tree is illustrated in Figure 2.2. The "root" of this decision tree begins with a decision maker selecting one of two alternatives (A_1 or A_2). If the decision maker selects alternative A_1, then three outcomes or states of nature are possible (S_1, S_2, or S_3) with probabilities (p_1, p_2, or p_3), respectively. If the decision maker selects alternative A_2, then three other outcomes or states of nature are possible (S_4, S_5, or S_6) with probabilities (p_4, p_5, or p_6), respectively. As indicated in Figure 2.2, the square represents a decision point, and the ovals represent alternatives available to the decision maker. This example can easily be extended to multiple stages; at any outcome (S_i), another decision node can be added that represents additional alternatives, outcomes, etc.

To evaluate the decision tree in Figure 2.2, first consider selecting alternative A_1. If A_1 is selected, the expected outcome is $(S_1)(p_1) + (S_2)(p_2) + (S_3)(p_3)$; if alternative A_2 is selected, then the expected outcome is $(S_4)(p_4) + (S_5)(p_5) + (S_6)(p_6)$. Working backward, the expected payoff can then be found for each alternative by subtracting the cost of each alternative from its respective expected outcome. If c_i denotes the cost of alternative i ($i = 1, 2$), then the expected value of each alternative is:

Expected value of alternative 1: $(S_1)(p_1) + (S_2)(p_2) + (S_3)(p_3) - c_1$
Expected value of alternative 2: $(S_4)(p_4) + (S_5)(p_5) + (S_6)(p_6) - c_2$

Typically, the values of the outcomes, S_i, are the discounted cash flows or NPV resulting from the given alternative and resultant outcome or state of nature. The estimated commercial value (ECV) of the project is the value of the alternative with the largest expected value.

To illustrate these concepts further, consider the case of an opera company trying to decide which opera to select for the opening performance of its season. For each opera, the company managers have estimated the possible demands (high, medium, low) and their respective revenues and probabilities. Assuming two possible choices (*Rigoletto* or *Falstaff*), the decision tree faced by the opera company is given in Figure 2.3.

If the opera company selects *Rigoletto,* its expected revenues would be $148,000 (.5 × $200K + .3 × $120K + .2 × $60K). If the company selects *Falstaff*, its expected

FIGURE 2.2
Decision Tree Example

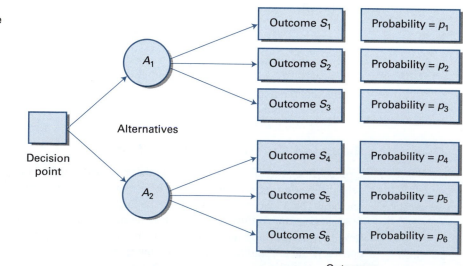

FIGURE 2.3
Opera Decision Tree
Example

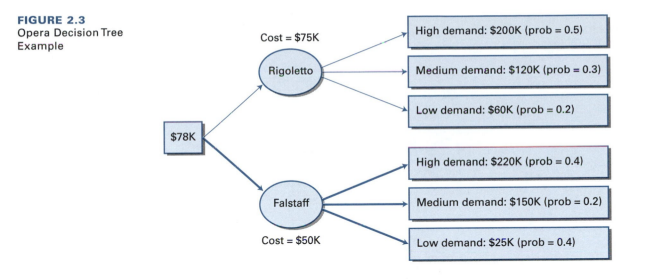

revenues would be $128,000 (.4 × $220K + .2 × $150K + .4 × $25K). Assuming that *Rigoletto* would cost an estimated $75,000 to perform (cast, set, director, etc.), the opera company would realize an estimated gross profit of $148,000 − $75,000 = $73,000. If it selects *Falstaff* (assuming it would cost approximately $50,000 to produce), the company's estimated gross profit would be $128,000 − $50,000 = $78,000. Thus, based on expected revenues only, the opera company could expect to make an additional $5,000 if it selects *Falstaff* to open the season (although there are still many good reasons why the company might select *Rigoletto* instead).

To illustrate an Expected Commercial Value (ECV) measure, consider the decision tree for a hypothetical product development project that is represented in Figure 2.4. In this case, there are two decision points: (1) to develop (or not develop) the product, and (2) to launch (or not launch) the product. If the product is developed, it could be a technical success (with probability p_t) or technical failure (with probability $1 − p_t$); if it is launched, it could be a commercial success (with probability p_c) or commercial failure (with probability $1 − p_c$). In Figure 2.4, assume that the organization does not launch the product if it is a technical failure (so that future cash flows are zero in this case). If the product is a commercial success, then all future cash flows are discounted back to the present time; these discounted cash flows are denoted by NPV.

Assuming that the cost to develop the product (to test its technical feasibility) is C_D and the cost to launch the product is C_L, then the expected value of launching the new product (assuming it is a technical success) is

$$\text{Expected Value of Launching} \mid \text{Technical Success} = \text{NPV}\,(p_c) + 0\,(1 − p_c) − C_L$$
$$= \text{NPV}\,(p_c) − C_L$$

Working backward, the expected value of developing the product is then

$$\text{ECV} = p_t\,[\text{NPV}\,(p_c) − C_L] − C_D$$

For example, assume that the design of a new product is expected to take three years and cost approximately $6M per year. At the end of the three years, the company will know if the product is a technical success; at the present time, its managers estimate an 80 percent likelihood that the product will be technically feasible. If technically successful, the product can be launched in year 4 at an estimated cost of $5.5M. If launched, the product would be a commercial success with probability 0.6 that would earn gross revenues of $15M per year for five years, but only $2M per year if it proves to a commercial failure.

FIGURE 2.4
Expected Commercial
Value (ECV) Defined

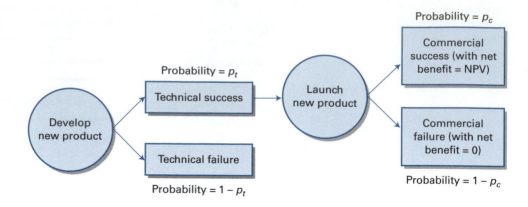

Assuming a discount rate of 10 percent, the expected cash flows for this project are indicated in Figure 2.5.

In the first three years, there is an annual negative cash flow of $6M; in year 4, the product is launched if it is a technical success (and incurs a one-time cost c_L of $5.5M). The expected cash flow in year 4 comes from the following calculation:

$$\text{Expected cash flow in year } 4 = 0.8 \, [(15 \times 0.6 + 2 \times 0.4) - 5.5] = 3.44$$

The net present value (NPV) of this proposed project is the sum of the discounted cash flows in the last column of Figure 2.5 that sum to $4.40M. Alternatively, the IRR for this project can be found; that is, the discount rate that results in an NPV value equal to zero. In this case, the IRR equals approximately 17.1 percent.

This example illustrates several advantages offered by the ECV measure. First, it explicitly considers the possibility that the project can be stopped at an intermediate stage (e.g., if the product is a technical failure). If the product is a commercial success, it uses the cash flows that are discounted to the present time, thereby adjusting for projects that have a potential launch many years from now. In addition, the ECV can be multiplied by a subjective factor that weights each project proposal by its relative strategic importance to the organization.

The ECV measure can be easily modified. For example, the forecasted cash flows used to calculate the discounted cash flows (NPV) could be adjusted by their respective probabilities to reflect an expected NPV. Alternatively, the decision tree in Figure 2.4 could be modified to reflect other alternatives or outcomes (for example, there could be more than two possible outcomes if the project is launched). Cooper et al. reported that some companies divided the ECV measure by a constraining resource (e.g., capital

FIGURE 2.5
ECV Calculations
Illustrated

Year	What's Happening	Commercial Success	Commercial Failure	Expected Annual Cash Flow	Discounted Cash Flow
1	Technical development			$ (6.00)	($5.45)
2	Technical development			$ (6.00)	($4.96)
3	Technical development			$ (6.00)	($4.51)
4	Product launch	$15	$ 2	$ 3.44	$2.35
5	Product launch	$15	$ 2	$ 7.84	$4.87
6	Product launch	$15	$ 2	$ 7.84	$4.43
7	Product launch	$15	$ 2	$ 7.84	$4.02
8	Product launch	$15	$ 2	$ 7.84	$3.66

resources) to define a ratio representing the return per unit of constraining resource (or "bang for buck"). This ratio was then used to rank various project proposals.

To further illustrate the ECV metric, consider a proposed new product development project described by Hodder and Riggs (1985). In the first phase, the product will be developed and the technical feasibility explored; it is estimated that this phase will cost $18 million per year and last for two years. There is a 60 percent probability that the company can successfully develop the new product. If successful, the second phase will be undertaken to explore the market feasibility of the product and develop marketing and logistics channels; this phase of the product development will require two years and cost $10 million per year. It is expected that the market research conducted in this phase will indicate sales potential of the new product; the sales potential could be high (with a 30 percent probability), medium (50 percent probability), or low (20 percent probability). If the sales potential is estimated to be low, the product will be dropped and manufacturing and sales will not be started. This new product development project is summarized in Figure 2.6.

If an IRR is calculated to evaluate this project (based on "standard" DCF), the table in Figure 2.7 is generated, with expected cash flows for the 24-year estimated life of the project.

The discount rate that results in a NPV = 0 in this case is 10.12 percent; that is, based on "standard" DCF, this project would be expected to return an average of 10.12 percent per year. Would you be willing to undertake such a risky project for an average return of 10.12 percent?

As previously mentioned, one criticism of DCF (and IRR) is the use of a single discount rate for the life of a project. To relax this assumption and avoid this criticism, a more sophisticated metric, the expected commercial value (ECV), is described. As will be indicated, the view of this proposed project changes dramatically when a more sophisticated measure like ECV is applied.

FIGURE 2.6
R&D Project Example
Defined

Phase I	Research and Product Development
	$18 million annual research cost for 2 years
	60% probability of success

Phase II	Market Development
	Undertaken only if product development is successful
	$10 million annual expenditure for 2 years to develop marketing and distribution channels (net of any revenues earned in test marketing)

Phase III	Sales
	Proceeds only if Phase I and II verify opportunity
	Production is subcontracted and all cash flows are after-tax and occur at year's end
	The results of Phase II (available at the end of year 4) identify the product's market potential as indicated below:

Product Demand	Product Life	Annual Net Cash Inflow	Probability
High	20 years	$24 million	0.3
Medium	10 years	$12 million	0.5
Low	Abandon project	None	0.2

FIGURE 2.7
Calculating DCF's for the R&D Project Example in Figure 2.6

Year	Expected Cash Flow (in $ million)
1	−18
2	−18
3	0.6(−10) = −6
4	0.6(−10) = −6
5 – 14	0.6(0.3 × 24 + 0.5 × 12) = 7.92
15 – 24	0.6(0.3 × 24) = 4.32

Now, consider the application of the ECV to the previous new product development project, for which an IRR equal to 10.12 percent was previously calculated. In this case, the decision tree is indicated in Figure 2.8.

In this case, we might assume that different discount rates apply for each phase of the project; that is, it is riskier to undertake the research and product development phase of the project than the market development phase since more information is available at the latter phase. Specifically, let's assume (following Hodder and Riggs) that we can sell the product to a third party if the market research indicates that sales for this product are likely to be either high or medium. How much would the product be worth at this point?

Since the product has been developed and the market research completed (and successful), there is much less risk associated with the manufacture and sales of this product. If we assume that a third party would be willing to use a discount rate of 5 percent at that point, the expected value of the product at the end of year 4 would be $136.06 million ($24 million/year for twenty years and $12 million/year for ten years). The cash flows for this project would then be as shown in Figure 2.9.

The IRR under these conditions is now 28.5 percent—a value that is almost three times as great as the initial IRR value we estimated. The difference is based on the use of differential discount rates for different project phases. The more sophisticated ECV measure makes this project appear much more attractive.

FIGURE 2.8
ECV Measure Defined for New Product Development Project Example

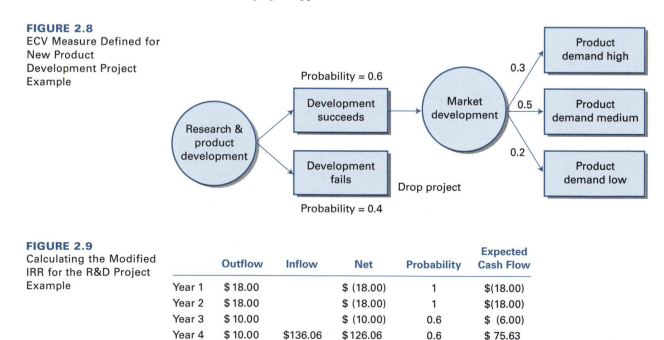

FIGURE 2.9
Calculating the Modified IRR for the R&D Project Example

	Outflow	Inflow	Net	Probability	Expected Cash Flow
Year 1	$ 18.00		$ (18.00)	1	$(18.00)
Year 2	$ 18.00		$ (18.00)	1	$(18.00)
Year 3	$ 10.00		$ (10.00)	0.6	$ (6.00)
Year 4	$ 10.00	$136.06	$ 126.06	0.6	$ 75.63

Real Options Approach

One of the most important aspects of the ECV measure is the concept that managers should think of proposed projects using an "options" perspective; that is, deciding to proceed with the R&D phase in the previous example merely gives managers an option (but not a commitment) to proceed with the subsequent market development phase. A related advantage is the recognition that a single discount rate is inappropriate to apply over the entire life of most projects.

Some organizations have gone one step further and applied options pricing theory (OPT) to formally evaluate proposed projects; Faulkner (2000) describes his experience at Eastman Kodak using OPT to evaluate R&D project proposals and the valuable insights that resulted. Faulkner notes, however, that application of OPT to new project proposals has some drawbacks; namely, the Black-Scholes formula (Brealey and Myers, 1988) is complex and difficult for most managers to understand, and is based on the assumption that future uncertainty can be modeled by a log-normal distribution (that may be an inappropriate assumption for many projects).

It is most important for project managers to have an "options" mind-set and retain as much flexibility as possible; real options theory indicates that greater uncertainty results in a greater expected project value if managers have the flexibility to respond to contingencies (Huchzermeier and Loch, 2001). Maintaining flexibility to dynamically change a project increases the expected value of a project as the uncertainty associated with a project increases.

One way to implement an options mind-set (without formal use of OPT) is to use a "stage-gate" or "toll-gate" approach. This approach requires that every project must pass through a gate with well-defined criteria at each stage. An example of a stage-gate approach used by a corporate IT division is given in Figure 2.10. According to Cooper et al. (2000), the process at each stage operates as follows:

> [At each stage], gatekeepers (senior management) judge the project against a list of criteria, such as strategic fit, technical feasibility, market attractiveness, and competitive advantage. If the discussion that centers on each criterion results in shrugged shoulders and comments like, "we're not sure," this is a sure signal that the quality of information is sub-standard: the project is recycled to the previous stage rather than being allowed to progress.

According to Cooper et al. (2000), companies that use a stage-gate approach have a 37.5 percent higher success rate at launch than companies not using such an approach and a 72 percent better chance of meeting profit objectives over the life of the product.

An options philosophy based on a toll-gate approach can also help with the difficult decision to pull the plug on a project. In many organizations, a stigma is attached to canceling a

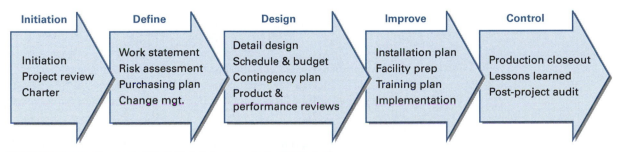

FIGURE 2.10 Example "Toll-Gate" Approach for IT Projects

project (that may be related to a perceived—or real—reduction in merit evaluation, pay, or even jobs). Given this bias, it may be difficult to cancel an ongoing project when changing environmental conditions or new technologies require that this should be done. A toll-gate approach, with definitive "go–no go" decisions at each gate, can help in this respect.

Increasingly, managers are exploring the application of options pricing theory to the valuation of R&D projects.

Scoring and Ranking Methods

While many numerical measures can be used to evaluate project proposals, most of these measures ignore unquantifiable factors (as well as some secondary costs and benefits) that may be difficult to measure directly. To include both quantitative and unquantitative factors, some organizations use scoring or ranking models that typically consist of a list of various attributes and weights associated with these attributes. Each attribute is scored by relevant managers and workers (for example, rated on a 1–10 scale). The choice of attributes, their respective weights, and the method of combining these scores and weights into a single measure is the key to a successful scoring method that can distinguish successful projects from unsuccessful projects.* A list of some potential attributes that have been used in such methods is given in Figure 2.11.

It should be noted that many of these attributes are related; that is, we would expect that market share (a "value" measure) and potential market demand (a "risk" measure) would be highly correlated. Correlated attributes have the effect of implicitly increasing the weight associated with the underlying factor(s). For example, in the list of attributes in Figure 2.11, it appears that at least four of the attributes are related to market demand for the new product. Thus, market demand might be the driving factor in determining the overall score for this proposal. To eliminate these implicit weights, it may be worthwhile to use a statistical methodology such as principal components (or factor) analysis to identify the natural or underlying "factors" in the data. These orthogonal factors can then be used as identifying attributes.

Given a list of (orthogonal) attributes for each proposed project, there are numerous ways to score these attributes. For example, each attribute can be rated on some scale (say, 1 to 7), evaluated on a yes or no basis, or used to rank each proposal (i.e., a forced ranking).

The wording of each attribute must also be carefully stated to reflect that a higher score represents a greater value (or vice versa, as long as there is consistency). For example, answering yes to the question asking if the project will increase profitability is certainly positive (and should increase the project score); answering yes to the question asking if a new facility is needed may be viewed as negative (and should lead to a lower project score).

Assuming a larger score is more desirable, a simple linear scheme can be used to convert all attribute scores to a common (0, 1) scale. In this case, assume that U is the upper bound of the scale and L is the lower bound. Then, given a score x_i assigned to the ith attribute, its value $v_i(x_i)$ is defined as:

$$v_i(x_i) = \frac{x_i - L}{U - L}$$

For example, assume that we are considering the probability that the project is a technical success, and it is rated as low, medium, or high. If we score x_i as 0, 1, or 2, respectively, the values $v_i(x_i)$ will be "translated" to 0, 0.5 or 1, respectively (since $L = 0$

---

* In some cases, forced ranking of proposal attributes may be used to help alleviate the objection stated by some managers that these models fail to adequately discriminate among project proposals.

FIGURE 2.11
Criteria for Possible
Scoring Models

Project name _____

Profitability/Value

1. Increase in profitability?
2. Increase in market share?
3. Will add knowledge to organization that can be leveraged by other projects?
4. Estimated NPV, ECV, etc.

Organization's Strategy

1. Consistent with organization's mission statement?
2. Impact on customers?

Risk

1. Probability of research being successful?
2. Probability of development being successful?
3. Probability of process success?
4. Probability of commercial success?
5. Overall risk of project
6. Adequate market demand?
7. Competitors in market

Organization Costs

1. Is new facility needed?
2. Can use current personnel?
3. Are external consultants needed?
4. New hires needed?

Miscellaneous Factors

1. Impact on environmental standards?
2. Impact on workforce safety?
3. Impact on quality?
4. Social/political implications

and $U = 2$). A similar result would be found if we rated an attribute on a $(1, 10)$ scale (in this case, for example, a response of 3 would be translated to a value of 0.33).

This simple linear transformation implies that the marginal benefit of any higher rating is constant; that is, moving from a medium score to a high score is just as valuable as moving from a low score to a medium score. When managers are not willing to assume such constant marginal benefits, a different transformation can be used. One possibility is to use an exponential scale, where the value of the attribute is given by

$$v_i(x_i) = \frac{1 - \exp(L - x_i)}{1 - \exp(L - U)}$$

For example, assume that responses to some attribute are given on a 7-point scale (e.g., rate the probability that this project will be a technical success on a scale from 1 to 7). The values of this attribute, using a linear and an exponential scale, are given in Figure 2.12. Note that a response of 1 is scored as a zero by both the linear and exponential scales, while a response of 2 receives a value of 0.17 using the linear scale but a much higher value of 0.63 using the exponential scale. Many other functions can be defined and used.

Since several of these schemes may be used within a single questionnaire, there must be a consistent method for converting these responses to a common scale if we want to aggregate the responses into a single overall score V_j for each jth project proposal. To

FIGURE 2.12
Attribute Values for a
Linear and Exponential
Scale

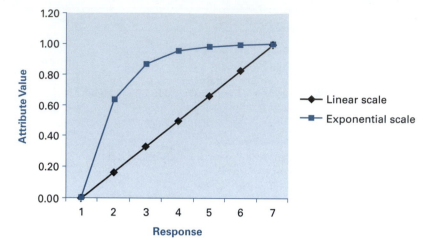

compute an overall score for each project under consideration, we can assign a nonnegative weight w_i to each ith attribute, where

$$0 \leq w_i \leq 1 \quad \text{and} \quad \sum_i w_i = 1$$

These weights reflect the relative trade-offs among the various attributes. Given the attribute values and weights, an overall score can be calculated for each proposed project; using an additive model, the overall project value V_j is defined as

$$V_j = \sum_i w_i v_i(x_i)$$

To illustrate how to use such an approach to develop a score for each proposed project, consider the example in Figure 2.13 that presents five attributes and their associated weights (w_i); these attributes include an assessment of the likelihood that the project will increase market share, whether or not a new facility is needed, etc. For the first, fourth, and fifth attributes, we rated these attributes on a 5-point scale. In the case of the second attribute ("Is a new facility needed?"), a yes response was scored as a 2 on our 5-point scale, while a no response was scored as a 4 (note that this is arbitrary; we could have scored a yes as a 1 and a no as a 5). In this way, a yes contributes to a lower value of the project's score since a new facility is viewed as a negative attribute, while a no response receives a higher and more positive value.

In similar fashion, the third attribute ("Are there safety concerns?") is scored so that a response of "likely" was given a value of 1 while an assessment that we are "unsure" received a value of 3 and an assessment that safety is not an issue received a score of 5. In this way, higher values on all five attributes contribute to a more favorable rating of the associated project.

Assume that we are considering two projects, A and B, and have rated each proposed project on the five attributes given in Figure 2.13. Hypothetical ratings for each of the five attributes as well as the converted values based on the use of a linear scale and an exponential scale are given in Figure 2.14. Finally, given the attribute weights (w_i) in Figure 2.13, we have calculated an overall project score (V_j) for each proposed project, where (using the linear scale), the score for Project A is calculated as:

Attribute	Measurement Scale								Attribute Weight
1. Does project increase market share?	Unlikely	1	2	3	4	5		Likely	30%
2. Is new facility needed?		Yes		No					15%
3. Are there safety concerns?		Likely	Unsure		No				10%
4. Likelihood of successful technical development?	Unlikely	1	2	3	4	5		Likely	20%
5. Likelihood of successful commercial development?	Unlikely	1	2	3	4	5		Likely	25%

FIGURE 2.13 Example Project Attributes and Measurement Scales

$$V_j = w_1 v_1(x_1) + \ldots + w_5 v_5(x_5)$$
$$= .3(.75) + .15(.25) + .10(0) + .2(.75) + .25(0)$$
$$= .413$$

As indicated in Figure 2.14, Project B has a higher overall score if either scale is used, implying that Project B would be favored over Project A using this approach. It is important to note that the difference between the two project scores is greater when the exponential scale is used; that is, the exponential scale makes Project B appear to be relatively more attractive than the linear scale.

For more information about different attribute scoring functions or combining these scores into an overall measure, see Keeney and Raiffa (1976). For a good description of how these (and other) functions were used to evaluate proposed projects at the nonprofit Monterey Bay aquarium, see Felli et al. (2000).

EVALUATING PROJECT PORTFOLIOS

Managers should always evaluate new project proposals with respect to the organization's project portfolio. In this regard, several questions arise that must be considered as part of any potential project adoption process:

- Is the proposed project consistent with the goals and mission of the organization?
- Does the project portfolio contribute to the organization's strategic objectives?
- Do the projects represent a mix of long-term and short-term projects?
- What is the impact on the organization's cash flows over time?
- How does the proposed project affect the organization's resource constraints?
- What is the impact of the proposed project on the organization's cash flows?

FIGURE 2.14
Example Project Ratings

Attribute	#1	#2	#3	#4	#5	Project Score (V_j)
Project A	4	Yes	Likely	4	1	
Project B	2	No	Unsure	3	4	
Linear Scale						
Project A	0.75	0.25	0.00	0.75	0.00	**0.413**
Project B	0.25	0.75	0.50	0.50	0.75	**0.525**
Exponential Scale						
Project A	0.97	0.64	0.00	0.97	0.00	**0.581**
Project B	0.64	0.97	0.88	0.88	0.97	**0.845**

Using the perspective of a project portfolio, project diversification becomes a primary consideration; a diversified project portfolio minimizing risks to an organization in the same way that a diversified financial portfolio minimizes market risk. For example, if an organization is considering several new project proposals, managers should select projects that represent a mix of new product and process development, market diversification, and a balance of technologies.

What happens when managers do not use a "portfolio perspective"? Wheelwright and Clark (1992) described a typical scenario in a large scientific instruments company. Motivated by rising budgets and declining numbers of successful projects, the company investigated and discovered that thirty development projects were under way, far more than the company could support. Since most of the projects were delayed and over budget, engineers and workers moved quickly from project to project, resulting in a crisis atmosphere that further delayed projects and compromised quality. According to Wheelwright and Clark, most of the projects had been selected on an ad hoc basis by engineers, who found the problems challenging; or by the marketing department, which was reacting to customer demands. Few of the projects contributed to the company's strategic objectives. After a thorough analysis, the company reduced its project portfolio to eight commercial development projects.

Assume that each project proposal is assigned a score representing its potential value (for example, NPV, expected NPV, a measure V_j from a scoring or ranking model, or some measure based on stock-options modeling such as the Black-Scholes model). Using this overall measure (that is assumed to be an unbiased and reasonably accurate representation of the project's value), many organizations rank the proposals under consideration[*] and select projects until resource constraints are no longer satisfied. This approach, however, fails to consider possible interrelationships among projects and ignores the risk of the portfolio.

A better approach recognizes that projects must be viewed in a multidimensional space. For example, some measure of risk can be associated with each proposal in addition to its estimated benefit; this measure could be the probability of technical success (p_t), commercial success (p_c), or some combination of the two. Given measures of risk and benefit (value), each proposed project can be graphed on these risk-return axes. One version of this graph is a two-dimensional bubble diagram; an illustration is given in Figure 2.15. There are many variations of bubble diagrams; some use three dimensions (e.g., NPV, risk, and expected duration), or different shapes and types of shading and colors to represent different types of projects. In Figure 2.15, for example, the type of shading represents a specific product line, while the size of the oval represents the resource requirements (e.g., R&D expenditures). Although bubble diagrams are useful for representing a set of projects and visualizing a project portfolio, they are less useful for selecting project proposals.

Under certain conditions, the project selection problem can be viewed as a mathematical programming model. This type of formulation assumes that the values of individual projects are independent and that the value of the portfolio is additive (i.e., the value of the overall portfolio is the sum of the projects' values).

In some cases, projects must be selected or rejected (binary choice); in other cases, projects can be funded at various levels. In the former case, the portfolio selection problem can be modeled using binary (0,1) decision variables. In the latter case, the mathematical programming model would use continuous decision variables between 0 and 1 that indicate the proportion of funding allocated to each project over some time horizon.

If the portfolio selection problem is modeled using binary (0, 1) variables, the problem is equivalent to a multidimensional knapsack problem. In the single dimensional

---

[*] Some organizations use a ratio, calculated by dividing the forecasted value of the project by some constraining resource, to rank the proposals.

FIGURE 2.15
Example of a
Risk–Reward
Bubble Diagram

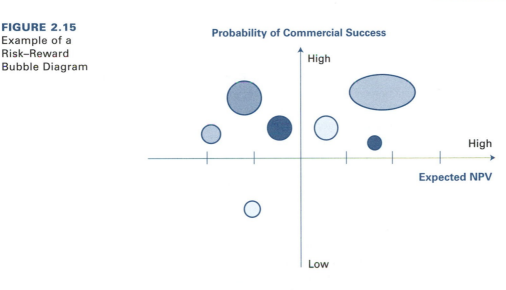

knapsack problem, there is a knapsack of given size or volume. A traveler wishes to pack items of known value and size into the knapsack to maximize the value of the selected items while not exceeding the size or volume limitations of the knapsack. In the multidimensional version of this problem, it is assumed that items are characterized by multiple characteristics: for example, size, category, color, etc. In this latter case, the traveler wants to select the set of items that maximize the value of the knapsack while simultaneously satisfying constraints on all dimensions (e.g., overall size, number of red items, etc.).

Numerous cases have been reported that used a knapsack formulation to model the project selection problem (see Fox et al., 1984; Martino, 1995; Loch et al., 2001). Beaujon et al. (2001) describe a recent application that was implemented by the General Motors R&D Center to evaluate between two hundred and four hundred projects over a one-year time horizon. The GM model used both binary and continuous decision variables; the latter model was implemented and solved as a spreadsheet model. Other approaches included a methodology used successfully by the Gas Research Institute over a fourteen-year period (Burnett et al.,1993) and a nonlinear integer programming model used by Bellcore to select R&D projects (Hoadley et al., 1993).

To illustrate these approaches, we will consider a simplified project selection model. In this case we assume that projects are either selected or not selected, although the model could be simplified by allowing projects to be funded at various levels (thereby implying the use of continuous variables). The binary decision variables in this model are y_j where

$$y_j = \begin{cases} 1 \text{ if project } j \text{ is selected} \\ 0 \text{ otherwise} \end{cases}$$

Assuming the score of each project is given by V_j, we wish to find the project portfolio that maximizes total value of the projects selected. Assuming that the value of the portfolio is the sum of the values of the projects selected from the set P of possible projects, the objective function becomes

$$\text{Maximize} \sum_{j \in P} V_j y_j$$

Any number and type of constraints can be added. If the organization is concerned with cash flows over the next T years, the following budget constraints can be included:

$$\sum_{j \in P} F_{jt} y_j \leq B_t \quad \text{for all } t = 0,1,\ldots, T$$

where F_{jt} denotes the forecasted cash flow from the jth project in year t, and B_t denotes the budget constraint in year t. Similarly, if projects are classified into various categories (e.g., relating to various organizational strategies), then additional constraints can be added relating to these categories. For example, assume that P_{IT} represents the set of IT-related projects and that management has specified that no more than 30 percent of all funded projects can be related to IT projects. Algebraically, this constraint becomes:

$$\sum_{j \in P_1} y_j - 0.3 \sum_{j \in P} y_j \leq 0$$

In similar fashion, additional constraints can be added to restrict the number of workers needed in various categories (e.g., engineers, accountants, carpenters), the number of new hires needed, total spending on R&D, and balance within the portfolio. In the model used by GM's R&D Center, additional constraints were included for precedence (e.g., Project B cannot be selected unless Project A is also selected), forced selection (when outside commitments dictate that a project must be selected), and a cap on additional spending.

For example, consider the simple two project selection problem discussed in the preceding section. Assume that both projects are expected to generate cash flows (both positive and negative) for four years; that is, $T = 4$. Forecasted cash flows for each project for the next four years as well as budget limitations on cash outflows for the projects' time horizon are given in Figure 2.16.

Given two binary decision variables, y_A and y_B, we can formulate the linear programming model for the two project selection problem. In this case, we will rate each project by the overall scores given in Figure 2.14 that were calculated using an exponential scale; that is, $V_A = .581$ and $V_B = 0.845$. Considering only cash flow constraints (that is, net cash outflows cannot exceed the budget limit in any year where positive values indicate cash outflows and negative values indicate cash inflows), the linear programming model becomes:

$$\text{Maximize } .581\, y_A + .845\, y_B$$

Subject to

$$\$40\, y_A + \$65\, y_B \leq \$120 \text{ (Year 1 constraint)}$$
$$-\$10\, y_A + \$25\, y_B \leq \$20 \text{ (Year 2 constraint)}$$
$$-\$20\, y_A - \$50\, y_B \leq \$40 \text{ (Year 3 constraint)}$$
$$-\$20\, y_A - \$50\, y_B \leq \$55 \text{ (Year 4 constraint)}$$
$$y_A, y_B = (0, 1)$$

FIGURE 2.16
Cash Flows for Two-Project Selection Problem

	Year (t)			
	1	2	3	4
Project A	($40)	$10	$20	$20
Project B	($65)	($25)	$50	$50
Budget limit (B_t)	$120	$20	$40	$55

SUPPORT FOR FORMAL PROJECT SELECTION METHODOLOGY

During our current series of visioning meetings for [our] office, we have been discussing how projects of varying size might affect delivery, profitability, and other measures of success for our group. We talked about large projects using up more than all of our resources over a longer period of time but leaving a gap at the beginning of the project when we are staffing up to handle a large workload but don't yet have the work, and at the end of a project when we don't have the work anymore and have to market to find more. On the other end of the spectrum are multiple small projects that require aggressive management to keep team members on task and to track budgets and schedules, but tend to even out the overall utilization because the projects are more flexible to schedule around. In the middle are medium-sized projects that take up a good part but not all of our staff but can be controlled if properly managed. It seems to me that there may be an optimal project size for our office and an LP [linear programming] program waiting to be modeled. Any suggestions?

Michael R. Shoberg, P.E.
Vice President
Barr Engineering Company

In this example, both projects are selected; even though Project B is preferred, the budget constraint for the second year requires that both projects be selected since the positive cash inflow from Project A offsets the relatively large cash outflow of Project B in that year.

This type of portfolio selection model can be formulated as a spreadsheet model (which was done for the GM R&D Center) and solved by a built-in optimization algorithm (i.e., Solver in Microsoft Excel). If a company knows the probability that each project will be successful, it can use the expected revenues instead of the project scores in the objective function. Once a project portfolio is identified, a simulation program can be used to identify a distribution of likely outcomes.

PROJECT PLANNING

Once an organization has decided to move forward with a project proposal, its managers must complete a project plan; the parts of most project plans are given in the "Outline of a Project Plan."

As indicated in the outline, an organization initially completes an executive summary/work statement that includes a statement of the project's goals and constraints if not already done as part of the project selection process. All technical specifications of the final product (or completed project), including detailed performance requirements, must be carefully described. The roles of the project team as well as the contractors and subcontractors are also specified. In general, the work statement stipulates how the project goals will be met and the constraints satisfied.

A procedures guide indicating all rules and procedures for the project should also be prepared as part of the planning phase. This guide should include information about who has responsibility for each subsystem as well as detailed information indicating who must give approval for each task. The relationships between the project and other parts of the organization are usually best specified by an organizational chart that indicates who has ultimate authority over the project. The procedures guide may also specify what accounting procedures will be used, personnel matters such as hiring and work practices, etc.

OUTLINE OF A PROJECT PLAN

1. Project Overview and Organization

1.1 Summary statement/project charter

    1.1.1 Specify mission statement.

    1.1.2 Define goals and constraints.

    1.1.3 Clearly define specifications of final product/service.

    1.1.4 Define project team composition.

1.2 Work breakdown structure (WBS)

    1.2.1 Define specific tasks or work packages.

    1.2.2 Identify responsible persons for each task.

    1.2.3 Specify task durations and due dates.

    1.2.4 Assign initial cost estimates to tasks.

1.3 Organization Plan

    1.3.1 Specify how project fits into organizational mission.

    1.3.2 Provide for oversight of project/reporting periods.

    1.3.3 Identify reporting milestones.

1.4. Subcontracting

    1.4.1 Specify types of contract and bidding process.

    1.4.2 Identify subcontractors if possible.

2. Project Scheduling

2.1 Time and schedule

    2.1.1 Define task precedence relationships.

    2.1.2 Find critical path and task starting and ending time.

    2.1.3 Identify slack times.

    2.1.4 Specify Gantt chart.

2.2 Project budget

    2.2.1 Identify cash flows.

    2.2.2 Determine method for tracking and controlling expenditures.

2.3 Resource allocation

    2.3.1 Finalize project team.

    2.3.2 Determine how workers and managers will be assigned to tasks.

    2.3.3 Specify responsible persons for approvals.

2.4 Equipment and material purchases

    2.4.1 Specify material purchases (timing and amounts).

    2.4.2 Determine appropriate equipment purchases and rentals.

3. Project Monitoring and Control

3.1 Cost control metrics

    3.1.1. Specify timing of periodic cost reports.

    3.1.2. Indicate communication documents.

3.2 Change orders

    3.2.1 Specify how change orders will be handled.

    3.2.2 Budget and schedule update procedures.

3.3 Milestone reports

    3.3.1 Specify major reviews and responsible persons.

4. Project Termination

4.1 Post-project evaluation

    4.1.1 Specify who will conduct post-project audits.

    4.1.2 Specify metrics for evaluating project success/failure.

Work Breakdown Structure (WBS)

The most important part of the planning phase is the development of the work breakdown structure (WBS). The WBS defines the set of independent tasks (also referred to as activities or work packages) that constitute the project in order to facilitate cost and time estimation, resource allocation, and monitoring and control systems. A WBS is a hierarchy that begins with the final end product(s) or deliverables and shows how this end product(s) can be subdivided into elemental work packages or tasks. The end product(s) (representing the goals of a project such as reports, products, buildings, software, etc.) is indicated at the first or highest level of the WBS. Successive levels provide increasingly detailed identification of individual work tasks that constitute the production of the end product(s).

The process of defining a WBS subdivides a project into smaller subprojects such that the sum of the smaller subprojects defines the larger project. A manager continues subdividing projects until she feels comfortable that she fully understands the nature of the subprojects and have them defined in a manner that is manageable and measurable. Generally, a manager does not subdivide projects into elemental tasks; for example, a project of writing documentation for a new software product could be broken into chapters, but probably should not be divided by specific pages or topics. A WBS is not a checklist for a manager to micro-manage a work package; it is an important tool for defining, monitoring, and understanding the nature and progress of a project.

Youker (1989) points out that the process of constructing a WBS is often difficult in practice since managers must consider both the product structure as well as the process structure (the life-cycle phases).[*] In addition, the definition of work packages has significant implications for worker scheduling and resource allocation, as well as budgeting and cost control. Improperly defining tasks is likely to result in serious problems once the project begins.

The WBS is analogous to a bill of materials used in manufacturing processes to identify assemblies, subassemblies, components, etc. that make up a finished product (or a recipe that defines ingredients in a menu item). For this reason, a WBS is sometimes referred to as a family tree or a "goes-into chart." Given this structure, it is logical that most WBSs are constructed in outline form, where tasks and subtasks form sections and subsections to indicate parts of the overall product. Following a typical outline format, the sections indicating tasks and subtasks are usually indented and numbered sequentially. These numbers are often assigned so that a whole number represents each end product. Any task listed under this end product would then be assigned a number consisting of this whole number, a decimal point, and another number. Any subtask listed under a task would be assigned the task number with an additional decimal point and number. For example, specific tasks under a third end product would be numbered 3.1, 3.2, etc., subtasks under task 3.1 might be numbered 3.1.1, 3.1.2, etc. In this way, any task or subtask can be traced immediately back to its end product and related to other tasks or subtasks. Note that the "Outline of a Project Plan" given earlier in this section constitutes a WBS.

A manager should begin the process of defining a WBS by first identifying the end product(s) that form the major headings. In most cases, these end products will take the form of a completed product such as a report, a computer program, a ship, or a building. While end products are usually defined in the initial project summary and work statement (if not a contract), managers should be careful that all end products are clearly defined in easily

---

[*] Youker states that the term *project breakdown structure* (PBS) is more appropriate than the term *work breakdown structure* (WBS).

understood terms. Note that the (proper) management of the project is frequently listed as a separate end product; thus, project management is often listed under a separate heading.

The second level of detail in a WBS should indicate major subsystems that define each end product. For example, if the end product is the creation of a new computer program, major tasks might include testing and debugging, documentation, etc.

The subsequent levels (i.e., the third, fourth, fifth, etc.) in a WBS reflect further subdivision of the subsystems indicated in the second level. In general, the number of levels in a WBS depends on the complexity of the particular end product(s). Three levels can define most projects, while projects with very complex end products may require four or even five levels. Moreover, the number of levels needed may vary for different end products within the same project (that is, one end product may require four levels while another may require only two levels).

The subtasks indicated at the lowest level of a WBS represent the smallest work efforts defined in a project; these tasks are also referred to as activities or work packages. These work packages correspond to the activities or tasks typically used by most project management software packages; they form the set of elemental tasks that are the basis for budgeting, scheduling, and controlling the project. It is usually assumed that no further subdivision of these work packages would be meaningful.

It may be difficult to decide how much detail should be shown in these work packages (another trade-off faced by project managers). According to Loch, each work package "should be selected so that it is small enough to be visualized as a complete entity for estimating purposes. On the other hand, the size of the task must be large enough to represent a measurable part of the whole project." In general, the definition of a work package should depend on various factors including, among others, the worker group involved (e.g., electricians, carpenters), the managerial responsibility for the work, the time needed to complete the work, the value of the work package, and the relationship of the task to the organization's structure and accounting system. On the other hand, a WBS should not define an extensive checklist that allows a project manager to micro-manage the project team.

Ideally, a work package should involve only one individual or a single skill group or department (although this is not always possible, of course). Several rules of thumb are widely used for defining work packages (some of these come from the influential *DoD and NASA Guide* published by the federal government in 1962). For example, the *DoD and NASA Guide* specifies that any work package should not exceed $100,000 in value or three months in duration. Another rule of thumb used by some organizations specifies that a work package should not exceed eighty employee hours of work. Another rule of thumb states that tasks should not exceed 2 percent of the total project length (e.g., if a total project is expected to take eight months, no individual task should take more than 0.16 month or approximately five days). The exact definition of work packages, however, may vary greatly from one project to another and is highly dependent on the specific nature of the project and end product(s). For example, in a warehouse location feasibility study, one work package might be defined as "find all available empty warehouses with more than ten thousand square feet"; this task might be estimated to require three days. In a large research and development project, however, a work package might consist of, say, testing a new drug that might be assigned a duration of four months.

In general, the following factors should be kept in mind when defining basic work packages:

- Workers and skill group(s) involved
- Managerial responsibility
- Ease of estimating time and costs
- Length of time

- Dollar value of task
- Relationship of task to project life cycle

When defining tasks, it is important to remember that work packages can always be aggregated (for example, for reporting purposes), but they cannot be easily disaggregated. Also remember that different levels of aggregation are needed for different purposes—top management, for example, is generally concerned only with milestones and very aggregate measures, while individual workers are concerned about specific tasks.

After completing the WBS, a manager normally estimates the duration of each task defined by the WBS. Direct costs are sometimes estimated with work packages as well; the resultant WBS is referred to as a costed WBS. In this case, the manager generally assumes that the sum of the tasks' estimated costs represent the total direct cost of the project.

To illustrate a WBS, consider the planning and execution of an auction to raise funds to support a charitable organization. In these auctions, individuals and businesses typically donate items and services that are subsequently auctioned off to the highest bidder on the night of the event. To initially plan such an event, a manager can create a two-level WBS outlining four basic functions that define the event:

- The event itself (e.g., location, entertainment, decorations, etc.)
- Procurement of items to be auctioned at the event
- Marketing of the event (e.g., sales of tickets, etc.)
- Corporate sponsorships

This WBS is represented in Figure 2.17 (note the definitions of levels 1 and 2).

In Figure 2.18, we extend the development of our hypothetical charity event to a three-level WBS. Note that we could easily extend this WBS to a four- or five-level WBS by subdividing, for example, the advertising function (1.3.2) into more specific tasks. In fact, the process of defining this event could be continued to almost any level of detail; but at some point, the marginal costs of additional levels and detail exceed the benefits.

It should also be noted that the WBS in Figure 2.18 is far from complete. First, the work packages or tasks specified at the lowest levels of the WBS are not well defined. For example, what does the task (1.3.2: Advertising) really mean? What type of advertising is planned? Will it be subcontracted? Likewise, what does "Corporate sponsorships" mean in task 1.4?

It is also important to note that precedence relationships are *not* indicated in most WBSs. For example, in Figure 2.18, we cannot print the auction catalog until most (if not all) item procurement is completed. However, this precedence relationship is not indicated in the WBS (but will be indicated in the precedence network discussed in Chapter 4).

Generally, a manager would like to define tasks such that a single resource is responsible for completing and managing the task. Is one person (or one group) responsible for acquiring all silent auction items? If not, that task should be further subdivided. In general, each work package/task defined in a WBS should be based on the product structure,

FIGURE 2.17
A Two-Level WBS

FIGURE 2.18
A Three-Level WBS

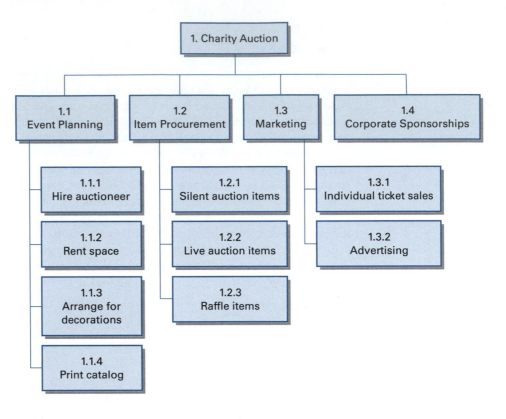

the organization structure, and the product life cycle; each work package or task should include the following:

■ A precise definition of the task to be done (this definition should use both a verb and a noun)

■ An estimate of the time needed to complete the task

■ The person(s) responsible for completing the task

■ The person(s) with authority for overseeing the task

■ An estimate of the cost of the task

■ Control protocols for project personnel

Estimating Task Costs and Durations

As part of the process of defining the tasks, it is necessary to estimate the cost and duration of the tasks identified at the lowest level of the WBS. Several methods are helpful when forecasting the duration and cost of an identified task. Most people usually base their judgments on previous experience with other similar tasks when trying to make such estimates. These estimates can be made using a formal benchmarking process, or they can be informally based on experience with previous projects. When estimating tasks for which there is little or no previous experience, a manager often relies on a modular approach (divide the task into smaller elemental units to simplify the estimation problem) or a parametric approach (consider those factors that will influence the duration and cost of a task).

For example, consider a project that requires drilling a deep-bore tunnel as part of a proposed light-rail system. Given information about soil conditions, tunnel requirements, etc., a manager or engineer may be able to estimate the cost and duration of a tunnel section based on her previous experience. Alternatively, she might subdivide the tunnel construction into smaller "pieces" or "elements" by knowing, for example, the average number of feet that can be bored in an eight-hour period. Extrapolating from this information, she could then estimate the cost and duration of the tunnel section.

When using the modular approach, the implication is that the smaller elements are homogeneous with respect to external conditions and internal requirements. Considering the deep-bore tunnel again as an example, the engineer might subdivide the tunnel-boring task into elemental pieces in which soil and rock conditions are the same and similar drilling equipment will be used.

Alternatively, a manager could use a parametric approach. Given a sufficient number of observations about drilling times and distances in different soil types, depths, etc., he could estimate an equation using regression analysis that determines the drilling distance as a function of these environmental variables (soil type, etc.). Once he knows the values of the independent variables, he can estimate task duration.

Occasionally, a manager must consider the fact that multiple similar tasks are involved in a project; these tasks use the same workers, who become more proficient as they repeat the tasks. In this case, the times (and costs) of these tasks should be reduced as learning occurs and the workers become more proficient.

To illustrate the effects of learning, assume that the manager wants to estimate the duration of several similar tasks that use the same worker(s). In this case, he can let $t(n)$ denote the duration of nth repetition of the task; that is, $t(1)$ is the time to complete the task for the first time, $t(2)$ is the time for the second time, etc. The rate of learning is indicated by the parameter β where $0 \leq \beta \leq 1$; that is, β indicates how quickly a worker is able to reduce the task duration time as she repeats the task. Given a value of β, a simple learning model states that the time needed for the nth repetition is given by

$$t(n) = t(1) \, n^{-\beta}$$

An example for $t(1) = 18$ hours and $\beta = 0.05$ and 0.20 is indicated in Figure 2.19. As indicated, task times are reduced significantly faster with the higher value of β indicating a higher rate of learning.

FIGURE 2.19
Task Duration Times
with Different Rates
of Learning

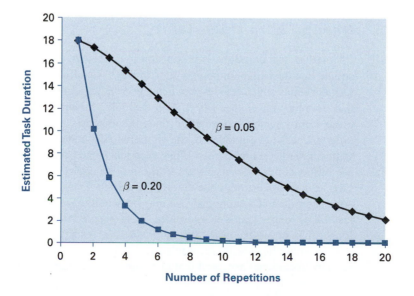

How is the value of β estimated? If the task duration times for the first and second repetition of the task are known—that is, $t(1)$ and $t(2)$—the value of β can be calculated by substituting these values into the preceding equation; that is,

$$t(2) = t(1)\, 2^{-\beta}$$

For example, assume that a worker needs ten hours to complete the task the first time (i.e., $t(1) = 10$ hours) and nine hours to complete the task on the second trial (i.e., $t(2) = 9.0$ hours). Then, using the preceding equation, we find that

$$9.0 = 10\left(2^{-\beta}\right)$$

$$2^{-\beta} = \frac{9}{10} = 0.9$$

$$-\beta \ln 2 = \ln (0.9) \;\Rightarrow\; \beta = \frac{0.1054}{0.693} = 0.152$$

We can then use this value of β to estimate the time needed to complete succeeding repetitions; that is, the values of $t(3)$, $t(4)$, etc. under the assumption that the rate of learning remains constant for all succeeding task repetitions.

This learning model, however, is unrealistic in the sense that $t(n)$ approaches zero as n gets very large; that is, the model assumes that workers can do the task in zero time if they have sufficient practice. To avoid this unrealistic assumption, we typically assume that there is an asymptote or limit on the task duration such that $t(n)$ approaches this limit as n (the number of repetitions) gets very large. To express this relationship algebraically, we can define an improved learning model as follows:

$$t(n) = t(1)\left[\delta + (1-\delta)n^{-\beta}\right]$$

where δ is known as an incompressibility factor and $0 \leq \delta \leq 1$. If $\delta = 0$, then the learning model is the same as the previous case; if $\delta = 1$, then $t(n) = t(1)$ and no learning takes place. In this case, the asymptote or limit as n gets very large is $\delta t(1)$. If it is assumed that $\beta = 0.152$, $t(1) = 10$ hours, and $\delta = .6$, the values of $t(n)$ are given in Figure 2.20 for forty repetitions of the task. As expected, the task duration times slowly approach 6.0 hours as the number of repetitions (n) increases.

Dealing with Uncertainty

Estimating task durations is an uncertain exercise at best. Research has clearly demonstrated that the human mind is limited in ways that affect our ability to accurately estimate task durations and costs—even when a person has a great deal of experience with a given task (Kahneman et al., 1982). For example, Silverman (1991) showed that humans process information sequentially; thus, if someone's most recent experience with a specific task was not a good one, she is likely to estimate the costs and durations associated with similar tasks higher than if her experience had been more positive. Likewise, people are influenced by the incentives in the project environment. For example, assume your boss asks you to estimate the duration of a specific task that you will have to complete at some later date. Knowing that you may be penalized (either implicitly or explicitly) if the task takes longer than you estimated, most people will estimate the duration of the task longer than necessary in order to allow themselves a buffer for contingencies.

To help alleviate these problems, the designers of PERT (Program Evaluation and Review Technique) assumed that task durations are random variables drawn from a beta

FIGURE 2.20
Example Task Durations
When Learning Occurs

Repetition (n)	$t(n)$
1	10.00
2	9.60
3	9.38
4	9.24
5	9.13
6	9.05
7	8.98
8	8.92
9	8.86
10	8.82
15	8.65
20	8.54
25	8.45
30	8.39
35	8.33
40	8.28

distribution (Malcolm et al., 1959). It would appear that the assumption of the beta distribution was an arbitrary (albeit reasonable) decision as indicated by Clark (1962).

To estimate the parameters of the beta distribution, managers are required to estimate three points for each task: the optimistic time, the pessimistic time, and the most likely time. Using these three time estimates, PERT designers gave two simple equations for calculating the expected duration (mean) and variance of each task. For any task, if

$$t^o = \text{optimistic time estimate}$$
$$t^p = \text{pessimistic time estimate}$$
$$t^m = \text{most likely time estimate}$$

then the expected task duration (which will be denoted by μ) is defined by

$$\mu = \frac{t^o + t^p + 4t^m}{6}$$

and the variance is given by

$$\sigma^2 = \frac{(t^p - t^o)^2}{36}$$

A beta distribution is a unimodal distribution that (unlike the normal distribution) reaches the x-axis. A beta distribution is not necessarily a symmetric distribution but may be skewed right or left depending on the values of the parameters. An example of a beta distribution is given in Figure 2.21.

For example, assume that a manager is trying to estimate the duration of a programming task. If he assumes that the task will take six days under the best possible circumstances, fourteen days under the worst circumstances, but most likely will require eleven days, then the expected duration of this task, μ_j, would be

$$\mu_j = \frac{6 + 14 + 4(11)}{6} = 10.67$$

with a standard deviation equal to

FIGURE 2.21
Beta Distribution
Illustrated

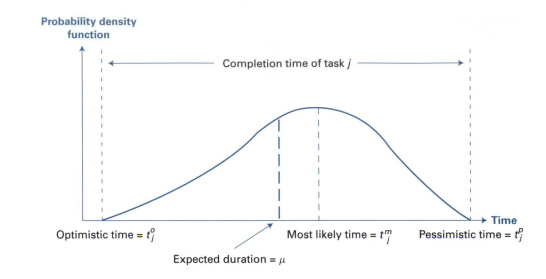

$$\sigma_j = \frac{(14-6)}{6} = 1.33$$

Many questions have been raised about these equations, the choice of the beta distribution, and the ability of managers/experts to accurately estimate the three required points. For example, can managers/experts accurately estimate the most optimistic and pessimistic times for all tasks? Since these times are the end points of the beta distribution, numerous researchers (Moder and Rodgers, 1968; Lau et al., 1996) have said it's doubtful that anyone can make accurate estimates of task durations they have never experienced (or not been aware of if they had). An additional problem results from the definition of the pessimistic time t^p (Perry and Greig, 1975) that requires the decision maker to not consider possible catastrophic events when making this estimate. Thus, the manager/expert must make an accurate appraisal for hundreds or thousands of tasks of the worst time that could occur under "normal" conditions (whatever these are). In addition, it has also been questioned whether managers/experts really understand the difference between a mode, t^m, and the median; as noted by Trout (1989), using the median instead of the mode would result in a significant distortion in the calculation of the mean and variance (at least without modifying the equations for calculating the mean and variance).

In response to these criticisms, some researchers (Moder and Rogers, 1968; Perry and Greig, 1975) have suggested that managers/experts estimate task durations at points that occur more frequently than the end points of the beta distribution. It is informative to consider their suggestion and its implications further.

Initially, note that the end points of the beta distribution can be viewed as fractiles t_α where

$$\text{Prob } (t \le t_\alpha) = \alpha$$

Using the PERT assumptions, the optimistic time estimate (t^o) corresponds to t_0 while the pessimistic time estimate (t^p) corresponds to t_{100}. Note that the mode is not a fractile measure while the median (t_{50}) is a fractile.

Moder and Rogers (1968) considered the use of other fractile measures, t_α and $t_{100-\alpha}$, in place of t_0 and t_{100}, respectively. They assumed that the definition of the mean would retain the same form, with the exception that the modified fractile measures would be used; that is,

$$\mu_j = \frac{t_\alpha + t_{100-\alpha} + 4t^m}{6}$$

Based on their study of several distributions (beta, triangular, uniform, normal, and exponential), these researchers suggested that the PERT formula for defining the standard deviation be modified so that the ratio of the range to the standard deviation $(t_{100-\alpha} - t_\alpha)/\sigma$ will be more robust with respect to the shape of the distribution and relative values of the mean and mode. Specifically, they suggested that the standard deviation be defined as

$$\sigma_\alpha = \frac{(t^P - t^o)}{K_\alpha}$$

where K_α is 3.2 for $\alpha = 5$ and $K_\alpha = 2.7$ for $\alpha = 10$. To test how well these values work in practice, Moder and Rogers presented "experience" data for refinishing a desk to four groups of subjects and asked them to estimate the parameters t_α, $t_{100-\alpha}$ (for $\alpha = 0$, 5, and 10) and t_m, as well as a single (point) estimate of the mean. The four groups of subjects included a group that had experience with the PERT model (PERT), a group with knowledge about statistics but not PERT (Technical), a group with limited knowledge of statistics and no work experience (Non-Tech A), and a group with limited knowledge of statistics but some work experience (Non-Tech B). The "experience" data presented to these individuals were random values drawn from a beta distribution with a mean of 17.16 and a variance of 5.29.

The results of Moder and Rogers' experiments are given in Figure 2.22. As indicated, subjects made more accurate estimates of the mean when asked to make three estimates of a task's duration rather than just a single-point estimate. These results imply that making three estimates forces subjects to think more carefully about the task in question, with a more accurate result. With respect to estimating the mean, the specific value of α was not significant. However, when estimating the standard deviation, the subjects were significantly closer to the true value when asked to estimate the 5th and 95th fractiles (the average variance in this case was 4.4). Thus, Moder and Rogers concluded that the equations for estimating the mean and standard deviation be modified from the original PERT model and should be:

FIGURE 2.22
Results of Moder and
Rogers' Experiments

		Average Estimates of Mean Duration		
	CPM	$\alpha = 0$	$\alpha = 5$	$\alpha = 10$
PERT	17.8	17.2	17.2	17.1
Technical	17.8	17.1	17.0	16.8
Non-Tech A	17.8	17.3	17.2	17.2
Non-Tech B	17.6	17.2	17.1	16.8
	17.75	17.2	17.125	16.975

	Average Estimates of Variance		
	$\alpha = 0$	$\alpha = 5$	$\alpha = 10$
PERT	2.6	5.1	3.1
Technical	2.6	4.8	3.2
Non-Tech A	2.1	3.5	2.4
Non-Tech B	2.7	4.1	2.7
	2.50	4.38	4.38

$$\mu = \frac{(t_{95} + t_5 + 4t_m)}{6}$$

and

$$\sigma = \frac{(t_{95} - t_5)}{3.2}$$

Numerous other researchers have studied the issue of how to best define the mean and standard deviation of task durations and questioned the formulae suggested by Moder and Rogers. Based on an analysis of the beta, gamma, and lognormal distributions, Perry and Greig (1975) suggest that the following formulas give better approximations for most distributions and most shapes:

$$\mu_j = \frac{t_{95} + t_5 + .95t^m}{2.95}$$

and

$$\sigma = \frac{(t_{95} - t_5)}{3.25}$$

Some researchers have pointed out that it may be difficult for a manager/expert to estimate the mode (assuming that he even knows the difference between the two measures). Since the mode is not a fractile measure (i.e., its value changes based on the shape of the distribution), it is inconsistent to ask a manager/expert to estimate two fractile measures and the mode (the difference can introduce considerable error into the estimated values for the mean and variance). Thus, these researchers suggest using the median (t_{50}) instead of the mode. In this case, Perry and Greig note that the following formula suggested by Pearson and Tukey (1965) will give an "extraordinarily accurate, distribution-free" estimate of the mean:

$$\mu = t_{50} + 0.185(t_{95} + t_5 - 2t_{50})$$

that, according to Perry and Greig, gives errors less than 0.5 percent for all unimodal distributions—except when the distribution is extremely leptokurtic. (The formula for estimating the standard deviation is not affected and remains equal to $(t_{95} - t_5)/3.25$.

Behavioral researchers in related fields have also suggested that more accurate estimates can be made by using fractiles. Hamption et al. (1973) and Solomon (1982) discuss the issues of training managers and structuring questions to give good fractile estimates. Based on this research, Lau et al. (1996) conclude that managers/experts be asked to provide seven fractile estimates for each task; they also point out that five fractiles, while giving less precise estimates of μ and σ, will usually suffice in practical applications. The fractiles suggested in each case are indicated in the following table (including the three-fractile formula suggested by Pearson and Tukey). (Pearson and Tukey also suggested a five-fractile estimation method based on an iterative scheme that was subsequently improved on by Keefer and Bodily.)

Based on extensive regression analyses of data generated from various beta distributions, Lau et al. suggest that the following formulas will result in estimates of μ and σ that are accurate for any beta distribution:

For five fractiles,

$$\mu = 0.4(t_{90} + t_{10} - t_{75} - t_{25}) + t_{50}$$

and

$$\sigma = 0.7(t_{90} - t_{10}) - 0.59(t_{75} - t_{25})$$

For seven fractiles,

$$\mu = 0.4(t_{99} + t_{01}) + 0.11(t_{90} + t_{10}) + 0.23(t_{75} + t_{25}) + 0.24\, t_{50}$$

and

$$\sigma = 0.2(t_{99} - t_{01}) - 0.6(t_{90} - t_{10}) + 1.2(t_{75} - t_{25})$$

It is useful to consider the advantages and disadvantages of each estimation method. First, empirical evidence indicates that human decision makers are better able to estimate the median than the mode; thus, it would appear that estimation schemes should be based on fractiles. Three fractiles, however, are limited because they provide no information about the shape (skewness, kurtosis) of the duration distribution—at least with respect to the beta distribution, since any beta distribution can be fit to any three fractiles. In addition, we have already mentioned that it is very difficult for managers/experts to accurately estimate the extreme points of any distribution (e.g., t_{01} and t_{99}). Thus, since empirical evidence indicates that managers/experts are more accurate at estimating central fractiles than extreme values, it would appear that a five-fractile estimation method offers the best compromise for accuracy and ease of implementation.

One other important point should be noted. *Any estimate of task duration or cost is influenced by the incentives faced by the individual making the estimate.* Consider, for example, the case when a person is asked to estimate a task that she will then be assigned to perform—and will be penalized (either implicitly or explicitly) if she takes more time (or resources) than she originally estimated. It is obvious that the individual is likely to "pad" her estimate in such a case. Furthermore, any organization having such a system is likely to have historical data that also reflect such padded estimates.

To avoid this estimation bias, managers should realize that task estimates are random variables and, as such, are likely to exceed their expected duration (or cost). If the duration of a task follows a symmetric beta distribution, then there is a 50 percent probability that the task duration could exceed its expected value under normal conditions. If an individual realizes that she will not be penalized if work exceeds the expected task duration, she is more likely to make an accurate estimate of task durations and costs. A manager can then use a risk and sensitivity analysis to determine the size and location of contingency buffers. This is discussed further in Chapter 6.

CONCLUSIONS

Perhaps the most important aspect of managing projects is selecting the right projects. We discussed some metrics that are frequently used to evaluate projects including the payback period, internal rate of return (IRR), and discounted cash flows (DCF)/net present value (NPV). We discussed the expected commercial value (ECV) metric and showed that only the ECV metric is able to explicitly incorporate different risk classes throughout the expected life of a project.

It is critical for project managers to retain an "options" mind-set; that is, to maintain the flexibility to adjust project resources (or delay or stop a project) even after a project has been initiated. This ability to dynamically respond to changing conditions will increase the expected value of a project as the uncertainty associated with a project increases. A stage-gate or toll-gate approach helps project managers institute such a mind-set.

We also discussed some of the key elements that constitute most project plans: project/executive summary and work statement, how to use a work breakdown structure (WBS) to define the basic work packages that constitute the project, and how to estimate the cost and duration of these work packages. Typically, information on project personnel and an organizational plan are also part of a project plan; information on project teams and organizational structures is given in the next chapter. In Chapters 4 and 5, we discuss the concepts of scheduling to minimize project makespan and project cost, respectively.

In addition, a project plan typically includes information on the monitoring system that will be used to control the project. Finally, a review procedure should be indicated that specifies how the project will be concluded and how, when, and who will conduct the post-project audit.

STUDY PROBLEMS

1. Suppose that your company has over a dozen projects to choose from—but can select only a limited few. What criteria would you suggest for ranking the projects? How would you ultimately decide which projects to select?

2. A popular metric for evaluating proposed projects is ROI (return on investment). How does ROI relate to NPV and ECV as defined in this chapter? Which of these metric(s) would you recommend? Defend your answer.

3. The owner of the Seattle Seabirds, a local badminton team, is planning to move the team to Los Angles where the television market for badminton is much larger and he can make more money. To organize the move to L.A., however, he has drawn the system diagram shown in Figure 2.23 indicating the tasks that must be completed.

   Using this diagram, construct a WBS indicating all tasks (i.e., work packages) that must be completed to move the Seabirds to Los Angeles. Indicate your estimate of the duration and cost of each task, and the duration and cost of the entire project.

FIGURE 2.23
Tasks Identified for
Moving Badminton Team

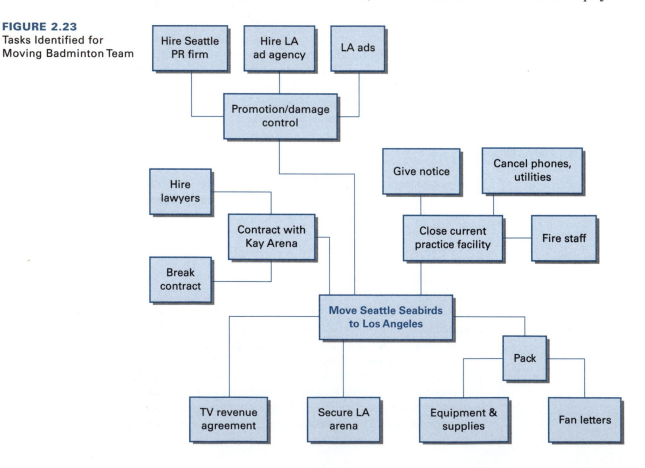

4. Wilden Wooley has decided to build a new garage attached to his home. Since his budget is limited, he has decided to work as his own contractor and hire individual workmen as needed. Wilden wants to know how long the whole project will take; more important (given the state of his finances), he wants to know what the garage will cost. In addition, the architect he wants to use is leaving town for an extended trip in a month; thus, Wilden wants to make sure that all jobs that must be done by the architect are completed before he leaves.

   After talking to several friends who have completed similar projects, Wilden begins planning for the new garage. He identifies the two major end products comprising the first level of the WBS as:

   - the garage
   - project management

   Having identified these two end products, Wilden is able to identify three major tasks that have to be completed:

   - legal issues resolution
   - architectural analysis
   - construction

   Wilden estimates that some parts of the first two tasks could be done concurrently, but that construction cannot begin until the first two tasks are in fact completed.

   Wilden decides that the first task (legal issues resolution) really consist of two individual subtasks: 1.1.1 checking zoning regulations, and 1.1.2 getting the necessary building permits. The architectural analysis is also subdivided into two subtasks: 1.2.1 initial architectural consultation and drawings, and 1.2.2 final blueprints. Finally, the construction of the garage itself can be subdivided into three subtasks: 1.3.1 foundation construction, 1.3.2 structure erection, and 1.3.3 electrical work.

   After talking to the architect, Wilden discovers that a zoning variance might be needed for the garage since he proposes to build it directly next to his property line. Thus, Wilden realizes that getting a zoning variance might add another subtask 1.1.3 under the first task (legal issues resolution). However, since there is some uncertainty about whether a zoning variance is needed, Wilden decides to construct two WBSs and plan for both contingencies.

   Figure 2.24 shows the second WBS that Wilden constructed, assuming that a zoning variance is needed. Since he is concerned about allocating both his and the architect's time, Wilden divided the subtask entitled zoning variance into three work packages: (1.1.3.1) get appropriate drawings and zoning variance application, (1.1.3.2) wait for response, and (1.1.3.3) pick up variance. Three work packages were defined since the architect was needed only to do the drawings and complete the application; no one would be needed during the wait, but no work could begin during this time; and Wilden would be needed to travel downtown and pick up the zoning variance when it was issued.

   How would you modify Wilden Wooley's WBS for his new garage if the city authorities required him to consult with a structural engineer before a building permit would be issued? How would you modify the WBS if the zoning authorities required him to get the approval of his neighbor before the zoning variance would be issued?

5. Estimate a cost for each task in the WBS in problem 4 in order to define a costed WBS. Using the costed WBS, develop a range of cost estimates that you feel are reasonable estimates of Wilden Wooley's project.

6. You have decided to paint a room that is approximately 10' × 20' in size. You have decided that all the walls and ceiling will be the same color and painted with a standard

FIGURE 2.24
WBS for Garage
Construction Project

Wilden Wooley's New Garage Construction Project

flat paint that is guaranteed to cover the existing paint with a single coat. The wood-
work around the four windows and two doors will be painted with a semigloss paint.
All paint and other supplies will be available at the start of the job. You have asked
friends and relatives who have done similar painting jobs for the time that they needed
to complete their painting jobs. Information on thirty-two similar painting jobs is given
in the following table.

Hours	Minutes	Hours	Minutes
27	25	31	52
38	25	19	15
33	12	26	27
17	44	30	27
26	7	25	21
22	1	24	28
14	2	32	58
30	27	32	1
28	30	13	43
21	13	42	45
23	59	22	57
27	44	32	15
23	15	32	31
37	6	27	15
17	54	26	11
17	13	21	52

Based on this information and your experience with similar jobs, estimate the
mean and variance of this task. How do your estimates vary if you use the (a)

standard PERT formulas, (b) the three-fractile approach, (c) the five-fractile approach, and (d) the seven-fractile approach? How many hours would you estimate if you were to submit a fixed cost bid for this painting job?

7. Assume that you have successfully completed the R&D phase of a new product development project. This phase took several years and cost an estimated $30 million, but resulted in a successful prototype product. Before your company can begin the marketing research phase, however, a long-time rival announces that it will have a similar product available in one year that will directly compete with your newly developed product.

   Your company estimates there is a 60 percent probability that your new product will be superior to your competitor's product. If your company's product is superior, you will earn a net profit of $10 million per year; otherwise, your company will lose $6 million per year. Senior marketing managers at your company estimate that your product will have a ten-year life span. Assuming a discount rate of 10 percent, calculate the NPV of your new product, assuming that you proceed immediately with the marketing research phase that is estimated to cost $10 million a year for two years (however, if you learn that your competitor's product is better than yours after one year, you will terminate the market research phase after one year).

   Compare your results to the case when you decide to wait for one year (to learn more about your competitor's product) before proceeding with the market research phase. If you wait a year, however, and your product is the superior product, it will have only a nine-year life span. What do you think is your best strategy?

8. Yash B'Gosh is a manager for a company that is considering four projects for possible adoption; two of the projects (A and C) are IT projects. Yash has estimated the cost per year for each project; these cost estimates are indicated in the following table. The company can fund any project in part or in total; however, it cannot change the funding percentage once the project has been started (for example, if Project A is funded at a 50 percent level, then this project will cost $20 in the first year, $5 in the second year, and $10 in the third and fourth years).

   The value of each project to the company is indicated by the project score; if the project is only partially funded, the project score is scaled proportionately (for example, if Project A is funded at a 50 percent level, the company gains $0.5 \times 0.741 = 0.3705$).

   Yash wants to select a project portfolio that maximizes the total score, subject to the budget constraints. In addition, top management has stated that funding on IT projects should not exceed 40 percent of total funding on projects over the next five years.

	1	2	3	4	5	Project Score
Project A (IT)	$ 40	$10	$20	$20	—	0.741
Project B	$ 65	$36	$30	$25	$30	0.845
Project C (IT)	$ 6	$ 8	$10	—	—	0.353
Project D	$ 20	$10	$20	$20	—	0.457
Available funds	$120	$40	$40	$55	$60	

a. Given the constraints, which projects should Yash recommend for funding? At what level?

b. Assume that Yash has the choice of delaying some of the projects as long as all selected projects can be completed in five years. Should Yash recommend that any project(s) be delayed; and if so, which projects and how long?

9. Assume in problem 8 that you can select a project only in its entirety or not at all (that is, you can fund a project only at 0 or 100 percent). How does this change your decisions in problem 8?

10. The Trid Soap Company is developing a radically new soap powder that is expected to take three years to develop and cost approximately $6M per year. At the end of the three years, Trid will know if the product is a technical success; at the present time, Trid managers estimate there is a 70 percent likelihood that they will be successful in developing the soap powder. Assuming the R&D succeeds, Trid can launch the product in year 4 at an estimated cost of $4M. The marketing VP estimates that if launched, the new product would be a commercial success with probability 0.6; if it is commercially successful, it would earn gross revenues of $15M per year for five years. If not a commercial success, the new soap powder would earn only an estimated $2M per year. Assuming an annual discount rate of 12 percent, what is the NPV of this project? Would you recommend that Trid proceed with this project?

11. In problem 10, assume that the first phase (the R&D phase) has proceeded very well; a successful prototype soap powder was successfully developed at the end of year 3 (at a cost of $6M each year). At the beginning of the fourth year (before the company begins developing test marketing), a long-time rival announces that it will have a similar product available next year.

    Trid Soap Company managers estimate a 75 percent probability that their product is superior to the competitor's product. If Trid's product is superior, they will earn a net profit of $12M per year; otherwise, the company will lose $3M per year. Trid senior managers are considering the possibility of suspending the project for a year to get more information on their competitor's product before launching the new soap powder. If they wait, however, and their product is superior, the life span of the new product would be reduced to four years. What would you recommend in this case (the cost to launch the new product is still $4M)? (Assume an annual discount rate of 12 percent.)

12. a. Assume that it takes a worker ten minutes to complete a task for the first time. If the incompressibility factor δ is 0.6 and the rate of learning parameter β is 0.152, how many repetitions are needed before the worker can complete a similar task in eight minutes or less?

    b. Assume that a worker works an eight-hour shift, and when she comes back the next day, she starts at 95 percent efficiency from the last time she performed the task in the previous day. How many total repetitions are needed before she can achieve the goal of eight minutes or less?

13. Consider planning an auction to raise funds to support a popular local charity. Are there other ways to define a two- and three-level WBS other than the ones given in Figures 2.17 and 2.18? Extend your three-level WBS to a four-level WBS. Estimate costs associated with the work packages defined by your four-level WBS.

REFERENCES

Brealey, R. and S. Myers. *Principles of Corporate Finance*. New York: McGraw-Hill, 1988.

Clark, C.E. "The PERT Model for the Distribution of an Activity Time," *Operations Research* 10 (1962): 405–6.

Cooper, R.G., S. Edgett, and E. Kleinschmidt. *Research Technology Management* (March–April 2000).

Faulkner, T. "Applying 'Options Thinking' to R&D Valuation," *Research-Technology Management* (May–June 1996): 50–56.

Fox, G.E., N.R. Baker, and J.L. Bryant. "Economic Models for R&D Project Selection in the Presence of Project Interactions," *Management Science* 30, no. 7 (1984): 890–904.

Hodder, J. and H.E. Riggs. "Pitfalls in Evaluating Risky Projects," *Harvard Business Review* (January–February 1985): 128–136.

Huchzermeier, A. and C. H. Loch. "Project Management Under Risk: Using the Real Options Approach to Evaluate Flexibility in R&D," *Management Science* 47, no. 1 (January 2001): 85–101.

Krakowski, M. "PERT and Parkinson's Law," *Interfaces* 5, no. 1 (November 1974).

Loch, C.H., M.T. Pich, M. Urbschat and C. Terwiesch. "Selecting R&D Projects at BMW: A Case Study of Adopting Mathematical Programming Models," *IEEE Transactions on Engineering Management* 48, no. 1 (2001): 70–80.

Malcolm, D.G., J.H. Roseboom, and C.E. Clark. "Application of a Technique for Research and Development Program Evaluation," *Operations Research* 7, no. 5 (September–October 1959): 646–669.

Moder, J.J. and E.G. Rodgers. "Judgment Estimates of the Moments of PERT Type Distributions," *Management Science* 15, no. 2 (October 1968): B76–B83.

Parkinson, C.N. *Parkinson's Law and Other Studies in Administration.* New York: Random House, Inc., 1957.

Wheelwright, S. C. and K. B. Clark. "Creating Project Plans to Focus," *Harvard Business Review* (March–April 1992): 70–82.

Youker, R. "A New Look at the WBS: Project Breakdown Structures (PBS)," *Project Management Journal* (1989): 54–59.

APPENDIX 2A. CHRISTOPHER COLUMBUS, INC. VOYAGE TO DISCOVER TRADE ROUTES TO ASIA

A time machine, recently invented by Dr. Bob N. Waters, has sent you back in time to January, 1492—place: Palos, Spain. Wanting to use the valuable knowledge gained from your project management course, you consider accepting a job with Christopher Columbus, Inc., which is a small startup company formed by Christopher Columbus to find and explore more efficient trade routes to Asia, spread Christianity, and lead an expedition to China.

After considering several other job offers, you decide to accept Columbus's offer to work as his project manager for a salary of $30/day (fully burdened). Columbus, who is generally viewed in local circles as a visionary crackpot who thinks that the world is round, wants to purchase three ships and sail west to find shorter trade routes to Asia. He wants to use this idea as the basis of a proposal to respond to the (attached) request for proposal (RFP) recently issued by King Ferdinand and Queen Isabella.

In addition to you, C. Columbus, Inc. already has a comptroller (Arturo Bayliner) and an administrative assistant (Juan de Puca) on its payroll. Arturo is paid $35/day and Juan de Puca is paid at $20/day, which were the average market salaries for comptrollers and administrative assistants in 1492 (in current dollars). While neither Bayliner, de Puca, nor you will be going on the voyage, all three of you will be working full time on administrative and public relations efforts until Columbus returns. Columbus is not accepting any salary for the project; instead, he has requested to be knighted, given the title Admiral of the Ocean Sea, and receive 10 percent of any new wealth if he is successful.

Before Columbus can submit a proposal to the king and queen (and, hopefully, start his voyage to find new trade routes to Asia), you recall from your project management class that it is necessary to complete a project plan. Before starting, you decided to interview Columbus in order to identify the major tasks that must be completed before the voyage can be started and get a better idea of times and costs involved. You also recall from your project management class that a work breakdown structure (WBS) might be helpful in this situation.

Columbus informs you that he is basically broke, so that no task can be started until funding is secured from King Ferdinand and Queen Isabella. Once funding is secured, however, Columbus will then hire the three ship captains himself; in turn, the captains will hire their own navigators. Juan de Puca will hire all regular crewmembers.

Spanish regulations require that no one can be hired until the positions have been advertised for at least two weeks in the local papers—as well as on the back of a wandering duck, known as the world wide webbed. After the positions have been advertised, interviews and hiring can begin. The current market rate for ship's captains is $60/day, navigators are paid $45/day, and crewmembers are paid $20/day.

Columbus wants to purchase three boats for this voyage; based on a *World Street Journal* article he recently read, three boats is the most cost effective fleet size. Columbus also indicated that he plans to name the three boats in his fleet as the Santa Maria, the Pinta, and the Nina (after his wife's family names).

After checking the local papers and posted ads, you have identified six boats for sale, their respective cost, crew sizes needed, and the probability that the boat will be able to successfully make the voyage to Asia, as shown in Figure 2A.1.

After inspecting the six boats for sale, Columbus determines that none of the boats have sails that are satisfactory for such a voyage; new ones will have to be made. The sail loft, which will make the sails, estimates that it will take approximately one month to make all primary sails as well as spare sails.

Since navigation is a critical issue, each captain will be responsible for hiring his own navigator, who, in turn, will be responsible for acquiring all necessary charts and navigation gear (e.g., compass, etc.). Because food and drink are important to the crews, they will be responsible for buying (at Spanish Costco) and stowing all edible items on the boats. Juan de Puca will purchase other (nonedible items), which the crews will stow.

After the captains have been hired, Columbus wants to purchase life insurance on the captains as well as himself. The largest insurance company in Europe at the time, Lords of London, estimates that life insurance premiums for anyone going on an ocean exploration to the ends of the earth are approximately 40 percent of total salary. The RFP also requires that Columbus purchase insurance policies on all three boats, with King Ferdinand and Queen Isabella as the beneficiaries. Columbus wants to purchase all insurance policies with the same company; he estimates that it will take one week to complete the negotiation on all policies.

After all hiring is completed and supplies are stowed onboard, Columbus plans to take his fleet on a shakedown cruise through the Mediterranean. He estimates that this will take approximately two weeks. Following the shakedown cruise, he estimates that it will take approximately three more weeks to make needed repairs and adjustments and replenish supplies. When all is ready, Columbus and his three ships will head west to look for trade routes to Asia. Columbus expects that each leg of the voyage will take three months, but he knows that this trip is very risky and estimates that there is only a 65 percent chance that each leg of the voyage could be completed in less than four months.

Columbus has asked you to prepare a proposal that he can present to King Ferdinand and Queen Isabella in response to their RFP. Please note that the RFP requests an executive summary as well as a statement of goals and constraints, a costed work breakdown structure (WBS), and a precedence network. Be sure that you can support your assumptions, because the king and queen have frequently been known to request documentation to support estimated time and costs. Your RFP should also clearly and concisely state why your project should be approved for funding.

Hear Ye, Hear Ye ... Request for Proposals (RFP)

King Ferdinand and Queen Isabella I hereby request formal proposals to explore new trade routes to Asia, spread Christianity, bring back gold and spices, and increase world trade.

Any submitted proposal should provide the following:

1. Executive summary (including contract specifications)
2. Statement of goals and constraints
3. Costed work breakdown structure
4. Precedence network
5. Estimate of project duration
6. Payment schedule

Requested Amount: $ _____

All proposals are due by the royal specified date.

FIGURE 2A.1
Available Boats for Sale
(*Palos Times-Gazette*,
January 1492)

Boat	Type of Boat	Probability of Not Sinking Before Reaching Asia	Cost	Crew Size
1	Schooner	0.80	$40,000	26
2	Carrack	0.95	$55,000	40
3	Caravel	0.70	$30,000	30
4	Carrack	0.90	$42,000	40
5	Caravel	0.30	$10,000	18
6	Schooner	0.85	$40,000	45

SAMPLE PROJECT INITIATION FORM

1. Project Name: _____

2. Date Submitted (mm/dd/yy): _____

3. Proposed Project Manager: _____

4. Requesting Division/Dept: _____

5. Provide brief problem description that the project addresses: _____
   _____
   _____

6. Briefly describe the benefits of this proposed project:
   _____
   _____

7. Estimate the total number of hours needed to complete proposed project: _____

8. Estimate the approximate cost of project: _____

9. Do you expect that all work will be done by in-house personnel?   ☐ Yes   ☐ No
   If answer to (9) is No, how will this work be accomplished? _____
   New hires? (Indicate number, type, approximate salary.) _____
   _____
   _____

   Subcontract? (Indicate approximate percentage of project subcontracted and what type
   of subcontractors will be needed.) _____
   _____
   _____

10. What are the project deliverables? _____
    _____
    _____

11. Will there be a significant increase in energy requirements? _____

12. Will any new facilities be needed? _____

13. Will there be any negative impact on workforce safety? Environmental standards?
    _____

14. What is impact on the organization's image? _____
    _____

Project Proposal Approval:

_____   _____

(Supervisory Management)   Date

CHAPTER 3

PROJECT TEAMS AND ORGANIZATIONAL RELATIONSHIPS

One implication of technology's increasing complexity is the need to have effective leadership and a closely integrated project team—a challenging task considering the variety of skills and disparate geographical locations that constitute most projects today. An emphasis on integrated project teams has been a cornerstone of project management for many years. In a study of twenty development projects that were conducted over four years and five companies, Bowen et al. (1994) concluded that successful projects occurred when project teams were able to work closely together to effectively solve technical problems and transfer this knowledge to the rest of the organization.

The findings by Bowen et al. (as well as others) have many implications for project managers, project teams, and the relationship between a project team and its organization. In this chapter, we explore these implications and other issues relating to:

- The role and responsibilities of the project manager
- The organization and dynamics of project teams
- The relationship between intra-organizational structure and project management
- Interorganizational relationships and project management

ROLES AND RESPONSIBILITIES OF THE PROJECT MANAGER AND PROJECT TEAM

Clearly, a project manager must have broad knowledge and experience that covers multiple areas. She has primary responsibility for maintaining effective communication among project team members, coordinating their efforts, and keeping them focused on the project goals. The project manager interacts with all stakeholders, including the client, subcontractors, and regulating organizations; these relationships are indicated in Figure 3.1.

The project manager must deal with top management to set realistic budget and resource constraints. In many cases, the project manager has no direct authority and must negotiate with functional managers for resources and funding. The project manager should also be involved in formulating and implementing any incentive programs for the project team. Clearly, the support of top management is a critical success factor because it gives a project manager some level of authority that would otherwise be missing.

As indicated in Figure 3.1, the project manager and the project team work together closely. The project manager must keep the team members fully informed and provide timely, accurate feedback. As part of this information, the project manager must keep the team members focused on the project goals, which are easy to forget in complex projects.

The project manager must communicate with external stakeholders in a timely and accurate manner. Outside stakeholders include the client, regulating organizations, and

FIGURE 3.1
Role of Project Manager
and Project Team to
Other Stakeholders

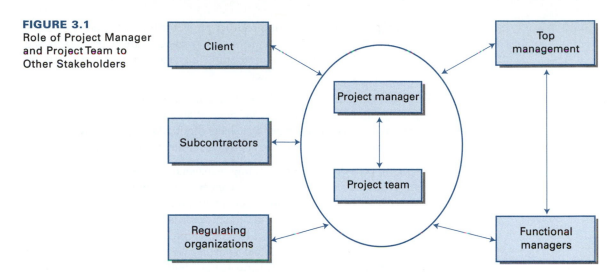

subcontractors, among others; relevant information includes project status updates, information on design changes and modifications, and changes in the schedule and budget.

The fact that project management is synonymous with change management creates stress for both the project manager as well as the project team. The current tendency for organizations to set tighter budget and schedule goals exacerbates the stress levels of both the team members and project managers. In addition, teams within an organization often compete with each other for resources and other priorities. As a result, it is not unusual for conflict to arise among project team members as well as between team members and other members of the organization.

Thamhain and Wilemon (1977a) identified seven basic areas that can serve as potential sources of conflict for project teams and managers:

- Scheduling and sequencing
- Administrative procedures
- Manpower (staffing) issues
- Budget and cost issues
- Personality conflicts
- Project priorities
- Technical opinions and performance trade-offs

Thamhain and Wilemon also note that the degree of conflict resulting from these sources varies over the life of a project (except for personality conflicts, which appear to be a constant factor over the life cycle of a project). In general, it appears that conflict is most intense during the third phase—scheduling and control—of a project (see Figure 1.1), when resource utilization is maximized (Posner, 1986).

Regarding specific courses of conflict, Posner (1986) reports that "disagreements over schedules resulted in the most intense conflict situations over the life of a project." Not surprisingly, Posner and others found that scheduling and budget issues become more critical as a project nears its due date. Posner also reported that the administrative procedures caused the least amount of conflict due to organizations' increasing experience with project management as an organizational form.

Several studies have examined the relationship between conflict management styles and project success or failure (Thamhain and Wilemon, 1977a; Evan, 1976; Hill, 1977).

Hill interviewed managers of forty-two high-conflict project teams that were viewed as high performance (twenty-six managers) or low performance (sixteen managers) and found that two factors differentiated high-performing managers from low-performing managers with respect to internal team conflict:

> the high performers reflected a much larger repertoire of responses [to conflict situations]. They simply had more ideas and choices about how to deal with conflict generally. Second, they seemed much less afraid of disagreements, and intimated much more willingness to approach conflict than avoid it.

Regarding specific behaviors, high-performing managers appeared to be better listeners who encouraged subordinates to voice their concerns when their frustration levels become high. Furthermore, they appeared to be genuinely more concerned about their subordinates' welfare and actively encouraged communication and expression. In general, high-performing managers tried to use conflict to increase project team productivity. It is interesting to note that several studies have found a positive correlation between intra-team conflict and project performance (Hill, 1975; Brown et al, 1990). This finding supports the task-oriented school of thought that project teams that have a great deal of harmony and camaraderie may be distracted from the goals of the project and will fail to meet targets and expectations (that is, some conflict is beneficial). On the other hand, the humanistic school of thought supports the belief that teams having positive characteristics and harmonious relationships will perform well (i.e., people perform better with less stress and conflict).

To test these opposing schools of thought, Brown et al. (1990) conducted an experiment at two different universities with forty-four MBA students who were enrolled in graduate project management courses. The students were divided into fourteen project teams; each team was self-selected and had from two to four members. The simulated project required each team to complete a total of fifty-two tasks that constitute the preoperational testing phase of a nuclear power plant (after completion of the physical structure and before the start of low-power testing). The entire project was reasonably complex and required teams to make decisions involving activity scheduling, resource allocation, staffing levels, overtime, equipment ordering, and project financing. The game had been calibrated so total cost (including costs of financing, interest fees, hiring and firing, fines for accidents and regulatory violations, labor, and so on) was a good measure of overall project performance. Since the performance in this project was a significant component of the course grade, the team members had a substantial incentive to perform well.

"The computers are fine, the staff's down."

This simulated project provided an unusual opportunity to examine group processes and characteristics in a controlled environment over time (in comparison to other studies that simply examined project performance at some time during the life of the project). Questionnaires were administered to all team members at the beginning of the game (before any work had started), at the end of the game (when the project was completed), and at weekly periods throughout the project (approximately seven weeks). The questionnaire consisted of a series of questions relating to group harmony, group decision-making effectiveness, the extent of an individual's contributions to the team, and individual attributes. All questions were simply worded and could be answered on a scale of 1–7 (where 1 = low and 7 = high). A summary of the questionnaire content is given in Figure 3.2.

After completing the project, the fourteen project teams were divided into two groups based on median project cost: high-performing (low cost) and low-performing (high cost) teams. An analysis of variance, with total cost as the dependent variable, demonstrated significant differences between the two groups ($F = 59.46$, $p < .0001$). The aggregate means for the questions in the first three categories were calculated for both high- and low-performing groups; the results for the questions in the Group Harmony category are indicated in Figure 3.3. Similar results were found for the questions in the other categories.

The results were somewhat surprising but indicated support for Hill's conjecture that some degree of internal conflict may lead to better team performance. As indicated in Figure 3.3, teams that ultimately performed better were *initially* lower in all measures of group harmony and cohesiveness. By the second week, however, internal conflict was significantly reduced within the higher-performing teams as their cohesiveness improved more or less steadily throughout the project. By the end of the project, there was no significant difference in group harmony and cohesiveness between the low- and high-performing teams.

FIGURE 3.2
Summary of
Questionnaire Content
Used by Brown et al.
(1990)

Summary of Questionnaire Content

Group Harmony
   Group cohesiveness
   Group cooperation
   Group motivation
   Group capability
   Member contribution
   Group conflict
   Your prediction of the likelihood of team success

Group Decision Making Effectiveness
   Quality of group decisions made so far
   Degree of group participation in decision making
   Speed of group decision making

Extent of Individual's Contribution to Group
   Technical expertise you contributed
   Group's use of your technical expertise
   Group process expertise you contributed
   Group's use of your group process expertise

Individual Attributes
   How do you see yourself fitting into the group?
   Do you see yourself as the:
      ● Leader
      ● Co-leader
      ● Assistant leader
      ● Highly active member
      ● Moderately active member
      ● Relatively inactive member
      ● Doormat

FIGURE 3.3
Aggregate Means for Questions Measuring Group Harmony (Brown et al., 1990)

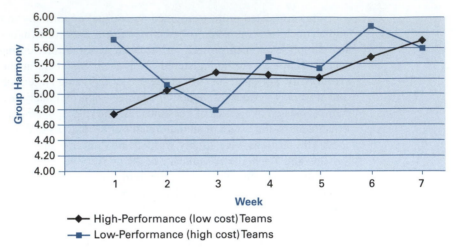

This pattern was consistent for the other questions on decision-making effectiveness and the extent of individual contributions; that is, the high-performing teams started with relatively low self-esteem but improved rapidly through the course of the project. It is interesting to note that the low-performing teams, on the other hand, did not appear to lose much group cohesiveness or camaraderie despite informal information throughout the project duration that their performance was possibly below average.

The study by Brown et al. is notable because the researchers were able to track and measure dimensions of group harmony and effectiveness throughout the life of a project (albeit a simulated project). Clearly, if results had been measured only at the end of the project, different conclusions would have emerged.

It is interesting to compare Brown's result with those of Keller (1986), who studied thirty-two project teams in the R&D division of a major American corporation. The projects were evaluated by a panel of seven managers on the basis of four performance criteria: technical quality, budget and cost performance, meeting an assigned schedule, and value to the company. Questionnaires were used to assess intra-team characteristics, including group cohesiveness, job satisfaction, self-esteem, innovative orientation, the quality of laboratory and technical equipment, the project manager's influence on administrative matters, functional managers' influence on technical aspects of the project, and the physical distances between team members. Keller found that group cohesiveness correlated positively and strongly with all four performance criteria; physical distance, job satisfaction, and innovative orientation correlated positively with at least one of the performance criteria. Keller observed no significant relationship between project performance and group size, the tenure of group members, or the nature of administrative and technical influence.

It should be noted that Keller studied these project teams twice—the first study represented a random snapshot of projects in a high-technology R&D organization, and the second study occurred one year later. Since the projects were at various stages of their respective life cycles during Keller's first study, it may be that Keller's observations and the findings by Brown et al. are not contradictory—especially given Brown's observation that group cohesiveness improved rapidly after the start of a project. In fact, Keller noted it was possible "that the relationship between cohesiveness and performance might have had a reverse causality, with high performance resulting in increased cohesiveness." (Keller, 1986). Thus, the high-performing teams in Keller's study may also have started with relatively lower measures of group cohesiveness and harmony.

In summary, it is reasonable to conclude that some degree of balance between group cohesiveness and group contentiousness is desirable. Clearly, too much conflict reduces effective communication and hampers team members' ability to work together. On the other hand, members of teams with long tenure and high cohesiveness tend to avoid asking each other the tough questions needed to keep projects on track. Effective project managers must balance this trade-off and ensure that their teams remain both harmonious *and* effective.

Characteristics of an Effective Project Team

An effective project team is more than just a group of individuals with a common goal. As in basketball teams or jazz bands, clearly some groups are more effective than others, even when the members of one team are individually less skilled. Coordination, hard work, motivation, and an ability to remain focused on important goals may be a team's most important qualities. The same is true for project teams.

It is interesting to note that Keller observed no significant relationship between group size and project performance. Others (e.g., Hughes, 1986) have observed that no teams fail for having too few members, but many fail for having too many members. Brooks' (1974) famous law states that "adding manpower to a late software project makes it later." What is the proper size of a project team?

In considering this issue of project team size, it is helpful to observe the interpersonal complexity that increases as the number of project team members increases. For example, assume that the number of interpersonal links is a surrogate measure for managerial complexity in a project; that is, the job of communicating and coordinating a project is directly related to the number of links existing among the members of a project team.

If there are two people on a project team, there is one link, as indicated in Figure 3.4. If there are three people, there are three links. In general, the number of interpersonal links on a team of M persons will be the number of combinations of M persons taken two at a time, or $_MC_2 = 0.5M(M-1)$. (If $M = 3$, then $_3C_2 = 0.5(3)(2) = 3$, as indicated in Figure 3.4.) In general, the number of interpersonal links increases as a function of the square of the number of persons on the team, as indicated in Figure 3.5. If communication complexity is related to the number of interpersonal links, it is not surprising that—as many observers have noted—projects become more difficult to manage as the size of project teams increases.

This simple analysis illustrates the trade-off between the complexity of intra-team communication and team size. A similar argument can be made for communication and

FIGURE 3.4
Project Team Size and
Interpersonal Links

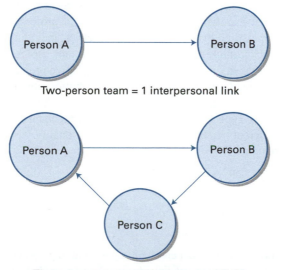

Two-person team = 1 interpersonal link

Three-person team = 3 interpersonal links

FIGURE 3.5
Number of Interpersonal
Links as a Function of
Team Size

coordination issues between the team and other stakeholders—both inside and outside the organization. This issue is revisited in Chapter 5, when we discuss the time-cost trade-off problem and introduce coordination costs that vary as a function of the number of interpersonal links.

Diversity of Project Teams

A multifunctional project team brings together many individuals with diverse skills, backgrounds, and philosophies. It often has members from both within and outside the organization (e.g., customers and suppliers may also be represented on a project team). With today's escalating technical complexity, it is increasingly important for a project team to include individuals with diverse expertise and backgrounds. The team's challenge is to establish an identity as a single unit, developing a group synergy that enables it to perform at a level greater than the sum of its parts.

Two questions remain. First, how should managers measure diversity when forming project teams? We typically measure diversity on such obvious metrics as educational backgrounds and professional experience, but are there other—and better—ways to measure diversity? Second, how much diversity is desirable? That is, is it possible for teams to be so diverse that they become dysfunctional?

With respect to the first question, project managers typically evaluate individuals on the basis of their experience, education, skills, and professional background. However, people can be measured by a variety of other metrics, including personality type, temperament, social background, gender, cultural background, etc. According to many observers (Smith, 2000), diversity is an important part of effective project teams; teams that are more diverse are more likely to make significant contributions and operate more effectively.

The idea of personality types became popular in the 1950s with the development of the Myers-Briggs Type Indicator—an evaluation mechanism for classifying individuals into sixteen different personality types. These personality types are based on four opposing characteristics:

- Extraversion vs. Introversion
- Intuition vs. Sensation
- Thinking vs. Feeling
- Judging vs. Perceiving

By measuring and mixing personality types within project teams, managers can encourage people to use both sides of their brains, thereby making them—and the team—more effective. A good description of these characteristics, the Myers-Briggs assessment instrument, and the resultant sixteen personality groups can be found in Keirsey and Bates (1984).

As teams become more diverse, they may become more difficult to manage (one reason for the popularity of team-building exercises is to promote interaction and interdependencies among group members). The question remains, however, whether there can be too much diversity; that is, can teams become so diverse that they become dysfunctional?

To test this hypothesis, Klein and Klastorin (1999) studied 188 criminal case juries in California over a seven-month period. The authors examined whether these juries were able to arrive at a verdict (that is, whether they "hung") as a function of the diversity of the jury. (No attempt was made to test the quality of the decisions made by juries that did not hang.)

Of the 188 criminal cases examined, a verdict was determined in 146 cases (22.3 percent of the cases had hung juries). Adjusting for the gender and ethnic category of the defendant, the authors found no significant relationship between gender diversity and likelihood that the jury would reach a verdict. They did, however, find a significant and positive relationship between the ethnic composition of the jury and the likelihood of reaching a verdict; based on ordinary least-squares regression, they estimated that only eight cases would have hung if the juries had been composed of a single ethnic group (adjusting for the defendant's ethnic group).

What are the implications of this study for project teams? While a jury is a type of project team, it is unique in many respects: (1) any member of the jury (at least in criminal cases) can cause the jury to hang, (2) members may not share common goals, and (3) jurors rarely know little if anything about each other. It should also be emphasized that this study considered the ability to reach a verdict (decision) and did not consider the quality of that decision (other studies have indicated that more diverse groups produce better decisions). Nevertheless, the study does suggest that increasing diversity may make it more difficult for a group to reach a decision in some situations. Clearly, the project manager's authority and the incentives given to the project team have a great deal of influence on the team's ability to reach a consensus. Nevertheless, to balance team efficiency and effectiveness, the project manager must be aware of these trade-offs when determining the team's composition.

Project Teams and Incentives

Both indirect and direct incentives may significantly affect the performance of a project team. There are, however, numerous questions and trade-offs that must be considered. For example, should individuals be given incentives for completing specific tasks, or should the entire project team be given incentives for meeting project milestones? Can project incentives be detrimental for the organization as a whole (for example, project-oriented incentives may make it more difficult to terminate a project that appears to be failing)? How should the incentives be structured (for example, should the project team be rewarded for completing a software project on time and budget even though the product fails in the marketplace)? How should incentives be changed if the project scope is modified or the schedule is compressed?

Project incentives also provide a means of prioritizing projects. As discussed in Chapter 10, project priorities generally result in reducing expected project duration or makespan in most multi-project environments. For more information on incentives, goals, and motivation, see Klein, (1991), Locke and Latham (1990), Mitchell and Silver (1990), and Rigg (1992).

Forming Project Teams

Concurrent engineering is a concept that has gained attention in recent years; it refers to an effort to reduce product development time based on the use of multifunctional teams that can anticipate—and resolve—difficult issues that are likely to occur during the product's life cycle (e.g., problems relating to manufacturing, serviceability, marketing, recycling). The key to concurrent engineering is to have a project team that reflects all aspects of the product's characteristics as well as its manufacturing process, customer base, and life cycle. Numerous products, including the Ford Taurus, were designed using a team-based concurrent engineering approach (Belson, 1994).

As mentioned previously, significant costs are associated with project teams—the larger the team, the higher the coordination and communication costs, as well as the direct labor costs. However, fewer team members may mean that some functions are not well represented on the team, resulting in a lengthier or inadequate design process. To form teams that balance the trade-offs between the team composition and the team members' characteristics, several researchers have suggested analytical approaches (Zakarian and Kusiak; 1999). To illustrate such an analytical approach, consider the following example.

A company wants to produce a new type of wireless personal digital assistant (PDA) that will allow a user to access e-mail and the Internet as well as keep track of her appointments, address book, etc. Given the characteristics of the product (that are presumably motivated by market/customer surveys), the project team designing this product must have team members who are knowledgeable in wireless technology, programming, operating systems for PDAs, liquid crystal display (LCD) technology, pattern recognition, and power supplies, among others. Given the possible members of the project team, a matrix can be used to identify possible members and their associated skills, as shown in Figure 3.6.

Let coefficients a_{ij} denote whether any ith potential team member has expertise with product characteristic j; that is,

$$a_{ij} = \begin{cases} 1 \text{ if person } i \text{ is qualified to work on characteristic j} \\ 0 \text{ otherwise} \end{cases}$$

Then, an integer programming model to minimize the number of people on the team can be formulated as follows:

$$\text{Minimize} \sum_{i=1}^{N} x_i$$

subject to:

$$\sum_{i=1}^{N} a_{ij} \, x_i \geq 1 \text{ for all } j \in J$$

$$x_i = (0, 1)$$

FIGURE 3.6
Example of Skill Set for Possible Project Team Members

	Jane	Moe	Larry	Barb	Curly
Wireless technology	X		X		
Programming languages		X			
Operating systems for PDAs			X	X	
Display (LCD) technology	X			X	
Pattern recognition					X
Power supplies				X	

where

$$x_i = \begin{cases} 1 \text{ if person } i \text{ is selected for the team} \\ 0 \text{ otherwise} \end{cases}$$

and J is the index set for the product characteristics.

The constraints in this problem guarantee that at least one person on the team has expertise relating to each product characteristic. This type of integer programming model is known as a set-covering problem; it has been used in a wide variety of problems, such as determining the location of emergency facilities, scheduling personnel to shifts, and designing examinations.* This example can be formulated as a spreadsheet model and solved using the Solver function in MS-Excel; the model and solution to this example are given in Figure 3.7. As indicated, the smallest possible team that can provide expertise in all needed areas consists of four persons: Jane, Moe, Barb, and Curly.

This model can be extended in numerous ways. For example, multiple project teams can be formed simultaneously, weights (w_i) can be added to the objective function to represent the cost or priority of each potential team member, or homogeneous groups of potential team members can be considered instead of specific individuals. Zakarian and Kusiak (1999) describe a more generalized approach that considers the tangible as well as intangible aspects of forming multifunctional teams and illustrates their methodology in the case of a new car development project.

FIGURE 3.7
A Set-Covering Model for Project Team Formation

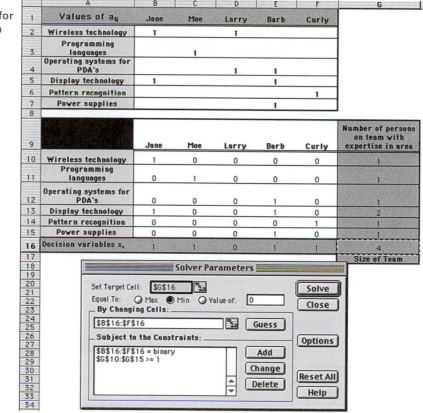

* For more information on set-covering problems, see W. Winston. *Operations Research: Applications and Algorithms*. Boston, Mass: PWS–Kent Publishing Company, 1991.

Extreme Programming

Extreme programming (known as XP) is an application of very closely integrated project teams to information technology (IT) projects. The project team defines and redefines the scope of the project while working on the coding tasks in small increments. Extreme programming is characterized by intense collaboration, extensive testing, and continuous communication.

Because communication among team members becomes increasingly difficult as the number of team members increases, extreme programming works best with teams of small or medium size. Part of extreme programming is "pair programming," in which two people write a section of computer code together at a single workstation. Having two programmers work on a section of code improves the quality of the code and makes it more understandable for other team members as well as for future programmers who may have to modify the code.

The client is typically an integral part of the project team. As the code is completed, it is released to the client, who then evaluates and tests the code. Once the code has achieved a certain level of functionality, the client begins implementation, which occurs concurrently with the final development and testing of the code.

ORGANIZATIONAL STRUCTURE AND PROJECT MANAGEMENT

Many researchers have considered the relationship between the structure of an organization and the impact on project outcome, especially for more complex and risky R&D projects (Allen, 1986; Katz and Allen, 1985; Might and Fischer, 1985; Larson and Gobeli, 1989; Ross and Staw, 1993). To discuss this relationship, it is first necessary to define organizational structures as they relate to project management. As defined by Might and Fischer (1985), different organizational structure types can be viewed as a continuum that ranges from a functional organization (where functional managers have most, if not all, of the authority) to project organizations (where project managers have most of the authority). This continuum of organizational structures is indicated in Figure 3.8.

Most of the continuum in Figure 3.8 defines some form of matrix organization. A matrix organization is an organization with two (or more) competing lines of authority or influence, in this case, functional managers (e.g., accounting, engineering, etc.) and project managers. The relative degree of authority given to each type of manager defines the organization's location on the continuum in Figure 3.8.

For example, consider a business school as a matrix organization, as indicated in Figure 3.9. The department chairs (e.g., accounting department chair, finance department chair, etc.) are the functional managers, while the associate deans serve as project

FIGURE 3.8
Organizational Structure
Continuum

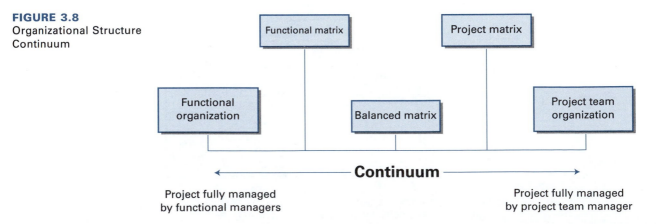

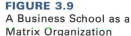

FIGURE 3.9
A Business School as a
Matrix Organization

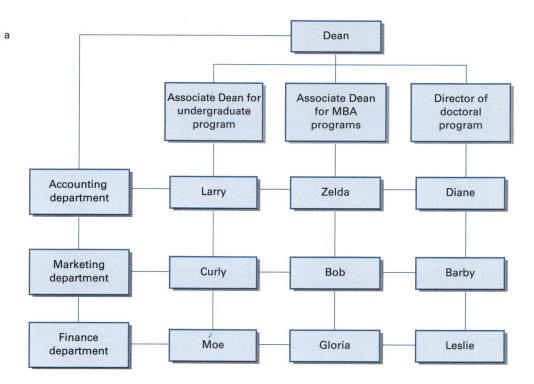

(program) managers. Whether the department chairs or associate deans have authority over such issues as hiring, promotion, teaching assignments, program design, etc. determines the precise type of matrix organization.

Larson and Gobeli (1989) have defined five types of organizational structures that exist along the continuum in Figure 3.8. Between the functional organization (where functional managers have total authority and project managers merely serve to coordinate, communicate, and persuade) and the project team organization (which is organized by projects and has no functional departments) lie the functional matrix, balanced matrix, and project matrix organizations. These three matrix organizations are defined as follows:

- **Functional matrix.** Project manager does not have direct authority over resource assignments; functional managers direct the design and work within their own departments.

- **Balanced matrix.** Functional and project managers share equal authority over design and resource allocation decisions.

- **Project matrix.** Project managers have direct authority over resource allocation and design issues; functional managers provide advice and consultation.

The issue of organizational type is a complex one with difficult trade-offs. On one hand, functional departments are the most effective way to keep technical workers in touch with their respective knowledge base (Allen, 1986). As technology continues rapidly evolving, it is critical for technical workers not only to remain knowledgeable about new developments in their respective fields but also to maintain their disciplinary support. On the other hand, as shown in Figure 3.8, intraproject coordination is facilitated by the organizational structures at the right-hand side of the continuum, which improve intraproject communication and reduce the barriers between disciplines.

As Allen observes, the choice of organizational structure should also depend on the duration and magnitude of workers' assignments in a project. For example, if workers' roles in any single project are relatively small (and so they are assigned to many different projects), it is generally ineffective to give project managers much authority over worker assignments (who sets priorities in this case?). A similar argument can be made when workers are assigned to projects for relatively short periods of time. When projects are scheduled for relatively long periods of time, however, it may be worthwhile to move the organization in the direction of the project team structure along the continuum in Figure 3.8. In either case, managers should remember Allen's (1986) warning:

> On a long project, engineers become very narrowly focused on the problems inherent in that project and come to know the application of their technologies to those problems extremely well. But since they are organizationally separated from colleagues in their specialty, they lose contact with other developments in those technologies.

The trade-off between organizational types often reflects the balance between technical excellence and project performance. Functional managers typically want to optimize product performance and design; project managers focus more on the cost and schedule of a project. This difference can result in conflict and problems, ranging from products that suffer from quality defects (to meet the cost and schedule goals) to promised products (so-called vaporware in the packaged software industry) that cannot be delivered (as a result of project managers who do not adequately understand technology).

Given the complexity of this trade-off, it is not surprising that matrix organizations have had vocal proponents and opponents emerging in the 1960s and becoming popular in the 1970s. In the early 1980s, Texas Instruments pulled back from the matrix organization citing it as one of the key reasons for the firm's economic decline (*Business Week*, 1982). Similarly, Xerox Corporation abandoned the matrix form in the 1980s claiming it created a deterrent to new product development (*Business Week*, 1984). Finally, Peters and Waterman (1982) claimed that a matrix organization is an unworkable structure that "…degenerates into anarchy and rapidly becomes bureaucratic and non-creative." Of the one hundred "excellent" companies they studied, Peters and Waterman reported that sixty-one either did not use or had reported a bad experience with a matrix organizational structure.

On the other hand, Stuckenbruck et al. (1981) presented several case studies of a bank and two public utilities in which the implementation of project management and a matrix structure resulted in successful outcomes (although the outcomes could have easily been less successful as noted by the authors). The authors identified a number of problems that arose as a result of implementing a matrix organization; these problems included:

- Conflict between some middle (functional) managers and project personnel
- Difficulties in defining lines of authority (the "two boss" problem)
- Problems with selecting project managers
- Problems of defining project management career paths
- Tension between functional and project personnel over the selection of appropriate PM scheduling and control tools

Other studies have compared project performance and organizational structure. Katz and Allen (1985) studied eighty-six R&D project teams in nine large U.S. organizations, including government laboratories and nonprofit firms as well as for-profit companies in the electronics, food processing, and aerospace industries. The researchers gave questionnaires to individuals in these organizations, asking them about the relative influence of functional versus project managers in the areas of (1) technical design, (2) salary increases and promotions, (3) work assignment process, and (4) overall conduct of the organization. At each organization, the researchers measured project performance by interviewing four or five managers who were above the project level to find out how they viewed the project team's performance.

Katz and Allen reported that project performance was not influenced by those who controlled the technical aspects of the project. Control over salaries and promotions, however, did have a significant impact on project performance. In this case, project performance was directly related to the influence of project managers; when functional managers had most control over salaries and promotions, project performance was significantly lower. In addition, the control of work assignments did not appear to be related to project performance; however, project performance was higher when project managers had greater influence in the organization than functional managers.

Might and Fischer (1985) surveyed managers of 103 development projects in thirty different organizations, using the six measures of project success defined in Chapter 1. Using data gathered from questionnaires, they compared the responses to the types of organizational structures indicated in Figure 3.8. (A matrix organization was defined as an organization where the project manager had project authority, but the functional managers held administrative authority.) Might and Fischer's results support previous findings that there is a significant (albeit small) relationship between organizational design and project outcomes. Specifically, they reported a significant and positive correlation between some type of matrix organization and the overall measure of project success as well as cost performance. Interestingly, they found that the use of matrix organizations was not related to schedule or technical performance. In fact, they reported that technical success did not appear to be related to organizational structure in any way.

A similar study was performed by Larson and Gobeli (1989), who gathered data on development projects by sending questionnaires to 855 randomly selected Project Management Institute (PMI) members. The 547 respondents (a 64 percent response rate) included project managers or directors of project management programs (30 percent), top managers (16 percent), functional managers (26 percent), and specialists working on projects (18 percent). The respondents worked in a cross section of industries (pharmaceuticals, aerospace, computer and data processing) that represented all five organizational structures indicated in Figure 3.7 (of the respondents, 13 percent indicated that they worked in a functional organization, 26 percent in a functional matrix organization, 16.5 percent in a balanced matrix organization, 28.5 percent in a project matrix, and 16 percent in a project team organization).

In Larson and Gobeli's study, respondents were asked to respond to a series of questions that related to a "recently completed development project they were familiar with." Each respondent was asked to evaluate his project as "unsuccessful," "marginal," or "successful" regarding four criteria: cost control, schedule, technical performance, and overall results. In addition, the researchers gathered information on possible confounding factors that are known to influence project success: the complexity of the project, the degree to which the objectives were clearly defined, whether new technologies were required, the priority given to the project within the organization, and whether sufficient resources were allocated to the project.

The responses were then given numerical values (higher values represented greater success). An analysis of variance was used to evaluate the responses, which are summarized in Figure 3.10; all results were significant at a $p < 0.01$ level. As indicated, the project matrix structure appeared to be the most effective structure for controlling cost, although the balanced matrix, project matrix, and project team structures were significantly better than the functional organization or functional matrix structures for controlling cost (based on the Scheffe results). As regards meeting the schedule goal, there was no significant difference between the project team and project matrix structures, which appeared to be better than a balanced matrix, which in turn was better than a functional matrix or functional organization.

FIGURE 3.10
Organizational Structure and Project Performance Data

Organizational Structure	N	Controlling Cost Ave (SD)	Meeting Schedule Ave (SD)	Technical Performance Ave (SD)	Overall Results Ave (SD)
A Functional Organization	71	1.76 (0.83)	1.77 (0.83)	2.30 (0.77)	1.96 (0.84)
B Functional Matrix	142	1.91 (0.77)	2.00 (0.85)	2.37 (0.73)	2.21 (0.75)
C Balanced Matrix	90	2.39 (0.73)	2.15 (0.82)	2.64 (0.61)	2.52 (0.61)
D Project Matrix	156	2.64 (0.76)	2.30 (0.79)	2.67 (0.57)	2.54 (0.66)
E Project Team	87	2.22 (0.82)	2.32 (0.83)	2.64 (0.61)	2.52 (0.70)
Total Sample	546	2.12 (0.79)	2.14 (0.83)	2.53 (0.66)	2.38 (0.70)
F-statistic		10.38*	6.94*	7.42*	11.45*
Scheffe Results		A,B < C,D,E E < D	A,B < C < D,E	A,B < C,D,E	A,B < C,D,E

* statistically significant at $p \leq 0.01$

With respect to technical performance and overall results, the balanced matrix, project matrix, and project team structures were equally effective and significantly better than the functional matrix or functional organizational structures.

In their regression model, Larson and Gobeli reported that only one confounding factor was significant: clearly defined objectives. In addition, they reported that organizational structure, while significant, explained only from 5 to7 percent of the total variance in project performance measures.

While all of these studies have significant limitations (e.g., the use of self-reported questionnaire data, analysis based on ongoing projects, etc.), several conclusions can be drawn from them. First, organizational structure does appear to have a significant—but small—impact on project performance. In general, it appears that a balanced matrix or project matrix organizational design is most effective; these designs give project managers greater levels of authority and responsibility while retaining functional units. This not only allows project managers to better control the dimensions of their projects but also signals the importance of the project from top management to all stakeholders.

SUBCONTRACTING AND PARTNERSHIPS

As part of the project planning process, project managers may specify that a subset of tasks (a subproject) will be subcontracted or outsourced to an outside organization(s). When making the decision to subcontract part or all of a project, the manager must consider the trade-offs. For example, if he outsources part (or all) of a project, he may lose the ability to develop critical skills for future innovations, thereby reducing future competitive advantages. On the other hand, he can reduce short-term costs by not having to hire new workers or by being able to allocate in-house workers to other projects.

When considering subcontracts, the project manager must answer the following questions:

- What part of the project will be subcontracted?
- How will she determine which subcontractors to use? Will she use a bidding system (auction) to select subcontractors? If so, what type of bidding system?
- What is the impact of the number of bidders on expected project cost?
- Will she use a prequalification list?
- What type of contract will be used?

- Will she offer incentives for finishing before a stated due date? Penalties for finishing beyond the due date?
- How will project team members communicate with the subcontractor(s)?
- What is the impact of project risk on expected project cost?

In most cases, an auction based on sealed bids is used to determine the successful bidder, given the asymmetry in information available to the stakeholders. In general, the subcontractor wants to submit a bid that is low enough to win the auction, yet high enough to earn a fair profit. The client, on the other hand, wants to secure the lowest possible bid while ensuring that the scope and quality of the subproject meet his expectations.

Although there are numerous variations, three basic types of contracts are generally used:

- Fixed-price contract
- Cost-plus contract
- Units contract

In a *fixed-price* contract, the subcontractor submits a bid for the subproject; if her bid is accepted, the subcontractor is expected to complete the tasks for that amount. If the costs exceed the contracted (fixed) amount, the subcontractor is liable for any cost difference over the bid amount (assuming that the project scope does not change). Since the subcontractor assumes all of the risk in a fixed-price contract, the client should expect that the cost of this subproject will exceed the cost of a similar in-house subproject. Also, since the subcontractor has incentives to reduce costs (and perhaps quality), it is imperative for the client to have in place an effective monitoring and quality control system.

In a *cost-plus* contract, the client agrees to reimburse the subcontractor for all documented (audited) costs incurred plus a percentage for overhead and profit. In this case, the client assumes most of the risk; if costs exceed budgeted amounts, the client is liable for any cost overruns. Since project costs are not guaranteed in a cost-plus contract, a client must have an effective monitoring and control system in place.

The fixed-price contract and the cost-plus contract are two (extreme) examples of incentive or risk-based contracts. In general, incentive contracts take the form:

$$\text{Payment to Subcontractor} = \text{Fixed Fee} + (1 - B) (\text{Project Cost})$$

where B is the percent of the project cost paid to the subcontractor by the client. If $B = 0$, the contract is a cost-plus contract; if $B = 1$, the contract is a fixed-price contract.

In a bidding situation, Samuelson (1986) identified two types of contracts:

- **Linear contract** When the client specifies a value of B and the subcontractor bids only on the fixed fee
- **Signalling contract** When the subcontractor bids on both the fixed fee and cost-sharing rate, B

Samuelson (1986) analyzed these contracts under assumptions that are generally consistent with most project bidding situations, and showed that a signalling contract is always preferred to a linear contract in the sense that it minimizes the expected cost for the client. He also showed that $0 < B < 1$ in an optimal contract (that is, the fixed-price and cost-plus contracts are not optimal).

Another contract type that is occasionally used is a *units* contract, in which the client agrees to pay the subcontractor a negotiated amount for each unit or item produced (although incentive contracts may be used to determine the unit rate). Quantity discounts are often negotiated as part of this type of contract; that is, the client pays a lower per-unit cost if she orders a number of units over a stated amount.

There are numerous variations on these contractual themes. For example, clients frequently include an incentive for completing a subproject before a stated due date, or a penalty fee if the subproject is completed after a stated due date. In other cases, a cost-plus contract could be written with a specified limit on the total costs of the subproject. In addition, change orders (legal amendments to the basic contract) are a common part of most projects; most subcontractors are aware that clients will make changes after a contract is signed. Since change orders can cause disruptions (and thereby increase costs) in other contractor projects, the amounts associated with change orders are frequently contentious.

A competitive bidding system is frequently used to select subcontractors. After specifying an RFB (request for bid) that specifies the tasks to be subcontracted, the client invites competitive bids. In some cases, only prequalified contractors are allowed to submit bids; prequalification requirements can range from a minimal requirement that the contractor be bonded to a more stringent requirement that the contractor has satisfactorily performed similar work in the past. The use of a prequalification list has trade-offs as well. On one hand, it can eliminate unqualified bidders who lowball a contract; on the other hand, it can discourage new contractors who are just getting started. In addition, some have charged that prequalification lists have been used to discriminate against women and ethnic minorities.

After receiving sealed bids for the subproject, a project manager must decide which subcontractor(s) to select. While many public projects are required by law to select the lowest bid, such practice has been criticized for allowing unscrupulous bidders to intentionally underbid and win the contract—and then raise the project price with large claims against change orders. Alternatively, some have suggested selecting the middle or average bid; other variations have been suggested and, in some cases, implemented. Given the information asymmetry between the client and subcontractors, it is little wonder that the design of the bidding process and selection of subcontractors is a "rigorous, difficult, and time-consuming process" (Pells, 1993).

Many competitive bidding systems fix the design specifications; thus, as indicated in Figure 1.4, a subcontractor can compete only on the basis of time and cost. To allow a subcontractor to consider design as well as cost and schedule in a competitive bidding situation, the client must specify clear design specifications so that the final product or subproject will perform in a desired manner. For example, a client might specify the operating characteristics of a power supply (input and output voltages, amperages, etc.) but leave it to the subcontractor to design both the circuitry and mechanical elements of the product.

Alternatively, some clients are using design-build teams; that is, identifying the subcontractors beforehand and including them as part of the project team along with customers and other stakeholders in the design of the product, process, or service. In this way, the entire team optimizes the trade-offs between design, schedule, and cost. Design-build teams have been successfully used by many private organizations as well as some public agencies.

When evaluating a bid, it is important for managers to consider all relevant costs associated with the subproject. If a subcontractor is allowed to consider design as part of the bidding process, then the nature of this design—including reliability, maintenance costs, operating costs, and even disposal costs—should be included in the subcontractor's bid. To evaluate such bids, some clients have used a point system or other approach similar to the methodologies discussed in Chapter 2.

An important subcontracting issue is to decide how to structure the RFBs, which in turn will affect the number of selected subcontractors. While some subcontracting decisions are straightforward (based on functional specialization), many other decisions are less clear. For example, consider a small hypothetical project consisting of five similar tasks {A, B, C, D, and E}. In this case, the client might consider issuing separate RFBs for each task, or separate RFBs for some subsets of tasks (for example, issue RFBs for task subsets {A, B} and {C, D, E}), or issue one RFB for all five tasks. When separate

LOSING FIRM EXCORIATES PROCEDURE IN HIGH-BID FERRY CONTRACT

A Tacoma shipbuilding firm says Washington State Ferries violated its own bidding guidelines and rules when it picked an Anacortes company to build two passenger-only ferries at the highest price offered.

"We have been in the shipbuilding business for 72 years now and have had our share or both victories and defeats ... (but) losing to the highest bidder is a relatively new experience," said Joe Martinac Jr., president of J.M. Martinac Shipbuilding Corp.

The company, one of four bidders vying for the state contract, submitted a bid of $18 million. Dakota Creek Industries of Anacortes, the apparent winner in last week's selection process, gave a bid of $19.4 million. No contract has been signed.

The two 143-foot vessels will be part of an expanded passenger-only fleet on Puget Sound.... Rather than award the job to the lowest bidder, the state judged the proposals on a point system, giving greater weight to performance and reliability than to price.

Source: Foster, G., *Seattle Post-Intelligencer,* Tuesday, 26 November 1996. Copyright 1996, *Seattle Post-Intelligencer*. Reprinted with permission.

RFBs are issued for each task, Gutierrez and Paul (1998) call this strategy "splitting"; when a single RFB is issued for all five tasks, they call this strategy "pooling".

The client must consider the trade-offs between splitting, pooling, or some combination of the two strategies. If the client uses more subcontractors, he reduces his risk by spreading the work over more subcontractors; in this case, the failure of one subcontractor is less disastrous than if a single subcontractor were used. On the other hand, economies of scale may be gained when using fewer subcontractors. In addition, communication and coordination costs are typically related to the number of subcontractors; as the number of subcontractors is reduced, communication is generally more efficient. Other factors (e.g., overhead and profit margins of subcontractors, the costs of evaluating multiple bids, cash flows) must also be considered.*

Gutierrez and Paul (1998) analyze the problem of pooling versus splitting subcontractors in a homogeneous project with the primary objective of minimizing the expected project completion time and the secondary objective of minimizing the variance of the project completion time (that is, project managers always prefer the scenario that results in the lowest expected completion time; when expected completion times are equal, they prefer the scenario that has the smaller variance). The authors also assume that each subcontractor submits a bid in response to each RFB and that the probability of a subcontractor winning a contract (i.e., having the lowest bid) is constant across RFBs. They consider two cases: (1) when tasks can be performed concurrently (no precedence relationships exist among the tasks) and (2) when tasks must be performed sequentially.

Assuming that the subcontractors perform all assigned tasks in a reasonably similar manner (that is, the subcontractors are consistent across tasks), Gutierrez and Paul show that splitting is the preferred strategy when tasks must be performed sequentially. Under their assumptions, the expected project duration is always the same for any strategy; however, they show that a splitting strategy will dominate all other strategies, including mixed strategies, with respect to the variance of project completion time.

* If there is a single RFB, a subcontractor is forced to bid on tasks that he may be unqualified to complete; in this case, it is likely that he would subcontract these tasks to another subcontractor. If multiple RFBs are issued, subcontractors only have to bid on those tasks they feel qualified to perform.

Conversely, these authors generally recommend pooling as the preferred strategy when tasks can be performed concurrently. While this is a more complicated case (under some conditions, the expected project duration can increase), most conditions will result in a smaller expected project duration and/or variance. For example, when a parallel project can be subdivided into identical subprojects, Gutierrez and Paul show that pooling will always minimize the expected project duration.

While it may be difficult to directly apply these results to more realistic projects, the authors raise important issues relating to bidding and subcontracting process, and provide valuable insights into the optimal structure of the bidding (auction) scheme that is ultimately adopted. Clearly, the subcontracting issue is a difficult and critical element of most project plans, and it frequently has a large impact on the ultimate success or failure of the project.

Partnerships and Alliances

More frequently, managers are recognizing that subcontractors are partners in managing complex projects. Such partnerships can provide a competitive advantage; organizations are forming partnerships where they might previously have operated in a competitive situation. For example, consider the "standard" model, whereby a client issues an RFB and then selects the contractor with the lowest bid. The client and the contractor are placed in a competitive situation; the client wants to minimize her payments while the contractor wants maximize his profits. Alternatively, the client and contractor can form an alliance for their mutual benefit; they can both participate in the project design and planning phase as well as in project scheduling and execution. Such an alliance can be viewed as an alternative organizational structure.

Cowan et al. (1992) describe numerous benefits from partnerships, including cost savings, reduction of project overhead, improvements in design based on knowledge sharing, and improved satisfaction of all stakeholders. As the authors note, however, alliances are not without risks. They require a greater degree of coordination and communication, and may result in conflict when managers in the partnership have to deal with corporate cultures that may be very different from their own. When personality types are compatible and trust can be established, project managers should carefully consider using project alliances.

CONCLUSIONS

The human factor in organizations is always a significant aspect of any management endeavor, including project management. How project teams are formed, how the organization rewards project team members, and how much importance an organization gives to a project all contribute greatly to the ultimate success or failure of a project.

STUDY PROBLEMS

1. Consider the formation of a project team. What characteristics do you feel members of the team should have? Should the team consist of members with similar training and background, or should team members have different skills and backgrounds? How should a project team operate? Who should have ultimate responsibility for the performance of the team?

2. Consider the relationship between a project team and the functional parts of an organization. Who should have responsibility for approving specific tasks? If an engineering task goes beyond its proposed duration and budget, who is responsible—the director of engineering or the project manager? In general, how do you think a company that is functionally organized should deal with projects?

REFERENCES

Allen, T.J. "Organizational Structure, Information Technology, and R&D Productivity," *IEEE Transactions on Engineering Management* EM-33, no. 4 (November 1986).

Belson, D. "Concurrent Engineering" in *Handbook of Design, Manufacturing, and Automation*. R.D. Dorf and A. Kusiak, eds. New York: John Wiley & Sons, Inc.

Bowen, K. K. Clark, C. Holloway, and S. Wheelwright. "Development Projects: The Engine of Renewal," *Harvard Business Review* (September–October 1994): 108–120.

Brooks, F. *The Mythical Man-Month: Essays on Software Engineering*. Addison-Wesley, 1995 (Anniversary Edition).

Brown, K. T. Klastorin, and J. Valluzzi. "Project Management Performance: A Comparison of Team Characteristics," *IEEE Transactions on Engineering Management* 37, no. 2 (May 1990): 117–125.

Business Week. "Cuts at Texas Instruments," 11 October 1982, 42.

Business Week. "How Xerox Speeds Up the Birth of New Products," 19 March 1984, 58–59.

Cowan, C., C. Gray, and E. Larson. "Project Partnering" *Project Management Journal*. Vol. XXII, No. 4 (December 1992): 5–11.

Evan, W.M. "Conflict and Performance in R&D Organizations," *Industrial Management Review* (Fall 1965): 37–46.

Gutierrez, G. and A. Paul. "Analysis of the Effects of Uncertainty, Risk-pooling, and Subcontracting Mechanisms on Project Performance," *Operations Research* 48 (1998): 927–938.

Hill, R.E. "Interpersonal Compatibility and Work Group Performance," *Journal of Applied Behavioral Science* 11, no. 2 (1975): 210–219.

Hill, R.E. "Managing Interpersonal Conflict in Project Teams," *Sloan Management Review* (Winter 1977): 45–61.

Hughes, M.W. "Why Projects Fail: The Effects of Ignoring the Obvious," *Industrial Engineering* (April 1986): 14–18.

Katz, R. and T. Allen. "Project Performance and the Locus of Influence in the R&D Matrix," *Academy of Management Journal* 28, no. 1 (1985): 67–87.

Keirsey, D. and M. Bates. *Please Understand Me: Character and Temperament Types*. Del Mar, Calif.: Prometheus Nemesis Book Company, 1984.

Keller, R.T. "Predictors of the Performance of Project Groups in R&D Organizations," *Academy of Management Journal* 29 (1986): 715–726.

Klein, J., "A Reexamination of Autonomy in Light of New Manufacturing Practices," *Human Relations* 44, no. 1 (1991): 21–38.

Klein, K. and T. Klastorin. "Do Diverse Juries Aid or Impede Justice?" *Wisconsin Law Review* 1999, no. 3 (1999): 553–569.

Larson, E. and D. Gobeli. "Significance of Project Management Structure on Development Success," *IEEE Transactions on Engineering Management* 36, no. 2 (May 1989).

Locke, E., and G. Latham. *A Theory of Goal Setting & Task Performance*. Englewood Cliffs, N.J.: Prentice-Hall, 1990.

Might, R.J. and W.A. Fischer. "The Role of Structural Factors in Determining Project Management Success," *IEEE Transactions on Engineering Management* EM-32, no. 2 (May 1985).

Mitchell, T. and W. Silver. "Individual and Group Goals When Workers are Interdependent: Effects on Task Strategies and Performance," *Journal of Applied Psychology* 75, no. 2 (1990): 185–193.

Pells, D. *The AMA Handbook of Project Management*. New York: AMACOM, 1993.

Peters, T. and R. Waterman. *In Search of Excellence*. New York: Harper and Row, 1982.

Posner, B. "What's All the Fighting About? Conflicts in Project Management," *IEEE Transactions on Engineering Management* EM-33, no. 4 (November 1986): 207–211.

Rigg, M. "Performance-Based Pay: Linking Work Objectives To Personal Interests," *Industrial Engineering* 24, no. 10 (1992): 26–27.

Ross, J. and B. Staw. "Organizational Escalation and Exit: Lessons from the Shoreham Nuclear Power Plant," *Academy of Management Journal* 36, no. 4 (1993): 701–732.

Samuelson, W. "Bidding for Contracts," *Management Science* 32, no. 12 (1986): 1533–1550.

Smith, K. A. *Project Management and Teamwork.* Burr Ridge, Ill.: McGraw-Hill Companies, Inc., 2000.

Stuckenbruck, L.D., H.B. Einstein, R.L. Day, and J.N. Salapatas. "The Implementation of Project Management: Three Case Histories" in Stuckenbruck, L.D. *The Implementation of Project Management: The Professional's Handbook,* 188–221. Reading, Mass.: Addison-Wesley Publishing Company, 1981.

Thaimhain, H.J. and D.L. Wilemon. "Leadership, Conflict, and Program Management Effectiveness," *Sloan Management Review* (Fall 1977): 69–89.

Zakarian, A. and A. Kusiak. "Forming Teams: An Analytical Approach," *IIE Transactions* 31 (1999): 85–97.

PRECEDENCE NETWORKS AND THE CRITICAL PATH METHOD (CPM)

In Chapter 2, we saw how a work breakdown structure (WBS) can be used to define tasks or work packages. These tasks form the basis for the project plan, including scheduling and budgeting that is normally used to establish initial cost and time goals.

As a result of the WBS, we have a list of tasks with an identifying name for each task and an estimate of task duration. Keep in mind that most project management (PM) software packages require a single estimate for each task's duration; that is, they assume that you know the exact duration of each task with no variation or uncertainty. In addition, PM software assumes that the tasks are independent in the sense that they can be started independently of each other.

After defining the set of tasks that define a project, project managers generally define the precedence relationships that exist among the tasks; that is, they must identify which tasks must precede (or succeed) other tasks. Assuming that task A must precede task B, we can define four types of precedence relationships:

- **Finish-to-start:** Task B cannot start until task A is completed.

- **Start-to-start:** Task B cannot start until task A has been started.

- **Finish-to-finish:** Task B cannot be completed until task A has been completed.

- **Start-to-finish:** Task B cannot be finished until task A has been started.

Most PM software packages allow the user to specify the type of precedence relationships; the default in most cases is the finish-to-start relationship. In addition, the user can usually specify a time lag between the start/finish of task A and the start/finish of task B. For example, if there is a two-day lag in a start-to-start relationship, task B cannot be started for at least two days after task A has been started. (A start-to-start relationship is especially useful when managers are overlapping phases of a new product development project. For example, a manager might want to start writing documentation on a new information technology (IT) product even though detailed design and programming have not been completed.) Throughout this chapter, we will assume that all precedence relationships are finish-to-start types; in Appendix 4B, however, we explore the start-to-start and the finish-to-finish relationships in more detail.

Once the tasks are defined, durations estimated, and precedence relationships specified, this information is displayed by a precedence network or diagram. Precedence networks are useful visual tools for displaying information about a project, including the current status of the project, the remaining work, and task assignments. Precedence networks are generated by most PM software products currently available.

PRECEDENCE NETWORKS DEFINED

There are two types of networks in use today; the first type uses nodes to represent tasks and arrows (arcs) to represent precedence relationships, while the second type uses arrows

83

or arcs to represent tasks and nodes to represent events/milestones. The first type of precedence network is known as an activity-on-node (AON) network and is typically used in most PM software. In addition, most project managers find the AON notation easier to explain and use—a definite benefit when communicating with nontechnical users.

Activity-on-Node (AON) Precedence Networks

The AON notation is best explained by use of an example. Consider a project with four tasks: A, B, C, and D. Assume that tasks A and B can start simultaneously; that is, their starts are independent of any other tasks. Furthermore, task C cannot be started until both tasks A and B have been completed, while task D cannot start until task B is finished. The AON network to represent these relationships is given in Figure 4.1.

In Figure 4.1, each task is indicated by a node (labeled A, B, C, and D), while arcs indicate precedence relationships. Note that two additional nodes have been added representing the start and end of the project. These tasks (indicated by a diamond in the network) are two milestones; milestones take zero time and cost nothing, but represent important events in the life of a project that are added for reporting and control purposes.

The START and END milestones must always be explicitly included since all precedence networks must start at a single node and end at a single node. In addition, cycles are not allowed among the tasks in these networks, where a cycle is a path that leads back to itself. For example, adding an arc from task C back to task A would result in an obvious cycle between tasks A and C; cycles indicate that there is a logical inconsistency among the precedence relationships that must be resolved before any further planning can occur.

It is usually difficult to determine if a cycle occurs in a large network by inspection. For example, adding an arc from task D to task A in the Figure 4.1 example would not result in a cycle or add any inconsistency. (It would, however, add redundant or unnecessary arcs.) All PM software packages can determine if there is a cycle in the precedence network; however, only the project manager can determine how such a cycle can be corrected. In addition, some PM software can determine which precedence arcs are redundant and can be removed. (If an arc is added from task D to task A, then the arc from START to task A as well as the arc from task B to task C become unnecessary and should be removed.)

Assuming that the precedence network has no cycles, there always exists one or more paths from START to END in every network. This type of network is known as an acyclic directed network; such a network is required for the calculations that form the basis of the critical path method (CPM).

Activity-on-Arc (AOA) Precedence Networks

The alternative method for representing precedence networks is the activity-on-arc (AOA) method. In this case, arcs in the network represent tasks, while the nodes represent events or points in time. In an AOA network, for example, an arbitrary task A would be represented as shown in Figure 4.2, where node i represents the possible start of task A and node j represents

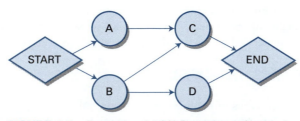

FIGURE 4.1 Example of AON Precedence Network

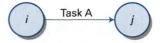

FIGURE 4.2 Task Representation in an AOA Network

the possible ending of task A. To illustrate further, assume that task A is expected to last eight days. If event i occurs at time 5, then the earliest time that event j (signaling the completion of task A) could occur is at time $(5 + 8) = 13$. In general, tasks in an AOA network are represented by their starting and ending events; that is, task A would be denoted by task (i, j).

At first, AOA notation is a bit more complicated to understand than AON notation. In some cases a dummy task must be used in AOA networks to accurately represent certain precedence relationships; a dummy task is a fictitious task that costs nothing and requires zero time. For example, if there are two (or more) tasks with the same starting and ending events, a dummy task must be used to differentiate between the two real tasks. To illustrate, consider a second task B that has the same starting and ending events as task A, as shown in Figure 4.3. In this case, a dummy or fictitious task (indicated by a dashed arrow) would be needed in order to properly represent tasks A and B in an AOA network, as shown in Figure 4.4.

In Figure 4.4, task A would be denoted as task (i, j), task B would be denoted as task (i, k), and the dummy task is denoted as task (k, j).

To further illustrate the differences between AON and AOA notation, consider the example precedence network in Figure 4.1. The same precedence relationships, expressed in an AOA network, are given in Figure 4.5. Note that in this case, a dummy task must be placed from node 1 to node 2 to correctly indicate that both tasks A and B precede task C (but only task B precedes task D).

In an AOA precedence network, the first event is always the start of the project while the last event is always the end of the project. Like AON networks, AOA networks must not have any cycles. In addition, we typically try to number the nodes (events) so that tasks proceed from a lower-numbered event to a higher-numbered event (for example, the dummy task that starts at event 1 and ends at event 2). As long as there are no cycles in a network, this can always be accomplished.

Regarding dummy tasks, it is generally best to remove redundant or unnecessary dummy tasks. In an AOA network, a dummy task is redundant if it is the only task starting or ending at a given event (except for the case when a dummy task is used to differentiate between two tasks having the same starting and ending events). For example, in Figure 4.5, the dummy task is not the only task starting from event 1 or ending at event 2; thus the dummy task in this example is not redundant but provides a unique precedence relationship and cannot be removed without changing the structure of the network.

Comparison of AOA versus AON Networks

Both AON and AOA networks have advantages and disadvantages. As indicated, AON networks are easier to explain and are more readily understood by nontechnical users. On the other hand, AOA networks were used for the initial Program Evaluation and Review

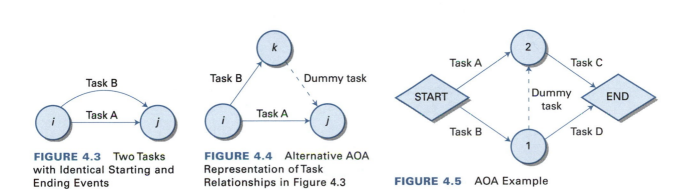

FIGURE 4.3 Two Tasks with Identical Starting and Ending Events

FIGURE 4.4 Alternative AOA Representation of Task Relationships in Figure 4.3

FIGURE 4.5 AOA Example

Technique (PERT) and CPM models developed in the 1950s, so the concept of an AOA network was established early. In addition, the PERT model discussed in Chapter 6 is based on the concept of events as defined in AOA networks.

AOA networks have other advantages as well. It is easier to store and transmit the structure of an AOA network than an AON network. For an AOA network, a simple list of all tasks with their respective starting and ending event numbers will suffice, while a list of tasks and their immediate predecessors must be specified for an AON network. For example, the following list of tasks will uniquely specify the AOA network in Figure 4.5:

- A: Task (START, 2)
- B: Task (START, 1)
- Dummy Task (1, 2)
- C: Task (2, END)
- D: Task (1, END)

In addition, an AOA network can be drawn using arc lengths that correspond to their respective durations. This type of visual aid can be very helpful when tracking a project's progress and budget.

Despite the relative advantages of AOA networks, we will use AON networks in this book for two significant reasons. As mentioned, AON networks are easier to understand and describe for nontechnical users. More important, however, is that most, if not all, PM software programs use AON networks. Thus, AON networks are used throughout this book (although the CPM calculations for an AOA network are provided at the end of this chapter).

CRITICAL PATH METHOD (CPM): CONCEPTS AND CALCULATIONS

As indicated, a network or arrow diagram can conveniently represent the precedence relationships among tasks in a project. We will also assume that the arcs in these AON networks represent finish-to-start relationships; that is, all preceding tasks must be completely finished before any succeeding tasks can begin.

To illustrate basic concepts of the critical path method (CPM), consider the AON project example in Figure 4.6, where diamond nodes represent milestones, circle nodes (with an identifying letter or word) represent tasks, and the arcs indicate precedence relationships. Also note that each task (node) indicates an expected duration for that task; in this example, expected durations are indicated in months. It is important to remember that the critical path calculations assume that these durations are deterministic (that is, known and constant). We will explore the implications of random task duration times in Chapter 6.

FIGURE 4.6
AON Network with Two
Paths Illustrated

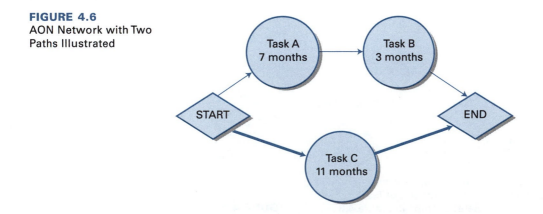

In this small example, it is clear that there are two paths through the network from the START node to the END node: START-A-B-END and START-C-END. Since all tasks must be finished to complete the entire project, it is clear that eleven months are needed to complete the project, assuming that milestones START and END require no time and that the durations of the three tasks are exactly as indicated. Thus, the minimum time needed to complete a project is equal to the length of the longest path through the network; this path is known as the **critical path** and is indicated by bold arrows. The project duration of eleven months, as defined by the length of the critical path, is also known as the project **makespan.**

This small example in Figure 4.6 also illustrates the concept of total slack or float. Since the tasks on path START-A-B-END require only ten months to complete, tasks A or B can be delayed by as much as one month without delaying the makespan of the project. Thus, the slack or float associated with both task A and task B is one month (this type of slack is known as total slack or total float). It should be noted that this slack is a path-dependent measure; that is, if the duration of task A is increased by one month (to eight months), the total slack of task B, as well as the total slack of task A, will be reduced from one month to zero.

The example in Figure 4.6 illustrates other concepts as well. For each task and milestone, program managers are usually interested in knowing the earliest time that each task can be started/finished as well as the latest time that each task can be started/completed, without delaying the project makespan. Assuming that the start of the project occurs at time 0, tasks A and C can start at time 0 since the START milestone takes zero time. The earliest starting time for the START milestone and the project, denoted by the notation ES_{START}, is zero. Task B can start as soon as task A is completed, so $ES_B = 7$. Likewise, task C can start as early as time 0, so $ES_C = 0$. Conversely, tasks B and C can be completed as late as time 11 (since eleven months are needed to complete the entire project, assuming that the END milestone also requires zero time). If we let LF_j denote the latest finish times for some task j, $LF_B = 11$ while $LF_A = 8$ indicating that task A, which precedes task B, can be completed as late as time 8. These calculations are indicated in Figure 4.7.

To illustrate these concepts in a larger project network and define the calculations more formally, consider the AON project example in Figure 4.8. In this example, expected durations are indicated in weeks; again, these durations are assumed to be known and constant.

As previously indicated, milestones are indicated by diamonds and always have zero duration. Again, the two milestones START and END indicate the unique starting and ending points of the network and the project.

FIGURE 4.7
AON Network Example with CPM Calculations Indicated

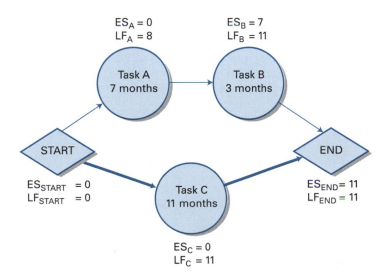

$ES_A = 0$
$LF_A = 8$

$ES_B = 7$
$LF_B = 11$

Task A
7 months

Task B
3 months

START

END

$ES_{START} = 0$
$LF_{START} = 0$

$ES_{END} = 11$
$LF_{END} = 11$

Task C
11 months

$ES_C = 0$
$LF_C = 11$

FIGURE 4.8
CPM Example Based on
AON Network

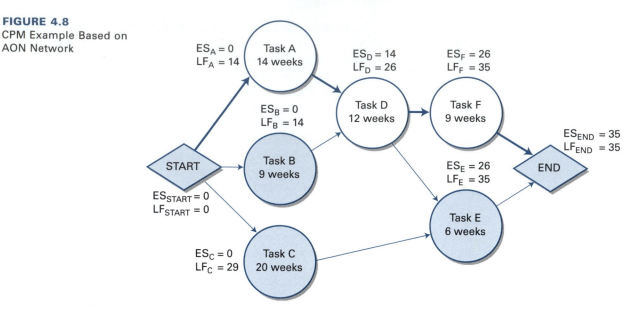

In this case, there are five paths through the network from START to END. These five paths, and their respective durations (that is, the sum of the task durations on each path), are given in Figure 4.9.

The longest (critical) path through the network (and therefore the minimum time needed to complete the project) is path 1, which takes thirty-five weeks. The heavy arrows and white nodes in Figure 4.8 indicate this critical path. Note that there may be more than one critical path in a project, but there must be at least one by definition.

Since realistically sized projects have far too many nodes to enumerate all possible paths, the developers of the critical path method (CPM) developed a methodology that could easily find the longest path in any project, no matter how large. As it turns out, this is a relatively easy problem that is based on the process of dynamic programming.

Two phases of the CPM calculations are needed to find the longest path(s) through a precedence network. In the first phase, we start at the START node and proceed forward through the network, finding the earliest time at each node that the task or milestone can begin. In the second phase of the calculations, we start at the END node and move backward through the network, finding the latest time that any task or milestone can finish.

In the first phase of the CPM calculations, the manager typically assumes that the milestone START begins at time zero, although this can be mapped onto a calendar after the calculations are completed. He then moves from node to succeeding node, at each stage asking himself this question: What is the earliest time that this task or milestone can start, given the earliest starting times for the preceding nodes? At each node, he wants to find the value of

$$ES_i = \text{Earliest starting time for node } i$$

FIGURE 4.9
Possible Paths Defined
for Example in Figure 4.7

Path	Tasks	Expected Duration (weeks)
1	START-A-D-F-END	35
2	START-A-D-E-END	32
3	START-B-D-F-END	30
4	START-B-D-E-END	27
5	START-C-E-END	26

Initially, $ES_{START} = 0$ by definition. The manager then moves to tasks A, B, and C that immediately follow the START node; clearly,

$$ES_A = ES_B = ES_C = 0$$

since the START milestone takes zero time. The manager then proceeds to task D. From the network, he knows that task D cannot start until tasks A and B are completed. Recall that task A can start at time 0 and needs fourteen weeks, and task B can start at time 0 and needs nine weeks. Thus, since task D cannot start until *both* tasks A and B are finished, the earliest starting time for task D must equal the maximum of the earliest finishing times for tasks A and B; that is,

$$ES_D = \max (ES_A + 14, ES_B + 9)$$
$$= \max (0 + 14, 0 + 9)$$
$$= 14$$

Likewise, the earliest starting time for task F is 26 $(ES_D + 12) = 26$ weeks, while the earliest starting time for task E is

$$ES_E = \max (ES_D + 12, ES_C + 20)$$
$$= \max (14 + 12, 0 + 20)$$
$$= 26$$

The earliest "starting" time for the ending milestone, END, is then

$$ES_{END} = \max (ES_F + 9, ES_E + 6)$$
$$= \max (26 + 9, 26 + 6)$$
$$= 35$$

In general, for the ith task that is immediately preceded by tasks j in set P_i, the early start time for task i is calculated using the following formula:

$$ES_i = \max \{ES_j + t_j \text{ for all tasks } j \text{ in set } P_i\}$$

where t_j = duration of task j.

Based on the value of ES_{END}, the program manager knows that the project cannot be completed in less than thirty-five weeks (the project makespan), given the estimated durations of the tasks in the project. The results of these calculations are indicated in Figure 4.8. He does not know, however, which tasks define the critical path(s) until he completes the second (backward) phase of the CPM calculations.

In the second (backward) phase of the calculations, the manager wants to find the latest times that any task or milestone can finish; he denotes this value by

$$LF_i = \text{Latest finish time for node } i$$

It is typical to set $LF_{END} = ES_{END}$ since the END milestone requires no time or cost; thus, $LF_{END} = 35$. The manager then proceeds to move backward through the network.

Since tasks E and F are the tasks that immediately precede the END node, he moves first to these nodes. In both cases, it is clear that these tasks can be finished as late as time 35 without delaying the latest finish time of the END node (and the project). Thus, $LF_F = LF_E = 35$, as indicated in Figure 4.8.

The manager then considers task D and asks: What is the latest time that this task can be finished without delaying the latest finish time of the tasks that follow (tasks F and E)? This is equivalent to calculating the latest starting times for tasks F and E. Since task F can be finished as late as time 35, it cannot be started any later than time $35 - 9 = 26$. Similarly, task E cannot be started any later than time $35 - 6 = 29$. Since task D cannot cause either task F or E to be late, the latest finish time for task D must be the smaller value of 29 or 26; that is,

$$\begin{aligned} LF_D &= \min (LF_F - 9, LF_E - 6) \\ &= \min (35 - 9, 35 - 6) \\ &= 26 \end{aligned}$$

The manager then continues in this fashion, calculating the latest finish times for tasks A, B, and C as follows:

$$\begin{aligned} LF_A &= LF_D - 12 = 26 - 12 = 14 \\ LF_B &= LF_D - 12 = 26 - 12 = 14 \end{aligned}$$

and

$$LF_C = LF_E - 9 = 35 - 6 = 29$$

Finally, he calculates the latest finish time for the START node of the project as follows:

$$\begin{aligned} LF_{START} &= \min (LF_A - 14, LF_B - 9, LF_C - 20) \\ &= \min (14 - 14, 14 - 9, 29 - 20) \\ &= \min (0, 5, 9) \\ &= 0 \end{aligned}$$

Clearly, the latest finish time for the START node must always equal zero, since the START and END nodes must lie on the critical (longest) path. In general, if tasks j in the set S_i immediately succeed task i, then the calculations for the latest finish times are found using the following formula:

$$LF_i = \min \{LF_j - t_j \text{ for all tasks } j \text{ in set } S_i\}$$

where t_j = duration of task j.

Spreadsheet Calculations

The CPM calculations for the example in Figure 4.8 are given in Figure 4.10. For each task and milestone in the project, the manager indicates the immediate predecessors and successors that form the basis of the calculations. Note that the values of the early start time (ES_i) and the latest finish times (LF_i) correspond to the values in Figure 4.8.

Once he finds the early start times (ES_i) and the latest finish times (LF_i) for each task, the manager can then calculate the earliest finish times (EF_i) and the latest starting times (LS_i) for all tasks. If ES_i represents the earliest time that task i can be started, then $ES_i + t_i$ represents the earliest time that the ith task can be completed (given that t_i represents the

Task or Milestone	Duration (t_i)	Immediate		Earliest		Latest	
		Predecessors (P_i)	Successors (S_i)	Start Time (ES_i)	Finish Time	Start Time	Finish Time (LF_i)
START	0	—	A, B, C	0	0	0	0
A	14	START	D	0	14	0	14
B	9	START	D	0	9	5	14
C	20	START	E	0	20	9	29
D	12	A, B	E, F	14	26	14	26
E	6	C, D	END	26	32	29	35
F	9	D	END	26	35	26	35
END	0	E, F	—	35	35	35	35

FIGURE 4.10 Early Start and Latest Finish Time Calculations for AON Example

task duration). Likewise, if LF_i denotes the latest completion time for the ith task, then $LF_i - t_i$ must equal the latest time that the ith task can be started. These values are indicated in Figure 4.10 and are easily calculated in a spreadsheet by adding (or subtracting) the column of task durations (t_i) to the column of the earliest starting times, ES_i (or the column of latest finish times, LF_i).

Slacks (Floats) Defined

Figure 4.10 (and Figure 4.8) indicates that task E, for example, can be started as early as time 26 but does not have to be completed until time 35. This leaves a time interval of $35 - 26 = 9$ weeks when this task can be completed. Since task E needs only six weeks, there are three weeks of "slack" or "float" in the time interval when this task can be performed. This also indicates that the duration of task E can slip up to three additional weeks before it negatively affects the latest finish time of the END task and the makespan of the project. Total slack is one measure used by many managers to identify those tasks that should be most carefully observed in order to keep the project on schedule.

In general, *total slack* is the time between a task's latest finish time (LF_i) and its earliest starting time (ES_i) minus the task duration. Algebraically, total slack is defined as follows:

$$\text{Total Slack for Task } i = LF_i - ES_i - t_i$$

with the values for total slack indicated in Figure 4.11. Note that any task having a total slack equal to zero is a critical task and therefore lies on the critical path.

There are other slack measures in addition to total slack. One useful measure is called *free slack;* this measure assumes that all tasks must be started at their earliest starting times. For example, consider task C in Figure 4.8. In this case, the earliest starting time for task C is zero. Since task E is the only task that follows task C and the earliest starting time for task E is 26, this means that task C must be finished by time 26 in order to avoid delaying the start of task E beyond its earliest starting time. Thus, the free slack for task C is defined as $(26 - 0 - 20) = 6$ weeks. In this case, the free slack is less than the total slack associated with task C. Also note that free slack can be zero while the total slack can be positive.

To define the free slack, we will define a value $ES_{i\min}$, where

$$ES_{i\min.} = \text{Minimum early start time of all tasks that immediately follow task } i$$
$$= \min \{ES_{j.} \text{ for all tasks } j \text{ in set } S_i\}$$

Then, the free slack FS_i can be defined as

$$\text{Free Slack}_i = (ES_{i\min.} - ES_i) - t_i = ES_{i\min} - EF_i$$

Task or Milestone	Duration (t_i)	Earliest Start Time (ES_i)	Latest Finish Time (LF_i)	Total Slack	Free Slack	Safety Slack	Independent Slack	Critical Task?
START	0	0	0	0	0	0	0	Yes
A	14	0	14	0	0	0	0	Yes
B	9	0	14	5	5	5	5	No
C	20	0	29	9	6	9	6	No
D	12	14	26	0	0	0	0	Yes
E	6	26	35	3	3	0	0	No
F	9	26	35	0	0	0	0	Yes
END	0	35	35	0	0	0	0	Yes

FIGURE 4.11   Slack (Float) Measures for the AON Example in Figure 4.8

Free slack is a useful measure for several reasons. First, many managers are risk averse and want to start all tasks at their earliest possible starting times. Free slack is therefore a good metric to measure the importance of noncritical tasks. Second, free slack can sometimes be useful in determining how much a critical task can be reduced or "crashed" before the critical path changes. This relationship is discussed in more detail in Chapter 5.

A third slack measure is called *safety slack*. This slack measure assumes that all noncritical tasks will be started at their latest starting times. For example, task C can be started as late as time 9 without delaying any succeeding task. Thus, the safety slack for task C is 9. In this case, safety slack is defined as

$$\text{Safety Slack}_i = (\text{LF}_i - \text{LF}_{i\max}) - t_i = \text{LS}_i - \text{LF}_{i\max}$$

where

$$\text{LF}_{i\max} = \text{Maximum late finish time of all tasks that immediately precede task } i$$
$$= \max \{\text{LF}_j \text{ for all tasks } j \text{ in set } P_i\}$$

For task D, $\text{LF}_{D\max} = \max \{\text{LF}_A, \text{LF}_B\} = \max \{14, 14\} = 14$. Thus, the safety slack for task D is

$$\text{Safety Slack}_D = \text{LF}_D - \text{LF}_{D\max} - 12 = 26 - 14 - 12 = 0$$

The values for all safety slacks are given in Figure 4.11. Note that the safety slack, as with all slack values, is always zero for tasks on the critical path.

A fourth slack measure is called the *independent slack*. Note that the other three slack measures are path-dependent measures; that is, if we change the duration of one task, the slack measures of other tasks will be affected. For example, if we increase the duration of task E from six weeks to seven weeks, not only will the total slack and the free slack of task E be reduced from three to two weeks, but the total slack and the safety slack of task C will be affected as well. The duration of task E has an impact on the slack values of task C because tasks C and E lie on the same path through the network and changing the duration of one task (in this case, task E) changes the duration of the entire path.

In some cases, however, task durations can be changed without affecting any other tasks in the project. This information can be very useful to a project manager, who must be concerned by these interaction effects. The amount of time that a task's duration can be increased without affecting any other task is known as the independent slack. Independent slack is defined as follows:

$$\text{Independent Slack}_i = \max \{0, (\text{ES}_{i\min} - \text{LF}_{i\max} - t_i)\}$$

where $\text{ES}_{i\min}$ and $\text{LF}_{i\max}$ were defined previously for the free and safety slacks.

The definition of independent slack requires that the value be nonnegative; since the value of $(\text{ES}_{i\min} - \text{LF}_{i\max} - t_i)$ could be negative, IS_i is arbitrarily defined to be equal to zero in this case. For task B, $\text{IS}_B = \max \{0, (14 - 0 - 9)\} = 5$. This value indicates that the duration of task B could be increased by as many as five weeks with no impact on the slacks of any other tasks in the project. All slack values are indicated in Figure 4.11.

Using the spreadsheets in Figures 4.10 and 4.11, the duration of various tasks in the network can be changed in order to observe how the critical path changes for the network in Figure 4.7. For example, if we make the duration of task C equal to thirty-one weeks, the critical path now becomes START-C-E-END with a duration of thirty-seven weeks. Other combinations can be easily explored. Except for the fact that this spreadsheet was designed for a specific network, the calculations in Figures 4.10 and 4.11 are basically the same as those performed by most PM software packages (e.g., Microsoft Project, etc.).

Linear Programming Formulations

As previously noted, a critical path in a project network is merely the longest path through the network from the START to the END milestone. Once the critical path is identified, program managers can find early starting times, latest starting times, slacks, and other measures that relate to the schedule and timing decisions (but ignore costs, resources, and workers that will be considered in later chapters).

Linear programming (LP) provides an alternative methodology for finding the critical path(s) in a precedence network. While it would be most unlikely to use an LP model to find the critical path(s) in a precedence network, an LP model gives us a framework that can be easily modified to consider more complex and realistic tradeoffs faced by most project managers. Thus, we will develop a basic linear programming model in this section and extend this framework in later chapters to include additional factors such as project costs, cash flows, penalty costs incurred if a project is completed after a given deadline, bonuses earned for finishing a project before a stated due date, etc.

The decision variables in our "basic" LP model are the starting times for each task (or milestone); we denote these variables as follows:

$$\text{START}_i = \text{starting time for task (milestone) } i$$

We must build constraints in the LP model to guarantee that sufficient time is allowed to complete each task at its given duration (denoted by t_i). For example, let's assume that some task i precedes a task j. Then, task j cannot start until task i is finished; that is, $\text{START}_j \geq \text{FINISH}_i$, where FINISH_i denotes the ending time of task i (FINISH_i is equal to $\text{START}_i + t_i$).

To illustrate further, consider the example in Figure 4.8. If task D is started at time 16, for example, then tasks E and F that immediately follow task D cannot start until time $16 + t_D = 16 + 12 = 28$ (i.e., when task D is finished). Algebraically, this is stated as follows:

$$\text{START}_E \geq \text{FINISH}_D \ (= \text{START}_D + t_D)$$

and

$$\text{START}_F \geq \text{FINISH}_D \ (= \text{START}_D + t_D)$$

We must have one constraint for each precedent constraint (arc) in the network; that is,

$$\text{START}_j \geq \text{FINISH}_i \text{ for all tasks } i \text{ in the set } P_j$$

where P_j is the set of all tasks that immediately precede task j. (For example, $P_E = \{D, C\}$).

In our LP model, we can include other considerations, including a lag parameter between tasks; that is, lag_{ij} denotes a minimum desired delay between the completion of task i (FINISH_i) and the start of task j. (Note that this could also be accomplished by adding a task between tasks i and j.) The LP model to find the minimum project makespan can then be stated as follows:

$$\text{Minimize END}$$

subject to:

$$\text{START}_j \geq \text{FINISH}_i + \text{lag}_{ij} \text{ for all tasks } i \text{ in the set } P_j$$
$$\text{START}_i \geq 0 \text{ for all tasks } i$$

This model can be formulated in an Excel spreadsheet and optimized using the Solver function. The spreadsheet, including the Solver dialog box, is given in Figure 4.12 for the example in Figure 4.8. In Figure 4.12, we minimize the variable END that represents the occurrence time of the end of the project (the project makespan). Note that the starting

FIGURE 4.12
LP Solution for Figure
4.7 Example (Minimize
Project Duration)

Task (Milestone)	Starting Times of Tasks (Milestones)		Duration (wks)	Ending Times of Tasks	
	Variable	Value		Variable	Value
START	START	0	0		
Task A	STARTA	0	14	FINISHA	14
Task B	STARTB	0	9	FINISHB	9
Task C	STARTC	0	20	FINISHC	20
Task D	STARTD	14	12	FINISHD	26
Task E	STARTE	29	6	FINISHE	35
Task F	STARTF	26	9	FINISHF	35
END	END	35	0		

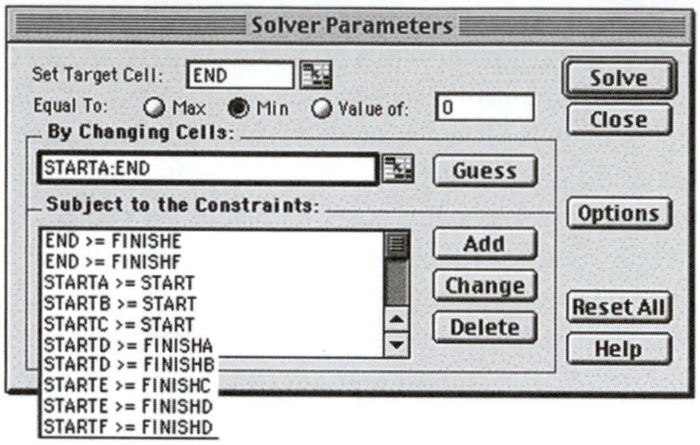

time of the project (START) is not a decision variable; that is, we set START = 0 in the spreadsheet such that all decision variables must be greater than or equal to zero.

As indicated in the Solver dialog box, we have labeled each cell in the spreadsheet that corresponds to a starting time ($START_j$) as well as the task ending times ($FINISH_j$). In this way, we can specify the ten precedence constraints (corresponding to the ten arcs in the precedence network) in Solver's constraint dialog box. Note that all lag values in this example were set to zero so that the LP solution would correspond to the calculations given in Figure 4.10. However, it is straightforward to add nonzero lags to the spreadsheet and rerun the model; any lag values less than the corresponding slack values will not increase project makespan.

The spreadsheet model in Figure 4.12 minimizes project makespan (END) and, of course, starts all critical tasks at their earliest starting times. Noncritical tasks, however, may be started at any time between their earliest and latest starting times. For example, consider task E in Figure 4.8. While the solution indicated in the spreadsheet starts this task at time 29, it could also be started at time 26 or time 27 or time 28—without changing the completion of the project at time 35.

If we are concerned about possible delays, we might want to ensure that all noncritical tasks are started at their earliest possible times. To do so, we can redefine the objective function in the LP model to include values of all $START_i$ variables. Using unit weights, the resultant LP model becomes:

Minimize $START_A + START_B + START_C + START_D + START_E + START_F + END$

subject to:

$$START_i \geq FINISH_j \text{ for all tasks } j \text{ in the set } P_i$$
$$START_i \geq 0 \text{ for all tasks}$$

The resultant solution is indicated in Figure 4.13; the Solver dialog box for this problem is the same one indicated in Figure 4.12, except that a different cell (corresponding to the sum of the starting times) is minimized (the minimum value indicated is equal to 101). Note that task E now starts at time 26—its early starting time. Using the task starting values given in Figure 4.12, the resultant total slack values equal the free slack values given in Figure 4.11 since all tasks are now starting at their earliest starting times.

FIGURE 4.13
Minimizing the Sum of
all Task Starting Times

Task (Milestone)	Starting Times of Tasks (Milestones)		Duration (wks)	Ending Times of Tasks	
	Variable	Value		Variable	Value
START	START	0	0		
Task A	STARTA	0	14	FINISHA	14
Task B	STARTB	0	9	FINISHB	9
Task C	STARTC	0	20	FINISHC	20
Task D	STARTD	14	12	FINISHD	26
Task E	STARTE	26	6	FINISHE	32
Task F	STARTF	26	9	FINISHF	35
END	END	35	0		

Sum of task starting times = 101

In similar fashion, we might want to set the starting times of noncritical tasks to their latest possible times so that the resultant slacks equal the safety slack for all tasks. While it might appear that the objective function

$$\text{Minimize} - \text{START}_A - \text{START}_B - \text{START}_C - \text{START}_D - \text{START}_E - \text{START}_F - \text{END}$$

accomplishes this goal, it does in fact *not* work correctly and will result in an unbounded solution to the LP model. This occurs because Solver will want to increase the values of all decision variables without bound (recall that all values must be nonnegative).

To avoid an unbounded solution, we must make certain that the value of the END variable is greater than the total value of ($\text{START}_A + \text{START}_B + \text{START}_C + \text{START}_D + \text{START}_E + \text{START}_F$). In general, attaching a weight to END that is an order of magnitude greater than the weights on the other variables will generally suffice; in this example, we can redefine the objective function as follows:

$$\text{Minimize } 10\,\text{END} - \text{START}_A - \text{START}_B - \text{START}_C - \text{START}_D - \text{START}_E - \text{START}_F$$

In this way, Solver places the highest priority in minimizing END (project makespan) and secondary priority in minimizing the variables START_A, START_B, … The resultant solution is given in Figure 4.14; using these task starting times, the resultant total slacks will equal the safety slacks.

PROJECT SCHEDULING AND GANTT CHARTS

Using the time estimates and CPM calculations, we can determine a planned schedule and budget (budgeting is discussed in Chapter 5). The results of the schedule are typically represented in a Gantt chart. To illustrate a Gantt chart, assume that we have a small project consisting of sixteen tasks; information on the status of these tasks is given in the spreadsheet in Figure 4.15.

A Gantt chart is merely a bar chart in which each task is represented by a horizontal bar; additional information can be included to represent critical tasks, work remaining, etc. Using the chart function in MS-Excel, we can draw a Gantt chart for the project information given in Figure 4.15; this Gantt chart is represented in Figure 4.16. Information on how to construct Gantt charts using MS-Excel is given in Appendix 4A.

Gantt charts can be customized in an unlimited number of ways. Part of a Gantt chart, produced by commercial PM software (Microsoft Project), is given in Figure 4.17. As indicated, the blue bars indicate critical tasks, the dark lines within the horizontal bars indicate completed work, and the arrows indicate precedence relationships. Note that diamonds are used to represent tasks that require zero time; these tasks are usually called milestones and denote significant events in the life of a project (e.g., project start, project end). Specific calendar dates are also indicated as well as the number of generic workers assigned to each task.

Gantt charts are useful for displaying the results of a CPM schedule. They can also serve as an effective control device by communicating the status of the project at any time.

FIGURE 4.14
LP Solution for Figure 4.8 Example: Latest Starting Times

Task (Milestone)	Starting Times of Tasks (Milestones)		Duration (wks)	Ending Times of Tasks	
	Variable	Value		Variable	Value
START	START	0	0		
Task A	STARTA	0	14	FINISHA	14
Task B	STARTB	5	9	FINISHB	14
Task C	STARTC	9	20	FINISHC	29
Task D	STARTD	14	12	FINISHD	26
Task E	STARTE	29	6	FINISHE	35
Task F	STARTF	26	9	FINISHF	35
END	END	35	0		

10 * END - (sum of task starting times) = 267

FIGURE 4.15
Status Information on Example Project

Tasks	Start Date	Days Completed	Days Remaining	Duration (days)
Build simulation	0	2	1	3
Collect data	0	4	2	6
Write software	0	3	0	3
Test software	0	3	1	4
Build computer	5	0	1	1
Build user interface	3	1	1	2
Integration test	3	1	4	5
Final test	12	0	9	9
Installation	10	0	4	4
Training	10	0	2	2
Vehicle test	12	0	2	2
Start production	10	0	8	8
Build	8	1	4	5
Install	14	0	7	7
First delivery	13	0	6	6
Total production	11	0	5	5

FIGURE 4.16
Excel Gantt Chart for Example Data in Figure 4.14

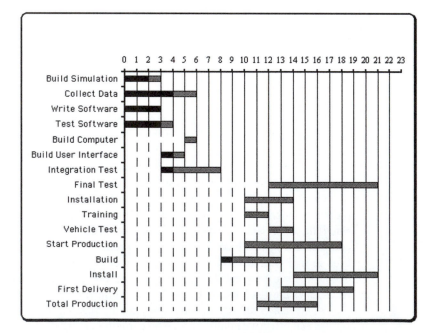

FIGURE 4.17
Gantt Chart Example (MS Project 2000)

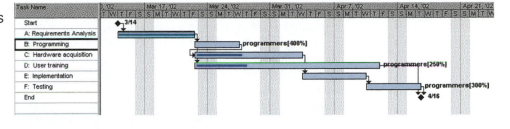

CPM CALCULATIONS FOR AOA NETWORKS

To illustrate the CPM calculations for AOA networks, we will consider the AOA network in Figure 4.5 with the addition of task duration estimates (in weeks). This AOA network is given in Figure 4.18.

In this example, there are four events (nodes): START, 1, 2, and END, and five tasks that can be uniquely identified by their starting and ending events:

$$\text{Task A} \equiv \text{Task (START, 2)}$$

$$\text{Task B} \equiv \text{Task (START, 1)}$$

$$\text{Task C} \equiv \text{Task (2, END)}$$

$$\text{Dummy task} \equiv \text{Task (1, 2)}$$

$$\text{Task D} \equiv \text{Task (1, END)}$$

Remember that the dummy task takes no time and uses no resources; it is used in AOA networks strictly to enforce correct precedence relationships.

In the case of AOA networks, we want to find the occurrence times of the events (nodes). Each event can start as early as possible; for example, assuming that the event START begins at time 0, event 1 cannot occur earlier than time 2 (since task B requires 2 weeks), but it could occur any time later. Likewise, the earliest occurrence time for event 2 is time 4 since there are two paths to event 2, and all tasks on both paths must be completed before the event can occur. In this latter case, the two paths between START and event 2 are

- **Path 1:** Task A (four weeks)
- **Path 2:** Task B (two weeks) + Dummy task (zero weeks)

Thus, the earliest occurrence time for event 2 is the maximum time of the two paths to the event; that is, the earliest occurrence time for event 2 is max (4, 2) = 4 weeks. In general, we will let T_i denote the occurrence time of event i and use a superscript E or L to denote the earliest or latest occurrence time, respectively. In this example,

$$T_2^E = \text{Earliest Occurrence Time of Event 2} = \max (4, 2) = 4 \text{ weeks}$$

FIGURE 4.18
AOA Network (Figure 4.5) with Task Durations

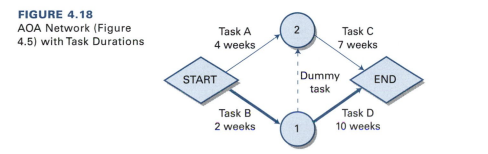

To find the earliest occurrence times of all events, we can make a forward pass through the AOA network in a similar fashion done with AON networks. Assuming that that $T_{START} = 0$, then we would move to event 1; clearly, the earliest occurrence time for event 1 is the time needed to complete task B, which is two weeks.

To find the earliest occurrence time of the ending event END, we must consider the two tasks that terminate at the event END, in this case, tasks C and D. The starting event of task C is event 2; the earliest occurrence time of this event is four weeks. Thus, the earliest time that task C can finish is 4 weeks + (duration of task C) = 4 weeks + 7 weeks = 11 weeks. Likewise, the earliest time that task D can finish is the earliest occurrence time of event 1 (at time 2) plus ten weeks for task D. The earliest occurrence time of event END is the larger of these two values since all tasks must be completed before the event can occur; that is,

$$T_{END}^E = \max (T_1^E + 10, \ T_2^E + 7) = \max (2 + 10, \ 4 + 7) = \max \ (12, 11) = 12$$

In general, if the duration of task (i, j) is denoted by t_{ij}, then the earliest occurrence time of event j is given by the following formula:

$$T_j^E = \max_{tasks \ (i, j)} \left(T_i^E + t_{ij} \right)$$

From the forward pass calculations, we know that the earliest time that the END event can occur is at time 12; this is the length of the longest or critical path through the network. (The forward pass will identify the length of the critical path but not the specific tasks on the critical path.) If we let the latest occurrence time of the END event equal the earliest occurrence time (that is, $T_{END}^E = T_{END}^L = 12$ weeks), then we can use a reverse or backward pass through the AOA network to find the latest occurrence times of all events.

In this example, if $T_{END}^L = 12$, then the latest time that event 2 can occur is 12 − (duration of task C) = 12 − 7 = 5 weeks. If event 2 occurs any later than time 5, it is clear that the ending event END would be delayed beyond time 12. Similarly, we can find the latest occurrence time of event 1. In this case, there are two tasks that start at event 1: the dummy task and task D. The latest time that the dummy task can be completed (the latest occurrence time of event 2) is 5, while the latest time that task D can be competed is time 12. Since these latest occurrence times cannot be delayed, the latest time that event 1 can occur is the smaller of (5 − duration of the dummy task) or (12 − 10); that is,

$$T_1^L = \min \ (5 - 0, \ 12 - 10) - \min \ (5, \ 2) = 2$$

In general, we find the latest occurrence times of all events using the recursive formula:

$$T_i^L = \min_{tasks \ (i, j)} \left(T_j^L - t_{ij} \right)$$

Using both recursive formulas to find the earliest and latest occurrence times for all events in an AOA network, we can then indicate these values in the network. In this example, these values are indicated in Figure 4.19.

Given the earliest and latest occurrence times, the slack values for each task are relatively straightforward to calculate in an AOA network. The total slack for task (i, j), which we can denote by TS_{ij}, is defined as follows:

$$TS_{ij} = \text{Total Slack for Task } (i, j) = T_j^L - T_i^E - t_{ij}$$

FIGURE 4.19
Example with Earliest
and Latest Occurrence
Times

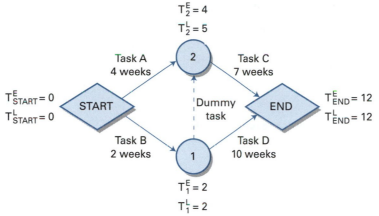

where t_{ij} is the duration of task (i, j). The other measures of slack defined for AON networks can be similarly defined:

$$FS_{ij} = \text{Free Slack for Task } (i, j) = T_j^E - T_i^E - t_{ij}$$

$$SS_{ij} = \text{Safety Slack for Task } (i, j) = T_j^L - T_i^L - t_{ij}$$

$$IS_{ij} = \text{Independent Slack for Task } (i, j) = \max\ (0, T_j^E - T_i^L - t_{ij})$$

For the example in Figure 4.19, the calculations for the four types of slack (float) are summarized in Figure 4.20. Verify the values in this table by your own calculations.

As indicated in Figure 4.20, any task that has a total slack equal to zero is on the critical path. Note that tasks B and D define the critical path in this case (with a total length equal to twelve weeks).

Mathematical Programming Formulation for AOA Networks

In this case, we define the occurrence times of each event to be the decision variables; that is,

$$x_i = \text{occurrence time for event } i$$

Since each task (i, j) is defined by a starting event i and an ending event j, we must guarantee in our basic linear programming model that sufficient time is allowed to perform each task; that is,

$$x_j - x_i \geq t_{ij} \quad \text{for each task } (i, j) \text{ in the network}$$

FIGURE 4.20
Slack Values for Example
in Figure 4.19

Task	Duration (t_{ij})	Earliest Start Time (T_i^E)	Latest Finish Time (T_j^L)	Total Slack TS_{ij}	Free Slack FS_{ij}	Safety Slack SS_{ij}	Independent Slack IS_{ij}
A: (START, 2)	4	0	5	1	0	1	0
B: (START, 1)	2	0	2	0	0	0	0
Dummy (1, 2)	0	2	5	3	2	3	2
C: (2, END)	7	4	12	1	1	0	0
D: (1, END)	10	2	12	0	0	0	0

If x_{END} is the final event (node) in the AOA network and we wish to minimize the project makespan, then the LP model is simply

$$\text{Minimize } x_{END}$$

subject to

$$x_j - x_i \geq t_{ij} \text{ for each task } (i, j) \text{ in the network}$$
$$x_i \geq 0$$

For the example in Figure 4.18, the LP model to minimize project makespan becomes:

$$\text{Minimize } x_{END}$$

subject to

$$x_2 - x_{START} \geq 4 \text{ (constraint for task A)}$$
$$x_1 - x_{START} \geq 2 \text{ (constraint for task B)}$$
$$x_2 - x_1 \geq 0 \text{ (constraint for dummy task)}$$
$$x_{END} - x_2 \geq 7 \text{ (constraint for task C)}$$
$$x_{END} - x_1 \geq 10 \text{ (constraint for task D)}$$
$$x_{START}, x_1, x_2, x_{END} \geq 0$$

CONCLUSIONS

Most, if not all, PM software packages find the critical path, total slack (or float) values, precedence network, and Gantt chart (as well as cost estimates, reports, etc.). Since most PM software packages are time oriented, they generally perform well in helping to schedule projects and tasks. However, most PM packages do not explicitly consider more complex issues relating to cash flows, penalty costs for missing a due date, payment schedules, etc. In addition, while most PM software packages have some capability for allocating resources (dollars, workers, equipment) to tasks, most of these resource allocation algorithms utilized by the packages are heuristic in nature and thereby do not guarantee optimal (or even good) solutions. These and other related issues are further described in the following chapters.

STUDY PROBLEMS

1. Construct both the AOA and the AON diagrams, which comprise activities A, B, C, ..., H, and satisfy the following precedence relationships:

   a. A, B, and C, the first activities of the project, can start simultaneously.

   b. Activity D can start immediately after tasks A and B are completed.

   c. Activity E succeeds task C.

   d. Activity F cannot be started until task A is completed.

   e. Activity E precedes tasks G and H.

   f. Activity D precedes task G.

2. A small research project is represented by an AOA network that is defined by the tasks in the following table. Construct the AOA network; clearly identify the earliest and latest occurrence times for each event. Find the total slack, free slack, safety slack, and independent slack for all tasks in the network.

Task Label	Events (i, j)	Duration
A	(1, 2)	5
B	(1, 3)	3
C	(1, 4)	4
D	(2, 4)	1
E	(3, 4)	2
F	(3, 5)	5
G	(3, 6)	9
H	(4, 6)	4
I	(5, 6)	2

3. For the AOA network in problem 2, construct the equivalent AON network and find the earliest starting and latest finish times for all tasks. Find the total slack, free slack, safety slack, and independent slack for all tasks in the network. Compare your results to the results found in problem 2.

4. For the AON network in problem 3, formulate and solve a linear programming model (using Solver in MS-Excel) to find the critical path and **free slack** (float) values, and the critical path and safety slack (float) values. Compare your results to those found in problems 2 and 3.

5. For the AON network in problem 3, formulate and solve a linear programming model (using Solver in MS-Excel) to find the critical path and **safety slack** (float) values. Compare your results to those found in problems 2 and 3.

6. Given the following AOA project network:

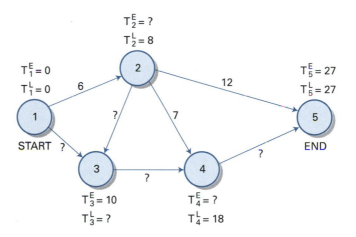

Given the earliest occurrence times (T_i^E) and the latest occurrence times (T_i^L) for each ith event, answer the following questions:

a. What is the duration of task (1, 3)?

b. What is the duration of task (2, 3)?

c. What is the total slack of task (3, 4)?

d. What is the safety slack of task (4, 5)?

e. What is the free slack of task (2, 5)?

f. What is the independent slack of task (2, 4)?

7. Prove or disprove the following two conjectures concerning slacks.

   a. Independent Slack = min (Free Slack, Safety Slack)

   b. Total Slack + Free Slack = Safety Slack + Independent Slack

8. Demand at the Wonder Widget Company (W2C) has recently decreased due to the economic slowdown. In response, the managers of W2C have shut down one of their production lines. However, management is concerned about how long it would take to restart the line when (and if) demand increases. They have come to you for help.

   After completing a careful study of the production process, you have determined from your work breakdown structure that there are ten distinct tasks that must be completed before the line can be restarted. These tasks are indicated below, along with their estimated duration (in days). Each task is represented by a unique identifying letter and by its starting and ending event numbers, which also indicate precedence. Event 1 is the starting event; event 10 is the ending event.

Task ID	Event Numbers	Duration (Days)
A	(1, 2)	5
B	(2, 3)	2
C	(2, 4)	4
D	(4, 5)	2
E	(4, 7)	8
F	(3, 5)	6
G	(7, 8)	5
H	(5, 7)	1
I	(8, 10)	3
J	(8, 9)	6

   Using this information, answer the following questions:

   a. If all tasks begin as early as possible, how much slack will remain for each task? If each task begins as late as possible, how much slack time will remain for each task? How much slack is associated with each task that is independent of any delays in the other tasks?

   b. Formulate and solve a linear programming model to find the critical path and free slack values. Compare your answer to the results found in part (a).

   c. How much does the duration of task D have to increase in order to change

      (i) the early start time of D?

      (ii) the early start time of I?

      (iii) the earliest possible completion time of the project?

   d. The production manager feels that you have made an error and that task C should be a predecessor to activity F.

      (i) Which activity will have their earliest start times changed? By how much?

      (ii) Which activities will have their latest start times changed? By how much?

9. A small project consists of six tasks; the immediate predecessors and task durations are given in the following table:

Task ID	Event Numbers	Duration (Days)
A	(1, 2)	5
B	(2, 3)	2
C	(2, 4)	4
D	(4, 5)	2
E	(4, 7)	8
F	(3, 5)	6
G	(7, 8)	5
H	(5, 7)	1
I	(8, 10)	3
J	(8, 9)	6

a. Draw an AON and an AOA precedence network for this project.

b. Using either network, find the following quantities: early and late starting times, early and late finishing times, total slack, free slack, safety slack, and independent slack.

APPENDIX 4A. DRAWING A GANTT CHART USING MS-EXCEL

Consider the Excel worksheet in Figure 4.15. (Note that the "Duration" is defined as the "Days Completed" plus the "Days Remaining".) Select the data to be plotted; in this case, we highlighted the data (including the task names) in the first four columns. Select a horizontal bar chart (100 percent stacked bar); a horizontal bar chart with 3-D effects could also be used. Basically, you now have a Gantt chart in which horizontal bars have three colors and task names appear along the vertical axis. The first part of each bar represents the time from day 0 to the starting date, the second part of the bar represents the number of days completed, and the third part of the bar represents the number of days remaining until the task's scheduled completion. (Note that some of the tasks have no work completed.)

Since we are not interested in the number of days from Day 0 until the start of each task, we want to make the first segment of each bar invisible. Do this by double-clicking on the first part of any bar; this should bring up the Patterns dialog box for the first data series. In the Patterns portion, set the colors to white (the background should already be white). Click OK, and you have a set of ghosts for your first data series.

In this example, we added vertical gridlines to the Gantt chart to make it easier to read dates. To do so, pull down the Chart menu, choose Gridlines, and select Major Gridlines for the x-axis. If you wish, you can also change the scale and, for example, add gridlines at each day. To change the scale, double-click on the horizontal scale; this will bring up the Patterns dialog box. Click on Scale and put a one in the major unit box. Excel will then draw vertical lines through the chart to delineate each time period (days in our example).

Finally, we want to reverse the vertical axis where the first task is listed at the bottom. To reverse the order, select the vertical axis and choose the Scale command. In the dialog box, select the check box labeled Categories in Reverse Order, and then click OK. Your Gantt chart (given in Figure 4.16) should now be complete.

APPENDIX 4B. ALTERNATIVE PRECEDENCE RELATIONSHIPS

In most projects, the finish-to-start precedence relationship is most often used when constructing a precedence network; the finish-to-start relationship implies that if task A precedes task B, then task B cannot be started until task A is completed. The critical path and slack calculations in this chapter were based on the assumption that all precedence relationships were finish-to-start.

However, the start-to-start and finish-to-finish relationships can be useful in many applications. In this appendix, we describe these relationships in more detail and show how the early start and latest finish time calculations are modified with these alternative precedence relationships. To illustrate the differences, we will use a modification of the Figure 4.8 example that is given in Figure 4B.1.

In this example, we will assume that the precedence relationship between task D and task E is no longer a finish-to-start relationship. We will first examine a start-to-start relationship and then a finish-to-finish relationship.

Start-to-Start Relationship

If the precedence relationship between tasks D and E is a start-to-start relationship, then task E cannot **start** until task D has been **started.** This implies that tasks D and E can now be performed at the same time, as long as task E is not started before task D. The calculations for the early start time for task E are now modified to reflect the case that task E can now start as soon as task D has started. Since the precedence relationship between tasks E and C is still a finish-to-start relationship, task E cannot start until task C is finished (at time $ES_C + t_C$) and task D has started (at time ES_D). Since both of these events must occur before task E can start, the early start time of task E (ES_E) is

$$ES_E = \max (ES_C + t_C, ES_D)$$
$$= \max (0 + 20, 14)$$
$$= 20$$

Recall that the early start time of task E was 26 when a finish-to-start relationship between tasks D and E was used. In general, the early start time for task i is calculated as

FIGURE 4B.1
Start-to-Start Precedence
Relationship Illustrated

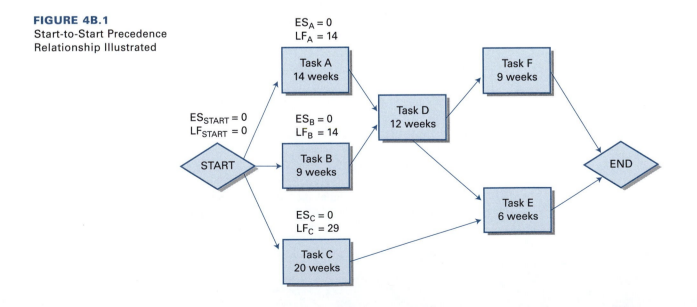

$$\text{ES}_i = \max \{\text{ES}_j + t_j \text{ for all tasks } j \text{ that precede task } i \text{ by a finish-to-start relationship;}$$
$$\text{ES}_j \text{ for all tasks } j \text{ that precede task } i \text{ by a start-to-start relationship}\}$$

When using start-to-start relationships, the calculations for finding the latest finish times are the same as those found using finish-to-start relationships (given in this chapter). Thus, the latest finish time for task E (LF_E) in the Figure 4B.1 example is equal to 35.

Given the latest finish times and early start times, the total slack can be calculated using the same approach given in this chapter; that is,

$$\text{Total Slack for Task } i = \text{LF}_i - \text{ES}_i - t_i$$

Thus, the total slack for task E is now $\text{TS}_E = 35 - 20 - 6 = 9$ weeks. (This compares to $35 - 26 - 6 = 3$ weeks when a finish-to-start relationship between tasks D and E was used.)

Finish-to-Finish Relationship

If the precedence relationship between tasks D and E is a finish-to-finish relationship, then task E cannot **finish** until task D has been **finished.** This implies that tasks D and E can be performed simultaneously as long as task E is not completed before the completion of task D.

If the precedence relationship between tasks D and E in Figure 4B.1 is now a finish-to-finish relationship as indicated in Figure 4B.2, the early start and latest finish calculations must be modified. The early start calculation for task D must allow sufficient time for task E to be completed as well as all tasks that follow task D. To do this, we assume that there is a directed arc from task E to task D; however, in this case, we subtract the duration of task D when considering task E. The early start time for task D is found as follows:

$$\begin{aligned}
\text{ES}_D &= \max (\text{ES}_A + t_A, \text{ES}_B + t_B, \text{ES}_E + t_E - t_D) \\
&= \max (0 + 14, 0 + 9, 20 + 6 - 12) \\
&= \max (14, 9, 14) \\
&= 14
\end{aligned}$$

Since we assume that the precedence relationship between tasks D and E is represented by a directed arc from task E to task D, the early start time for task E is defined in the usual fashion; that is, $\text{ES}_E = \text{ES}_C + t_C = 0 + 22 = 22$.

The latest finish time for task D is calculated in the usual fashion; that is, $\text{LF}_D = \text{LF}_F - t_F = 35 - 9 = 26$. To find the latest finish time for task E, we must allow sufficient time

FIGURE 4B.2
Finish-to-Finish
Precedence Relationship
Illustrated

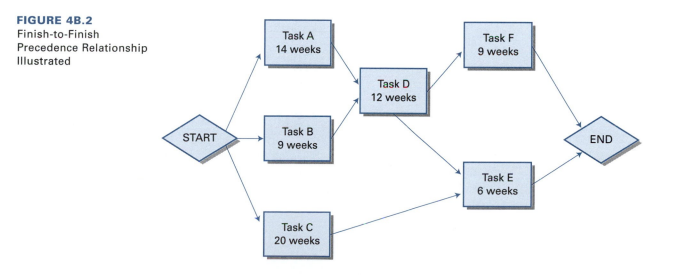

for all tasks following task D to be completed (since task E cannot be completed until task D is completed). Thus, the latest finish time of task E is calculated as follows:

$$LF_E = \min (LF_{END} - 0, LF_D)$$
$$= \min (35 - 0, 26)$$
$$= 26$$

Given the latest finish times and early start times, the slack values for all tasks can be found directly.

Additional Study Problems

B1. Use the following AON precedence network (and given task durations) to find the slack values in parts (a) and (b).

Task	Immediate Predecessor	Duration
A	—	8
B	—	5
C	—	2
D	B, C	3
E	A, D	10
F	—	13

a. Assuming that tasks A, B, C, and D follow a finish-to-start relationship with a lag of 1 day, find the following values:

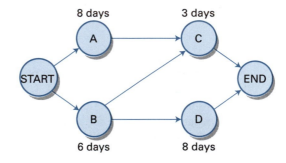

b. Assuming that tasks A, B, C, and D follow a start-to-start relationship with zero lag, find the following slack values:

Task	Total Slack
A	
B	
C	
D	

B2. For the example in Figure 4B.1, find the early start times, latest finish times, and total slack values for all tasks under the assumption that task C now requires twenty-two weeks.

CHAPTER 5

PLANNING TO MINIMIZE COSTS

As we discussed in the first chapter, projects are frequently evaluated on cost and time only; that is, was the project completed within the planned schedule and within the allotted budget? While these criteria ignore the obvious issues of project functionality, quality, etc. (recall the Mars Lander project discussed in the first chapter), we will consider the relationship between cost and time in more detail in this chapter.

When planning a project, the fundamental goal should always be to maximize the difference between the discounted project benefits and project cost. For example, consider a project when bonuses (incentives) are offered if the project is completed before a stated date. In this case, the extra costs of reducing the project's duration to meet this date may be greater than the bonus that would be earned. If so, it would not make economic sense to reduce the project to take advantage of the offered incentives.

When calculating total cost, a manager must consider all relevant costs when finding the best project plan. In addition to standard costs, she must consider penalty costs for violating a stated due date, earliness rewards for finishing before a stated due date, and cash flows. The latter is important not only for defining the value of the project but also for maintaining liquidity of the organization.

We generally make the assumption that managers can influence task (and project) duration by assigning additional resources (e.g., people, equipment) to reduce the duration of critical tasks. Reducing a project in this fashion is generally referred to as *crashing* the project (although this term is not used in the aerospace industry, for obvious reasons). Thus, the project manager's job is to assign appropriate resources to all tasks to minimize the sum of all costs; that is, to find the optimal trade-off among the costs indicated earlier.

It should be noted that some projects appear to violate the "minimum total cost project plan" rule. For example, consider the case when a company wants to develop a new product as quickly as possible in order to maximize its market share. Or the case when a company loses money on an R&D project that it feels will lead to future contracts (e.g., the so-called loss leader). It may appear in the short run that these projects violate the minimum-cost project plan goal. In both cases, however, the organization is following the minimum total cost rule, because it incurs a high penalty (delay) cost if the new product is not brought to market by a certain date, or if the R&D project is not completed on time. In both of these examples, minimizing project makespan (e.g., duration) is synonymous with minimizing project cost.

In this chapter, we discuss the trade-offs between time and cost that a project manager must consider. We also consider several models that can be used to analyze these trade-offs. In the first section, we examine the budgeting process in general and see how budgets can be affected by scheduling decisions. In the following section, we consider how scheduling decisions can dramatically affect cash flows and net present value. In the third section, we discuss the general time-cost trade-off problem and examine a model and associated spreadsheet for analyzing these trade-offs.

PROJECT BUDGETING

The budget is a critical planning document and communication link among all project stakeholders, including the project team and the functional departments of an organization. A budget firmly establishes the goals and resource assignments that typically affect all parts of the organization, including other projects. As a planning and communication tool, the budget should never be viewed as set in stone, but should be modified periodically as new information becomes available and the project plan is updated. Most project management (PM) software allows you to keep one baseline version of the budget to compare to the updated budget.

As discussed in the first chapter, budgets often play an important role in judging a project's success or failure. While using budgets in this fashion may be shortsighted, it is nevertheless a common practice (did the project meet its schedule and cost goals?). When a project fails to meet its budget goal, it is helpful to keep in mind that this failure may be due to poor project management, poor budgeting, or simply a changing environment.

Budgets that are created by starting with cost estimates for the lowest-level work breakdown schedule (WBS) tasks are called bottom-up budgets since they start with the smallest work packages and aggregate these tasks to define a final budget. This process of aggregating WBS tasks explains why WBS packages are often viewed as the basic building blocks of the project budget and schedule. Conversely, budgets can begin with an overall allocation and be subsequently subdivided and allocated to various components of a project. For example, many firms develop budgets by product line and then subdivide these budgeted amounts to specific projects within product lines. When budgets are created in this latter fashion, they are referred to as top-down budgets.

In practice, a combination of bottom-up and top-down budget processes are used. Top management typically indicates a budget constraint, while project managers use a bottom-up approach to estimate aggregate costs. The result is usually an iterative process that refines the budget as well as the scope and design of the project. For example, if project managers find the amount allocated by top management inadequate, they must renegotiate the budget or redefine the project scope and definition in order to find an adequate compromise.

Budgets are typically stated in monetary units but any measurable units (e.g., worker-hours) can be used. Budgets should also indicate how resource costs will be allocated to various functional units (e.g., number of carpenter hours). In addition, project milestones should be clearly indicated as part of the budget.

Budgets are generally updated regularly. The planning horizon and update frequency are important issues; typically, a rolling horizon is used (for example, the budget is updated every quarter for the next twelve months). The question of how often to update a budget has no clear answer and is dependent on factors such as the length, cost, and priority of the project.

Typically, four types of costs should be considered in the context of the budget:

- Direct costs
- Material costs
- Overhead and indirect costs
- Penalty and/or bonus costs

Direct costs relate to resource costs that vary directly with the duration of a specific task; direct costs are typically measured in monetary units (e.g., francs or dollars) but may be measured in worker-hours or some other unit, as long as it is measurable and consistent. Estimates of direct labor costs are frequently based on the concept of a standard cost, which is management's estimate of the expected number of direct labor hours and cost per hour to produce a single unit. Standard costs and hours may be estimated from accumulated data and experience within the organization, shared information from other organizations (usually through professional organizations or consultants), or time and motion studies.

When estimating standard costs and hours, care must be given to ensure that the costs are accurate estimates of the resources that will be actually assigned to tasks. For example, when preparing budget forecasts in response to many governmental RFBs (requests for bids), regulations frequently require that project planners use the average cost for a given resource (e.g., programmers, technical support personnel, secretaries). Consider the case when the scheduler assumes that certain senior individuals (who are paid above-average salaries) will be assigned to a project, but then fails to communicate this information to the person(s) preparing the budget. In this case, actual labor costs will exceed the budgeted amount for all tasks where these workers are assigned.

Material costs reflect the cost of acquiring materials needed to complete specific defined work packages (materials such as pencils and notepads are part of overhead costs). Again, standard costs may be used to estimate material costs to produce a single unit. These standard costs, however, typically ignore such issues as quantity discounts and holding costs. These and other related issues are discussed in more detail in later sections of this chapter.

Overhead costs refer to the administrative costs of the organization that are allocated to support the project (e.g., electrical power, security personnel, library). These costs may be based on a standard allocation rate. For example, assume that a company incurs $1M in overhead costs during a year and expects to have a total of 25,000 worker-hours allocated to various projects. In this case, the organization might allocate $40 in overhead costs for each worker-hour used ($1M divided by 25,000); if one project uses 1,500 worker-hours in direct labor, a total of 1,500(40) = $60,000 would be charged to that project for overhead. Other allocation schemes are possible, including systems based on activity-based costing (ABC). For more information on ABC, see Jiambalvo (2001).

Indirect costs refer to those costs that can be attributed to the project but are not directly related to a specific task. For example, construction projects typically involve security fencing around the perimeter of the construction site that is rented for the duration of the project. Other indirect costs include the cost of the project managers and support staff, consultants, security personnel, etc. These costs are usually allocated per time period (i.e., per month, per quarter) for the duration of the project.

In addition, project managers must consider any penalty costs that are assessed for violating stated due dates, as well as bonuses that are offered for completing a project early (before a stated due date). These costs constitute an important part of the budget.

Budget Uncertainties

One of the difficult issues relating to budget preparation is how to incorporate uncertainty. Since there is always uncertainty concerning such factors as schedule delays, worker availability, material ordering, etc, project planners should try to explicitly recognize these uncertainties in the budget. One method for including these uncertainties is to prepare a range or confidence interval for the budget; that is, given estimates of various uncertainties, what is a 99 (or 95 or 90) percent probability that the budget will be within some lower and upper bounds? When these bounds are explicitly defined, all project stakeholders are made aware of the risks associated with any budget/forecast.

Budget Example

To illustrate the bottom-up budget process, consider the example given by the precedence network in Figure 4.8. In this case, we will assume that there are two resource types, A and B. Resource types generally refer to homogeneous groups of workers (e.g., programmers, carpenters, electricians, plumbers, etc.) or equipment (types of machines), although specific workers could be used just as easily. We will assume that workers of resource type A are paid $400 per week, while workers of resource type B are paid $600 per week. (A week represents a standard forty-hour workweek.) If workers in each resource group are not equally paid, then resource groups could be subdivided into smaller—and more homogeneous—groups. For example, consider programmers Bob and Zelda. If their hourly salaries are different, "Bob" would define one resource type and "Zelda" would define a second resource type.

The number of each resource type needed by each task is indicated in Figure 5.1. The information on task durations and early and late start times were taken directly from the information in Figure 4.8.

In this example, we assume that all materials must be available before a task can be started, so we arbitrarily allocate the material costs to the first week of each task. (Note that material costs could be subdivided and allocated to any number of weeks, if desired.) We also assume that the indicated number of workers is needed for all weeks that the task is performed; this assumption is consistent with the heuristics we used to define tasks in a WBS. Obviously, other assumptions could be used to allocate costs and/or workers per week.

To illustrate the budget calculations, consider task A. In the first week, this task requires $340 in material costs, in addition to $800 for two workers of resource type A (at $400 per worker), resulting in a total direct cost of $1,140 for the first week. In each of the 13 weeks that follow, task A requires only $800 (2 type A workers × $400/worker) for direct labor costs.

If we specify when the noncritical tasks will be started, the weekly costs per task can be indicated directly. The spreadsheet in Figure 5.2 indicates the expected direct costs for this project for the first twelve weeks if the noncritical tasks are started at their earliest starting times; the spreadsheet in Figure 5.3 indicates the cash flows when the noncritical tasks are started at their latest starting times. The entire spreadsheet, indicating the budgeted cash flows for the entire 35-week project duration, is available on the CD-ROM accompanying this book.

The cumulative cash flows can be graphed when noncritical tasks are started at their earliest and their latest starting times. While noncritical tasks could be started at any time between their earliest and latest starting times, these values represent the boundaries of project cash flows (at least based on the current estimated task costs and durations). These two cumulative cash flows are indicated in Figure 5.4.

FIGURE 5.1
Resource Requirements for the Example in Figure 4.8

Task or Milestone	Duration (t_j)	Early Start Time (ES_j)	Latest Start Time (LS_j)	Number of Resource A Workers	Number of Resource B Workers	Material Costs
START	0	0	0	—	—	$ —
A	14	0	0	2	0	$ 340
B	9	0	5	4	12	$ 125
C	20	0	9	3	14	$ —
D	12	14	14	0	8	$ 200
E	6	26	29	1	0	$ 560
F	9	26	26	4	10	$ 90
END	0	35	35	—	—	$ —

Task	1	2	3	4	5	6	7	8	9	10	11	12
A	1,140	800	800	800	800	800	800	800	800	800	800	800
B	8,925	8,800	8,800	8,800	8,800	8,800	8,800	8,800	8,800			
C	9,600	9,600	9,600	9,600	9,600	9,600	9,600	9,600	9,600	9,600	9,600	9,600
D												
E												
F												
Weekly subtotals	19,665	19,200	19,200	19,200	19,200	19,200	19,200	19,200	19,200	10,400	10,400	10,400
Cumulative	19,665	38,865	58,065	77,265	96,465	115,665	134,865	154,065	173,265	183,665	194,065	204,465

FIGURE 5.2 Project Cash Flows for the First 12 Weeks When Noncritical Tasks Start at Earliest Starting Times

Task	1	2	3	4	5	6	7	8	9	10	11	12
A	1,140	800	800	800	800	800	800	800	800	800	800	800
B					8,925	8,800	8,800	8,800	8,800	8,800	8,800	8,800
C									9,600	9,600	9,600	9,600
D												
E												
F												
Weekly subtotals	1,140	800	800	800	9,725	9,600	9,600	9,600	19,200	19,200	19,200	19,200
Cumulative	1,140	1,940	2,740	3,540	13,265	22,865	32,465	42,065	61,265	80,465	99,665	118,865

FIGURE 5.3 Project Cash Flows When Noncritical Tasks Start at Latest Starting Times

FIGURE 5.4
Cumulative Costs for
Early Start and Late Start
Schedules

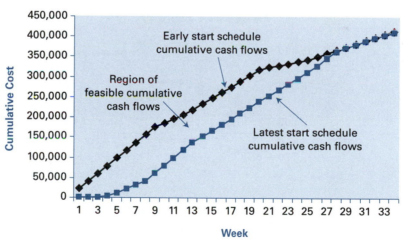

The graph of cumulative resource utilization that is illustrated by Figure 5.4 is provided by some PM software packages. In addition, the graph of actual expenditures is usually included in this graph, with the implication that as long as actual expenditures remain in the region of "feasible" cumulative cash flows, project costs are within acceptable limits. However, the reader should be wary when interpreting such graphs. For example, an indication that actual cumulative expenditures are outside of the feasible region might indicate that the project is over budget—or simply ahead of schedule. This is discussed further in Chapter 9, which deals with issues relating to monitoring and control systems.

In addition to cumulative costs, it may be helpful to graph projected cash flows based on the early start and late start schedules in Figures 5.2 and 5.3. As indicated in Figure 5.5, there may be a considerable difference in cash flows between these two schedules; that difference may be significant to an organization's liquidity as well as to the net present value of the project portfolio. In general, managers should be careful about scheduling noncritical tasks when considering and planning the budget.

MANAGING CASH FLOWS

Typically, project managers negotiate a schedule of payments with the client before the project is started. For example, consider a consulting project that is planned for a client organization. At certain milestones, the client organization has agreed to make partial payments to the consulting company (for example, when certain progress reports are submitted); at other times (say, at the end of each month), the consulting company has to pay for expenses such as the salaries of the personnel who are doing the work.

Assuming a positive time value of money (i.e., money is worth more today than tomorrow), the project manager would then like to schedule the tasks in a project so that her company's payments are made as late as possible while its receipts occur as early as possible. In this way, she hopes to maximize the project's net present value or some related goal.

To consider the impact of cash flows on a project's net present value, consider the example given in Figure 5.6. To simplify, assume that task durations are fixed (in months), although it is straightforward to extend this approach to more complex situations.

FIGURE 5.5
Weekly Cash Flows with the Early Start and Late Start Schedules

FIGURE 5.6
Activity-on-Node (AON)
Cash Flow Example

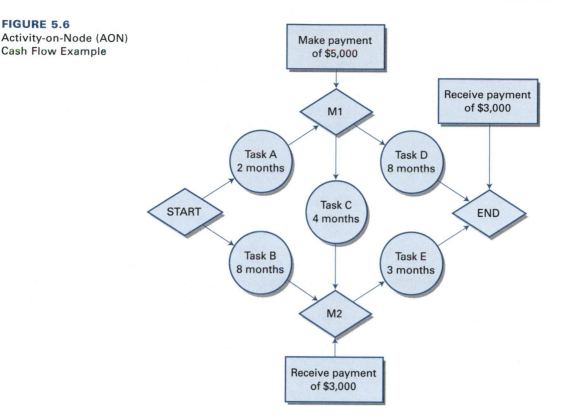

As indicated in Figure 5.6 and the following table, there are three milestones that represent cash payments or receipts.

Milestone	Event
M1	Pay $5,000 in salaries and/or materials
M2	Receive payment of $3,000
END	Receive final payment of $3,000

Following our usual assumptions, no task can be started until the preceding tasks (or milestones) have been completed; in this case, tasks C and D cannot be started until the $5,000 payment is made at milestone M1. Likewise, task E cannot be started until the $3,000 payment is received at milestone M2. Also note that the net profit for this project (ignoring the time value of money) appears to be $6,000 − $5,000 = $1,000.

If we ignore cost considerations, the critical path is eleven months, as indicated in Figure 5.6. Considering cash flows, however, we want to take into account the scheduling of milestones and tasks so that accounts payable (e.g., the $5,000 payment at M1) are made as late as possible and accounts receivable (e.g., the $3,000 payments at milestones M2 and END, respectively) are made as early as possible. From Figure 5.6, we can see that milestone M1 is not on the critical path, so the $5,000 payment could be made as late as time 3 (the latest finish time for M1) without delaying project completion time. In real-world projects, however, it is generally not possible to merely schedule accounts payable at their latest occurrence times and accounts receivable at their earliest occurrence times. Such milestones are usually interdependent, so rescheduling one milestone may affect other milestones and tasks. The linear programming (LP) model developed in Chapter 4 can easily be adapted to consider these interactions.

Intuitively, we want to schedule accounts payable as late as possible and accounts receivable as early as possible. Two factors are a concern: the magnitude of the payment and the timing. Thus, assuming that accounts receivable defines positive cash flows and accounts payable defines negative cash flows, we can define a measure called dollar-months (or dollar-days, etc.) that is simply the product of each cash flow times its respective occurrence time. In the Figure 5.6 example, dollar-months for the $5,000 payment made at milestone M1 is $5,000 s_{M1}$; total dollar-months for this example is defined as:

$$\text{Dollar-Months} = -5000s_{M1} + 3000s_{M2} + 3000s_{END}$$

By minimizing total dollar-months, we will attempt to schedule accounts payable (e.g., the $5,000 payment) as late as possible and the accounts receivable (e.g., the $3,000 payments) as early as possible. The Excel model defined in Chapter 4 can be easily modified to minimize dollar-months; the modified spreadsheet model and resultant solution are given in Figure 5.7 (the precedence constraints are indicated in the Solver constraint box).

In the spreadsheet, the value for total dollar-months is given in the column marked "Dollar-Months." The solution given in Figure 5.7 was found by minimizing this value (which by itself has no real meaning or direct interpretation). In this case, the values of the milestone starting times (denoted by s_j) show an interesting finding; namely, the solution that minimizes dollar-months delays the project completion time to month 12. (Remember that the critical path in this example was eleven months.) Such a delay allows the project manager to delay the payment of $5,000 to time 5 and reduces the delay between the $3,000 payment and the $3,000 that is received at time 8. This result was not intuitively evident, even in this small example.

The measure of dollar-months that we used is closely related to the more common measure of net present value (NPV). Using a monthly discount rate, r, equal to .0167 (corresponding to an annual discount rate of 20 percent), we calculated the NPV of all three cash flows (based on the event times). In this example, the total NPV of the project is defined as:

$$\text{NPV} = \frac{-5000}{(1+r)^{s_{M1}}} + \frac{3000}{(1+r)^{s_{M2}}} + \frac{3000}{(1+r)^{s_{END}}}$$

The values of each discounted cash flow are given in the appropriate cells under the NPV heading. When we resolved the model in Figure 5.7 to maximize total project NPV, we found the same solution that was calculated when we minimized total dollar-months (that is, the project was delayed to twelve months).

In fact, the criterion of minimizing dollar-months is closely related to maximizing NPV. The relationship between these two criteria is explained in more detail in Appendix 5A at

FIGURE 5.7
Excel Spreadsheet for
Cash Flow Example

| Annual discount rate = | 20% |
| Monthly discount rate = | 1.67% |

Activity	Duration (mos)	Start Time	Finish Time	Cash Flow	Dollar-Months	NPV
START*	0	0		–		
Task A	2	0.5	2.5	–		
Task B	8	0	8	–		
M 1*	0	4	4	$ (5,000)	$ (20,000)	$ (4,680.11)
Task C	4	4	8	–		
M 2*	0	8	8	$ 3,000	$ 24,000	$ 2,628.41
Task D	8	4	12	–		
Task E	3	8.5	11.5	–		
END*	0	12		$ 3,000	$ 36,000	$ 2,460.24
					$ 40,000	$ 408.55

*denotes milestone

the end of this chapter. As indicated in the appendix, the measure of dollar-months is a reasonably good surrogate measure for NPV under conditions when the discount rate is reasonably small. In addition, it allows for a linear model to be used which, for large projects, could save significant computational time. It is also a useful measure when it is difficult to determine a precise value of the discount rate (e.g., in the case of nonprofit organizations).

Many researchers have studied the relationship between cash flows and task scheduling in deterministic projects, including Russell (1986); Grinold (1972); Yang et al (1993); Smith-Daniels and Aquilano (1987); Smith-Daniels and Smith-Daniels (1987); Elmaghraby and Herroelen (1990); and Rosenblatt and Roll (1986). Rosenblatt and Buss (1997) studied the effect of delaying tasks in a stochastic project and showed that delaying tasks in a stochastic environment can also increase expected present value of a project under some conditions.

Finally, note that the approach discussed in this section is also useful when negotiating payments and setting milestones in the project planning phase (when the project manager has such flexibility). When the timing of milestones (including due dates) is negotiated, the model suggested here could be useful when scheduling accounts payable and accounts receivable.

PROJECT COMPRESSION: TIME-COST TRADE-OFFS

As noted in Chapter 1 and illustrated by the diagram in Figure 1.2, effective project management requires trade-offs between the design and specifications of a project and the time and cost to complete the project. Such trade-offs, especially in the face of an uncertain and rapidly changing technological environment, can be difficult to make. In this section, we discuss these trade-offs in more detail while focusing on the time-cost trade-off under the assumption that the design and specifications of the project are held constant.

There are many reasons to reduce the duration of a project (including the need to get a new product to market quickly or balance resource requirements among several projects). *In general, managers want to schedule a project so that total expected costs are minimized.* Several types of costs must be considered when reducing a project's duration, including direct labor costs associated with each task, indirect or overhead costs, and bonus or penalty costs for completing the project early or late, respectively. Initially, we will consider the trade-off between direct costs and overhead and indirect costs; we will then show how our approach can be extended to include other costs.

It is typically assumed that there is an inverse relationship between direct costs associated with a given task and the estimated duration of that task. For example, the project manager can reduce the time needed to complete a task by assigning more workers to the task, buying or leasing faster (and presumably more costly) equipment, assigning overtime, etc.

This inverse relationship generally holds—at least over a range. For example, consider the observation made by Brooks (1995) with respect to software development projects:

> Observe that for the programmer, as for the chef, the urgency of the patron may govern the scheduled completion of the task, but it cannot govern the actual completion. An omelet, promised in ten minutes, may appear to be progressing nicely. But when it has not set in ten minutes, the customer has two choices—wait or eat it raw. Software customers have the same choices.
>
> The cook has another choice; he can turn up the heat. The result is often an omelet nothing can save—burned in one part, raw in another. (p. 21)

The problem, of course, is that project managers frequently continue to add resources to a task even after that task has reached the limit on how far its duration can be reduced. Omelets, concrete, and software may take a specified amount of time that no number of chefs, workers, or programmers can reduce. In real-world projects, estimating how far a task can be reduced is a rough approximation at best; it is not always clear when a task has reached this "crash limit." Given this uncertainty, along with pressure to meet target due dates, it is not surprising that project managers frequently continue to add resources to a task beyond the point that it is economically sensible.

To illustrate the basic trade-off between time and direct cost, consider the precedence network in Figure 5.8 with information about the cost and duration to perform each task under "normal" conditions. This normal cost and duration represents the combination of direct costs and task duration that is initially estimated in the WBS. This point represents the smallest direct cost for completing any task; we assume that it is technically or politically impossible to perform any task at a lower direct cost.

Figure 5.8 also indicates the marginal cost of reducing the duration of any task by one week. Thus, the total direct cost to complete task B in four weeks is $85 + 2($5) = $95. In this example, assume that all four tasks can be reduced by a maximum of two weeks only.

Using the normal durations for the tasks in Figure 5.8, the project will take twenty-two weeks (as indicated by the critical path: START-A-C-END). The total direct cost to complete the project in twenty-two weeks is $320, which is the sum of the normal costs. Now assume that we want to reduce the project duration by one week—to twenty-one weeks. Clearly, we want to achieve this schedule reduction at the minimum possible increase in direct costs.

While task D has the smallest marginal direct cost ($4), reducing task D would not reduce the project duration since task D is not on the critical path. Thus, decreasing the duration of task D would only result in increasing slack values; this practice is avoided by most rational organizations. Thus, we can only consider reducing the duration of task A or task C (the critical tasks); since task A has the smaller marginal cost, we would reduce task A from seven weeks to six weeks and increase total project direct costs by $8 (to a total of $328). The project duration is now reduced to twenty-one weeks and there are two critical paths: START-A-C-END, and START-B-C-END.

To reduce the project duration further (to twenty weeks), we must again consider all critical tasks: A, B, and C (ignoring milestones that cannot be reduced). In this case, task B has the smallest marginal cost ($5) of these three tasks; however, reducing task B by one week will result in reducing only one of the critical paths. Since the critical path START-A-C-END will remain at twenty-one weeks, there will be no reduction in project duration. It is important to remember that *all* critical paths must be reduced in order to achieve a reduction in project duration.

Since task A has the second smallest marginal cost value ($8), we might consider reducing both tasks A and B at a total increase of direct costs equal to $13. Since both critical paths are reduced, the project duration would be reduced by one week. However, we note that task

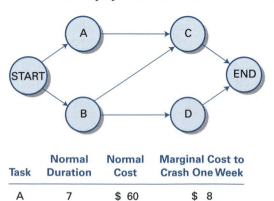

FIGURE 5.8
Reducing Project
Duration by Increasing
Direct Costs

Task	Normal Duration	Normal Cost	Marginal Cost to Crash One Week
A	7	$ 60	$ 8
B	6	$ 85	$ 5
C	15	$ 55	$ 10
D	10	$120	$ 4

C lies on both critical paths; thus, a one-week reduction in task C will reduce the project by one week at a marginal cost increase of $10. Since this is less than $13, we would decide to reduce task C by one week and increase total project direct costs to $338 (= $328 + $10).

We could continue reducing project duration in this manner until the project is at eighteen weeks. At that point, there is at least one critical path (START-A-C-END) that cannot be reduced any further. The steps to reduce this project from twenty-two weeks to eighteen weeks are summarized in Figure 5.9.

Note also that the marginal direct costs increase at an increasing rate as the project duration is reduced (i.e., the first week of project reduction costs $8, the second week costs $10, etc.) even though the marginal costs associated with each task are constant. This is because we reduce the least expensive tasks first, leaving the more expensive tasks to a later time.

As indicated by this small example, the choice of tasks to reduce at each time period is not always evident (e.g., choosing which tasks to crash when reducing the project duration from twenty-one to twenty weeks). In larger and more realistic projects, the problem of finding which tasks to reduce can be a difficult combinatorial problem. Most PM software programs offer little if any assistance in this regard.

Linear Time-Cost Trade-offs

There is a way, however, to formulate a linear programming (LP) model that will find the set of tasks to crash at each iteration. In this case, assume that the marginal cost to crash a task is constant (as in the previous example). Alternatively, project managers sometimes estimate both a normal point for each task as well as a crash point that defines the smallest possible task duration (and corresponding maximum direct cost). At the crash point, it is assumed to be technologically impossible to reduce the task duration any further, even if infinite resources are allocated to the task. Assuming a linear relationship between the normal and crash points (that is, a constant marginal cost to crash a task), the time-cost trade-off is indicated for a generic jth task in Figure 5.10.

The marginal cost to reduce the task duration by one time unit is represented by the slope of the line in Figure 5.10, which is denoted by b_j. As indicated in Figure 5.3, we will use the following notation:

$$t_j^N = \text{normal task duration}$$

$$t_j^c = \text{minimum possible (crash) task duration}$$

$$C_j^N = \text{normal direct costs}$$

$$C_j^c = \text{direct costs at crash point}$$

FIGURE 5.9
Example Project Duration Reduction

Project Duration (weeks)	Crital Path(s)	Task(s) Reduced	Direct Labor Cost
22 weeks	START-A-C-END	—	$320
21 weeks	START-A-C-END START-B-C-END	A	$328
20 weeks	START-A-C-END START-B-C-END	C	$338
19 weeks	START-A-C-END START-B-C-END	C	$348
18 weeks	START-A-C-END START-B-C-END	A, B	$361

FIGURE 5.10
Time-Cost Trade-off for
Task j

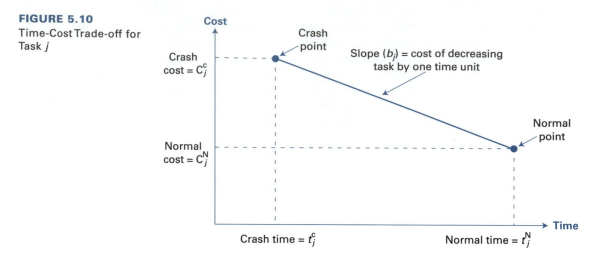

Assuming a linear relationship between the normal and crash points, the marginal cost of reducing the task duration is the slope b_j, defined as:

$$b_j = \frac{C_j^N - C_j^c}{t_j^N - t_j^c}$$

Note that the slope is negative, indicating that increasing direct costs reduce task duration.

Using this linear time-cost trade-off, we can revisit the combinatorial problem to find which task(s) to crash for a given project duration. Assume that T_{max} is the desired project duration. Then the problem of finding the task durations that minimize total direct costs (subject to the constraint that the project duration must equal T_{max}) can be formulated by modifying the linear programming (LP) model as described in Chapter 4.

In this modified model, there are now two sets of decision variables (occurrence times of tasks and milestones, and task duration times):

$$s_j = \text{starting time for task } j$$
$$\text{END} = \text{project completion time}$$
$$t_j = \text{duration of task } j$$

For all tasks in the project, the task time t_j (now a decision variable) must lie between the normal duration t_j^N and the crash duration t_j^c. The precedence constraints used in the previous LP model remain unchanged.

For any jth task, the direct cost can be found knowing the value of t_j. From Figure 5.10, the direct cost associated with task duration t_j is

$$C_j^N + b_j(t_j - t_j^N) = C_j^N + b_j t_j - b_j t_j^N$$

where $b_j \leq 0$. Thus, the total direct cost for the project is

$$\text{Minimize} \sum_j b_j t_j$$

$$t_j^c \leq t_j \leq t_j^N \quad \text{for all tasks } j \text{ in project}$$

Since the second term in this cost function is a constant, we can drop the term from the objective function. The modified linear programming problem to find task starting times and task durations that will minimize total direct costs for a given project duration T_{max} can then be stated as

$$\sum_j b_j t_j + \sum_i (C_j^{N} - b_j t_j^{N})$$

subject to

$$t^c_j \leq t_j \leq t^N_j \quad \text{for all tasks j in project}$$
$$s_j \geq s_i + t_i \quad \text{for all tasks } i \text{ in the set } P_j$$
$$\text{END} \leq T_{max}$$
$$s_i \geq 0 \quad \text{for all tasks } i$$

The spreadsheet and Solver model for this problem is given in Figure 5.11 for the problem in Figure 5.8 when $T_{max} = 19$ weeks. (Note that the "lag" variables were omitted from this formulation but could be easily added.) The solution for a duration of nineteen weeks is the same solution given in the table in Figure 5.9: total direct costs equal $348, task A has been reduced by one week, and task C has been reduced by two weeks.

We can now consider the trade-off between direct costs and other project costs. For example, we might want to reduce project duration in order to reduce the overhead or indirect charges. Conceptually, this trade-off is represented in Figure 5.12. As indicated, we would like to schedule the project at the point of minimum total cost.

The LP model used to minimize direct costs can easily be expanded to include other costs. For example, if c_I denotes the overhead and indirect costs per week, then the objective function to minimize total direct and indirect costs can be written as follows:

$$\text{Minimize} \sum_j b_j t_j + c_I \text{END}$$

Similarly, a penalty cost for completing the project after a due date (or a bonus for completing the project early), can be added to the model. Again, let T_{max} denote a given

FIGURE 5.11
Solver Model for Crashing Example

Task Starting Times		Duration (t j)		Task Finish Times	Normal		Crash	Slope (bj)
Variables	Values	Variables	Values		Duration	Cost	Duration	
START	0			0	0	$ -	0	-
STARTA	0	tA	6	6	7	$ 60	5	$ 8
STARTB	0	tB	6	6	6	$ 85	4	$ 5
STARTC	6	tC	13	19	15	$ 55	13	$ 10
STARTD	9	tD	10	19	10	$ 120	8	$ 4
END	19			19	0	$ -	0	-
Tmax	19					$ 320		

	Task A	Task B	Task C	Task D
Direct Cost/Task=	$ 68	$ 85	$ 75	$ 120

Total Direct Costs =	$ 348

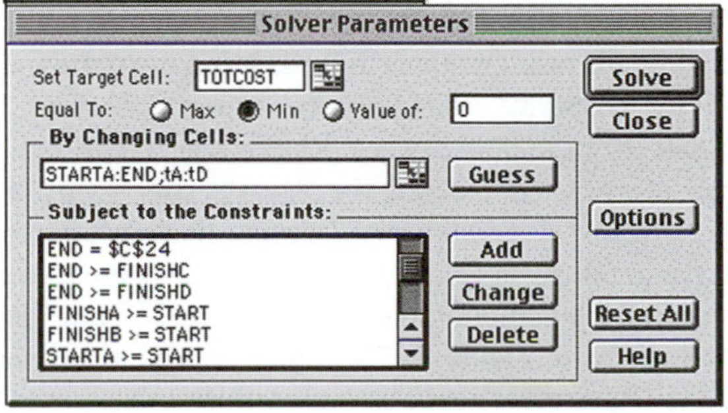

FIGURE 5.12
Total Cost versus
Project Duration

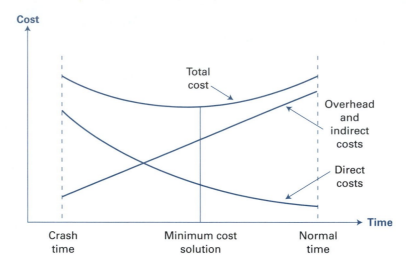

due date. If P is the penalty cost per week if the project is delayed beyond the due date T_{max}, then the objective function can be modified to include this penalty cost,

$$\text{Minimize} \sum_j b_j t_j + c_I \text{END} + \text{PL}$$

where

$L =$ the number of weeks the project is delayed beyond Tmax
$= \max(0, \text{END} - \text{Tmax})$

The value L is referred to as the tardiness of the project. While L could be defined in a Solver model using the max function, it is also possible to define L using a linear relationship. In this case, the objective function remains the same but an additional constraint is added to the LP model:

$$\text{END} - L \leq \text{T}_{max}$$

Since all variables (including L) must be nonnegative, L represents the number of weeks that the project is completed past the due date. If the project is finished before the due date (i.e., $\text{END} < T_{max}$), then L will be set to zero since the objective in this model is cost minimization.

The modified spreadsheet model that minimizes total costs for the previous example is given in Figure 5.13. While the due date T_{max} remains at nineteen weeks, we no longer use T_{max} to define a "hard" constraint (that is, we removed the constraint that END ≤ 19). Thus the only remaining constraints in this model were the precedence constraints and the constraints that require the task durations to be between the normal and crash times.

To define the costs, we set P (the penalty cost per week for completing the project after the due date T_{max}) to $5 per week. The overhead and indirect cost, c_I, was set to $7. The max function was used to define the penalty costs, if any. As indicated in Figure 5.13, the total minimum cost, is equal to $481. In the final solution task A is crashed one week (to six weeks), and task C is crashed two weeks (to thirteen weeks).

A bonus paid for completing the project before the due date could easily be added to the spreadsheet model in Figure 5.13 using an approach similar to the one used to define the penalty cost. Other costs could be included in a similar manner.

FIGURE 5.13
Spreadsheet Model for
Minimizing Total Costs in
Example Problem

Task	Normal Duration	Normal Cost	Marginal Cost to Crash One Week
A	7	$60	$8
B	6	$85	$5
C	15	$55	$10
D	10	$120	$4

Decision variables: t_j = Duration of task
 $START_j$ = Starting time of task j

Parameters: Overhead cost/wk = $7
 Penalty cost/wk = $5

Task Starting Times		Duration (t_j)		Task Finish Times	Normal		Crash	Slope (b_j)	
Variables	Values	Variables	Values		Duration	Cost	Duration		
START	0			0	0	$ -	0	$ -	
STARTA	0	t_A	6	6	7	$ 60	5	$ 8	
STARTB	0	t_B	6	6	6	$ 85	4	$ 5	
STARTC	6	t_C	13	19	15	$ 55	13	$ 10	
STARTD	9	t_D	10	19	10	$ 120	8	$ 4	
END	19			19	0	$ -	0	$ -	
						$ 320			

	Task A	Task B	Task C	Task D
Direct Cost/Task=	$ 68	$ 85	$ 75	$ 120

Total Direct Costs =	$ 348
Overhead costs =	$ 133
Penalty costs =	$ -
Total Cost =	$ 481

Nonlinear Time-Cost Trade-offs

In Figure 5.10, we assumed that the trade-off between the normal and the crash points is linear; that is, the marginal cost of reducing task duration is constant. This is not always the case, of course; sometimes the marginal costs increase (or decrease) as the task duration is reduced. In Figure 5.14, two alternative cases are illustrated; in the first case, marginal costs increase at an increasing rate (a convex function). This would occur when the initial reduction in task duration time is relatively easy; for example, existing personnel can work overtime. However, the amount of overtime that can be used may be limited (perhaps by union restrictions). Thus, further reductions in task durations might require that additional workers are hired or more costly equipment is purchased. In any event, the marginal cost of reducing the task duration further would be increased.

In the second case illustrated in Figure 5.14 (concave function), the marginal cost is reduced as the task duration is reduced. This might occur when expensive equipment is required to achieve an initial reduction in task durations; for example, a company may have to rent a concrete pump to decrease the time needed to pour a cement foundation in a construction project. Once the pump is rented, additional workers can be hired at a relatively smaller cost to assist with the frame construction and concrete work.

FIGURE 5.14
Nonlinear Time-Cost
Trade-offs

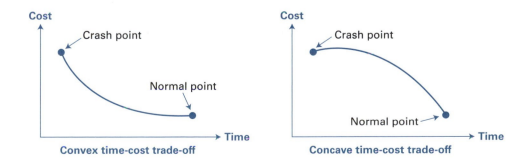

Convex time-cost trade-off   Concave time-cost trade-off

The linear programming model illustrated in Figure 5.13 can easily be modified to accommodate the convex time-cost trade-off case. The concave time-cost trade-off is somewhat more complicated and beyond the scope of this text. The interested reader is referred to Levy and Wiest (1977).

In either case, we can approximate the nonlinear time-cost trade-off curve by using a number of linear functions. For example, consider the convex time-cost trade-off illustrated in Figure 5.15. In this case, we use two linear functions to approximate the nonlinear convex function; each linear function defines a subtask that has its own normal and crash points. The original task j is defined by the sum of these two subtasks.

In the example in Figure 5.15, we want to reduce subtask j_2 initially (since its marginal cost is less than the marginal cost of subtask j_1). After reducing the duration of subtask j_2 to zero, we can then reduce the duration of subtask j_1 from t_j' to the overall crash time t_j^c. Thus, the normal and crash points for the two subtasks are shown in Figure 5.16.

For example, consider modifying the example in Figure 5.8. In that example, recall that task C could be reduced for a maximum of two weeks (from fifteen to thirteen weeks) at a marginal cost of $10 per week. Now, however, assume that the cost of reducing task C for the second week increases to $13.50 (the cost to crash the first week remains at $10).

To include this new information, we modify the spreadsheet in Figure 5.13 to split task C into two subtasks C1 and C2 (see Figure 5.17). The normal duration of subtask C2 is set equal to $15 - 14 = 1$ week, with a crash duration equal to 0. The normal duration of subtask C1 is fourteen weeks with a crash duration equal to 13. Since the slopes are already known ($10 and $13.50, respectively), this information can be placed directly into the modified spreadsheet model. Note that the duration of task C is now defined by the sum of the two subtasks, t_{C1} and t_{C2}. The modified spreadsheet model to minimize total costs that are defined by the sum of direct costs and overhead and indirect costs (charged at $11 per week) is given in Figure 5.17.

FIGURE 5.15
Convex Time-Cost Trade-off

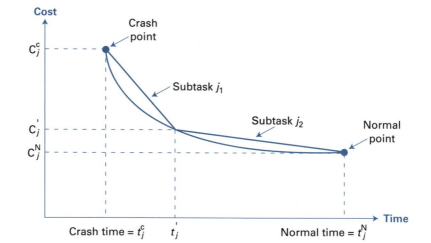

FIGURE 5.16
Normal and Crash Points for the Two Subtasks in Figure 5.15

	Normal		Crash	
	Duration	**Cost**	**Duration**	**Cost**
Subtask j_2	$t_j^N - t_j'$	C_j^N	0	C_j'
Subtask j_1	t_j'	0	t_j^c	$C_j^c - C_j'$
Task j	t_j^N	C_j^N	t_j^c	C_j^c

FIGURE 5.17

Modified Spreadsheet
Model with Convex
Time-Cost Trade-off

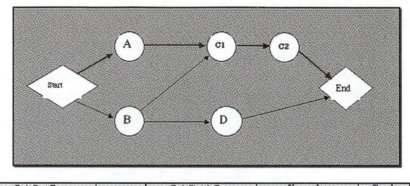

Task Start Times			Task Finish Times		Normal		Crash	
Variables	Values	Duration	Variables	Values	Duration	Cost	Duration	Slope (bj)
START	0				0	$ -	0	-
STARTA	0	6	FINISHA	6	7	$60	5	$8
STARTB	0	6	FINISHB	6	6	$85	4	$5
STARTC1	6	14	FINISHC1	20	14	$0	13	$13.5
STARTC2	20	0	FINISHC2	20	1	$55	0	$10.0
STARTD	8	10	FINISHD	17.9	10	$120	8	$4
END	20				0	$ -	0	-
						$320		

	Task A	Task B	Task C1	Task C2	Task C	Task D
Direct Cost/Task=	$68	$85	$0	$65.0	$65.0	$120.0
Overhead Cost/wk =	$11					

Total Direct Costs =	$338
Overhead costs =	$220
Total Cost =	$558

In the indicated solution, the project is crashed two weeks to minimize total costs; task A is crashed one week, and task C is crashed one week from fifteen weeks to fourteen weeks (subtask C2 is crashed to 0 and subtask C1 is not crashed at all). This is because these tasks can be reduced at a marginal cost of $8 (for task A) and $10 (for task C2), thereby reducing the overhead cost by $2 \times \$11 = \$22$. Any additional project compression would cost more (at $13/week for compressing tasks A and B) than could be saved in overhead and indirect costs (at $11 per week).

Discrete Time-Cost Trade-offs

In some cases, tasks can be performed only at certain discrete modes or points. In a software development project, for example, the manager might have only specific programmers available for this project and must assign one of these programmers to the project. In this case, each mode represents a specific worker and indicates an estimate of the time needed by each individual (and their associated cost) to complete the task in a satisfactory manner.

Figure 5.18 illustrates the case when there are three possible modes for performing some task j. The task times at each point (mode) are denoted by t_j^k, where k denotes the number of the point (in Figure 5.18, $k = 1, 2, 3$); the associated costs are similarly denoted by C_j^k.

To modify the Solver model with discrete modes, it is necessary to use binary (e.g., 0 or 1) decision variables, y_{jk}, where:

$$y_{jk} = \begin{cases} 1 & \text{if task } j \text{ is performed at mode/point } k \\ 0 & \text{otherwise} \end{cases}$$

If we want to minimize total direct costs, for example, the linear programming formation is straightforward. If the task is done at mode k, the duration and cost of task j is equal to $t_j^k y_{jk}$ and $C_j^k y_{jk}$, respectively. Including multiple choice constraints that require

FIGURE 5.18
Discrete Time-Cost
Trade-off

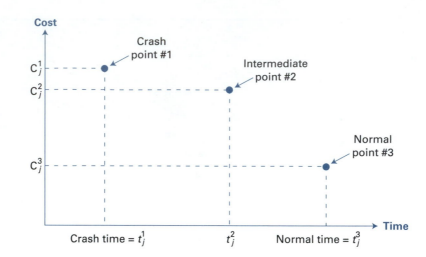

only one y_{jk} variable to equal one (so that the task is performed at one mode or point), the linear programming formulation becomes:

$$\text{Minimize Total Direct Cost} = \sum_{j}\sum_{k=1}^{3} C_j^{\,k}\, y_{jk}$$

subject to

$$\sum_{k=1}^{3} y_{jk} = 1 \quad \text{for all tasks } j$$

$$S_j \geq S_i + \sum_{k=1}^{3} t_j^{\,k}\, y_{jk} \quad \text{for all } j \in P_i$$

$$y_{jk} = (0,1) \text{ for all tasks } j$$

$$S_j \geq 0 \quad \text{for all tasks } j$$

where S_j denotes the starting time of task j. The spreadsheet for the example problem in Figure 5.8 is given in Figure 5.19 when the four tasks must be done at either their normal or crash points only. Note that task durations, t_j, are not decision variables in this model; the decision variables are task starting times, S_j, and the binary decision variables y_{jk}.

Since there are only two possible modes for each task in this example, we need only a single binary variable for each task (in addition to continuous variables representing the task starting times). If Y_{jN} denotes the binary variable indicating if the task is performed at the normal time and cost, $Y_{jC} = 1 - Y_{jN}$ indicates if the task is conversely performed at the crash time and cost. Thus, there are six continuous decision variables in our spreadsheet indicating the starting times of the four tasks and two milestones (START and END) and four binary decision variables.

As indicated in Figure 5.19, we want to minimize total project costs that are defined by the sum of the direct costs, and indirect and overhead costs (that are charged at $11/week). The optimal solution indicates that three tasks (A, B, and D) are performed at their normal duration times and costs, while task C is set to its crash point (thirteen weeks with a corresponding direct labor cost of $75). The minimum total cost is $560, and the project will be completed in twenty weeks.

It is interesting to compare these results to the solution in Figure 5.17, when continuous (but nonlinear) time-cost trade-offs were allowed between the normal and crash

FIGURE 5.19
Discrete Time-Cost
Trade-off Example

Task Starting Times		Duration	Task Finish Times	
Variables	**Values**		**Variables**	**Values**
START	0			
STARTA	0	7	FINISHA	7
STARTB	0	6	FINISHB	6
STARTC	7	13	FINISHC	20
STARTD	6	10	FINISHD	16
END	20			

	NORMAL		Binary Var	CRASH		Binary Var
	Duration	**Cost**	**YjN**	**Duration**	**Cost**	**YjC**
Task A	7	$ 60	1	5	$ 76	0
Task B	6	$ 85	1	4	$ 95	0
Task C	15	$ 55	0	13	$ 75	1
Task D	10	$ 120	1	8	$ 128	0

Direct Cost/Task=	$ 60	$ 85	$ 75	$ 120
Overhead Cost/wk =	$ 11			

Total Direct Costs =	$ 340
Overhead costs =	$ 220
Total Cost =	$ 560

points. When tasks are restricted to discrete modes, the minimum total cost will always be at least as great as the continuous case since the discrete problem has more restrictions. In this example, the discrete case is more costly than the continuous case ($560 versus $558) although both projects were compressed to twenty weeks.

Time-Cost Trade-offs with Coordination and Communication Considerations

In his book, Brooks (1995) stated that "Adding manpower to a late software project makes it later." This statement has become known as Brooks's Law and is consistent with similar observations, for example, Hughes's (1986) observation that many projects have failed for having too many people but none had ever failed for having too few people. Why is this so? If there were an inverse relationship between task duration and direct cost, we would think that adding resources (e.g., programmers) to a project would reduce task and project duration.

Brooks's Law and Hughes's observations are based on the fact that increased communication and coordination time frequently results from adding more workers to a task. As we discussed in Chapter 3, the number of interpersonal relationships increases exponentially as more people are added to a task or project team. At some point, the additional communication and coordination burden resulting from additional workers becomes counterproductive and actually starts to increase the overall task duration. This is especially true in software projects for which computer code must be coordinated and integrated into a final product.

To illustrate what happens when coordination times are included in the usual time-cost trade-off, consider a small software development project to develop a computer program that requires approximately 50,000 lines of Perl code.* Assume that a typical programmer can write 1,500 lines of code per week. Following the discussion in Chapter 3 on the number of interpersonal links between members of a project team, we assume that coordination time (in weeks) is defined by $_MC_2 = M(M - 1)/2$, where M is the number of programmers hired for the project.

As the project manager hires more programmers, their individual tasks and associated work times are reduced. However, as indicated in Figure 5.20, the marginal reduction in programming time is offset by the marginal increase in coordination time as more programmers

---

* Lines of code is not a particularly good metric for software projects, but is used here nevertheless.

FIGURE 5.20

Time-Cost Trade-off with Coordination

Number of Programmers	Number of Weeks Coding	Number of Coordination Weeks	Total Number of Weeks
1	33.33	0	33.33
2	16.67	1	17.67
3	11.11	3	14.11
4	8.33	6	14.33
5	6.67	10	16.67
6	5.56	15	20.56
7	4.76	21	25.76
8	4.17	28	32.17
9	3.70	36	39.70
10	3.33	45	48.33
11	3.03	55	58.03

are added to the project. As indicated, the total time for this hypothetical project is minimized with three programmers (with an associated project duration of 14.11 weeks), whereas the project duration actually increases to 14.33 weeks when four programmers are hired. While the relationship in this example is an approximation, of course, the concept clearly holds and may explain both Hughes's and Brooks's observations.

MATERIAL AND INVENTORY COSTS

In Chapter 2, we saw that material costs should be considered when determining a budget for a project and learned that material costs can be a significant factor when estimating project costs. In addition, material costs can dramatically affect cash flows depending on when materials are ordered and delivered; conversely, materials can delay a project if they are not available at the needed time.

Generally, we assume that a task cannot be started until all necessary materials are available. Since delays due to material unavailability can be costly, it seems obvious that low-cost items (office supplies, nuts and bolts, etc.) would be ordered well in advance of a task and stored until needed. These items are generally classified as "Type C" items; for more information about material classification schemes, see Nahmias (1997) or Davis et al. (2003).

It is costly to hold materials in inventory; costs include not only deterioration, depletion, insurance, and spoilage but also the opportunity cost incurred by having resources invested in materials instead of revenue-generating options (e.g., bonds). Given that this opportunity cost constitutes much of the cost of holding materials in stock, most organizations use an annual inventory carrying-cost rate to calculate the cost of holding one unit of material in stock for a year. Typical values of annual inventory carrying-cost rates range from 15 percent to 40 percent.

In a project environment, materials are consumed during the duration of a task and turned into components, subassemblies, or final products. If we assume that the value of the components, subassemblies, final products, etc. is greater than the value of the materials used to create these products, then we can always reduce material holding costs by delaying a task (although other costs might increase). That is, if a task adds value to raw materials and holding costs are proportional to the value of the product, then it follows that holding costs are always reduced by holding raw materials instead of finished (or intermediate) products.

What are the implications of this assumption? In a deterministic environment, this implies that all tasks that have significant material costs should be postponed as much as possible (i.e., to start at their latest starting times). However, is this always the case?

Should the project manager ever consider delaying the project in order to save holding or ordering costs? If a task requires some materials, should she ever consider splitting this requirement into two or more orders?

To consider these issues, consider the example in Figure 5.21. As indicated, there are six tasks in the project; two of these tasks (B and E) require the use of a single raw material. Task B requires 2 units of this raw material, while task E requires 30 units. Task duration times and the latest starting times of all six tasks are indicated in Figure 5.21; the critical path is 17 weeks (START-A-B-C-END).

Following the usual assumptions relating to inventory management (Davis et al., 2003), we assume that there is a fixed cost associated with placing an order that is denoted by S. To simplify this discussion, assume that the cost of holding raw materials is proportional to the number of raw material "unit-weeks," although this value could be converted to actual costs if we know the inventory carrying-cost rate and the cost of the materials. Following our previous discussion, assume also that it is more costly to hold the intermediate or final product that results from a task than the raw materials used to create this intermediate/final product. Finally, assume that the project can be delayed at a cost of P per week.

Clearly, one possible option for ordering the 32 units or raw materials is to order all materials at the beginning of the project and hold them until needed (i.e., until time 4 for task B and time 12 for task E, assuming that these tasks are started at their latest starting times). If we adopt this ordering option, the associated cost would be equal to $S + (4 \times 2 = 8)$ unit-wks $+ (30 \times 12 = 360)$ unit-wks $= S + 368$ unit-wks. (Assume that the raw material holding costs accrue only until a task is started; this assumption is not restrictive and can be easily relaxed.)

Since the project is deterministic, however, there seems to be little reason why we should hold the raw materials from time zero. If we were to have all 32 units delivered at time 4, they would be readily available when needed for each task (that is, they would be available at time 4 for task B and at time 12 for task E). In this case, the holding cost would be reduced to $S + (30 \text{ units}) (8 \text{ weeks}) = S + 240$ unit-wks. (Again, it would reduce raw material holding costs if we started task E before its latest starting time; however, it would be more costly to hold the finished product from this task than the associated raw materials.)

Another option would be to have the materials delivered in two shipments. Given this option, we would want to have the units for task B delivered at time 4 and the units for task E delivered at time 12. In this way, the material costs would be equal to $(2S)$ and there would be no raw material holding costs, since the raw materials are delivered "just-in-time." This option also indicates why we would never split our orders, for example, order

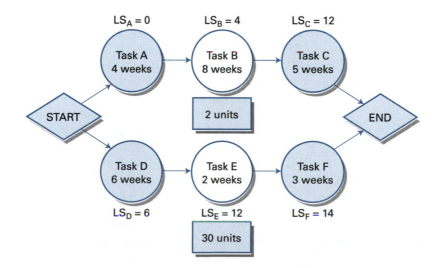

FIGURE 5.21
Material Management
Example

12 units at time 4 and 22 units at time 12. In this latter case, we would incur a fixed order cost equal to ($2S$) (since two shipments would be made), but we would also incur a holding cost of (10 units) (8 weeks) = 80 unit-wks since 10 of the units delivered at time 4 would have to be held until time 12 for use in performing task E.

We can also consider the possibility of delaying the project in order to save holding costs. One possibility is to have all 32 units delivered at time 12; in this way we incur only S in fixed ordering costs, and most of the units (30 units) incur no holding cost since they would be delivered just-in-time for task E. Or do they incur a holding cost?

Considering this case further, we realize that if the materials are not delivered until time 12, task B will be delayed 8 weeks beyond its current latest starting time (time 4). Since task B is on the critical path, the completion time of the project will be delayed by 8 weeks to 25 weeks (17 weeks plus an 8-week delay). Since the project is now delayed until time 25, the latest starting time of task E is delayed until time 20 ($25 - 3 - 2$).

Since we assumed that the cost of holding finished goods or work in progress is more costly than holding raw materials (and thereby want to start all tasks at their latest starting times to reduce holding costs), the cost of this policy can be calculated as follows:

- The fixed cost of placing the order = S.
- The holding cost of raw materials associated with task E = (30 units) × (20 − 12 weeks) = 240 unit-wks.
- The penalty cost for delaying the completion of the project by 8 weeks = $8P$.

You should note that the cost of this policy ($S + 240$ unit-wks + $8P$) is exactly $8P$ more costly than the policy of having all 32 units delivered at time 4. This is not a coincidence; as shown by Smith-Daniels (1987), we would never want to delay a project to save on holding costs as long as the project delay cost P is greater than zero.

Thus, there are only two viable alternatives in this case:

- Order all 32 units at time 4 (with cost = $S + 240$ unit-wks).
- Order 2 units at time 4 and 30 units at time 12 9 (with cost = $2S$).

To compare these two alternatives, you would have to know the value of S and the weekly unit holding or carrying cost, which would be defined as the number of unit-weeks times the cost per unit times the weekly inventory carrying cost rate. The important point, however, is that there are only two alternatives to consider; these options dominate all other alternatives.

This example has other implications. First, there are only two times when we would consider having units delivered—either time 4 and/or time 12. Furthermore, as we have shown, we would never split an order. Thus, at time 4, we would order units for time 4, or the units for time 4 and the units for time 12. If there were other tasks that needed the same materials at some later time, we could consider including this amount in the order at time 4 as well. This type of problem is well known in the operations management literature (Davis et al., 2003; Nahmias, 1997).

There is one other important implication. A widely used material management system is known as a material requirements planning (MRP) system; MRP systems are integral parts of many enterprise resource planning (ERP) systems (Shtub, 1999) In an MRP system, a master production schedule (MPS) is used to forecast demand for end items; these demands are then used with a bill of materials to generate demands for subassemblies, components, and raw materials. The result is a forecast of demands for subassemblies etc. that are needed at specific time periods.

The problem in MRP is to find appropriate lot sizes for these materials; that is, knowing which forecasts should be combined into a single order. The same logic we used for analyzing material ordering decisions in the example project is used in MRP systems; i.e., orders are never split, and a manager should only consider combining some number of subsequent orders.

Since the problems of managing materials in projects are so similar to those problems found in MRP systems, MRP (and many ERP systems) can used for managing material ordering decisions and material flows in a project environment. For more details about MRP systems, the interested reader should see Nahmias (1997) or Davis et al. (2003).

STUDY PROBLEMS

1. The president of Walla Walla Boat Company, Mr. Seymore Books, has agreed to build a new sailboat for a consortium that plans to enter the boat in the next America's Cup Race. The project network, which consists of five tasks and four milestones, is the same network given in Figure 5.6 with the following task durations:

   ■ Task A: 1 month
   ■ Task B: 10 months
   ■ Task C: 4 months
   ■ Task D: 9 months
   ■ Task E: 2 months

   Mr. Books estimates that a cash payment of $5000 will have to be made at milestone M1, while the consortium has agreed to pay Walla Walla $3000 at milestone M2 and $3000 when the boat is completed and delivered. Mr. Books wants to schedule the project in order to maximize the net present value of the cash flows, but isn't certain of an appropriate discount rate to use in this case. Thus, he has decided instead to simply treat money as a resource that can be spent or collected at various times and schedule the tasks (and milestones) to minimize dollar-months. Mr. Books claims that minimizing dollar-months is nearly equivalent to maximizing NPV.

   What is the makespan of this project based on the critical path? If Mr. Books minimizes total dollar-months, what is the makespan of the project? If Mr. Books maximizes the NPV of the project, assuming an annual discount rate of 20 percent, what is the project makespan?

2. a. Mr. Books is concerned about delaying the delivery of the America's Cup boat in Problem 1. How much does the $5000 payment made at milestone M1 have to be *decreased* such that the project will NOT be delayed beyond its critical path and still maximize the NPV of the project?

   b. A total of $6000 will be paid by the client in Problem 1 ($3000 at milestone M2 and $3000 at the end of the project). If the client pays more than $3000 at milestone M2 and less at the end of the project (but still only pays a total of $6000), will this reduce the project makespan of the solution that maximizes the NPV (assume that a payment of $5000 is still made at milestone M1)? If so, how much would have to be paid at milestone M2?

3. Izzi Bright must complete a project with seven identified tasks; the precedence relationships among these tasks and their expected durations are indicated in the following AON diagram. Three tasks (tasks 3, 4, and 5) in this project require a specific resource for completion; all needed resources must be available at the site before a task can be started.

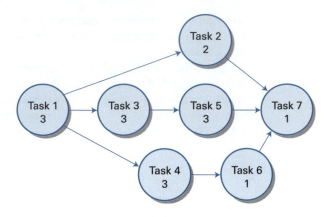

The number of resource units needed by tasks 3, 4, and 5 as well as the estimated value of the completed tasks is given in the following table.

Task	No. of Units Needed	Value of Completed Task
3	10	$4000
4	10	$3000
5	12	$4500

Each resource unit costs $100; no quantity discounts are available. In addition, it costs $2 per unit per time period to hold this resource in stock, and it costs $45 just to place an order for materials (independent of the number of units ordered). Once a task is completed, the holding cost per time period is estimated at 2 percent of the value of the completed task (e.g., it would cost $80 to hold completed task 3 for one time period). If the project is not completed on time, it will cost $5 for each time period that the project is delayed.

When should each task in the project be started, and when (and how many) resources should be ordered to minimize total project costs?

4. Rob D. Store, chairperson of the Marketing Department, has made a list of all the tasks that must be completed by his staff before the end of the academic year. Given the number of days remaining in the semester, he is beginning to panic. Luckily, he has studied project management and wants to apply CPM concepts. Using the data shown, reduce the project completion time by four days. Assume a linear time-cost trade-off for each task and show, step by step, how you arrived at your schedule. Also indicate the critical path.

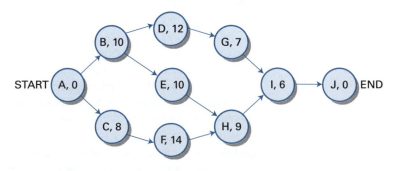

Activity	Normal Time (days)	Normal Cost ($)	Crash Time (days)	Crash Cost ($)
B	10	100	9	110
C	8	80	7	100
D	12	120	10	140
E	10	100	7	120
F	14	140	12	190
G	7	70	5	100
H	9	90	6	150
I	6	60	5	80

5. Dr. Denton Fender, a noted geologist, has discovered a site that she believes may hold a large deposit of natural gas. To test for the possible presence of natural gas, she proposes to drill a test hole, set off a small explosive charge, and use the resulting seismic pattern to indicate the likely presence or absence of natural gas. The process of testing a likely site has been divided into five tasks that are indicated in the following AON precedence network.

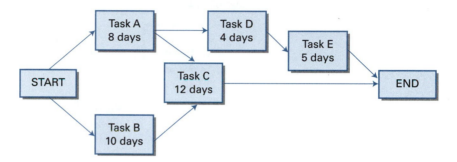

Dr. Fender has estimated the times and costs of each task assuming normal conditions, as well as the times and costs of each task assuming a crashed or reduced condition. This information is indicated in the table that follows.

Task	Normal Duration	Normal Cost	Crash Duration	Crash Cost	Slope
START	0	—	0	—	—
Task A	8	$ 100	6	$ 200	$ 50
Task B	10	$ 70	5	$ 170	$ 20
Task C	12	$ 260	8	$ 500	$ 60
Task D	4	$ 80	4	$ 80	—
Task E	5	$ 100	2	$ 175	$ 25
END	0	—	0	—	—

Under normal conditions, Dr. Fender estimates that the test procedure would take twenty-two days (the length of the critical path under normal conditions) and cost $610 in direct costs.

a. Given the importance of new sources of natural gas, she wants to consider possible shorter scenarios; thus, she would like you to reduce the project one day at a time and calculate the minimum direct cost associated with each day. Summarize your findings in a table. What is the shortest possible time needed for this project?

b. If overhead (indirect) charges are $50 per day, what would be the project duration that minimizes the sum of direct and indirect charges?

c. Formulate and solve a linear programming model using Solver in MS-Excel for solving the problem in part (b). Compare your answer to the solution you found in part (b).

d. Assume that an incentive (bonus) is now offered if the project is completed in nineteen days. Assuming that the overhead (indirect) charges in part (b) remain in effect, how large would the incentive have to be to make it financially attractive for Dr. Fender to complete this project in nineteen days?

6. In the following AON project network, the estimated normal durations for each task are indicated at each node. Each task in this project can be compressed by a maximum of two weeks; each week's decrease will cost an amount that is equal to its estimated normal duration (for example, the duration of task A can be reduced to six weeks by spending an additional $7, or it can be reduced to five weeks for an additional cost of $14).

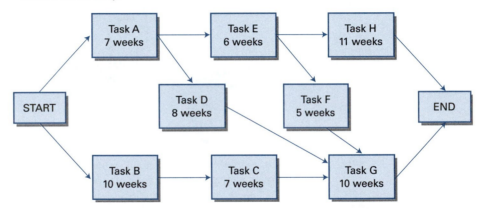

a. Which tasks should be compressed if we want to reduce the project three weeks at the smallest possible total direct cost? What is the marginal increase in total direct costs for each week that we decrease the project duration?

b. If the project is completed after twenty weeks, a penalty fee of $9 per week is assessed for each week late. However, if the project is completed before week 20, there is a $5 bonus paid for each week early. Find the project duration that minimizes total costs (where total cost includes direct labor costs, late fees, and earliness bonus). Defend your answer.

REFERENCES

Brooks, F. *The Mythical Man-Month: Essays on Software Engineering.* Boston: Addison-Wesley, 1995 (Anniversary Edition).

Davis, M., N. Aquilano, and R. Chase. *Fundamentals of Operations Management.* 4th ed. New York: McGraw-Hill, 2003.

Grinold, R. C. "The Payment Scheduling Problem." *Naval Research Logistics Quarterly* 19 (1972): 132–42.

Elmaghraby, S. E., and W. S. Herroelen. "The Scheduling of Activities to Maximize the Net Present Value of Projects." *European Journal of Operational Research* 49 (1990): 35–49.

Hughes, M. W. "Why Projects Fail: The Effects of Ignoring the Obvious." *Industrial Engineering,* April 1986, 14–18.

Jiambalvo, J. *Managerial Accounting.* (New York: Wiley, 2001).

Levy, F., G. L. Thompson, and J.D. Wiest. "The ABC's of the Critical Path Method." *Harvard Business Review* (September–October 1963): 98–108.

Nahmias, S. *Production and Operations Analysis.* 3d ed. Chicago: Richard D. Irwin, 1997.

Roemer, T., R. Ahmadi, and R. Wang. "Time-Cost Trade-offs in Overlapped Product Development." *Operations Research* 48, no. 6 (November–December 2000): 858–65.

Rosenblatt, M. J., and A. Buss. "Activity Delay in Stochastic Project Networks." *Operations Research* 45, no. 1 (1997): 126–39.

Rosenblatt, M. J., and Y. Roll. "A Future Value Approach to Determining Project Duration." *IIE Transactions* 17 (1986): 164–67.

Russell, R. A. "A Comparison of Heuristics for Scheduling Projects with Cash Flows and Resource Restrictions." *Management Science* 32 (1986): 1291–1300.

Shtub, A. *Enterprise Resource Planning (ERP): The Dynamics of Operations Management.* Boston: Kluwer Academic Publishers, 1999.

Smith-Daniels, D. "Optimal Project Scheduling with Material Ordering." *IIE Transactions* 19, no. 2 (1987).

Smith-Daniels, D., and N. J. Aquilano. "The Use of a Late Start Resource Constrained Project Schedule to Improve Project Net Present Value." *Decision Sciences* 18 (1987): 617–30.

Smith-Daniels, D., and V. Smith-Daniels. "Maximizing the Net Present Value of a Project Subject to Materials and Capital Constraints." *Journal of Operations Management* 7 (1987): 33–45.

Yang, K. K., F. B. Talbot, and J. H. Patterson. "Scheduling a Project to Maximize Its Net Present Value: An Integer Programming Approach." *European Journal of Operational Research* 64 (1993): 188–98.

APPENDIX 5A. THE RELATIONSHIP BETWEEN NET PRESENT VALUE AND DOLLAR-MONTHS

Let F_i denote the ith cash flow (such that a positive cash flow represents an account receivable and a negative case flow represents an account payable) that occurs at some time s_i. If r denotes the discount rate, then the present value of F_i is defined as

$$\frac{F_i}{(1+r)^{s_i}}$$

If there are M such cash flows over the life of a project, the net present value (NPV) of a project is simply the sum of the M cash flows, or

$$\text{NPV} = \sum_{i=1}^{M} \frac{F_i}{(1+r)^{s_i}}$$

which is maximized subject to the constraints

$$s_j \geq s_i + t_i \text{ for all tasks } i \text{ in the set } P_j$$

Now, assume that we have a function $f(x)$ and some point a where the function $f(x)$ is continuously differentiable. Then, letting the first derivative of $f(x)$ at point a be denoted by $f'(a)$, the second derivative by $f''(a)$, the third derivative by $f'''(a)$, etc., the function $f(x)$ can be approximated by the polynomial

$$f(a) + f'(a)(x-a) + \frac{f''(a)}{2!}(x-a)^2 + \frac{f'''(a)}{3!}(x-a)^3 + \ldots + \frac{f^{(n)}(a)}{n!}(x-a)^n + \ldots$$

which is called a Taylor series expansion of $f(x)$ at the point a.

The present value of F_i, that is defined as $F_i(1+r)^{-si}$, is of the form b^u. Since the first derivative of b^u with respect to x is defined as:

$$\frac{d(b^u)}{dx} = b^u (\ln b) \frac{du}{dx}$$

then the first derivative of the present value of F_i, with respect to s_i, is

$$\frac{d[F_i(1+r)^{-s_i}]}{ds_i} = -F_i(1+r)^{-s_i}\ln(1+r)$$

Given some constant a and using only the linear term in the Taylor series expansion, the problem of maximizing the net present value can be approximated by

$$\text{Maximize}\sum_{i=1}^{M} -F_i[(1+r)^{-a_i}\ln(1+r)]s_i$$

Letting

$$g_i = (1+r)^{-a_i}\ln(1+r)$$

the problem of maximizing the net present value of the project (given the M cash flows) can be rewritten as:

$$\text{Maximize}\sum_{i=1}^{M} -F_i g_i s_i \equiv \text{Minimize}\sum_{i=1}^{M} F_i g_i s_i$$

If the values of $g_i = 1$, then the objective function is exactly equivalent to minimizing dollar-months.

How should the constants a_i (and terms g_i) be defined? Theoretically, the values of a_i should equal the optimal values of s_i, which of course are unknown. However, because the function $(F_I g_i s_i)$ is convex, the following iterative scheme can be used to find the optimal values of a_i (and s_i) because the process will converge to an optimal solution (generally within three or four iterations).

Step 1. Initially set all values of $a_i = 1$ (or equal to the values of s_i found by minimizing dollar-days).

$$\text{Minimize}\sum_{i=1}^{M} F_i g_i s_i$$

Step 2. Calculate the values of g_i and solve the linear programming problem subject to precedence constraints.

Step 3. If

$$\sum_{i=1}^{M} |a_i - s_i| \le \varepsilon$$

where ε is some small positive number, then STOP; the optimal solution has been found. Otherwise, set the values of a_i equal to the optimal values of s_i and repeat Step 2.

PLANNING WITH UNCERTAINTY

In the first chapter, we briefly discussed the history of project management (PM) systems including PERT (generally known as Program Evaluation and Review Technique), which was reportedly developed between 1956 and 1958 by the consulting firm Booz Allen Hamilton for the U.S. Navy's Special Projects Office to assist with the development and deployment of the Polaris Fleet Ballistic Missile program. Since that time, PERT has gained widespread visibility, application, and criticism.

According to Malcolm et al. (1959), the initial PERT (first known as Program Evaluation Research Task) system was developed to provide "management with integrated and quantitative evaluation of: (a) progress to date …, (b) validity of established plans and schedules …, and (c) effects of changes proposed in established plans." A somewhat different perspective on the history of PERT is given by Craven (2001), who was the chief scientist of the Special Projects Office at the time PERT was developed. According to Craven:

> A new management system was invented on the spot that included the now famous PERT program (progress evaluation and reporting technique). Its origin came from a directive from Admiral Raborn that a new management program was to be established to give the contractors the illusion that they were being managed and that the name of the program was to be PERT in honor of his new bride, whose nickname was Pert.

However it was developed, PERT remains well known today, although its application is limited. The motivation behind the development of PERT, however, remains sound; namely, to develop a PM system that explicitly considers the fact that task duration times are random variables and gives managers a way to explicitly respond to the question: If milestone X is met by a given date, what is the probability that milestone Y will be met by another (given) date?

In this chapter, we will discuss the approach that was developed to support the Polaris missile and submarine project in the 1950s. We will refer to this model as "Classic PERT" and discuss the methodology as well as its advantages and many limitations. We will also discuss some important implications that follow when task times are assumed to be random variables. Finally, we will examine alternative methodologies, based on Monte Carlo simulation and Goldratt's theory of constraints, that are replacing Classic PERT and avoid most of the limitations of that approach.

CLASSIC PERT DEFINED

The PERT system developed for the Special Projects Office (Classic PERT) assumes that task duration times can be described by a beta distribution as discussed in Chapter 2.

Following that discussion, Classic PERT assumes that managers can estimate three points for each task:

t^o = most optimistic time estimate
t^p = most pessimistic time estimate
t^m = most likely time estimate

Using these three time estimates, the expected duration or mean (denoted by μ) and variance (denoted by σ^2) of each task can be calculated using the following simple approximation formulas:

$$\mu = \frac{t^o + t^p + 4t^m}{6}$$

and

$$\sigma^2 = \frac{(t^p - t^o)^2}{36}$$

Recall from the discussion in Chapter 2 that the beta distribution is a unimodal distribution that is not necessarily symmetric but may be skewed right or left depending on the values of the parameters. An example of a beta distribution is given in Figure 2.21.

For example, consider again a programming task that the project manager thinks will take six days under the best possible circumstances, fourteen days under the worst circumstances, but most likely will require eleven days. Using the PERT approximation formulas, the expected duration of task j, μ_j, would be

$$\mu_j = \frac{6 + 14 + 4(11)}{6} = 10.67$$

with a standard deviation equal to

$$\sigma_j = \frac{(14 - 6)}{6} = 1.33$$

While a number of problems arise concerning the use of these formulas (see Chapter 2 for a discussion of these issues), the designers of the Classic PERT model used these formulas nevertheless to calculate the means and standard deviations of each task. The means were then substituted into the critical path model (CPM) described in Chapter 4, and the expected longest path through the precedence network was calculated; this path was then used to calculate various probabilities that milestones would be completed by some given date. To describe the Classic PERT model in more detail, we will use the example in Figure 6.1 to illustrate the calculations as well as the limitations of the Classic PERT model.

The example in Figure 6.1 assumes that managers have estimated the optimistic, pessimistic, and most likely durations for all six tasks in this information technology (IT) project. With these estimates, the equations for μ and σ^2 were used to calculate the mean/expected value and variance, respectively. The template for these calculations is provided on the CD-ROM accompanying this text, so that you can verify these equations and calculations.

The Classic PERT model assumes that task durations are statistically independent random variables that follow a beta distribution. Given this assumption, a project manager can find the expected duration of any path in the precedence network by summing the expected durations of all tasks on that path. For example, consider path (START-A-D-END); the expected duration of that path is 0 + 6.67 + 14.33 + 0 = 23.33. Since it is

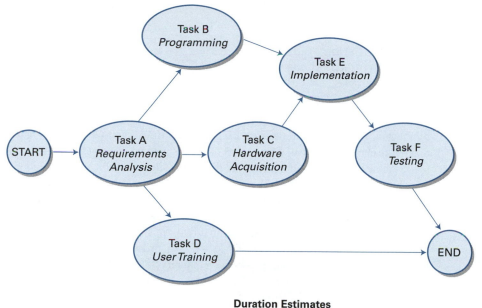

Task	Description	Predecessors	Duration Estimates			Expected Duration	Variance
			Optimistic	Pessimistic	Likely		
A	Requirements analysis	none	2	14	6	6.67	4.00
B	Programming	A	4	12	7	7.33	1.78
C	Hardware acquisition	A	2	13	8	7.83	3.36
D	User training	A	12	18	14	14.33	1.00
E	Implementation	B,C	3	7	5	5.00	0.44
F	Testing	E	3	7	4	4.33	0.44
END	End of project	D,F	0	0	0	0.00	0.00

FIGURE 6.1 Classic PERT Example 1

assumed that tasks are statistically independent, the variances can also be summed (*not* the standard deviations) to find the variance associated with any path.

Examining the precedence network in Figure 6.1, we can see that there are three paths through the precedence network. The three paths through the example precedence network and their associated expected durations and variances are given in the table in Figure 6.2.

The Classic PERT model assumes that the path with the greatest expected value is the critical path; this path is used for all further calculations. If two or more paths have the same expected durations, the path with the greatest variance defines the critical path. As indicated in Figure 6.2, path (START-A-C-E-F-END) defines the critical path with the longest expected duration in the example in Figure 6.1; using the Classic PERT approach, the manager would assume that the expected duration of this project is 23.83 weeks with a variance of 8.25 weeks.

Now let's say that the project manager wants to find the probability that the project will be completed in, say, 25 weeks; that is, he wants to find

$$\Pr[\mathrm{ES}_{\mathrm{END}} \leq 25]$$

the probability that the early start time of END milestone will be less than or equal to 25. Since the task durations are random variables, $\mathrm{ES}_{\mathrm{END}}$ is also a random variable that is defined

FIGURE 6.2
Paths in Classic PERT
Example Precedence
Network

Path	Expected Early Start	Variance
START A-B-E-F-END	23.33	6.67
START A-C-E-F-END	23.83	8.25
START A-D-END	21.00	5.00

by the sum of the task durations on the expected critical path CP (START-A-C-E-F-END); that is, the expected value of ES_{END} is 23.83 weeks with an associated variance of 8.25 weeks.

Since ES_{END} is a random variable defined by the sum of a series of independent beta distributions, ES_{END} is defined by a normal distribution according to the central limit theorem that states that the sum of a large number of independent random variables converges to a normal distribution. While there are not a "large number" of tasks defining the longest expected path in this example, in a real-world project there are generally enough tasks to satisfy this requirement. Thus, we will proceed with the assumption that our example networks have enough tasks such that any value of ES_i can be described by a normal distribution. The Classic PERT model then defines the expected project duration and variance of the project duration as follows:

$$\text{Expected Project Duration} = E[ES_{END}] = \left(\sum_{\text{tasks } j \text{ on path CP}} \mu_j \right)$$

and

$$\text{Variance of Project Duration} = \text{Var}[ES_{END}] = \left(\sum_{\text{tasks } j \text{ on path CP}} \sigma_j^2 \right)$$

Knowing that ES_{END} can be described by a normal distribution with a mean of 23.83 weeks and a variance of 8.25 weeks, we can find the probability that the project will be completed within 25 weeks (the "Due Date"). To use a standard normal table (based on a normal distribution with a mean of zero and a variance of one), we compute the associated z-score as follows:

$$\Pr(ES_{END} \leq \text{Due Date}) = \Pr\left(z \leq \frac{\text{Due Date} - E[ES_{END}]}{\text{Var}[ES_{END}]} \right)$$
$$= \Pr\left(z \leq \frac{25 - 23.83}{\sqrt{8.25}} \right)$$
$$= \Pr(z \leq 0.41)$$

Using the standard normal table in Appendix 6A, we find that $\Pr(z \leq 0.41) = 0.658$; that is, there is almost a 0.66 probability that the project will be completed within 25 weeks (conversely, there is a 34 percent probability that the project will exceed 25 weeks). The spreadsheet calculations, showing the corresponding z-scores and probabilities for various due dates, are given in Figure 6.3.

According to the Classic PERT model, there is virtually no likelihood that the project in Figure 6.1 will be completed within 15 weeks. There is almost certainty (99.8 percent probability) that the project will be completed within 32 weeks.

The Classic PERT model can be used to estimate the probability that any task will be completed by a given due date. For example, consider task D (user training). In this case,

FIGURE 6.3
Classic PERT
Calculations That Project
Example Is Completed
within Given Due Date

Due Date	z_i	$Pr(z_i)$
15	–3.07	0.001
20	–1.33	0.091
25	0.41	0.658
28	1.45	0.927
32	2.84	0.998

there is only one path (through task A) that precedes task D, so the mean and variance of task A defines the mean and variance for ES_D. In general, the project manager would find the longest expected path to a task in question and use the sum of the tasks' expected durations and variances on that path; that is,

$$\text{Expected early start time of task } k = E[ES_k] = \max_s \left\{ \sum_{\text{tasks } j \text{ on path } s} \mu_j \right\}$$

where there exists $s = 1,\ldots, N_k$ paths between the milestone START and task k.

Limitations of the Classic PERT Model

The Classic PERT model has been criticized on many dimensions, including the problems associated with accurately estimating the most optimistic, most pessimistic, and most likely times for each task (this issue was discussed in Chapter 2). A related problem is associated with the apparently arbitrary choice of the beta distribution and the formulas used to approximate the mean and variances of the tasks. An additional problem is the assumption that task durations are independent, which of course is frequently not true.

However, the most significant problem with the Classic PERT model is illustrated by the simple example with four tasks given in Figure 6.4. In this example, assume that the project manager knows the means and variances of all four tasks so that she can ignore the problems associated with estimating these values.

As we discussed, the Classic PERT model assumes that the critical path is the path with the longest expected duration; it is easy to see in Figure 6.4 that this critical path is START-B-D-END, which has an expected duration of 15 and a variance of 5; that is,

FIGURE 6.4
Classic PERT Example 2

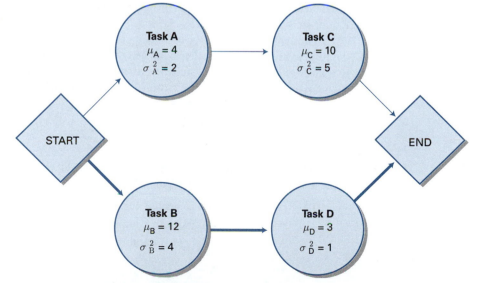

$$E[ES_{END}] = 15 \text{ and } Var[ES_{END}] = 5$$

According to the Classic PERT model, the probability that the project will be completed by, say, time 17 (the due date) is

$$Pr(ES_{END} \leq 17) = Pr\left(z \leq \frac{17-15}{\sqrt{5}}\right) = Pr(z \leq 0.894) = 0.81$$

that is, there is an 81 percent probability that the project will be completed within 17 time periods.

In this example, however, there are two paths between START and END milestones. The second path (START-A-C-END) is ignored by the Classic PERT model since its expected duration is less than the expected duration of the path (START-B-D-END); however, we see that this path has an expected duration of 14 and a variance of 7. Assuming there are a sufficient number of tasks to use a normal approximation, a manager can compute the probability that the tasks on this path will be completed within 17 time periods:

$$Pr(z \leq \frac{17-14}{\sqrt{7}} = Pr(z \leq 1.134) = 0.872$$

In reality of course, all tasks on *both* paths must be completed within 17 time periods for the project to be completed within 17 time periods. Since the two paths do not overlap in this example, it is reasonable to assume that the paths are independent; thus, the real probability that the project will be completed within 17 time periods is the product of the two probabilities: $0.81 \times 0.872 = 0.706$.

By multiplying probabilities that are less than one, the product will always be less than either individual probability; that is, the true probability that the example project in Figure 6.4 will be completed within 17 time periods is only 70.6 percent.

This illustrates the major problem with the Classic PERT model: whenever there are parallel paths, it always gives optimistic estimates because it considers only a single path through the precedence network. While the Classic PERT approximation may be close if there is only one dominant path, this is rarely the case in real-world projects due to various factors that are discussed in the next section.

The limitations of the Classic PERT model can be further illustrated by an example with discrete probabilities; in this case, assume that the project manager knows the precise durations of each task and their respective probabilities. This example (Classic PERT Example 3) is given in Figure 6.5.

In this case, there are four tasks that can take the durations indicated in the table with the respective probabilities. The expected duration of each task is indicated in the respective node on the precedence network; these values are computed by simply multiplying each duration times its respective probability and summing these products; for example,

$$E[B] = \sum_{i=1}^{2} x_i \, Pr(X = x_i) = 2(0.2) + 12(0.8) = 10.0$$

In Example 3, there are three paths from the START to the END; using the calculated expected task durations, the expected durations of each path are:

    START-A-D-END: Expected duration = 17.3
    START-B-D-END: Expected duration = 19.3
    START-C-END: Expected duration = 19.0

FIGURE 6.5
Classic PERT Example 3

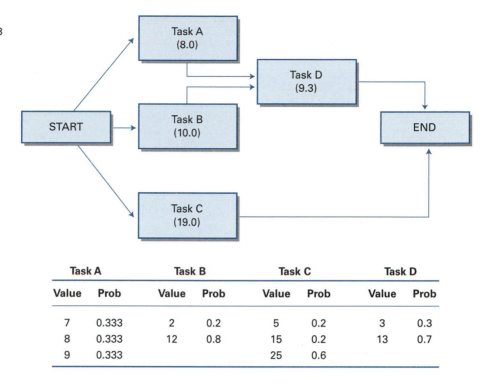

Task A		Task B		Task C		Task D	
Value	Prob	Value	Prob	Value	Prob	Value	Prob
7	0.333	2	0.2	5	0.2	3	0.3
8	0.333	12	0.8	15	0.2	13	0.7
9	0.333			25	0.6		

According to the Classic PERT model, path (START-B-D-END) is the critical path; the project will be expected to take 19.3 weeks, and tasks B and D are the tasks of greatest concern (since they lie on the critical path).

Since there are a finite number of durations for each task, we can enumerate all possible combinations of task durations (and probabilities) to find the exact distribution of project completion times. Since task A can take 3 values, task B can take 2 possible values, task C can take 3 values, and task D can take 2 values, there are a total of $3 \times 2 \times 3 \times 2 = 36$ possible combinations. These 36 combinations are given in the table in Figure 6.6.

For each combination in the table in Figure 6.6, we find the duration of the three paths through the network and indicate the longest path. The probability of each combination is calculated by multiplying the probabilities of each associated task duration; for example, in the first combination, the probability that task A duration is 7, task B duration is 2, task C duration is 5, and task D duration is 3 is $(0.333) \times (0.2) \times (0.2) \times (0.3) = 0.004$. The longest path associated with these values is the path START-A-B-END, which has a value of 10.

We can use the data in the table in Figure 6.6 to compute the true project expected duration by multiplying the probabilities of each combination times its respective longest path. In this case, we find that the expected value is 23.22 weeks—a value that is more than 20 percent greater than the 19.3 weeks given by the Classic PERT model. A manager using the Classic PERT model to estimate the expected project duration would be using an estimate that is significantly less than the true value.

Using the information in Figure 6.6, we can calculate the probabilities for all possible project durations; this information is summarized for both the probabilities and cumulative probabilities in the table in Figure 6.7.

Since Classic PERT assumes that the project duration follows a normal distribution with a mean of 19.3 weeks, this implies a 50 percent probability that the project would be

Combination	Task A Value	Task A Prob	Task B Value	Task B Prob	Task C Value	Task C Prob	Task D Value	Task D Prob	Critical Path	Prob of CP	Length of CP
1	7	0.333	2	0.2	5	0.2	3	0.3	A,D	0.004	10
2	7	0.333	2	0.2	5	0.2	12	0.7	A,D	0.009	19
3	7	0.333	2	0.2	15	0.2	3	0.3	C	0.004	15
4	7	0.333	2	0.2	15	0.2	12	0.7	A,D	0.009	19
5	7	0.333	2	0.2	25	0.6	3	0.3	C	0.012	25
6	7	0.333	2	0.2	25	0.6	12	0.7	C	0.028	25
7	7	0.333	12	0.8	5	0.2	3	0.3	B,D	0.016	15
8	7	0.333	12	0.8	5	0.2	12	0.7	B,D	0.037	24
9	7	0.333	12	0.8	15	0.2	3	0.3	B,D	0.016	15
10	7	0.333	12	0.8	15	0.2	12	0.7	B,D	0.037	24
11	8	0.333	12	0.8	25	0.6	3	0.3	C	0.048	25
12	8	0.333	12	0.8	25	0.6	12	0.7	C	0.112	25
13	8	0.333	2	0.2	5	0.2	3	0.3	A,D	0.004	11
14	8	0.333	2	0.2	5	0.2	12	0.7	A,D	0.009	20
15	8	0.333	2	0.2	15	0.2	3	0.3	C	0.004	15
16	8	0.333	2	0.2	15	0.2	12	0.7	A,D	0.009	20
17	8	0.333	2	0.2	25	0.6	3	0.3	C	0.012	25
18	8	0.333	2	0.2	25	0.6	12	0.7	C	0.028	25
19	8	0.333	12	0.8	5	0.2	3	0.3	B,D	0.016	15
20	8	0.333	12	0.8	5	0.2	12	0.7	B,D	0.037	24
21	8	0.333	12	0.8	15	0.2	3	0.3	B,D	0.016	15
22	8	0.333	12	0.8	15	0.2	12	0.7	B,D	0.037	24
23	8	0.333	12	0.8	25	0.6	3	0.3	C	0.048	25
24	9	0.333	12	0.8	25	0.6	12	0.7	C	0.112	25
25	9	0.333	2	0.2	5	0.2	3	0.3	A,D	0.004	12
26	9	0.333	2	0.2	5	0.2	12	0.7	A,D	0.009	21
27	9	0.333	2	0.2	15	0.2	3	0.3	C	0.004	15
28	9	0.333	2	0.2	15	0.2	12	0.7	A,D	0.009	21
29	9	0.333	2	0.2	25	0.6	3	0.3	C	0.012	25
30	9	0.333	2	0.2	25	0.6	12	0.7	C	0.028	25
31	9	0.333	12	0.8	5	0.2	3	0.3	B,D	0.016	15
32	9	0.333	12	0.8	5	0.2	12	0.7	B,D	0.037	24
33	9	0.333	12	0.8	15	0.2	3	0.3	B,D	0.016	15
34	9	0.333	12	0.8	15	0.2	12	0.7	B,D	0.037	24
35	9	0.333	12	0.8	25	0.6	3	0.3	C	0.048	25
36	9	0.333	12	0.8	25	0.6	12	0.7	C	0.112	25

FIGURE 6.6 Thirty-six Combinations for Classic PERT Example 3

completed by that time. In reality, however, the cumulative probabilities in Figure 6.7 indicate that the project will need 25 weeks to have at least a 50 percent probability of being completed on time. Again, Classic PERT results in a sizeable error.

Recall that the Classic PERT model identified tasks B and D to be the critical tasks; presumably, these are the tasks that managers would most closely monitor. Using the table in Figure 6.6, however, we can calculate the true likelihood that each task will be a critical task. To calculate the probability that task A is a critical task, we simply add the probabilities of each combination that identifies task A as a critical task (combinations 1,

Length of CP	Prob	Cumulative Prob
10	0.004	**0.00**
11	0.004	**0.01**
12	0.004	**0.01**
15	0.108	**0.12**
19	0.019	**0.14**
20	0.019	**0.16**
21	0.019	**0.18**
24	0.224	**0.40**
25	0.599	**1.00**

FIGURE 6.7 Possible Critical Paths in Classic PERT Example 3

Task A	Task B	Task C	Task D
0.068	0.320	0.611	0.388

FIGURE 6.8 Criticality Indices for Tasks in Example 3

2, 4, etc.). Repeating this process for each task, we find the probabilities shown in Figure 6.8. The probability that a task lies on the critical path is sometimes referred to as a **criticality index.**

Interestingly, neither task B nor task D has the greatest likelihood of being critical; task C has the greatest likelihood by far (0.611 versus 0.388 for task D and 0.32 for task B). In this small example this result occurs because task C has a 60 percent probability of having a duration equal to 25, which is longer than any other possible path. However, there is rarely a dominant task or path in larger and more realistic project networks; again, managers who follow the Classic PERT model may be seriously misled.

MONTE-CARLO SIMULATION MODELS

Given that task durations in real world projects are, in fact, random and the Classic PERT model is flawed, how should a manager determine project plan? One alternative is to use a Monte-Carlo simulation model.

Monte-Carlo simulation (with discrete events) is a process that repeatedly sets values for each random variable by sampling from each variable's respective distribution; these values are then used to compute the critical path, slack values, etc. For example, let's assume that task duration times follow a beta distribution as described in the second chapter. For each simulation run, we set the duration of each task by "drawing" a value from its respective distribution (that is, values near the mode t^m are more likely to appear than values in the tail of the distribution near the optimistic time estimate t^o or the pessimistic time estimate t^p). In other words, the selection of each task duration is determined by the respective probability distribution of each task. After selecting task durations, we can easily calculate the critical path, early and late start times, slacks, etc. We repeat this process numerous times and use these results to calculate statistics of interest (e.g., criticality indices).

To illustrate a Monte-Carlo simulation approach, we will describe two examples: Classic PERT Example 1 with continuous random variables, and Classic PERT Example 3 with discrete random variables. In the first case, we will assume that task duration times can be described by a normal distribution using the estimates of the mean and variance calculated from the equations in "Classic PERT Defined." To generate a normally distributed random variable t_j with mean μ_j and variance σ_j^2 for each task j, we can use the following equation (Naylor et al, 1968):

$$t_j = \mu_j + \sigma_j \left(\sum_{k=1}^{12} \text{RAND}_k - 6 \right)$$

where RAND_k is the kth random number that is generated by the Excel RAND function from a uniform distribution over the interval [0, 1].

Values for one run are indicated in the table in Figure 6.9; the expected durations and variances for all tasks were found using the formulas in "Classic PERT Defined." Using the generated values (e.g., $t_A = 8.24$, $t_B = 8.18$, etc.), we can find the early start times, latest finish times, etc. for this trial. Note that the project will take 26.44 weeks to complete with the set of selected task durations.

Using the TABLE function in Excel, we can build a table that gives the results of multiple runs. The results of 200 Monte-Carlo simulation trials for this example is given in Figure 6.10; this spreadsheet model is also on the CD-ROM that accompanies this text.

For each run, the value of the critical path is given, as well as the values of a binary variable for each task indicating if that task is critical or not. These binary variables, $t(j)$ for task j, are more formally defined as:

$$t(j) = \begin{cases} 1 & \text{if } TS(j) = 0 \\ 0 & \text{otherwise} \end{cases}$$

where $TS(j)$ = total slack of task j.

Given the values of $t(j)$ over the 200 runs, we can estimate the probability that any task will lie on the critical path by summing the 200 values of $t(j)$ and dividing by the number of runs (200). These probabilities (previously identified as criticality indices) are indicated in Figure 6.10

According to the Classic PERT model, the expected critical path is START-A-C-E-F-END (task A is not included in the table in Figure 6.10 since it lies on all three paths and therefore must be critical). Note that the probability that task C is critical is 40 percent while the probability that task B (not identified as a critical task by the Classic PERT model) is 51 percent. The likelihood that tasks E and F will be critical is almost double the probability that task B will lie on the critical path.

The Monte-Carlo simulation finds that the expected project duration of this project is equal to 27.65 weeks—a value that is significantly greater than the expected project duration (23.83) weeks determined by the Classic PERT model. It is interesting to note that the Classic PERT model estimated the project variance at 8.25 weeks while the Monte-Carlo simulation model estimates the variance at a considerably higher value of 18.022 weeks.

Since Monte-Carlo simulation represents sampling (with replacement), we can estimate confidence intervals for all values calculated from the simulation model. Assuming that we are most interested in project makespan, we can use the sample mean project makespan (27.65 weeks) and sample variance (18.022 weeks) to find the desired confidence intervals.

FIGURE 6.9
One Monte-Carlo
Simulation Trial for
Classic PERT Example 1

Task	Task Duration (Normal Distribution)	Early Start	Latest Finish	Total Slack	Expected Duration	Variance
A	8.24	0	8.24	0.00	6.67	4.00
B	8.18	8.24	16.41	0.00	7.33	1.76
C	6.87	8.24	16.41	1.30	7.83	3.36
D	13.52	8.24	26.44	4.68	14.33	1.00
E	4.81	16.41	21.23	0.00	5.00	0.44
F	5.22	21.33	26.44	0.00	4.33	0.44
END	0.00	26.44	26.44	0.00	0.00	0.00

FIGURE 6.10
Results from 200 Monte-Carlo Simulation Runs

Run	Project Duration	t (B)	t (C)	t (D)	t (E)	t (F)
1	29.35	1	0	0	1	1
2	29.97	1	0	0	1	1
3	25.37	1	0	0	1	1
4	30.87	0	1	0	1	1
5	35.26	0	1	0	1	1
194	28.57	1	0	0	1	1
195	31.76	0	1	0	1	1
196	27.22	0	1	0	1	1
197	28.63	0	1	0	1	1
198	24.94	0	1	0	1	1
199	27.45	0	1	0	1	1
200	31.18	0	1	0	1	1
Ave	27.65	51.0%	55.0%	9.0%	91.0%	91.0%
Var	18.022					

Assume that we want to find a two-sided 95 percent confidence interval for the project makespan; that is, we want to find an interval that will have a 95 percent probability of containing the true project makespan. Using a normal approximation, we find that the appropriate standard normal z-score $z_{0.025}$ is equal to 1.96; thus, the confidence interval is defined as

$$\overline{X} \pm z_{0.025} \ s_{\bar{x}} = \overline{X} \pm 1.96 \ s_{\overline{X}}$$

where $\overline{X}$ is the sample mean and $s_{\bar{x}}$ is the estimated standard error of the mean that is equal to $s/\sqrt{n}$, where s is the sample standard deviation and n is the number of trials. Given that $\overline{X} = 27.65$, $s = \sqrt{18.02} = 4.25$, and $n = 200$ trials, the 95 and 99 percent confidence intervals for the project makespan are given in Figure 6.11. Greater precision (that is, smaller confidence intervals) can be found by increasing the number of trials (n).

Monte-Carlo Simulation with Discrete Probability Distributions

To illustrate a case where the task durations are described by discrete probability distributions, we can consider the Classic PERT example 3 given in Figure 6.5. Since this example is small, we could enumerate all 36 possible combinations (in Figure 6.6) and find the true expected project duration as well as the probability that each task will be critical, etc. In larger real-world projects, however, managers cannot enumerate all possible combinations and thus would have to resort to a sampling (Monte Carlo) approach.

We can construct a Monte-Carlo model for Classic PERT example 3 (Figure 6.5), again using the RAND function. In this example, recall that task A can take three possible values (7, 8, or 9 weeks) with equal probability. To generate one of the values using the RAND function, we create a spreadsheet using an IF statement that sets the duration of task A equal to 7 weeks if RAND is between 0 and 0.33, to 8 weeks if RAND is between 0.33 and 0.67, and to 9 weeks

FIGURE 6.11
Confidence Limits on Project Duration (Makespan)

Project Makespan	Lower Limit	Upper Limit
95% Confidence interval	27.07	28.24
99% Confidence interval	26.88	28.43

if RAND is between 0.67 and 0. (Since RAND generates a continuous number between 0 and 1, we do not have to concern ourselves with the possibility that RAND = 0.33 or 0.67 exactly.)

The results of this Monte Carlo process are informative. Averaging the 100 critical path values, we find a value of 23.12 weeks for the expected critical path. This value compares favorably with the true expected critical path value of 23.22 weeks that we found from the calculations in Figure 6.7. From our runs, we can also generate a distribution of critical path values similar to the table in Figure 6.7. The distribution of critical path (and project) durations found from the Monte-Carlo simulations is given in Figure 6.10.

A comparison between the tables in Figures 6.7 and 6.12 indicate a high degree of similarity. The probability that the project will be completed in less than 20 weeks is 12 percent by the Monte Carlo simulation, compared to 16 percent in reality. The difference between the two tables occurs because the Monte-Carlo statistics were based on a sample of only 100 trials; as we increase the number of trials, the variance associated with each statistic decreases and the values in the two tables will converge.

Using the $t(j)$ variables calculated in each Monte-Carlo trial, we can estimate the probability that each task will lie on the critical path. These values are given in Figure 6.13; as indicated, task C has the greatest likelihood of lying on the critical path (with a probability equal to 0.59), while task A has the least likely probability of being a critical task (with a probability equal to 0.10). These values compare favorably to the true values of 61.1 percent and 6.8 percent for tasks C and A, respectively.

Monte-Carlo simulation is relatively easy to apply for large-scale and complex projects. Given the speed and memory capabilities of current microcomputers, it takes relatively little time to simulate several thousand runs for large real-world projects. Several simulation products are available, including the @Risk product that was created by Palisades Corporation for use with Microsoft Project. These simulation products generate task durations from a large number of possible probability distributions (user specified) and then calculate the statistics of interest for each trial. The results of these trials are summarized and reported in a fashion similar to that used for our spreadsheet simulation model; however, these simulation packages give the user more options and can accommodate much larger projects than are possible in a standard spreadsheet.

New Product Development Example: Cycling in Precedence Networks

Monte-Carlo simulation models use the critical path calculations described in Chapter 4 for each simulation run that represents a random sample of task durations. That is, for any choice of task durations, we calculate the critical path, slack values, costs, etc. and evaluate the distribution of these values over all simulation runs. In some projects, however, other uncertainties in the project must be considered. For example, the results from one task might indicate that some of the previous tasks would have to be repeated, resulting

FIGURE 6.12
Distribution of Critical Path Durations Determined by 100 Monte-Carlo Trials

Length of Critical Path	Probability	Cumulative Probability
10	0.01	0.01
15	0.08	0.09
19	0.02	0.11
20	0.01	0.12
21	0.01	0.13
24	0.24	0.37
25	0.63	1.00

Task	Predecessors	t (1)	Pr [t(1)]	t (2)	Pr [t(2)]	t (3)	Pr [t(3)]	Random #
START	none	0	1.0		0.667	9	1.0	0.203
A	Start	7	0.333	8	1.00			0.243
B	Start	2	0.2	12	0.40	25	1.0	0.176
C	Start	5	0.2	15	1.000			0.446
D	A,B	3	0.3	12				0.046
END	C,D	0	1.0					0.510

Task	Duration	Early Start	Latest Finish	Total Slack	Expected Duration
START	0	0	0	0	0
A	7	0	22	15	8
B	2	0	22	20	10
C	25	0	25	0	19
D	3	7	25	15	9.3
END	0	25	25	0	0

Run	Critical Path	t (A)	t (B)	t (C)	t (D)
1	25	0	0	1	0
2	15	0	1	0	1
3	25	0	0	1	0
4	25	0	0	1	0
5	25	0	0	1	0
6	25	0	0	1	0
7	15	0	1	1	1
8	25	0	0	1	0
9	24	0	1	0	1
10	21	1	0	0	1
11	25	0	0	1	0
12	24	0	1	0	1
13	25	0	0	1	0
14	25	0	0	1	0
96	24	0	1	0	1
97	24	0	1	0	1
98	24	0	1	0	1
99	25	0	0	1	0
100	25	0	0	1	0
Averages	23.12	10.0%	33.0%	59.0%	43.0%

FIGURE 6.13   Monte-Carlo Spreadsheet Model for Classic PERT Example 3

in a cycle in the precedence network. This is not uncommon in new product development (NPD) projects where a prototype product or service might fail a beta test or marketing research hurdle, resulting in redesign or retest of the new product or service. This case is illustrated in the example in Figure 6.14, which illustrates an NPD project through the beta test phase. As indicated, there is a 0.25 probability that the beta test will fail; if this occurs, all previous design tasks—including "Design of physical unit," "Electronics design," and "Software"—must be repeated.

Critical path calculations cannot accommodate cycles in a precedence network such as the one indicated in Figure 6.14; most PM software packages check for—and disallow—any cycles in the network. Thus, a manager must modify the network so that he can compute the critical path and associated calculations for each simulation run.

One way to achieve this is to assume that *at most* one redesign cycle may be needed if the beta test fails, and indicate all the redesign tasks as a new task in the network (alternatively, all the design tasks could be repeated by adding five new tasks to the network). This redesign task is then added to a modified network, as indicated in Figure 6.15. Note that there is still a 0.25 probability of branching to this redesign task and a 0.75 probability that the beta test will succeed and the redesign task will be bypassed.

To model the probabilistic branching from "Beta test prototype" to "Beta test fails" or "End," assume that the arcs in the precedence network are the "standard" finish-to-start relationships and modify the duration of the "Beta test fails" task; that is, there is now a 0.75 probability that the duration of "Beta test fails" is zero and a 0.25 probability that the duration of that task is an estimated value. Thus, by modifying the duration of the task "Beta test fails" appropriately, the manager can analyze the issue of probabilistic branching (and possible cycling) in a precedence network.

Note that this framework can be extended to include multiple cycles if the manager wishes. For example, she could add another task, "Beta test fails for a second time," between "Beta test fails" and "End" to indicate a possible second redesign effort. More cycles could be added in a similar fashion (although it is not clear how many redesign cycles would be allowed before the NPD project would be canceled).

The Monte-Carlo simulation model for the modified NPD project in Figure 6.15 is given in Figure 6.16. In this example, assume that the project manager has only two estimates of task durations—an optimistic and a pessimistic duration—and that task durations follow a uniform distribution between these two extremes. He then uses task durations to determine direct labor costs based on the number of resource types and associated costs indicated in Figure 6.16. For each simulation run, he finds the project

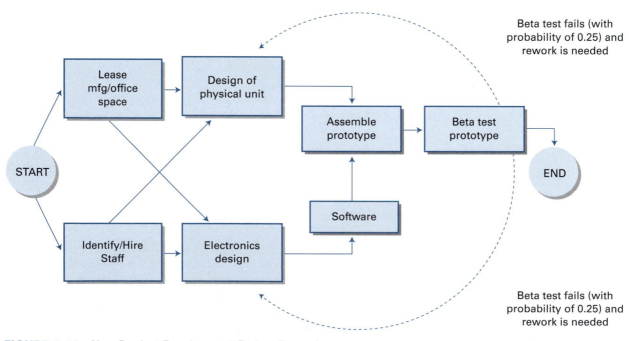

FIGURE 6.14 New Product Development Project Example

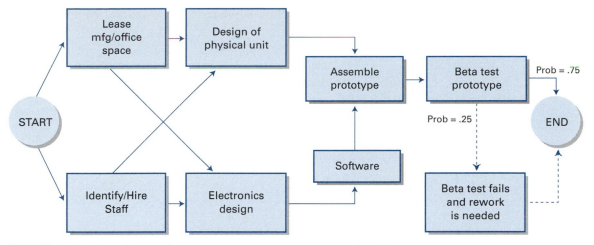

FIGURE 6.15 New Product Development Precedence Network Modified

FIGURE 6.16
Monte Carlo Simulation
Model for NPD Example

Task ID	Description	Predecessors	Duration Estimates (wks) Optimistic	Pessimistic	Expected Duration	Variance	Random #
A	Lease Mfg/Office space	START	2	4	3.0	0.11	0.36
B	Identify/hire staff	START	2	3	2.5	0.03	0.69
C	Design of physical unit	A, B	10	15	12.5	0.69	0.08
D	Electronics design	A, B	3	8	5.5	0.69	0.90
E	Software	D	6	12	9.0	1.00	0.78
F	Assemble prototype	C, E	3	4	3.5	0.03	0.49
G	Beta test prototype	F	5	5	5.0	0.00	0.67
H	Rework if beta test fails	G	20	25	22.5	0.69	0.06
END	End of project	G, H	0	0	0.0	0.00	0.58

Notes:
Task A: (Lease mfg/office space): Performed by project manager
Task B: (Identify/hire staff) performed by HR folks
Task C: (Design of the physical unit) is performed by 2 mechanical engineers whose time is billed at $1600/wk (each engineer)
Task D: (Electronics Design) is performed by 3 electrical engineers (each billed at $1750/wk) and 1 technician ($800/wk)
Task E: (Software) is subcontracted to software development firm for fixed cost of $25,000
Task F: (Assemble prototype) is performed by task C and D engineers and technician (billed at same rate)
Task G: (Beta test prototype) is performed testing group (billed at $1400/wk)
Task H: (Beta test rework) is performed by engineering design group ($9250/week) and testing group ($1400/wk)

Direct Labor Cost Calculations

Task ID	Description	Duration (wks)	Early start time	Early finish time	Latest finish time	Total Slack	Mech Eng cost	Electrical Eng cost	Technician cost	Testing Group
A	Lease Mfg/Office space	2.7	0	2.7	2.7	0.0				
B	Identify/hire staff	2.7	0	2.7	2.7	0.0				
C	Design of physical unit	10.4	2.7	13.1	20.9	7.8	$ 33,244.17			
D	Electronics design	7.5	2.7	10.2	10.2	0.0		$ 39,381.37	$ 6,000.97	
E	Software	10.7	10.2	20.9	20.9	0.0	$ 25,000.00			
F	Assemble prototype	3.5	20.9	24.4	24.4	0.0	$ 11,180.11	$ 18,342.37	$ 2,795.03	
G	Beta test prototype	5.0	24.4	29.4	29.4	0.0				$ 7,000.00
H	Rework if beta test fails	0.0	29.4	29.4	29.4	0.0	$ -	$ -	$ -	$ -
END	End of project	0.0	29.4	29.4	29.4					

Run	Expected Project Makespan	Expected Direct Costs	t(A)	t(B)	t(c)	t(D)	t(E)	t(F)	t(G)	t(H)
1	29.39	$ 142,944.02	1	0	0	1	1	1	1	1
2	23.79	$ 133,215.15	1	0	0	1	1	1	1	1
199	26.11	$ 129,198.83	0	1	0	1	1	1	1	1
200	28.29	$ 136,917.12	1	0	0	1	1	1	1	1
Mean	31.69	$190,233.76	0.69	0.30	0.22	0.78	0.78	1.00	1.00	1.00
St Dev	9.68	$100,358.92	0.46	0.46	0.42	0.42	0.42	0.00	0.00	0.00

makespan, direct labor cost, and total slack associated with each task in the project. The result of 200 simulation runs is indicated in Figure 6.16.

THE THEORY OF CONSTRAINTS AND THE PROJECT BUFFER

In his book "Critical Chain," Goldratt (1997) applied the theory of constraints (TOC) to managing complex projects and presented an alternative to Monte-Carlo simulation. Fundamentally, Goldratt's approach is based on the deterministic critical path method (CPM) with the addition of buffers to deal with the uncertainty associated with task durations. As described by Goldratt (1997), Newbold (1998), and Leach (2000), among others, a project manager must first identify the critical chain—the set of tasks that includes resource requirements as well as precedence dependencies and determines the overall duration of the project. The critical chain is the resource constrained critical path discussed in Chapter 8.

Applying the theory of constraints to project management, Goldratt advocates the following:

- Use deterministic CPM model with buffers to deal with any uncertainties.
- Place a buffer at the end of a project schedule to protect the customer's completion schedule.
- Exploit constraining resources (make certain that resources are fully utilized).
- Avoid wasting slack time by encouraging early task completions.
- Develop a plan and stick to it.
- Carefully monitor the status of the buffer(s) and communicate this status to other project team members on a regular basis.
- Make certain that the project team is 100 percent focused on critical chain tasks.

Goldratt also recognizes the problems associated with estimating task durations needed to create an initial project plan. To avoid estimation bias, he recommends using the median to remove "padding" from estimates and avoid wasting slack (counter to Parkinson's Law). Calculating the median, however, requires that managers estimate the optimistic and pessimistic durations for each task as well as the skewness of the probability distribution describing the task duration. Difficulties associated with estimating task durations were discussed in Chapter 2.

Applying the theory of constraints, Goldratt suggests adding buffers at various points along the critical chain to protect the completion schedule. According to Newbold (1998), there should be three types of buffers: a project buffer, feeding buffers, and resource buffers (feeding buffers and resource buffers are discussed in Chapter 8 under "Resource Allocation and the Critical Chain"). The project buffer is placed after the last task in the project to protect the project schedule. Since task durations are random, placing a buffer at the end of the project and removing contingencies from individual tasks (by using the median duration and starting all tasks at their earliest starting times) allows a project manager to pool the risks and random fluctuations associated with all tasks. To illustrate, consider a simple project with two tasks A and B that must be completed by the same worker (or crew) sequentially. Assume that the duration of task A is described by a normal distribution with a mean of 20 days and a standard deviation of 5 days, while the duration of task B is also described by a normal distribution with a mean of 30 days and a standard deviation of 8 days.

If the project manager wants to make certain that each task has a 95 percent probability of being completed on time (corresponding to a z-score = 1.64 using the table in Appendix 6A), she would allow 20 + 1.64 (5) = 28.2 days to complete task A, and 30 + 1.64 (8) = 43.12 days to complete task B. Thus, the total buffer built into the schedule in this case would be 8.2 + 13.12 = 21.32 days.

However, the manager recognizes that she can treat the two tasks as a single task and gain considerable efficiencies. To combine the two tasks, the manager would add the task means and variances (assuming that the two original tasks are statistically independent) resulting in the combined task having a mean equal to 50 days (30 days + 20 days) and a variance equal to 89 days (25 days + 64 days). If there are a sufficient number of tasks involved, the manager could reasonably assume that the duration of the combined task is N(50, 89) = N(50, 9.4). Now, if the manager wants a 95 percent probability that the project will be completed on time, she could promise that the project will be completed in 65.47 days (50 days + 1.64 × 9.4 days) instead of the previous due date of 71.32 days. Thus, the manager has saved 71.32 – 65.47 = 5.85 days by using a single project buffer equal to 15.47

days instead of the individual buffers for each task and still maintained the same probability of completing the project on time.

According to Newbold (1998), the size of the project buffer is unclear; in fact, he states, "In practice, we want buffer sizes that are good enough. We could certainly go into great detail with formulas and calculations, worst-case and best-case timings, and so on. This would not be worth the trouble. The data just aren't good enough to support precision or complex calculations." Nevertheless, Newbold suggests that for those "who want a scientific approach to sizing buffers" the project buffer be set to

$$\sqrt{\sum_{\text{tasks } k \text{ on critical chain}} (t_k^p - \mu_k)^2}$$

where t_k^p is the most pessimistic estimate of task k's duration and μ_k is the mean duration (or the median, following Goldratt's suggestion). According to Newbold, such a buffer would represent approximately two standard deviations, such that 90 percent of projects would be completed with the allotted time (assuming a normal distribution).

To illustrate such a project buffer, consider Classic PERT Example 1 in Figure 6.1. The modified project network, with the addition of a project buffer, is given in Figure 6.17.

Using the expected task durations, the project manager applies deterministic CPM and finds that START-A-C-E-F-END is the critical path (note that this is the same process followed by Classic PERT). The expected duration of this path is 23.83 weeks with a variance of 8.25 weeks. Using the estimated pessimistic task durations and the calculated expected durations (Figure 6.1), the manager computes the size of the project buffer following Newbold's suggestion; the computations are indicated in the table given in Figure 6.18.

Thus, the project buffer equals 9.57 weeks, since

$$\text{Buffer} = \sqrt{\sum_{\text{tasks } k \text{ on critical chain}} (t_k^p - \mu_k)^2} = \sqrt{91.59} = 9.57 \text{ weeks}$$

Goldratt, Newbold, and others then suggest setting the customer due date by adding the project buffer to the length of the critical path found from the Classic PERT model; in

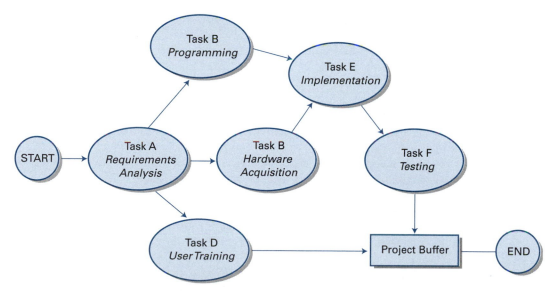

FIGURE 6.17 Classic PERT Example 1 with Project Buffer

FIGURE 6.18

Calculating a Time Buffer for PERT Example 1

Critical Task	Description	Pessimistic Time Estimate, t^p	Expected Duration, μ	$t^p - \mu$	$(t^p - \mu)^2$
A	Requirements analysis	14	6.67	7.33	53.73
C	Hardware acquisition	13	7.83	5.17	26.73
E	Implementation	7	5.00	2.00	4.00
F	Testing	7	4.33	2.67	7.13
					91.59

this example, the manager would expect the project to be completed in $23.83 + 9.57 = 33.4$ weeks. However, using the information from a Monte-Carlo simulation, he can calculate the probability that the project will in fact be completed within 33.4 weeks. In this case, a Monte-Carlo simulation with 200 replications estimates that the expected project makespan is 27.6 weeks with a variance of 18.2 weeks. Assuming that project makespan is normally distributed, the probability that the project is completed by the promised due date is

$$\Pr[z \leq 1.36] = 0.91$$

In PERT example 3, the manager can add a project buffer as well. Since tasks B and D lie on the expected critical path (using deterministic CPM), the project buffer (following Newbold's suggested calculations) is equal to:

$$\text{Buffer} = \sqrt{\sum_{\text{tasks B\&D}} (t_k^p - \mu_k)^2} = \sqrt{(12-10)^2 + (12-9.3)^2} = \sqrt{11.29} = 3.36$$

The expected project duration is then $19.3 + 3.36 = 22.66$ weeks; according to the table in Figure 6.7, there is only an 18 percent chance that the project will be completed within this time (recall that the true expected duration of this project is 23.22 weeks). While the use of a project buffer is certainly better than only relying on Classic PERT calculations, the expected project duration may still be overly optimistic.

OTHER IMPLICATIONS OF PROJECT UNCERTAINTY

When we recognize that task durations are in fact random variables, we find numerous implications that are managerially significant (and sometimes counterintuitive). To illustrate, we will initially consider a simple project with two tasks that can be performed simultaneously as indicated in Figure 6.19. The durations of both tasks are random variables described by a symmetric distribution (e.g., normal) with a mean duration of 30 days. We will also assume that there is a given due date (denoted by D) that is 30 days.

If there is no uncertainty (i.e., task durations are deterministic), the project makespan is clearly 30 days and we would not expect the project to be delayed beyond its due date. Since the task durations are random, however, the project would be delayed if either task were delayed beyond 30 days. Since we assumed that both task durations are described by a symmetric distribution with a mean of 30 days, we know that the probability that each task will be completed within 30 days is 50 percent. Thus, the probability that this project will be delayed is

$$\Pr[\text{Project delay}] = \Pr[\text{at least 1 task} > 30 \text{ days}]$$
$$= 1 - \Pr[\text{neither task is delayed}]$$

FIGURE 6.19
Project Example

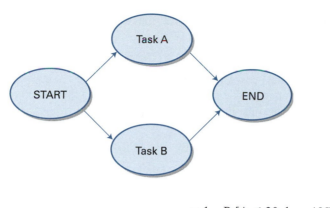

$$= 1 - \Pr[A \le 30 \text{ days AND } B \le 30 \text{ days}]$$
$$= 1 - (0.5)(0.5)$$
$$= 0.75$$

That is, there is a 75 percent probability that the project will be delayed beyond its due date.

What happens to the probability that the project will be delayed if there are more than two tasks in parallel (even though the durations of all tasks are described by the same symmetric distribution with a mean of 30 days)? In general, the probability of project delay is $1 - (0.5)^N$, where N is the number of tasks; the probability of a project delay is given in the as a function of N in Figure 6.20. As indicated, there is a 99.2 percent probability that the project will be delayed when there are as few as seven tasks in parallel.

Worker Behavior and Expected Project Duration

Professor C. N. Parkinson (1957) observed in 1957 that "Work expands so as to fill the time available for its completion"—a dictum that is fittingly known as Parkinson's Law. Krakowski (1974) discussed the implications of Parkinson's Law in a humorous manner, describing how Parkinson's Law implies that all slack values will always equal zero. Gutierrez and Kouvelis (1991) used Parkinson's Law in a more serious manner to analyze worker behavior and its impact on deadlines, actual work content, and expected project duration.

Following Gutierrez and Kouvelis, we can consider the implications of Parkinson's Law by examining a simple project consisting of two tasks that must be completed sequentially; we assume that both tasks are performed by the same worker or subcontractor. The durations of both tasks are random variables T_i with expected durations $E[T_i]$ for $i = 1, 2$.

FIGURE 6.20
Probability of Project
Delay when Tasks Are
Performed
Simultaneously

Number of Tasks (N)	Probability of Project Delay
2	75.0%
3	87.5%
4	93.8%
5	96.9%
6	98.4%
7	99.2%
8	99.6%
9	99.8%
10	99.9%

Assuming independence, it is clear that the expected makespan of the project (denoted by T) is simply equal to the sum of the two expected durations of the two tasks; that is,

$$E[T] = E[T_1] + E[T_2]$$

What happens when workers/subcontractors are given a deadline, D? Parkinson's Law states that work expands (if necessary) such that the project will never be completed before the deadline D. Thus, the expected project makespan, which is now a function of D, is defined as

$$E[T(D)] = E(T_1) + E(T_2) + E\{\max[0, (D - T_1 - T_2)]\}$$

To illustrate, consider the example in Figure 6.21, in which task durations are given by the discrete probabilities. As indicated, the expected duration of the first task is 8 days and the expected duration of the second task is 16 days such that

$$E[T] = E[T_1] + E[T_2] = 8 + 16 = 24 \text{ days}$$

Assume that we set a deadline D = 24 days, representing a "reasonable" deadline for workers or subcontractors. In this case, we can enumerate the six possible project durations or realizations; since we are assuming that work expands to fill the time allotted, any choice of task durations that are shorter than the deadline will expand to 24 days. The calculations are indicated in Figure 6.22.

Using the project makespan calculations and their respective probabilities, we find the expected project duration is now equal to 25.0 days; that is, it is likely that we have delayed the project simply by setting a due date.

Following this approach, we can investigate the impact of other worker behavior as well. For example, assume that we have procrastinating workers who wait until the last possible time to start a task but do not delay once they begin work. Thus, if a procrastinating worker in our Figure 6.21 example completes the first task in 7 days, she would delay starting the following task by one day since she expected the second task to take only 16 days. The calculations for the procrastinating worker are given in Figure 6.23.

The expected project duration for the procrastinating worker is equal to

$$E'[T(D)] = E(T_1) + E(T_2) + E(\max\{0, [D - T_1 - E(T_2)]\})$$
$$= 8 + 16 + 1 \, (.3) = 24.3 \text{ days}$$

In general, we can show that

$$E[T(D)] \geq E'[T(D)] \geq D$$

This somewhat surprising result has several implications. First, managers should expect the project to be completed later than the deadline if workers either procrastinate or follow Parkinson's Law. This occurs even when the first task is completed earlier than expected and the deadline is "reasonably" set equal to the sum of the tasks' expected durations. Second,

Values of T_1	Prob	Values of T_2	Prob
7	0.3	14	0.5
8	0.4	18	0.5
9	0.3		
	8.0		**16.0**

FIGURE 6.21 Worker Behavior Example

Values of T_1	Prob	Values of T_2	Prob	Project Makespan	Prob
7	0.3	14	0.5	24	0.15
7	0.3	18	0.5	25	0.15
8	0.4	14	0.5	24	0.20
8	0.4	18	0.5	26	0.20
9	0.3	14	0.5	24	0.15
9	0.3	18	0.5	27	0.15

FIGURE 6.22 Worker Behavior Following Parkinson's Law

FIGURE 6.23
Procrastinating Worker
Behavior

Values of T_1	Prob	E [Delay] = $\max[0, D - T_1 - E(T2)]$	E [Makespan]
7	0.3	1	24
8	0.4	0	24
9	0.3	0	25

procrastinating workers will usually complete a project before "expanding" workers, imply-ing that managers might want to keep workers as busy as possible to avoid slack time.

As noted by Gutierrez and Kouvelis, managers can reduce these negative conse-quences by setting deadlines as tight as possible. However, unreasonably tight deadlines may have other negative effects for both workers and managers, including stress and res-ignations. Again, managers must make optimal trade-offs.

Task Variation and Expected Project Duration

It should be apparent that variation in task durations and costs makes projects more diffi-cult to manage and can result in unexpected consequences. One example of the negative effects of increasing task variance is the conjecture made by Schonberger (1981), who hypothesized that an increase in the *variability* of task durations will result in an increase of the *expected* project duration. A small example illustrates both Schonberger's hypoth-esis as well as the reasoning supporting his hypothesis.

Assume that we have a project with two tasks (tasks A and B) that can be performed simultaneously; task durations are random variables that can only take a limited number of discrete choices. Details for this example are given in Figure 6.24.

As indicated, the expected duration of task A is 14 (with a variance of 0.8 days) while the expected duration of task B is 12.5 days (with a variance of 6.3 days). In a determin-istic world, the project would take 14 days, that is, the length of the expected critical path. In this case, however, we can enumerate all six realizations and find the true value of the

FIGURE 6.24
Example of Effects of
Task Variation

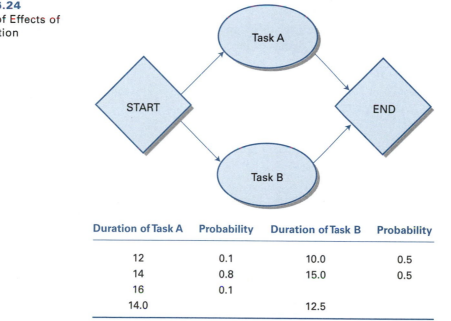

Duration of Task A	Probability	Duration of Task B	Probability
12	0.1	10.0	0.5
14	0.8	15.0	0.5
16	0.1		
14.0		12.5	

expected project duration; these calculations are given in Figure 6.22. Multiplying the probability of each realization times its associated makespan and summing these values results in an expected project makespan of 14.55 days.

To test Schonberger's hypothesis, we can increase the variance—but not the mean—of task A by changing the probabilities associated with each duration value. The new probabilities are given in Figure 6.25.

Using the modified probabilities in Figure 6.25, the variance of task A has now increased to 2.4 days (the mean remains at 14 days). To measure the effect of this change on the expected project duration, we can repeat the calculations in Figure 6.26 with the modified probabilities in Figure 6.25 (note that the values listed under Max[A, B] do not change). We now find that the expected project duration has increased to 14.65 days.

It is possible to show that whenever task variances are increased, the modified expected project makespan will be greater than or equal to the current project makespan if there are tasks that can be completed in parallel. (For example, if tasks A and B were to be completed sequentially, the increase in task variance would have no impact on expected project makespan). The examples in Figures 6.21 through 6.23 also illustrate that if one task has a duration that is much greater (or lesser) than the other task, a change in task variance will have little if any impact on expected project makespan. This can be seen by changing the possible durations of task B to, say, 100 days and 150 days (instead of 10 and 15) with equal probabilities. Gutierrez and Paul (1998) investigated these relationships in detail and developed general conditions when increased task variability results in increased expected project makespan.

The example illustrates why (and perhaps where) managers may want to make efforts to reduce task variation. The Monte-Carlo simulation models described in this chapter can help managers assess this potential impact.

PROJECT COMPRESSION WITH UNCERTAIN TASK DURATIONS

In Chapter 5, under "Project Compression: Time-Cost Trade-offs," we discussed the issue of compressing a project to find the optimal trade-off between direct costs on one hand and indirect/overhead costs (and possibly penalty costs and earliness bonuses) on the other when task durations are assumed to be deterministic. When task durations are stochastic, the processes described in the previous chapter must be modified.

FIGURE 6.25
Increased Variance of Task A

Realization	Task A Duration	Task B Duration	Probability	Max (A,B)
1	12	10	0.05	12
2	14	10	0.4	14
3	16	10	0.05	16
4	12	15	0.05	15
5	14	15	0.4	15
6	16	15	0.05	16

FIGURE 6.26
Calculation of Expected Project Makespan

Task A Duration	Probability	Task B Duration	Probability
12	0.3	10	0.5
14	0.4	15	0.5
16	0.3		
14.0		12.5	

Johnson and Schou (1990) describe three rules for compressing projects with stochastic networks; these rules indicate which task(s) should be selected and crashed when iteratively compressing a project. (Recall in Chapter 5 we showed that such an iterative procedure does not necessarily result in an optimal solution.) These three rules are described as follows:

- **Rule 1:** Select the task on the expected critical path with the smallest slope (that is, the lowest marginal cost of crashing per time period).
- **Rule 2:** Select the task with the largest criticality index.
- **Rule 3:** Select the task that has the lowest expected marginal cost of crashing per time period.

Rule 1 is based on the rule used in the previous chapter to compress projects when task durations are deterministic and we assume a linear time-cost trade-off. To calculate the slope in this case, we must estimate the optimistic, pessimistic, and most likely times for both normal and crash conditions and find the expected normal task duration (denoted $E[t^N]$) and the expected crash task duration (denoted $E[t^C]$)) using the formulas for the Classic PERT model described earlier in this chapter (and in Chapter 2). Letting C^N denote the total expected cost of performing the task at its normal duration and C^C denote the total cost of performing the task at its expected crash duration, the absolute value of the marginal cost or slope is then calculated (similar to Chapter 5) as follows:

$$\text{Marginal cost (slope) of crashing task one time period} = \left| \frac{C^N - C^C}{E\left[t^N\right] - E\left[t^C\right]} \right|$$

Rule 2 is based on work by Van Slyke (1963), who suggested choosing the task with the greatest criticality index. This rule is motivated by the idea that the task with the highest criticality index has the greatest probability of being a critical task; hence, crashing that task has the greatest probability of compressing the project. After crashing the task (and presumably the project), the manager should recalculate the criticality indices before repeating the process and continuing to compress the project. If there is a tie, one of the other rules can be used to break the tie.

Rule 3 is a modification of Rule 1 that includes the criticality indices in the calculations. By multiplying the difference $\{E[t^N] - E[t^C]\}$ times the criticality index, we find the expected time that the project can be compressed. This value is used to find the marginal cost of crashing each task as follows:

$$\text{Marginal cost (slope) of crashing task one time period} = \left| \frac{C^N - C^C}{CI\left\{E[t^N] - E[t^C]\right\}} \right|$$

where CI denotes the criticality index. The task with the smallest value is selected for compression. In similar fashion to Rule 2, the critical index (CI) should be recalculated after each project compression step.

Johnson and Schou point out that specific project conditions will determine which rule works best. For example, if one dominant expected critical path is significantly longer than any other path in a project, the first rule will probably work well. The second rule suffers from the limitation that no cost information is included, but it should work well if the marginal costs are similar for all tasks. The third rule combines the advantages of the first two rules, but (like Rule 1) suffers from the difficulties of estimating the values of $E[t^N]$ and $E[t^C]$ that were described in Chapter 2.

CONCLUSIONS

Throughout this book, the random nature of task durations is emphasized. Since most PM software is based on the assumption that task durations are deterministic, a prudent manager must exercise caution when using these tools and interpreting their results.

In any effort to develop a tool that explicitly recognizes randomness, Classic PERT was developed. If there is only a single dominant path through a precedence network, the results from the Classic PERT model may be reasonably accurate (see Elmaghraby *et al.*, 1999; Gutierrez and Paul, 2001; and Cho and Yum, 1997 for more discussion on the concept of a dominant path when task durations are random). When a single path is not dominant, however, Classic PERT usually provides overly optimistic results that can be quite misleading. To correct for this bias, increasing numbers of managers are using Monte-Carlo simulation and/or the concept of a project buffer advocated by Goldratt and others.

STUDY PROBLEMS

1. Consider the following project network:

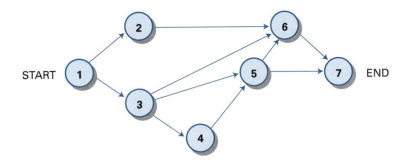

For each activity in this network, three estimates for the time required (in months) are given in the following table:

Activity	Optimistic Estimate	Most Likely Estimate	Pessimistic Estimate
(1,2)	8	9	10
(1,3)	6	7	9
(2,6)	9	12	15
(3,4)	5	5	5
(3,5)	8	10	11
(3,6)	11	15	20
(4,5)	3	4	6
(5,6)	5	6	8
(5,7)	8	10	12
(6,7)	4	5	10

The original schedule for the respective events had been set based on the most likely estimates; these estimates are given in the following table (assuming that the project begins at time 0). For the events in this project, management has requested the following information; respond by completing the following table:

Event Number	Earliest Time		Original Schedule	z score	Probability of Meeting Schedule
	Expected Value	Variance			
1			0	—	—
2			9		
3			8		
4			12		
5			18		
6			25		
7			30		

2. Rob D. Store is an accountant who prepares tax returns for customers who submit their income information via the Internet. One of Rob's problems is to figure out when he can promise customers that their tax returns will be ready for their signatures and filing.

   Rob (who has studied project management in his MBA program) knows there are four tasks that must be completed for each tax return. He is also aware that the durations of these tasks are uncertain and vary according to known probabilities. The precedence relationships and possible task durations are given in this table:

Task	Days	Prob
Task (1,2)	2	0.6
	3	0.2
	4	0.2
Task (1,3)	1	0.1
	4	0.9
Task (2,4)	7	0.6
	9	0.4
Task (3,4)	10	0.5
	2	0.5

   a. If Rob uses the classic PERT model and wants to give a customer a due date that has at least a 60 percent chance of occurring, what is the earliest date that Rob can promise the customer's tax return will be completed?

   b. In reality, what is the earliest date that Rob should promise the tax return will be completed with at least a 60 percent probability that this will occur?

3. Dr. Denton Fender has the following activity-on node (AON) precedence network for a small car repair project:

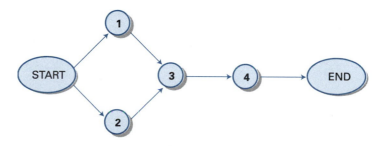

She has come up with the following estimates:

	Duration (Wks)		
Task	Optimistic	Most Likely	Pessimistic
1	2	7	8
2	1	3	8
3	4	9	11
4	5	9	16

a. According to the classic PERT model, what is the minimum project makespan that has at least a 90 percent chance of occurring?

b. Assume that the formula for computing the standard deviation of any task j (σ_j) is modified to the following:

$$\sigma_j = \frac{t_p - t_o}{10.2}$$

where t_o = optimistic time, and t_p = pessimistic time.

Using this modified formula for estimating the standard deviation of task duration, what is the probability that the project will be completed within 26 weeks (based on the classic PERT model)?

4. Duncan Tank is a plumber who has been given a small project that is represented by the following AON precedence network. Duncan is uncertain about the duration of each task; however, he has estimated several possible durations and their respective probabilities that follow the precedence network.

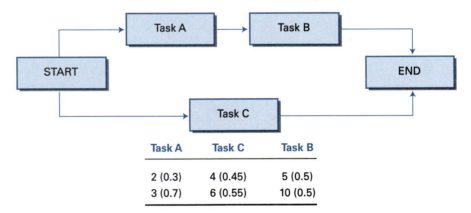

Task A	Task C	Task B
2 (0.3)	4 (0.45)	5 (0.5)
3 (0.7)	6 (0.55)	10 (0.5)

a. If Duncan uses the classic PERT model and wants to give his customer a due date that has at least a 60 percent chance of occurring, what is the earliest date he Duncan can promise that the project will be completed?

b. In reality, what is the earliest date that Duncan should promise the project will be completed with at least a 60 percent probability that this will occur?

5. A project manager has the following AON precedence network for a small project:

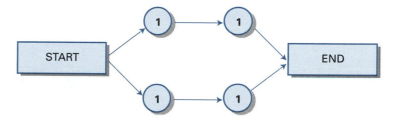

Time estimates are as follows:

	Duration (Wks)		
Task	Optimistic	Most Likely	Pessimistic
1	4	6	14
2	1	3	11
3	2	9	16
4	1	3	8

a. Find the expected duration of the project and its variance, according to the Classic PERT model.

b. Based on the Classic PERT model, what is the probability that the project will be completed within 13 weeks?

c. What is the true probability that the project will be completed within 13 weeks?

6. A small project is composed of seven activities whose time estimates are listed in the following table. Activities are identified by their beginning (i) and ending (j) node numbers.

		Estimated Duration (Wks)		
i	j	Optimistic	Most Likely	Pessimistic
1	2	1	1	7
1	3	1	4	7
1	4	2	7	9
2	5	1	1	1
3	5	2	2	14
4	6	2	6	10
5	6	3	3	15

a. Using the classic PERT model, what is the probability that the project will be completed two weeks earlier than its expected duration?

b. Based on the classic PERT model, what due date has a 90 percent chance (or greater) of being met?

c. A major criticism of the classic PERT model is that it relies only on the longest expected path in the precedence network. One possible solution that has been suggested is to use both the longest path and the second-longest path to calculate the expected project duration. If this approach was used in this problem, what is the probability that the project will be completed within 16 weeks?

7. For the new product development (NPD) project indicated in Figure 6.15, calculate the expected critical path and compare your results to the simulation results given in Figure 6.16. What do you conclude?

8. For the new product development (NPD) project indicated in Figure 6.15, modify the precedence network to allow the possibility that the prototype design task may have to be repeated at most two times. Modify the simulation model appropriately (using the spreadsheet on the CD-ROM accompanying the book) and compare your results to those in Figure 6.16.

REFERENCES

Charnes, A., W. W. Cooper, and G. L. Thompson. "Critical Path Analyses via Chance Constrained and Stochastic Programming." *Operations Research* 12 (1964): 460–70.

Cho, J. G., and B. J. Yum. "An Uncertainty Importance Measure of Activities in PERT Networks" *International Journal of Production Research* 35 (1997): 2737–57.

Craven, J. P. *The Silent War: The Cold War Battle beneath the Sea.* New York: Simon & Schuster, 2001.

Elmaghraby, S. E. "On the Expected Duration of PERT Type Networks." *Management Science* 1, no. 3 (1967): 299–306.

Elmaghraby, S. E., Y. Fathi, and M. R. Taner. "On the Sensitivity of Project Variability to Activity Mean Duration." *Journal of Production Economics* 62 (1999): 219–32.

Goldratt, E. *Critical Chain.* Great Barrington, Mass.: North River Press, 1997.

Gutierrez, G., and P. Kouvelis. "Parkinson's Law and Its Implications for Project Management." *Management Science* 37, no. 8 (August 1991): 990–1001.

Gutierrez, G., and A. Paul. "Analysis of the Effects of Uncertainty, Risk-pooling, and Subcontracting Mechanisms on Project Performance." *Operations Research* 48 (1998): 927–38.

Gutierrez, G., and A. Paul. "Robustness to Variability in Project Networks." *IIE Transactions* 33 (2001): 649–60.

Johnson, G., and C. D. Shou. "Expediting Projects in PERT with Stochastic Time Estimates." *Project Management Journal* XXI, no. 2 (June 1990): 29–33.

Krakowski, M. "PERT and Parkinson's Law." *Interfaces* 5, no. 1 (November 1974): 35–40.

Leach. L. P. *Critical Chain Project Management.* Norwood, Mass.: Artech House, 2000.

Malcolm, D. G., J. H. Roseboom, and C. E. Clark. "Application of a Technique for Research and Development Program Evaluation." *Operations Research* 7, no. 5 (September–October 1959): 646–69.

Naylor, T., J. Balintfy, D. Burdick, and K. Chu. *Computer Simulation Techniques.* New York: Wiley, 1968.

Newbold, R.C. *Project Management in the Fast Lane: Applying the Theory of Constraints.* Boca Raton, Fla.: St. Lucie Press, 1998.

Parkinson, C. N. *Parkinson's Law and Other Studies in Administration.* New York: Random House, 1957.

Schonberger, R. I. "Why Projects Are 'Always' Late: A Rationale Based on Manual Simulation of a PERT/CPM Network." *Interfaces* 11, no. 5 (1981): 66–70.

Van Slyke, R. M. "Monte Carlo Methods and the PERT Problem." *Operations Research* 11 (1963): 839–60.

APPENDIX 6A. STANDARD NORMAL DISTRIBUTION TABLE (POSITIVE VALUES OF *z*)

z	0	0.01	0.02	0.03	0.04	0.05	0.06	0.07	0.08	0.09
0.0	0.500	0.504	0.508	0.512	0.516	0.520	0.524	0.528	0.532	0.536
0.1	0.540	0.544	0.548	0.552	0.556	0.560	0.564	0.567	0.571	0.575
0.2	0.579	0.583	0.587	0.591	0.595	0.599	0.603	0.606	0.610	0.614
0.3	0.618	0.622	0.626	0.629	0.633	0.637	0.641	0.644	0.648	0.652
0.4	0.655	0.659	0.663	0.666	0.670	0.674	0.677	0.681	0.684	0.688
0.5	0.691	0.695	0.698	0.702	0.705	0.709	0.712	0.716	0.719	0.722
0.6	0.726	0.729	0.732	0.736	0.739	0.742	0.745	0.749	0.752	0.755
0.7	0.758	0.761	0.764	0.767	0.770	0.773	0.776	0.779	0.782	0.785
0.8	0.788	0.791	0.794	0.797	0.800	0.802	0.805	0.808	0.811	0.813
0.9	0.816	0.819	0.821	0.824	0.826	0.829	0.831	0.834	0.836	0.839
1.0	0.841	0.844	0.846	0.848	0.851	0.853	0.855	0.858	0.860	0.862
1.1	0.864	0.867	0.869	0.871	0.873	0.875	0.877	0.879	0.881	0.883
1.2	0.885	0.887	0.889	0.891	0.893	0.894	0.896	0.898	0.900	0.901
1.3	0.903	0.905	0.907	0.908	0.910	0.911	0.913	0.915	0.916	0.918
1.4	0.919	0.921	0.922	0.924	0.925	0.926	0.928	0.929	0.931	0.932
1.5	0.933	0.934	0.936	0.937	0.938	0.939	0.941	0.942	0.943	0.944
1.6	0.945	0.946	0.947	0.948	0.949	0.951	0.952	0.953	0.954	0.954
1.7	0.955	0.956	0.957	0.958	0.959	0.960	0.961	0.962	0.962	0.963
1.8	0.964	0.965	0.966	0.966	0.967	0.968	0.969	0.969	0.970	0.971
1.9	0.971	0.972	0.973	0.973	0.974	0.974	0.975	0.976	0.976	0.977
2.0	0.977	0.978	0.978	0.979	0.979	0.980	0.980	0.981	0.981	0.982
2.1	0.982	0.983	0.983	0.983	0.984	0.984	0.985	0.985	0.985	0.986
2.2	0.986	0.986	0.987	0.987	0.987	0.988	0.988	0.988	0.989	0.989
2.3	0.989	0.990	0.990	0.990	0.990	0.991	0.991	0.991	0.991	0.992
2.4	0.992	0.992	0.992	0.992	0.993	0.993	0.993	0.993	0.993	0.994
2.5	0.994	0.994	0.994	0.994	0.994	0.995	0.995	0.995	0.995	0.995
2.6	0.995	0.995	0.996	0.996	0.996	0.996	0.996	0.996	0.996	0.996
2.7	0.997	0.997	0.997	0.997	0.997	0.997	0.997	0.997	0.997	0.997
2.8	0.997	0.998	0.998	0.998	0.998	0.998	0.998	0.998	0.998	0.998
2.9	0.998	0.998	0.998	0.998	0.998	0.998	0.998	0.999	0.999	0.999
3.0	0.999	0.999	0.999	0.999	0.999	0.999	0.999	0.999	0.999	0.999

APPENDIX 6A (CONT'D). STANDARD NORMAL DISTRIBUTION TABLE (NEGATIVE VALUES OF z)

z	0.09	0.08	0.07	0.06	0.05	0.04	0.03	0.02	0.01	0
-3.0	0.002	0.002	0.002	0.002	0.002	0.002	0.001	0.001	0.001	0.001
-2.9	0.002	0.002	0.002	0.002	0.002	0.002	0.002	0.002	0.002	0.002
-2.8	0.003	0.003	0.003	0.003	0.003	0.003	0.003	0.003	0.003	0.003
-2.7	0005	0.004	0.004	0.004	0.004	0.004	0.004	0.004	0.004	0.005
-2.6	0.006	0.006	0.006	0.006	0.005	0.005	0.005	0.005	0.005	0.006
-2.5	0.008	0.008	0.008	0.007	0.006	0.007	0.007	0.007	0.006	0.008
-2.4	0.010	0.010	0.010	0.010	0.007	0.009	0.009	0.009	0.008	0.011
-2.3	0.014	0.013	0.013	0.013	0.009	0.012	0.012	0.011	0.011	0.014
-2.2	0.017	0.017	0.017	0.016	0.012	0.015	0.015	0.015	0.014	0.018
-2.1	0.022	0.022	0.021	0.021	0.016	0.020	0.019	0.019	0.018	0.023
-2.0	0.028	0.027	0.027	0.026	0.020	0.025	0.024	0.024	0.023	0.029
-1.9	0.035	0.034	0.034	0.033	0.026	0.031	0.031	0.030	0.029	0.036
-1.8	0.044	0.043	0.042	0.041	0.032	0.039	0.038	0.038	0.037	0.045
-1.7	0.054	0.053	0.052	0.051	0.040	0.048	0.047	0.046	0.046	0.055
-1.6	0.066	0.064	0.063	0.062	0.049	0.059	0.058	0.057	0.056	0.067
-1.5	0.079	0.078	0.076	0.075	0.061	0.072	0.071	0.069	0.068	0.081
-1.4	0.095	0.093	0.092	0.090	0.074	0.087	0.085	0.084	0.082	0.097
-1.3	0.113	0.111	0.109	0.107	0.089	0.104	0.102	0.100	0.099	0.115
-1.2	0.133	0.131	0.129	0.127	0.106	0.123	0.121	0.119	0.117	0.136
-1.1	0.156	0.154	0.152	0.149	0.125	0.145	0.142	0.140	0.138	0.159
-1.0	0.181	0.179	0.176	0.174	0.147	0.169	0.166	0.164	0.161	0.184
-0.9	0.209	0.206	0.203	0.200	0.171	0.195	0.192	0.189	0.187	0.212
-0.8	0.239	0.236	0.233	0.230	0.198	0.224	0.221	0.218	0.215	0.242
-0.7	0.271	0.268	0.264	0.261	0.227	0.255	0.251	0.248	0.245	0.274
-0.6	0.305	0.302	0.298	0.295	0.258	0.288	0.284	0.281	0.278	0.309
-0.5	0.341	0.337	0.334	0.330	0.291	0.323	0.319	0.316	0.312	0.345
-0.4	0.378	0.374	0.371	0.367	0.326	0.359	0.356	0.352	0.348	0.382
-0.3	0.417	0.413	0.409	0.405	0.401	0.397	0.394	0.390	0.386	0.421
-0.2	0.456	0.452	0.448	0.444	0.440	0.436	0.433	0.429	0.425	0.998
-0.1	0.496	0.492	0.488	0.484	0.480	0.476	0.472	0.468	0.464	0.460
0.0	0.536	0.532	0.528	0.524	0.520	0.516	0.512	0.508	0.504	0.500

CHAPTER 7

RISK MANAGEMENT

A critical part of managing any project is defining, analyzing, and managing project risk. Every project has some degree of risk, although it is often overlooked by many project managers (with disturbing results). In this chapter, we consider the issues associated with planning, analyzing, and mitigating risks. Finally, we examine a brief case study that illustrates the nature of many project risks and possible strategies to manage these risks.

As discussed in Chapter 2, many organizations select a portfolio of projects to minimize overall project risk; that is, they select a "balanced" portfolio to offset risks associated with staffing, resources, hardware, etc. in the same way that an individual would diversify an investment portfolio. Subcontracting a part (or all) of the project is another way to manage risks; the type of contract written with a subcontractor has significant implications for allocating risks among project stakeholders. For example, a fixed-price contract shifts most risks associated with the subproject to the subcontractor, while a cost-plus contract places most risks with the client.

In general, there are two elements that define risk in projects: (1) the probability of an adverse event or outcome, and (2) the severity or cost of that event or outcome. In other words, what can happen (and how much can it cost), and what is the likelihood of such an event occurring?

The likelihood of most events is influenced by both exogenous as well as endogenous factors; for example, bad weather or bad management can equally delay the completion of a project. Organizations may be able to directly address endogenous factors (e.g., by replacing managers), but generally find it more difficult to influence the likelihood of environmental or exogenous factors. Sometimes the likelihood of an adverse event can be influenced by the actions of an organization, but some uncertainty may remain. In general, sources of exogenous uncertainty include:

- Changes in technology
- Government regulations or policies
- Unexpected losses due to deterioration, theft, etc.
- Market fluctuations in prices and supplies
- Legal and contractual issues
- Natural hazards such as weather delays, earthquakes, etc.

Endogenous risks include random variations in component performance, inaccurate or incomplete data, personnel issues, impacts of other projects, and cash flows, as well as an inability to accurately forecast due to a lack of data, experience, or foresight.

Huchzermeier and Loch (2001) identify five sources of uncertainty or variability that are commonly associated with R&D projects:

- Schedule variability (task durations are random)

- Budget variability (costs may vary)
- Performance variability (the product under development may not achieve its targeted specifications)
- Market requirement variability (product specifications required by the market may change)
- Market payoff variability (the market payoff may change due to competition, environmental changes, etc.)

These variations can result from both endogenous as well as exogenous effects. R&D managers must maintain as much flexibility as possible in order to respond to changes in these factors.

Some organizations make distinctions among adverse events based on the projected magnitude of their possible impact. In this case, they will classify potential risks into categories (e.g., small, medium, large) such that greater attention can be focused on adverse events with large potential costs. Other managers, however, feel that such an approach can be misleading and believe that all risks should be considered and monitored carefully.

How can an organization avoid or reduce the potential costs associated with adverse events or outcomes? Obviously, the first step is to identify adverse events as well as the likelihood of these events and their associated impacts. For each identified risk/event, managers should identify two possible actions:

- **Preventive action:** What to do in anticipation of an adverse event to reduce the likelihood of the undesirable event from occurring or mitigate its effect.
- **Contingency plan:** What to do if the undesirable event occurs.

For example, suppose a company is considering a project in a foreign market; if the company has signed a fixed-price contract, fluctuations in the foreign exchange rate could adversely affect the project's expected profitability. As a preventive plan, the organization could consider using financial derivatives such as forward contracts and options to hedge against the currency risk; as a contingency plan, the organization could plan to reduce the scope of the project if exchange rates do in fact change and make the project less profitable.

Associated with the contingency action is an identified "trigger point" that specifies the time and conditions under which the contingency action will be implemented. For example, consider an enterprise resource planning (ERP) implementation project. One possible risk is a delay in the acquisition of necessary hardware to run the system; to mitigate this possibility, a project manager may decide to acquire the necessary hardware as early as possible (preventive action) or, if the hardware is still delayed, to rent the needed hardware (contingency plan). The manager should also identify a given date (trigger point) on which rental contracts will be negotiated if the hardware is not available by that time.

For each possible adverse event it is helpful to create a chart, clearly specifying each undesirable event/outcome, its associated probability and additional cost, and preventive plans and contingency actions. An example of such a chart is illustrated in Figure 7.1.

The likelihood of an event can be estimated by a single number, a range (e.g., the probability is less than 70 percent), or a qualitative assessment (e.g., low, medium, or high). The expected additional cost can be estimated in similar fashion. To the table in Figure 7.1, a column can also be added that specifies the trigger point for each contingency action.

TOOLS FOR ANALYZING PROJECT RISK

There are several useful tools for analyzing project risk. One is a **tornado diagram,** which represents a sensitivity analysis of the input variables. Each input variable is varied

Undesirable Event/Outcome	Probability of Event	Expected Additional Cost	Preventive Plan	Contingency Action
Market survey inadequate			Add incentive to questionnaire	Hire market research firm
Key personnel leave organization			Treat key personnel kindly	Hire replacements
Poorly written instruction manual			Have writers work closely with end-users	Sub contract task
Hardware is not delivered on time			Schedule delivery as soon as possible	Rent computer time/storage space

FIGURE 7.1   Risk Analysis Example

sequentially; initially, each variable is set to an estimated low value and then to an estimated high value. For each estimate of the input variable, the overall project value is calculated. In the example given in Figure 7.2, assume that a proposed project is expected to cost a total of $1,500 based on the managers' best estimates. To test the sensitivity to changes in certain key parameters (e.g., wage rate, interest rates, etc.), the project planners varied each factor from a low to high estimate, while holding all other factors constant, and calculated the resulting impact on total project cost. For example, assume the project planners felt that the direct labor wage rate could increase or decrease by as much as 8 percent over the life of the project. In this case, the expected cost of the project would increase to $1,760 (if the direct wage rate increased) or fall to $1,260 (if the wage rate decreased). As a result of this sensitivity analysis, since wage rate for direct labor had the greatest impact on the variability of potential project cost, wage rate is listed at the top of the diagram. Each factor that could affect project cost is listed in decreasing order of its potential impact. The resultant diagram resembles a tornado—hence the name.

Tornado diagrams suffer from the fact that they are calculated by varying one factor at a time while holding all other input variables constant. A **sensitivity chart** considers changes in all input variables simultaneously. In this case, the manager varies all input variables simultaneously by choosing factor values randomly from their specified ranges. For example, he can use a random-number generator to set the value of the wage rate, the number of direct labor hours, and so on. (Random-number generators in spreadsheet programs generate a random number between zero and one from a uniform distribution.)

FIGURE 7.2   Tornado Diagram Example

Spreadsheet add-on programs, such as Crystal Ball* or @Risk, allow the user to generate random numbers from a variety of distributions. Given these values for input variables, the manager then calculates the project cost. This procedure can then be repeated for multiple sets of sample values, resulting in a value for each input variable and a corresponding project cost. A correlation coefficient between each set of input variables and the project cost can be calculated and reported, as indicated in the example in Figure 7.3. In this case, it appears that project cost is most highly correlated with changes in the direct labor wage rate. Thus, management may want to most closely watch the value of this input variable, because it has the greatest potential for increasing project cost.

Several observations can be made about this chart. First, note that one factor (early completion bonus) has a negative correlation with project cost. This is not surprising; it indicates that a larger bonus will provide a greater incentive to complete the project early—which, it appears, will reduce total project cost. Second, the simple method of sampling (known as Monte Carlo simulation) used to create this sensitivity chart assumes that all factors (wage rate, direct labor hours, etc.) are statistically independent. This may not always be true. For example, if the manager increases the number of material units needed, she may also have to increase the number of direct labor hours. The assumption that input variables are statistically independent, however, is a limitation of these charts.

CONTRACT TYPES AND RELATIVE RISK

As discussed in Chapter 2, the client or owner of a project can negotiate several types of contracts. All contracts have implications for managing risk. For example, the *fixed-price* contract requires a contractor to absorb all costs that exceed the negotiated contract price. Since the contractor is accepting this risk in this case, the client should expect to pay a higher price than if he agrees to absorb cost overruns.

In contrast, the *cost-plus* contract specifies that the client will pay the contractor for whatever time and materials (T&M) are required to complete the project's design. Since the client is assuming all of the risk in this case, she should expect to negotiate a lower initial price than with a fixed-price contract.

There are, of course, many variations of these contract types. The client and contractor could negotiate a fixed-price contract with a clause that requires the client to pay a

FIGURE 7.3
Sensitivity Chart

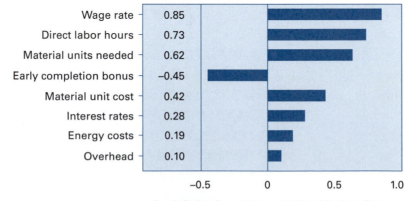

Rank Order Correlation with Total Project Cost

* Crystal Ball refers to a series of risk analysis tools produced by Decisioneering that use Monte Carlo simulation in conjunction with Excel spreadsheets. @Risk is a similar product produced by Palisade Corporation.

higher rate if labor and/or material costs rise above a certain level. Or the client and contractor could negotiate a contract for part of the project, with the understanding that the remainder of the project will be negotiated at some later date. Contract incentives also determine how project risks are allocated. A fixed-price contract with a specified penalty if the project is delayed beyond some due date shifts some of the risk to the contractor. On the other hand, some of this risk may be mitigated by an "earliness" incentive that provides a bonus payment to the contractor if the project is completed before a specified date. Several contract types and their relative risks are indicated in Figure 7.4 (this is not an exhaustive list of contract types).

VAN ALLEN CONSTRUCTION COMPANY

The Van Allen Construction Company is hoping to sign a contract in the next few months to build a new soccer stadium where the Louisiana Superdome now stands. Hopeful of getting this contract, managers at Van Allen have started planning the first phase of the project (i.e., demolition of the Superdome).

The demolition project consists of nine tasks, which are indicated in the following table. Also indicated are the normal times (in weeks) and normal costs (in hundreds of dollars), as well as the crash times and crash costs. Indirect charges (e.g., security fencing around the perimeter site) and overhead charges will cost approximately $12 (hundred) per week.

Task	Immediate Predecessors	Crash Time	Crash Cost	Normal Time	Normal Cost
A	—	3	$60	5	$40
B	—	1	$50	5	$30
C	B	5	$70	10	$40
D	A	2	$60	7	$40
E	A	2	$50	6	$30
F	C, D	5	$90	11	$60
G	C, D	4	$60	6	$30
H	G	1	$40	5	$20
I	E, G	1	$50	4	$20

The project manager has become aware that workers may strike during the demolition project. If such a strike occurs, no one will cross the picket line, and the demolition project will be stopped for the duration of the strike (overhead and indirect charges, however, will continue to accrue during the strike). To get more information about this potential strike, the project manager has hired a consultant who specializes in labor relations. The consultant reported that the probability of a strike is between 60 and 80 percent. If a strike does occur, she estimates the duration of the strike is as follows.

Strike Duration	Probability
3 wks	0.45
4 wks	0.30
5 wks	0.25

The consultant has also stated that if a strike should occur, it is equally likely that the strike would start at any time during the demolition project, and that there would be no more than one strike during the project's life. Given this information, how should the Van Allen Company manage this risk? Should the company take any preventive actions or plan some contingency actions? If so, what do you recommend?

FIGURE 7.4
Relative Risk and
Contract Types

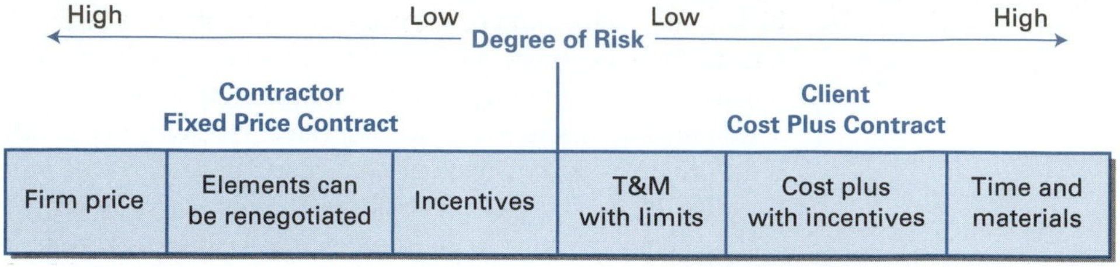

High		Low	Low		High
←		Degree of Risk			→

Contractor				**Client**	
Fixed Price Contract				**Cost Plus Contract**	
Firm price	Elements can be renegotiated	Incentives	T&M with limits	Cost plus with incentives	Time and materials

RISK MANAGEMENT CASE STUDY

To illustrate elements of risk analysis in project management (PM), we can consider the Van Allen Construction Company "caselet." The discussion that follows the caselet is intended to stimulate the reader to think further about issues relating to risk planning and management; it is *not* intended to present an exhaustive plan for dealing with potential disruptive events. The caselet is based on a real project that had a well-defined deadline and began under the threat of a potential worker strike (that did in fact materialize). The names and scenario in this caselet have been changed to protect proprietary information.

The Van Allen caselet illustrates some important issues about managing project risk. First, based on prior information or simply her experience, the project manager was able to identify the risk event (a possible strike). Furthermore, she had sufficient preliminary information about a possible strike that caused her to hire a management consultant who, in turn, was able to provide additional information about the likelihood and cost of a strike.

The actions of the project manager illustrate the three main factors associated with managing project risks:

- **Risk identification:** Identify possible adverse events.
- **Risk probability:** Estimate the likelihood of the event occurring.
- **Risk assessment:** Estimate all costs associated with the adverse event.

Once the project manager recognizes that a strike may occur, she must then determine a *risk mitigation plan.* Before formulating such a plan, the project manager may want to determine the motivating cause of the possible strike. Has the contract for a group of workers expired (or is it about to expire)? Is the potential strike a result of too much overwork? Too little pay? Have there been other worker complaints? Does the company have safety issues that are adversely affecting worker morale? Can other factors be identified that may be contributing to the possibility of a strike?

Once the project manager has identified possible causes, she should consider an *impact analysis* that shows the expected short-term and long-term effects of the strike on the project and organization (e.g., will a strike on the Superdome demolition project affect other Van Allen projects in Louisiana? How much will a delay cost?). The risk mitigation plan should contain information on preventive actions as well as on contingency plans. (The trigger point in this situation is straightforward; contingency plans will be implemented if the strike occurs.)

As part of the preventive actions, the project manager may want to consider these strategies:

- Negotiate directly with the workers involved to reduce the likelihood of a strike.
- Try to rewrite the project contract so that the client assumes any losses resulting from a strike.
- Try to purchase an insurance policy to cover any financial losses incurred by a strike.

- Compress the project beyond the time that minimizes total project costs.

The last two preventive actions are similar; in both cases, the project manager will incur additional costs to ensure the likelihood that the project will be completed on time. By compressing the project beyond the cost minimization point, the project manager will be building in a time buffer that can be used to offset a strike if it should occur.

In the case of a strike, this adverse event may be motivated by issues that are company-wide and out of the project manager's scope of responsibility. If so, there may be little that a project manager can do directly to reduce the likelihood of a strike occurring. If a strike does occur, possible contingency plans include the following:

- Hire non-union labor.
- Assign Van Allen managers to work on the project.
- Do nothing (i.e., suspend work until the strike is over).

Using a Cost Model to Assess and Manage Risks

The cost model described in Chapter 5 can be useful for better understanding the risks in the Van Allen case as well as the preventive actions and contingency plans. Following the model discussed in Chapter 5, we want to consider the trade-off between direct costs and overhead and indirect costs to minimize total project costs. Ignoring the possibility of a strike, the project manager should plan to complete this project in seventeen weeks to minimize total costs (if all tasks were performed at their normal durations, the project would take twenty-six weeks). The spreadsheet model and minimum-cost solution are given in Figure 7.5; note that tasks B, C, D, F, and H are compressed beyond their normal durations in the minimum-cost solution.

As we discussed in Chapter 5, the solution in Figure 7.5 represents the trade-off between the increase in direct costs resulting from crashing tasks B, C, D, F, and H, and the reduction in indirect and overhead costs resulting from reducing the expected project duration from twenty-six weeks (no crashing) to seventeen weeks. At seventeen weeks,

Task	Task Duration (tj)	Immediate Predecessors	Starting Times	Finish Times	Crash Time	Crash Cost	Normal Time	Normal Cost	Slope (bj)	Marginal Cost Incr
START	0	—	0							
A	5	START	0.0	5.0	3	$ 60	5	$ 40	$ 10	$ 0.00
B	1	START	0.0	1.0	1	$ 50	5	$ 30	$ 5	$20.00
C	6	B	1.0	7.0	5	$ 70	10	$ 40	$ 6	$24.00
D	2	A	5.0	7.0	2	$ 60	7	$ 40	$ 4	$20.00
E	6	A	6.0	12.0	2	$ 50	6	$ 30	$ 5	$ 0.00
F	10	C, D	7.0	17.0	5	$ 90	11	$ 60	$ 5	$ 5.00
G	6	C, D	7.0	13.0	4	$ 60	6	$ 30	$ 15	$ 0.00
H	4	G	13.0	17.0	1	$ 40	5	$ 20	$ 5	$ 5.00
I	4	E, G	13.0	17.0	1	$ 50	4	$ 20	$ 10	$ 0.00
END	0	F, I, H	17.0	17.0						
Totals						$530.00		$310.00	$310.00	$74.00

Indirect cost/wk = $ 12.00   **Total direct cost = $384.00**
Indirect costs = $204.00

FIGURE 7.5 Minimum Cost Solution for Van Allen Company (No Strike Considered)

the total direct labor cost is $384 and indirect/overhead costs are 17 weeks × $12/week = $204, resulting in a total minimum cost of $588. If the manager tried to compress the project any further to sixteen weeks, she would have to crash tasks A and C (in addition to tasks B, D, F, and H) at an additional marginal cost of $16 (bringing direct labor costs to $400). Since the company would save only $12 in indirect and overhead costs, it would not be worthwhile to compress the project beyond seventeen weeks.

We can now modify the spreadsheet model to include the possibility of a strike or other disruptive event (Figure 7.6). Based on the information provided by the management consultant, the expected duration of the strike is 3.80 weeks, as indicated in the table. Since the manager also knows there is a 70 percent chance that the strike will occur, she can multiply 0.70 times 3.80 weeks and add this expected value to the duration of the project. Since she assumes that all work on the project will cease during the strike (but indirect/overhead charges will continue to accrue), she uses the modified project duration to adjust the indirect/overhead cost cell and resolve the Solver model. The new solution is given in Figure 7.6.

Examining the optimal solution in Figure 7.6, we note that the manager would still plan to complete the project in 17 weeks. In fact, rerunning this model with various probabilities indicates that the solution does not change even if the probability of a strike is 1.0. Why is this so? As indicated in Figure 7.5, managers compress a project until the marginal increase in direct costs meets or exceeds the marginal savings in indirect/overhead costs. Adding the expected duration of the strike to the project duration merely adds a constant to the total project cost (equal to 3.80 weeks times $12/week = $31.92 such that the total project cost is now increased to $619.92, as indicated in Figure 7.6). The expected project duration is now 19.66 weeks; however, if the project manager tries to reduce the expected project duration, it will cost her more ($16) than the realized savings ($12 in overhead costs).

The managerial insights from this analysis are clear. Based on the spreadsheet model in Figure 7.6, it would not be worthwhile for the project manager to compress the project beyond seventeen weeks *even if she knows that the probability of a strike is one*. As long as the likelihood of the disruptive event is constant, a preventive plan should not include additional project compression.

Task	Task Duration (tj)	Immediate Predecessors	Starting Times	Finish Times	Crash Time	Crash Cost	Normal Time	Normal Cost	Slope (bj)	Marginal Cost Incr
START	0	—	0							
A	5	START	0.0	5.0	3	$ 60	5	$ 40	$ 10	$ 0.00
B	1	START	0.0	1.0	1	$ 50	5	$ 30	$ 5	$20.00
C	6	B	1.0	7.0	5	$ 70	10	$ 40	$ 6	$24.00
D	2	A	5.0	7.0	2	$ 60	7	$ 40	$ 4	$20.00
E	6	A	7.0	13.0	2	$ 50	6	$ 30	$ 5	$ 0.00
F	10	C, D	7.0	17.0	5	$ 90	11	$ 60	$ 5	$ 5.00
G	6	C, D	7.0	13.0	4	$ 60	6	$ 30	$ 15	$ 0.00
H	4	G	13.0	17.0	1	$ 40	5	$ 20	$ 5	$ 5.00
I	4	E, G	13.0	17.0	1	$ 50	4	$ 20	$ 10	$ 0.00
END	0	F, I, H	17.0	17.0						
Totals						**$530.00**		**$310.00**		**$74.00**

Indirect cost/wk = $ 12.00   Total direct cost = $384.00

Prob of strike = 0.70   Indirect costs = $235.92

Total cost = $619.92

FIGURE 7.6 Minimum Cost Solution for Van Allen Company (Strike Considered)

However, this result may change if the nature of the problem changes. For example, the manager may want to plan to compress the project beyond seventeen weeks if there is a project due date and the Van Allen Company incurs a penalty if the project is completed after this due date. Alternatively, the probability of a strike may no longer be constant but may vary throughout the project life (a typical occurrence with many risk events). Alternatively, the likelihood of a strike may increase as the project duration increases. The spreadsheet model in Figure 7.6 provides an important tool to analyze and better understand the implications of these requirements. Some of these extensions are considered further in the study problems.

RISKS IN NEW PRODUCT DEVELOPMENT PROJECTS

Riek (2001) identified three types of risks that he observed while studying fifteen new product development (NPD) efforts, and categorized these risks into the following taxonomy:

- Technical risk
- Commercial risk
- Risks associated with product development personnel

Technical risk is the risk associated with the development and application of new technologies. With respect to technical risk, Riek cautioned about the need to clearly understand all development steps in a new technology development project, and not to "cut corners" during such a process. He also emphasized the need for PM training and risk management planning. With respect to commercial risk, Riek documented several cases where the technology was ahead (or behind) its time, or secondary or tertiary effects were overlooked, or competitive technologies were not fully appreciated. Other documented problems were directly related to personnel issues, including the loss of key personnel to competing organizations and poor allocation and scheduling policies.

Ahmadi and Wang (1999) describe problems associated with the development of liquid-propellant rocket engines at the Rocketdyne Division of Rockwell International. They describe how managers at Rockwell International control development risks (including time and costs) through careful management of the product design process. A key part of this process is the management of the monitoring and control of the design process; the authors point out that both over- and under-control are likely to result in failure. They develop a methodology, based on the work by Ha and Porteus (1995), that tries to determine the optimal review policy for new product development projects.

Since the nature and likelihood of various risk events change throughout the life of a project, managers must closely monitor the project—especially during the design phase. It is essential for project managers to identify all risk events, if possible, because they will affect the project's final cost, schedule, and design.

STUDY PROBLEMS

1. The management consultant on the Van Allen project has discovered that the labor contract is in effect until the beginning of week 14; that is, the strike would occur only at the beginning of week 14, if at all. Would this change your decisions? If so, how?

2. The project manager at the Van Allen Company now thinks that the likelihood of a strike increases as the duration of the project increases. Specifically, she estimates the probability of a strike during the course of the project to be as follows:

$$\text{Probability of Strike} = \text{END}/(\text{END} + 4)$$

where END is the project duration. Would this assumption change her preventive plans? If so, how?

3. Assume that the Van Allen Company has a deadline of twenty weeks to complete the Superdome demolition project. In this case, the state will fine the Van Allen Company $3.5 (hundreds) for each week the demolition project is delayed. How does this affect your recommendation (assume that the probability of a strike is 0.70)?

4. To get the demolition project completed as quickly as possible, the state of Louisiana is considering adding an incentive clause to Van Allen's contract. Specifically, the incentive clause would reward the company with a bonus of $5.0 (hundreds) for each week that the project is completed before week 18. What would you now recommend to Van Allen? Why? (Assume that the probability of a strike is constant at 0.70.)

REFERENCES

Ahmadi, R., and R. H. Wang. "Managing Development Risk in Product Design Processes." *Operations Research* 47, no. 2 (March–April, 1999): 235–46.

Ha, A., and E. Porteus. "Optimal Timing of Reviews in Concurrent Design for Manufacturability." *Management Science* 41, no. 9 (September 1995): 1431–47.

Huchzermeier, A., and C. H. Loch. "Project Management Under Risk: Using the Real Options Approach to Evaluate Flexibility in R&D." *Management Science* 47, no. 1 (January 2001): 85–101.

Riek. R. F. "From Experience: Capturing Hard-Won NPD Lessons in Checklists." *Journal of Product Innovation Management* 18 (2001): 301–13.

CHAPTER 8

RESOURCE MANAGEMENT

In most of the previous discussion in this book, we assumed that resources (i.e., workers, machines, money) were available in unlimited quantities. Since this assumption is generally not true, project managers must know how to manage limited resources; in fact, managing limited resources may be a project manager's greatest challenge. In this chapter, we will examine and discuss problems associated with limited resources. To motivate discussion on this topic, we initially present the Date Dilemma "caselet."

The Date Dilemma caselet is designed to illustrate some important points relating to the definition of tasks and the fact that a project may be "resource constrained." In the Date Dilemma caselet, the constraining resource is Jim, and he is clearly the only one available. Note that there are other resources in the case, but they are not constraining; for example, the case assumes that Jim has as many available ovens as he needs. Resources add precedence constraints to a project; since Jim can perform only one task at a time, the tasks assigned to Jim must be performed sequentially. This case illustrates the important point that the concept of a critical path, as discussed in Chapter 4, must be significantly modified when resources are introduced and considered.

In general, two overall problems are associated with resource management: (1) the resource leveling problem and (2) the resource allocation problem. The resource leveling problem refers to the scheduling of noncritical activities in order to minimize the peak resource requirements and smooth out or level resource utilization over the life of the project. The resource allocation problem, on the other hand, refers to the case when there are sufficient resources to complete a project within the critical time. Assuming that additional resources are not available, the project manager wants to find the minimum time (or cost) needed to complete the project within his resource constraints.

THE RESOURCE LEVELING PROBLEM

To illustrate the resource leveling problem, consider the problem represented by the AON precedence network in Figure 8.1. As indicated, the critical path is START-A-D-G-END with a project makespan (defined by the critical path) equal to thirteen weeks. In this example we will consider only one resource, denoted generically as "workers"; however, we could easily extend our analysis to multiple resources by simply repeating our approach for each resource.

In the resource leveling problem, the project manager wants to schedule noncritical tasks to minimize the maximum number of workers the company must hire throughout the project (obviously, the critical tasks cannot be delayed without delaying the project). To better understand how the manager might schedule noncritical tasks, we can first examine what happens if she schedules all noncritical tasks to start at their earliest starting times. A spreadsheet indicating the number of workers needed each week for the early start schedule, with the resulting histogram, is given in Figure 8.2. Note that tasks A, D, and G are critical tasks.

As indicated in both the spreadsheet as well as the frequency histogram, the largest number of workers needed in any week is 21 (week 4). In weeks 3 and 5, the number of workers

THE DATE DILEMMA*

Jim Gantt isn't paying attention in his accounting class; he's thinking about his date tonight. He is making dinner for a special someone at his apartment, and he is bothered by the thought that he might not have enough time to get everything ready for the special evening. His accounting class lasts until 5:30 P.M., and his date is arriving at exactly 7:00 P.M.; she is very prompt and dislikes it when people are late. Jim knows it will take him eight minutes to walk home and about an hour and twenty minutes to do his laundry and get dressed. Other than that, he hopes he can fit all the other chores in by seven o'clock.

Jim made a list of things he had to do by seven and the amount of time he thought each would take. Here is Jim's list:

Walk home	8 minutes
Do laundry	1 hour 20 minutes
Clean dining room floor	35 minutes
Borrow friend's Beatles' album	5 minutes
Make bed	2 minutes
Pick up wine	10 minutes
Pick up ice cream	3 minutes
Defrost cheesecake	42 minutes
Bake potatoes	55 minutes
Prepare and cook salmon	24 minutes
Prepare and heat bread	15 minutes
Make salad	10 minutes
Set table	5 minutes
TOTAL	**4 hours 54 minutes**

Jim realizes it won't take almost five hours to prepare everything since some activities include waiting time that can be made productive. However, he is doubtful that nearly five hours of chores can be condensed down to ninety minutes.

Doing the laundry will take five minutes to collect and carry to the laundry room in his apartment complex, twenty-five minutes to wash, three minutes to transfer the wash to the dryer, forty minutes for drying, and seven minutes to fetch and fold plus get dressed. Jim figures it will take five minutes to swing by his friend's apartment to borrow a Beatles' album if he does it on one of the return trips from the laundry room (otherwise it will take longer). He also figures it would be best to pick up the wine and ice cream on the same trip to the shopping center in order to save time and gas.

The dining room floor will take ten minutes to wash and twenty-five minutes to dry. Defrosting the cheesecake will take forty minutes with an extra minute on each end for removing it from the freezer and replacing it in the refrigerator. Of the fifty-five minutes to bake the potatoes, Jim is allowing four minutes for scrubbing and buttering the skins. Because Jim bought the salmon whole, he figures it will take nine minutes to wash, cut into steaks, and season with spices and another fifteen minutes to cook. The bread will take five minutes to butter, season, and put in foil with ten minutes for heating.

Since he plans to serve dinner precisely at seven, Jim wants all heated food to be ready just before his date arrives (Jim allows two additional minutes to remove all heated food from the oven and place it on serving dishes). Other than this, all food should be prepared as late as possible. Jim is unconcerned about leaving his apartment while food is cooking.

Although Jim knows there are enough ovens in the kitchen so that cooking times can overlap, he realizes he can't set the table while the dining room floor is wet.

It is 4:20 and Jim is considering cutting out of class at the break in ten minutes. Although Jim considers tonight's date more important than his accounting class, he recalls how he got burned on the last midterm. If at all possible, Jim wants to stay for the entire class and still complete all his chores before his seven o'clock date.

(continued)

*This caselet was written by Jack Eisenhauer.

THE DATE DILEMMA (CONT'D)

Questions

1. Should Jim cut out of his accounting class at the break? If not, will he have enough time to do all his chores before seven o'clock?

2. Prepare a network diagram describing the order that allows Jim to carry out his chores in the shortest total time. Which activities are critical?

3. Prepare a Gantt chart illustrating the time slot for each activity.

4. Can you think of any mathematical programming formulation that will help solve Jim's problem?

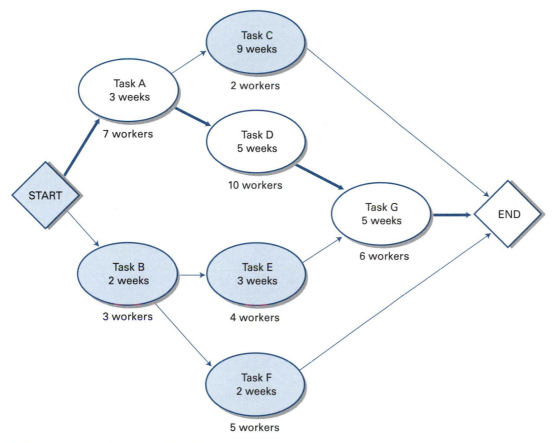

FIGURE 8.1   Resource Leveling Example

needed is reduced to 16. The frequency histogram generated by Microsoft Project for the early scheduling problem is given in Figure 8.3. Note the dotted line indicating the current day/time, as well as the horizontal line indicating the constraint on the number of available workers.

What happens if the project manager schedules all noncritical tasks to start at their latest starting times? The results of this schedule are given in Figure 8.4; as indicated, the maximum number of workers needed in any week is now reduced to 16. In other words, the latest starting schedule represents a better utilization of workers from the perspective of reducing the maximum (peak) requirements.

	Week												
	1	**2**	**3**	**4**	**5**	**6**	**7**	**8**	**9**	**10**	**11**	**12**	**13**
Task A	7	7	7										
Task B	3	3											
Task C				2	2	2	2	2	2	2	2	2	
Task D				10	10	10	10	10					
Task E			4	4	4								
Task F			5	5									
Task G									6	6	6	6	6
Total workers needed each week	10	10	16	21	16	12	12	12	8	8	8	8	6

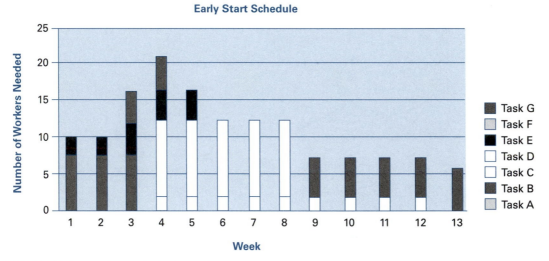

FIGURE 8.2 Earliest Scheduling of Noncritical Tasks in Example

Note that the total worker-weeks needed for either the early start or latest start schedule is 147 worker-weeks (found by adding the total number of workers needed each week over the life of the project). The number of worker-weeks is the same regardless of the scheduling of the noncritical tasks.

Is there any other schedule that reduces the maximum number of workers needed in any week below 16? To investigate this possibility, a project manager can attempt to reschedule the noncritical tasks between their respective earliest and latest starting times. If she begins with the earliest starting schedule given in Figure 8.2, it is clear that she should consider rescheduling only tasks C, E, and F (since task D is a critical task, it cannot be delayed without delaying the completion of the project). Task F has the largest total slack (12 − 3 = 9 weeks) since it can be started as late as week 12. However, the requirement of sixteen workers is a result of tasks C, D, and E being scheduled concurrently; a careful analysis of this problem indicates that these three tasks must overlap by at least one week. Thus, it appears that the project manager cannot reduce the maximum worker requirement below 16 without delaying the project's completion beyond thirteen weeks.

The frequency histograms indicated in Figures 8.2, 8.3, and 8.4 are also known as *resource profiles* or *skyline profiles*. When compared to actual resource utilization, they

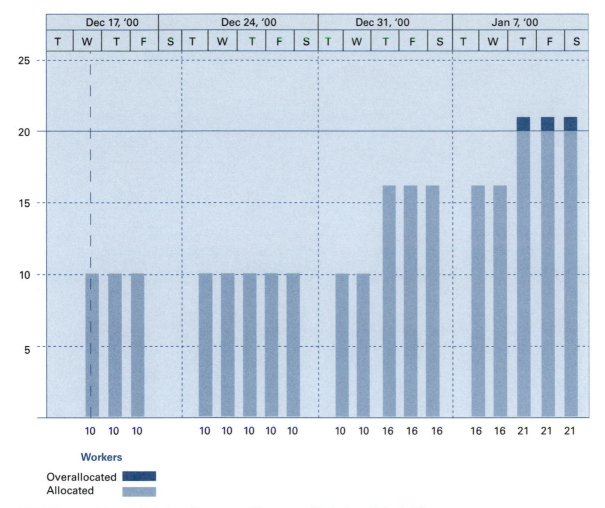

FIGURE 8.3 Microsoft Project Frequency Histogram (Early Start Schedule)

can be useful as communication and control devices as well as planning tools. These histograms are frequently available in most computerized project management (PM) software packages.

The resource leveling problem is important for many reasons. A "level" worker requirement can minimize hiring and firing costs, which can be substantial. A "level" budget can maximize interest earnings on unspent monies. The resource leveling problem is especially significant in repetitive manufacturing environments. For example, consider the case when the project in Figure 8.1 represents the assembly of a product that must be produced on a dedicated assembly line with a cycle time of, say, thirteen weeks. In this case, the workers represent the size of the crew that will be needed to staff such a line. If the project manager uses the early start schedule, he will have to hire a crew of twenty-one people; on the other hand, a project manager who uses the latest starting schedule would only have to hire a crew of sixteen persons. Understanding the nature of the resource leveling problem may allow the project manager to devise a scheme that uses fewer than sixteen persons (e.g., by hiring part-time workers or overlapping work on multiple copies of the product). This issue is further explored in study problem 8.2 at the end of this chapter.

The resource leveling problem is usually complicated, of course, by the existence of several resources that must be leveled at the same time. As might be expected, scheduling

	Week												
	1	**2**	**3**	**4**	**5**	**6**	**7**	**8**	**9**	**10**	**11**	**12**	**13**
Task A	7	7	7										
Task B				3	3								
Task C					2	2	2	2	2	2	2	2	2
Task D				10	10	10	10	10					
Task E						4	4	4					
Task F												5	5
Task G									6	6	6	6	6
Total workers needed each week	7	7	7	13	15	16	16	16	8	8	8	13	13

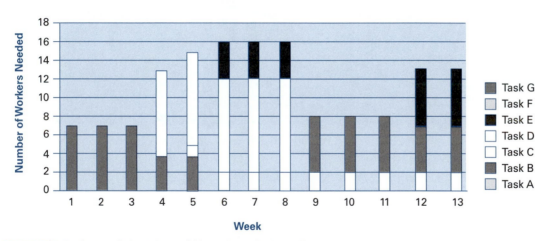

Latest Schedule

FIGURE 8.4 Latest Scheduling of Noncritical Tasks in Example

the noncritical tasks to level one resource "unlevels" some other resource. While some researchers have suggested mathematical programming models for solving this problem, these models are generally impractical for any reasonably sized problem and are rarely used in practice. Thus, project managers usually rely on heuristics (rules of thumb) to help them find an acceptable solution.

THE RESOURCE ALLOCATION PROBLEM

The resource allocation problem is concerned with allocating scarce resources to tasks to meet certain goals (e.g., complete the project as early as possible, minimize total costs, or maximize net present value of the project). It is assumed that these resources (which may be workers or equipment or money) are limited in quantity, or rate, or both. In fact, we often distinguish among resource allocation problems by the type of resource present in the problem. In general, we define two types of resources:

■ **Renewable resources.** A limit on the rate at which resources can be used (e.g., maximum number of workers per day).

■ **Nonrenewable resources.** A limit on the total resource consumption over the life of the project (e.g., a budget limit).

Renewable resources, limited by the rate at which they can be used per time period, are referred to as "renewable" since they are renewed each time period. For example, if ten workers are available for a project, each morning the ten workers are renewed and can be reallocated if necessary (assuming none quit or become ill, of course). Nonrenewable resources are limited by their total consumption; for example, dollars (or pounds, marks, euros, etc.) are a nonrenewable resource when there is a constraint on the total budget but no limit on the daily spending rate. Finally, resources that are constrained by both rate and total consumption are known as *doubly constrained resources.* For example, when there is a limit on both the total budget as well as an expenditure rate, money is a doubly constrained resource.

Most (though not all) resource allocation problems are exceedingly difficult to solve. However, much work has been done to find optimization approaches to reasonably sized problems (for an example of a real-world, spreadsheet-based optimization model that was used to assign managers to construction projects, see LeBlanc et al. 2000). Objective functions in this work have included (1) project makespan, (2) tardiness (i.e., time past a deadline), (3) lateness (i.e., time before and after a deadline), (4) total cost, (5) balanced workload, and (6) net present value. Demeulemeester and Herroelen (1992) developed a relatively efficient procedure for minimizing project makespan based on branch and bound (for further discussion, see Sprecher and Drexl, 1999). Many other variations have been considered; for example, Talbot (1982) developed an optimization algorithm to minimize project cost that combined the renewable resource problem and the time-cost trade-off problem. In his work, Talbot modeled each task using a discrete time-cost trade-off (as indicated in Figure 5.7c) and placed limits on the rate at which resources could be used as well as on total resource consumption. For more information, see Ozdamar and Ulusoy (1995), Brucker et al. (1999), Herroelen et al. (1998), Talbot and Patterson (1978), and Demeulemeester and Herroelen (2002).

Given the difficulty of solving renewable resource allocation problems, it is not surprising that heuristics are widely used. We will consider a small project example to illustrate two heuristic approaches to minimizing project duration when there is a constraint on renewable resources. Despite the simplicity of these approaches, our discussion illustrates some important points about the resource allocation problem, including the concept of a "critical chain" introduced by Goldratt (1997). The example (in Figure 8.5) consists of five tasks that use a single generic resource, denoted as "workers"; we assume that no more than nine workers are available each week.

Given a maximum of nine workers available each week, we are interested in the following questions that could be relevant to project managers:

■ Can the project be completed within twelve weeks (the length of the critical path) using no more than nine workers?

■ If the project cannot be completed within twelve weeks, how many more workers will be needed to meet the twelve-week deadline?

■ If the manager cannot hire more than nine workers, what is the minimum project delay he will incur?

To answer these questions, we start with a straightforward approach suggested by Baker (1974) to find a lower bound on either the minimum number of workers needed to complete the project in twelve weeks, or the minimum number of weeks needed to complete the project with nine workers. These bounds may not be tight, but they are easy to calculate and frequently provide useful information to a project manager in the planning stage of a project. Although this approach is illustrated with an example having only a single

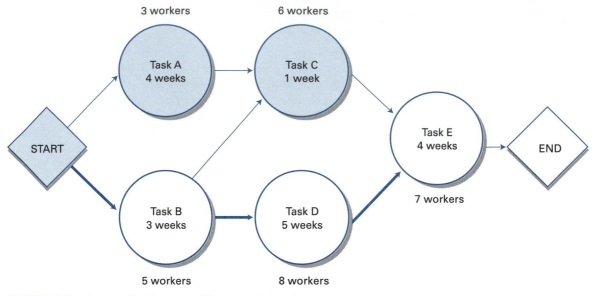

FIGURE 8.5 Renewable Resource Allocation Example

resource type, the project manager would merely repeat this analysis for each resource type if several resource types were being considered, and use the largest lower bound found from all resources.

To define these lower bounds, we consider initially the early start schedule and the latest start schedule. Figure 8.6 represents the early start schedule using activity-on-arc (AOA) notation; each task is denoted by an arrow whose length indicates the duration of the respective task (e.g., task B requires three weeks). Note that the number of available workers is first exceeded in week 4, when eleven workers are needed.

As indicated in Figure 8.6, a total of 101 worker-weeks are needed to complete this project in twelve weeks (sum of the number of workers needed each week). This total number of worker-weeks is constant for any scheduling of noncritical tasks, as in Figure 8.7, where the late start time schedule is indicated.

It appears from the early and late starting schedules that this project cannot be completed in twelve weeks with only nine workers (since both schedules need more than nine workers in at least one week). However, this information may be misleading; the manager may be able to reschedule noncritical tasks between their early and late starting times, thus creating a schedule that does not require more than nine workers in any week.

Is it possible to create a schedule that completes the project in twelve weeks without using more than nine workers in any week? To see if such a schedule is possible (without actually solving the problem), Baker (1974) suggested an elegant test that a manager can easily calculate, using little more than pencil and paper.

To illustrate Baker's approach, we will let the total number of worker-weeks be denoted by W (W is equal to 101 worker-weeks in this problem). Also, let R denote the number of available workers (per week) such that $R = 9$ workers in this example, and let D denote the target completion date of the project ($D = 12$ weeks in this example). Since we have a maximum of (9 workers) × (12 weeks) = 108 worker-weeks available during the project, we know that for any schedule to be feasible,

$$W \leq DR$$

Since $W = 101$ worker-weeks, it would appear that a 12-week schedule *might* be feasible since $101 \leq 108$.

Early Start Schedule

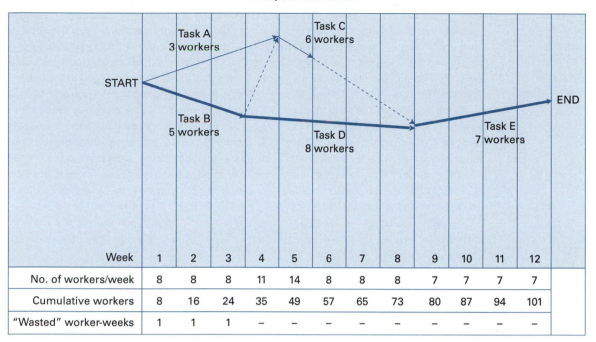

Week	1	2	3	4	5	6	7	8	9	10	11	12
No. of workers/week	8	8	8	11	14	8	8	8	7	7	7	7
Cumulative workers	8	16	24	35	49	57	65	73	80	87	94	101
"Wasted" worker-weeks	1	1	1	–	–	–	–	–	–	–	–	–

FIGURE 8.6 Early Start Schedule for the Resource Allocation Example

Late Start Schedule

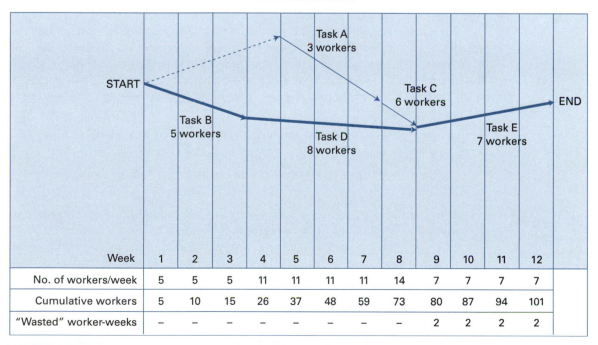

Week	1	2	3	4	5	6	7	8	9	10	11	12
No. of workers/week	5	5	5	11	11	11	11	14	7	7	7	7
Cumulative workers	5	10	15	26	37	48	59	73	80	87	94	101
"Wasted" worker-weeks	–	–	–	–	–	–	–	–	2	2	2	2

FIGURE 8.7 Late Start Time Schedule for Noncritical Tasks

However, it is possible to improve this bound by examining the early start and late start schedules. First, let's consider the early start schedule in Figure 8.5. Note that the project manager uses only eight workers in week 1 in the early start schedule, even though nine workers are available. Since all tasks in the early start schedule are shifted as far to the left as possible in the Gantt chart, it is impossible to find any other schedule that satisfies the precedence constraints and uses more than eight workers in the first week. Thus, one worker is "wasted" in week 1; that is, there is no way this worker can be used on this project without changing the precedence constraints. If we then move to week 2, we again see that another worker is wasted (i.e., not used). As long as the number of workers used per week is less than or equal to the number of workers available (nine workers), the manager can continue moving to sequentially higher weeks. In this example, he needs eleven workers in week 4 so he must stop at this point; though a future week may require fewer than nine workers, the manager might be able to reschedule noncritical tasks to shift workers to those weeks. So, based on the early start schedule, the project has a total of 3 (1 + 1 + 1) wasted worker-weeks.

To summarize the calculations to find the number of wasted worker-weeks from the early start schedule, let $r_E(t)$ denote the number of workers needed in time period t by the early start schedule. Then,

1. Let T_E = smallest value of t such that $r_E(t) > R$ (the number of available workers). In this example, $T_E = 4$.
2. For each value of $t = 1, ..., T_E - 1$, the number of wasted worker-weeks is equal to $[R - r_E(t)]$.
3. Sum the wasted worker-weeks (which, in this example, equal 3).

The calculations for the wasted worker-weeks from the early start schedule are summarized in the spreadsheet in Figure 8.6.

The procedure is similar for the latest start schedule, except that the project manager starts with the last week and works backward to the first week. For example, only seven workers are used in week 12 in the late starting schedule in Figure 8.7; thus, $9 - 7 = 2$ workers are wasted and (since the tasks in the late start schedule are shifted as far to the right as possible) cannot be used.

The calculations for finding the number of wasted worker-weeks from the late start schedule are summarized in the following equations. In this case, let $r_L(t)$ denote the number of resource units used in each time period t for the late start schedule, and let T_L denote the largest value of t such that $r_L(t) > R$. In the example in Figure 8.6, $T_L = 8$ since $r_L(8) = 14$. Then the number of wasted worker-weeks found from the late start schedule can be calculated as follows:

1. Let T_L = largest value of t such that $r_L(t) > R$. In this example, $T_L = 8$.
2. For each value of $t = D, D - 1, ..., T_L + 1$, find $[R - r_L(t)]$.
3. Sum the wasted worker-weeks (in the example, this sum is equal to 2 + 2 + 2 + 2 = 8).

Note that the calculations for wasted worker-weeks from the late start schedule are summarized in the third row of the spreadsheet in Figure 8.7.

Previously, we indicated that the project would require a total of 101 worker-weeks to complete, regardless of the schedule. However, we now know that the project has a total of 3 + 8 = 11 wasted worker-weeks that are impossible to utilize in any schedule. Thus, the manager must reduce the available worker-weeks by 11 to reflect these wasted resources. The basic relationship now becomes:

$$W \leq DR - \sum_{u=1}^{T_E-1} [R - r_E(t)] - \sum_{u=T_L+1}^{D} [R - r_L(t)]$$

Since $(D\,R - 3 - 8) = (108 - 11) = 97$, which is clearly less than $W\ (= 101)$, we now know that no feasible schedule can be created, using only nine workers, that will be completed within twelve weeks (i.e., the manager will either have to delay the project *or* increase the number of available workers).

Let's assume that the manager does not want to hire more than nine workers. Can we say anything about the minimum project duration that is possible with nine workers? Using the preceding calculations, a lower bound on the project duration is easily calculated.

In this case, we know the number of available workers ($R = 9$) but do not know the project duration, D. Thus, the basic relationship now becomes

$$101 \text{ worker-weeks} \leq 9\,D - 11 \text{ "wasted" worker-weeks}$$
$$9\,D \geq 112$$
$$D \geq 112\,/\,9 = 12.44 \text{ weeks}$$

If the manager requires an integer number of weeks, then the project cannot be completed in less than thirteen weeks unless he hires more than nine workers. In addition to providing project managers with valuable information concerning minimum project duration, Baker's approach also gives them an improved starting point when searching for a feasible schedule.

Similarly, we can find a lower bound on the number of workers needed to complete the project in twelve weeks (assuming that this is now a requirement). In this case, $D = 12$ weeks and the number of resources R is unknown; the basic relationship now becomes

$$101 + 11 \leq 12\,R$$

which implies that *at least* ten workers are needed to complete the project in twelve weeks (9.33 workers rounded up to the nearest integer).

FINDING FEASIBLE SOLUTIONS FOR THE RENEWABLE RESOURCE ALLOCATION PROBLEM

In most project planning situations, there is a constraint on either the available resources or the project due date; but as we saw in the previous section, the project manager cannot generally satisfy both constraints. To explore some methods for solving the resource allocation problem, we will assume that there is a constraint on the number of available resources and try to find a schedule that minimizes the project delay. Conversely, we could hold the due date fixed and try to find the smallest number of additional resources would be needed to meet the due date. Procedures for solving the former problem can usually be easily modified to solve the latter problem.

Given the complexity of the resource allocation problem, managers typically rely on heuristic algorithms for finding a feasible schedule. Some heuristics are quite straightforward and some are quite complex. By definition, none can guarantee an optimal solution (i.e., minimize the project delay); however, given the myriad complexities faced by real-world project managers, a process that can easily and quickly generate multiple alternative solutions for a manager to consider can be most useful.

There are numerous ways to classify heuristic algorithms. The most efficient algorithms are called "single pass"; these algorithms schedule one task at a time until all tasks have been scheduled. Since the starting times of each task are fixed once the task has been scheduled, these algorithms have a complexity of order N (where N is the number of tasks in the project).

As in most algorithms, some method is needed for ranking or ordering tasks. While an unlimited number of metrics can be defined, typical measures are based on task durations, slacks, and/or resource requirements. Several commonly used metrics are defined here, although they represent only a small subset of possible metrics. To define these measures, we will use R_j^k to denote the number of units of resource type k that is required by task j.

- FCFS: First come, first served = Choose the first available task (if tie, choose randomly)
- TRU: Total resource utilization = $\sum_k R_j^k$

- GRD: (Greatest) resource utilization × task duration = $t_j \max_k \left(R_j^k \right)$
- GTS: (Greatest) total number of successors
- SPT: Shortest processing time = $\min (t_j)$
- MINSLK: Minimum total slack
- $ACTIM_j$: Longest path from task j to end of project
- $ACTRES_j$: Longest "path value" from task j to end of project, where each "path value" is defined by the product of each task's duration times total resources
- ROT (Resources over Time): Longest "path value" from task j to end of project, where each "path value" is defined by the ratio of resources over duration

We will use task B in the Figure 8.5 example project to illustrate the calculation of these measures. Since there is only one resource (workers) in this problem, TRU equals the number of workers. To find other measures for any jth task, the project manager must identify all paths from task j to the end of the project; for task B, there are two paths: path (C, E, End) and path (D, E, END). GTS_B (greatest number of successors from task B to the "END" milestone) is then equal to max (2, 2) = 2. The sum of the total slacks for path (C, E) is 7 + 0 = 7; the sum of the total slacks on path (D, E) is 0 (since tasks D and E are on the critical path). Thus, the value of $MINSLK_B$ is equal to the minimum of these two path slacks; that is, $MINSLK_B$ = min (7, 0) = 0.

The $ACTIM_j$ measure is defined as the longest path from task j to the end of the project. Since there is only one path from task A to the end of the project, $ACTIM_A$ = 5; for task B, where there are two possible paths to the end of the project,

$$ACTIM_B = \max (1 + 4, 5 + 4) = \max (5, 9) = 9$$

The ACTRES measure, proposed by Bedworth (1973), was an attempt to improve the ACTIM measure by including resources. To compute the $ACTRES_j$ measure, we use "worker-weeks" for each task on the path(s) from task j to the end of the project; for task B in this example,

$$ACTRES_B = \max (6 + 28, 40 + 28) = \max (34, 68) = 68$$

The ROT_j measure is similar to ACTRES but uses the ratio of resources over duration for each task on the path(s) from task j to the end of the project. For task B, given that there are two paths (C, E) and (D, E) from task B to the end of the project,

$$ROT_B = \max (6/1 + 7/4, 8/5 + 7/4) = \max (7.75, 3.35) = 7.75$$

Most of these metrics are relatively easy to compute, although most have serious shortcomings. For example, the TRU (total resources utilized) measure simply uses the number of resources required by each task; for example, if a task requires two technicians and one brain surgeon, it would be equally weighted (with a weight equal to three) with a task that requires one technician and two brain surgeons (since resources are not weighted by their relative values). Obviously, the TRU measure could be modified to account for relative weights, but there may be some question about how to account for these weights themselves.

Given these criticisms, researchers have proposed many other measures, most of which are variations or combinations of the simple measures previously indicated (it is been estimated that over one hundred different metrics have been proposed). For example, Whitehouse and Brown (1979) proposed a measure that is a weighted combination of the ACTIM and ACTRES measures; they denoted this measure by $GENRES_j$ and defined it as

$$GENRES_j = w\, ACTIM_j + (1 - w)\, ACTRES_j$$

where $0 \leq w \leq 1$ represents the relative weight on either the ACTIM or ACTRES measures. Similarly, Elsayed (1982, 1984) suggested two other measures utilizing ROT:

- ROT-ACTIM $= (w)\, ROT + (1 - w)\, ACTIM$
- ROT-ACTRES $= (w)\, ROT + (1 - w)\, ACTRES$

where w is once again a weighting factor that varies from 0 to 1.

The table in Figure 8.8 summarizes the calculation of several of these measures for the example in Figure 8.5. Readers should verify the calculation of these measures.

All of these measures (e.g., ACTIM, ACTRES, and ROT) can be normalized to a (0, 1) scale by dividing each measure by the largest respective value. For example, the ROT measures could be normalized by dividing all ROT measures in the ROT column by 7.75, the ACTIM measures could be normalized by dividing by 9, etc. If there are multiple resource types, the metrics can be extended by summing all resource requirements for each task. Because of scale differences, however, it would be prudent to convert all resources to a common measurement scale. Alternatively, managers could treat each resource independently, compute a separate metric for each resource type, and utilize an appropriate scheduling algorithm for each measure. The best solution would be retained for possible implementation.

HEURISTIC ALGORITHMS FOR THE RENEWABLE RESOURCE ALLOCATION PROBLEM

Single-pass heuristics for the renewable resource allocation problem can be classified by how they implement the ranking measures that were previously described. These heuristics proceed in numerous ways, including:

- **Fixed versus dynamic task ordering.** In a fixed ordering, the tasks are ordered prior to the scheduling process; this ordering does not change during the scheduling process. Alternatively, the ranking of tasks can be modified dynamically as the scheduling process proceeds.

- **Scheduling process can be "task-based" versus "time-based."** In a task-based approach (also known as serial heuristics), the tasks are ordered and scheduled sequentially to start as early as resource and precedence constraints will allow. Once all tasks are scheduled, the process stops. Time-based algorithms (also known as parallel heuristics) consider each time

FIGURE 8.8
Calculation of Ranking Measures of Example Problem

Task	TRU: Workers	Duration (weeks)	Total Slack (TSj)	ROT$_j$	ACTIM$_j$	GENRES$_j$ (w = 0.5)
A	3	4	3	7.75	34	19.5
B	5	3	0*	7.75	68	38.5
C	6	1	3	1.75	28	16.0
D	8	5	0*	1.75	28	16.0
E	7	4	0*	0.00	0	0.0

period sequentially; at each time period, project managers define and order the set of tasks whose precedence constraints have been satisfied. From this feasible set, they select as many tasks to start at this time as resource requirements will allow. They then consider the next time period, and continue in this fashion until all tasks have been scheduled.

- **Forward or backward scheduling process.** Project managers generally schedule each task at its earliest starting time and build a feasible schedule from the beginning of the project; however, some algorithms schedule tasks from the end of the project and work backward.

In our discussion, we assume that tasks cannot be split or stopped prematurely once work has started (that is, jobs are "nonpreemptive"). However, project managers should always think about splitting tasks whenever possible and redefining the work breakdown structure (WBS) as described in Chapter 2. It should be noted that most commercial software packages assume that tasks cannot be split or preempted.

We will use the example in Figure 8.5 to illustrate both a task-based and a time-based approach. In both cases, the ACTRES measure is arbitrarily used to order tasks; clearly, the final results could differ if the project manager used a different measure to rank tasks. The manager's goal in both cases is to find the shortest possible project duration that can be achieved with no more than nine workers.

Task-Based Algorithms (Serial Heuristics)

The manager initially places the tasks in lexicographic order, using ACTRES to break ties. A lexicographic ordering is an ordered list of the tasks such that precedence constraints are satisfied for each successive task in the list. For the example in Figure 8.5, the manager starts with tasks A and B since they follow the START milestone; he would rank task B first, since its ACTRES value (68) is greater than $ACTRES_A$ ($ACTRES_A = 34$). Following tasks A and B are tasks C and D; in this case, however, both tasks have the same ACTRES value (28). The manager chooses task C randomly by flipping a fair coin. Thus, the final lexicographic ordering of the five tasks in Figure 8.5 (using the ACTRES measure) is B, A, C, D, E.

The manager then schedules each task in order, scheduling each task to start at its earliest possible time. Clearly, task B can start at the beginning of week 1. Task A can be started at the same time because these tasks can overlap, and use a total of eight workers. Task C (next in the list) can then start at the beginning of week 5 when both tasks A and B are completed. The schedule at this point is represented in Figure 8.9.

According to the precedence constraints, task D could also start at the beginning of week 5 since tasks C and D can theoretically be performed simultaneously. However, task D cannot start until task C is completed, because tasks D and C use a total of fourteen workers; thus, the manager will start task D at the beginning of week 6. Since tasks D and E cannot be performed simultaneously, he cannot start task E until the beginning of week 11 when task D is completed. The manager has thus found a feasible schedule requiring a total of fourteen weeks to complete; this schedule is given in Figure 8.10.

The algorithm can be repeated with a different lexicographic ordering (using a different metric to break ties). Since the process is quite efficient, numerous schedules can be generated and considered by the project manager and project team.

Time-Based Algorithms (Parallel Heuristics)

Alternatively, the project manager can find a feasible schedule using a time-based approach. In this case, she starts at $t = 0$ (beginning of week 1) and places all tasks whose

FIGURE 8.9
Partial Schedule for Task-
Based Heuristic

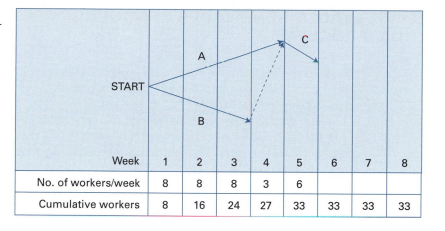

Week	1	2	3	4	5	6	7	8
No. of workers/week	8	8	8	3	6			
Cumulative workers	8	16	24	27	33	33	33	33

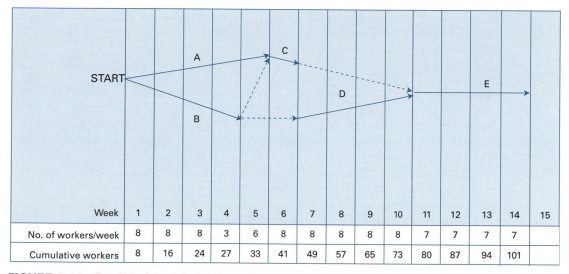

Week	1	2	3	4	5	6	7	8	9	10	11	12	13	14	15
No. of workers/week	8	8	8	3	6	8	8	8	8	8	7	7	7	7	
Cumulative workers	8	16	24	27	33	41	49	57	65	73	80	87	94	101	

FIGURE 8.10   Feasible Schedule for Example Problem

predecessor tasks have been scheduled in a "fit" list. At time $t = 0$, the fit list is set {A, B}. Again, the manager uses some measure to order the tasks in the list and schedule the tasks to start at the beginning of week 1 in that order. In this case, tasks A and B will be scheduled to start at the beginning of week 1. At time $t = 3$ (beginning of week 4), task B is completed; the manager can consider another fit list, which in this case includes only task {D}. Thus, she schedules task D to start at the beginning of week 4. At the beginning of week 5 (when task A is completed), the fit list consists of task {C}; however, this task cannot be started due to resource limitation. When task D is finished (at the end of week 9), she schedules task C for one week, which is then followed by task E.

To summarize the process for a time-based algorithm, a time counter (t) is incremented from $t = 0$ until all tasks are scheduled. For each value of t, the project manager lists those tasks whose predecessor tasks have been scheduled and rank orders these tasks by some metric. She then schedules as many tasks as resources allow, considering each task in order. When no additional tasks can be scheduled from this list, she increments the time counter (t) and repeats the process until all tasks have been scheduled. For the example in Figure 8.5, the resulting schedule would be the same as the schedule given in Figure 8.10, except that task C would be scheduled before task D. The project, however, would require 14 weeks to complete.

AN EASILY SOLVABLE RENEWABLE RESOURCE ALLOCATION PROBLEM

In an interesting example, Fox (1990) presented a problem to illustrate why the concept of a critical path should not be used for project planning. A modified version of his problem is given in Figure 8.11.

As indicated in this problem, there are two crews—the blue crew and the gray crew—and six tasks. Each crew can perform only one task at a time; task durations are known and given in Figure 8.11. The question is, what sequence should the crews use to process their respective tasks?

This example illustrates several important issues relating to resource allocation and project management. First, the critical path is clearly ten days; however, we know that this project cannot be completed in ten days (assuming that no additional crews can be added) since it will take the blue crew at least eleven days just to complete their tasks. However, we frequently use information from the critical path calculations to sequence the tasks. For example, let's assume that the project manager calculates total slacks and decides to use this information to sequence the blue crew's tasks. Ordering tasks in ascending order by total slack results in the following sequence (for the blue crew):

$$A1, B1, C1$$

since $TS_{A1} = 0$, $TS_{B1} = 2$, and $TS_{C1} = 3$. Assuming that the gray crew follows the same sequence, the resultant project schedule is given in Figure 8.12. As indicated, a total of twenty days are required to complete this project. Note that the gray crew has no delays between tasks (once they start working on task A2), but delays could occur if the tasks' durations were different.

It is interesting to note that the solution in Figure 8.12 is the same solution found by Microsoft Project using the "Resource leveling" function (a heuristic for solving the renewable resource allocation problem). Since that function is based on total slack calculations, it is not surprising that the program arrives at the same solution given in Figure 8.12.

Is there another sequence that will result in a shorter project makespan? A careful examination of the problem in Figure 8.11 indicates that the problem occurs because the blue crew effectively blocks the gray crew from starting work until the blue crew has completed at least one task. Thus, it seems reasonable to start the blue crew with their shortest task and in this way minimize the gray crew's delay. If we follow this logic, the project

FIGURE 8.11
Solvable Renewable
Resource Allocation
Example

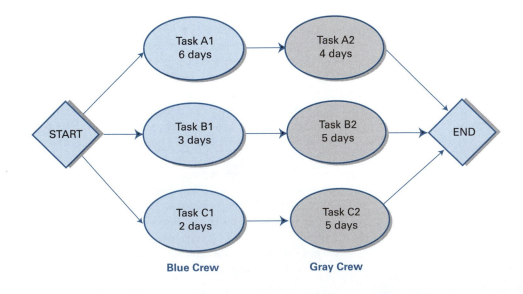

manager would have the blue crew start with task C1 and work on their tasks in the order C1, B1, A1. If the gray crew follows the same sequence (that is, C2, B2, A2), the solution is indicated in Figure 8.13. Note that this sequence results in a reduced project makespan of sixteen days.

Does this reasoning (sequence the blue crew's tasks in ascending order of processing times) always result in a solution that minimizes the project makespan? The general answer is no. However, this problem has a structure that allows us to easily find—and verify—an optimal solution.

The key in this example is to recognize that this problem is closely related to a flow-shop scheduling problem. A flow shop is a group of workstations (e.g., machines, workers) that produce parts, components, or subassemblies where all items produced in this shop must be processed through the workstations in the same order. In this case, we will consider only a flow shop with exactly two workstations, as represented in Figure 8.14. Furthermore, the flow shop is classified as a "static" flow shop—all jobs that must be processed by these workstations are available at the beginning of the processing period; the alternative is a "dynamic" flow shop, where jobs arrive for processing at various times.

To illustrate a static flow-shop problem, we will assume that five jobs must be processed by two workstations; the processing times on each workstation are given in Figure 8.14. The question in this case is how to determine the job processing sequence that will minimize the total time makespan needed to process all five jobs on both workstations.

There are 5! = 5 × 4 × 3 × 2 × 1 = 120 possible job sequences. However, solving this problem in general by complete enumeration quickly becomes intractable (with ten jobs, there are a total of 3,628,800 possible sequences). However, when there are only two workstations, there is a very straightforward method for finding a sequence that will minimize the total processing time needed (for any number of jobs). The procedure, known as Johnson's Rule (Johnson, 1954), is as follows:

1. Find the job-workstation combination with the smallest processing time. If there is a tie, choose one job-workstation combination arbitrarily.

2. If this job-workstation combination occurs on workstation 1, assign the job to the first available place in the sequence.

3. If this job-workstation combination occurs on workstation 2, assign the job to the last available place in the sequence.

4. Cross out this job and repeat the process.

FIGURE 8.12
Project Schedule Using Total Slack to Sequence Tasks

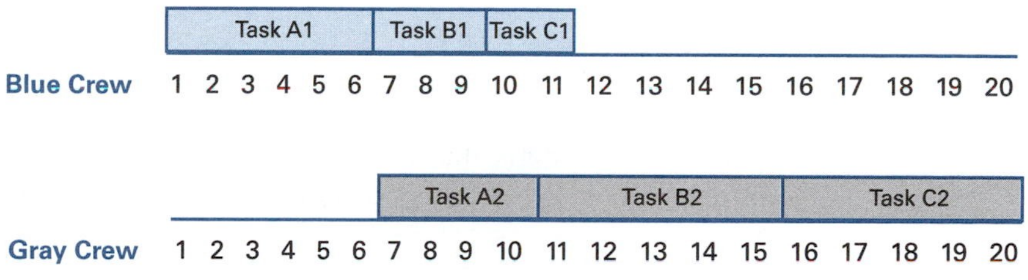

FIGURE 8.13
Project Schedule Following C, B, A Sequence

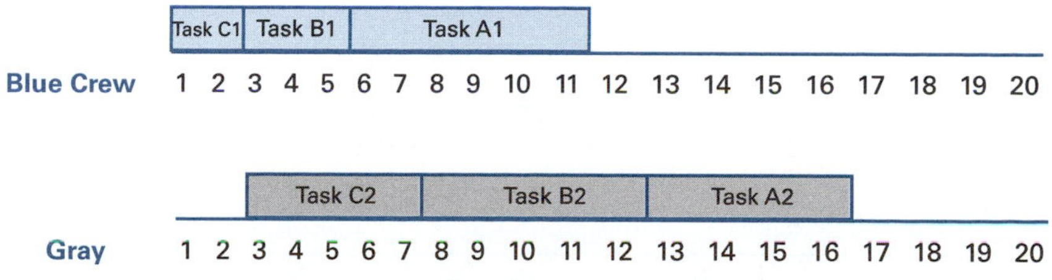

For the example in Figure 8.14, the job-workstation with the smallest processing time would be the (job 4–workstation 1) combination with a processing time equal to 4. Thus, job 4 would be placed first in the sequence and eliminated from further consideration. The next job with the smallest processing time would be the (job 3–workstation 1) combination with a processing time equal to 6. Job 3 would then be placed second in the sequence (since job 4 has already been sequenced first) and eliminated from further consideration. The next job would be the (job 1–workstation 1) combination. From the remaining two jobs (jobs 2 and 5), the smallest processing time is the (job 5–workstation 2) combination. Since this processing time occurred on workstation 2, we would schedule job 5 at the end of the sequence. The only remaining job (job 2) would then be placed in the fourth position. The final sequence would be Jobs (4, 3, 1, 2, 5), resulting in a minimum makespan of 16.

We can now see the relationship between the flow-shop problem and the project scheduling problem proposed by Fox. Each work crew (the gray crew and the blue crew) represents a workstation in the flow shop. The tasks in the project represent three jobs—A, B, and C—that must be processed (in order) at each workstation. Applying Johnson's Rule to the project scheduling problem in Figure 8.11, we see that the smallest processing time is the duration of task C1 (two days); thus, the blue crew is instructed to work on task C1 first. Of the two remaining tasks (A and B), the smallest remaining processing time is three days, that is, the duration of task B1. Thus, the blue crew should start task B when it has completed task C1. The overall sequence is (C, B, A), resulting in a minimum project makespan of 66, as indicated in Figure 8.13.

The relationship between project scheduling problems and job (and flow) shop scheduling problems has been known for many years (see Davis et al., 1999, for a good discussion). Unfortunately, Johnson's Rule holds only for the two-workstation flow-shop problem (and a special case with three workstations). When there are more than three workstations the problem rapidly increases in combinatorial complexity, so that heuristic algorithms are most frequently used. Nevertheless, important insights are possible by recognizing the relationship between flow shop and project scheduling problems. For more information about Johnson's Rule and job and flow-shop scheduling, see Nahamias (1997) or Davis et al. (1999).

RESOURCE ALLOCATION AND THE CRITICAL CHAIN

Recognizing the importance of the resource allocation problem, Goldratt (1997) introduced the concept of a "critical chain" that relates resource dependencies to the concept of a critical path. For example, in the Date Dilemma caselet described at the beginning of this chapter, Jim Gantt's assigned tasks form a chain (since he can perform only one task at a time) that defines the project duration. If Jim is delayed in completing any of his assigned tasks, the project will be delayed and require more than his allotted ninety minutes.

The Date Dilemma illustrates the theory of constraints (TOC) that was originally defined by Goldratt and Cox (1992) for process management and recently applied to

FIGURE 8.14
A Flow Shop with
Two Workstations
and Five Jobs

Job	Work Station #1 Processing Time	Work Station #2 Processing Time
1	10	14
2	13	20
3	6	8
4	4	8
5	19	12

project management by Goldratt (1997), Newbold (1998), and Leach (2000). The theory of constraints, as defined by Leach, contains five steps:

1. Identify the project's constraints.
2. Exploit the project's constraints.
3. Subordinate other decisions to support the constraining resource(s).
4. Improve the constraining resource(s).
5. Repeat steps 1 through 4 for other resources as they become constraining.

According to Goldratt, the goal of project management is to minimize project duration (makespan). To minimize the makespan in the Date Dilemma case, Jim must keep busy at all times since his activities define the minimum project duration of 90 minutes. Thus, Jim's tasks define the critical chain in this case.

To illustrate the concept of the critical chain further, consider the problem in Figure 8.11. This problem can be represented by a precedence network that indicates the optimal sequence and includes resource dependencies as well as precedence relationships; the result is given in Figure 8.15. Note that the critical chain (START-C1-C2-B2-A2-END) representing the optimal task sequence defines the minimum project makespan of sixteen days.

This example can be used to illustrate other concepts relating the application of TOC to project management. Once the critical chain is identified, Goldratt et al. advocate adding buffers to "protect" the tasks on this chain and reduce the likelihood that the project will not be delayed. Two factors can delay the project: either (1) work is delayed and not available for processing at the correct time, or (2) resources (gold or purple crew) are not available at their needed time. For example, if the gold crew takes more than three days to complete task B1, the processing of task B2 may be delayed.

To reduce the likelihood of either event, Newbold et al. recommend adding two types* of buffers to the project:

- **Resource buffers** to ensure resource availability
- **Feeding buffers** to ensure work availability

Resource buffers make certain that resources (e.g., crews) are available when needed; Newbold refers to these buffers as "wake-up calls" to alert the crews that they will be needed soon for a critical task. Resource buffers are added to the precedence network just before a crew starts working on a critical task; in the example in Figure 8.15, a resource buffer would be added before task C1 and before task C2 to alert the blue and gray crews, respectively, that they will soon be needed for critical tasks.

Feeding buffers are added whenever a noncritical task precedes a critical task to ensure that the critical task can proceed without delay. In the example in Figure 8.15, a feeding buffer would be added between task B1 and task B2, and a second feeding buffer would be added between task A1 and task A2. These buffers add time (but do not delay the project) to ensure that tasks B2 and A2 are started promptly at the beginning of day 8 and day 13, respectively. The modified precedence network, showing the feeding and resource buffers, is given in Figure 8.16.

RESOURCE ALLOCATION CAPABILITIES OF COMMERCIAL SOFTWARE PACKAGES

It was previously noted that Microsoft Project, using the built-in resource allocation function, found the suboptimal solution in Figure 8.12 (with a solution of twenty days) for the

---

* Recall that in Chapter 6, "The Theory of Constraints and the Project Buffer," we discussed the concept of a project buffer—the third type of buffer advocated by Newbold.

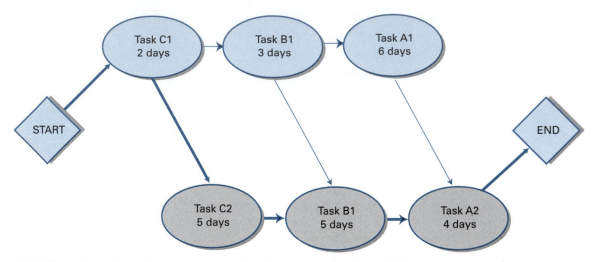

FIGURE 8.15   Critical Chain Represented for the Example in Figure 8.11

problem in Figure 8.11. How well do commercial software packages perform on renewable resource allocation problems in general? To answer this question, Kolisch (1999) tested seven commercial PM software packages on a series of randomly generated renewable resource allocation problems and compared their solutions to known optimal solutions.

Kolisch's analysis was performed on 160 randomly generated test problems that varied the number of tasks (10, 20, or 30), the number of resource types (2, 3, or 4), the complexity of the precedence network, the average number of resource types used by each task, and the proportion of resource demand and availability. Consistent with our discussion, he assumed that all tasks were nonpreemptive and task durations were deterministic. The criterion for evaluating each software package was project makespan.

For each problem, Kolisch found the optimal solution using the branch and bound algorithm developed by Demeulemeester and Herroelen (1992) and then solved each problem using seven different commercial software packages. Letting π_p^* denote the optimal makespan for test problem p, he defined

$$\pi_{ps} = \frac{\pi_{ps} - \pi_p^*}{\pi_p^*}$$

as the metric to evaluate each commercial software package, where π_{ps} is the makespan found by software package s for test problem p. The seven commercial software packages and Kolisch's results are given in Figure 8.17. The value of refers to the average of the π_{ps} values (percent deviation from the optimal solution) over all 160 test problems.

Kolisch reports that the seven commercial software packages found the optimal solution in 45 percent of the projects tested. Furthermore, he reported that the performance deteriorates as the number of tasks and the number of constrained resources increases, but performance improves as the number of precedence relationships increase. Based on a number of parametric and nonparametric statistical tests, Kolisch concluded that these commercial packages can be classified into four groups with respect to their ability to solve a renewable resource allocation problem; in the first class, he included Primavera Project Planner, CA Super-Project, and Time Line; in the second class, he included Time Line, Project Scheduler, and Microsoft Project (Time Line overlapped the first and second classes). Project Manager Workbench and Artemis Schedule Publisher, which he felt performed poorly overall, defined the third and fourth classes, respectively.

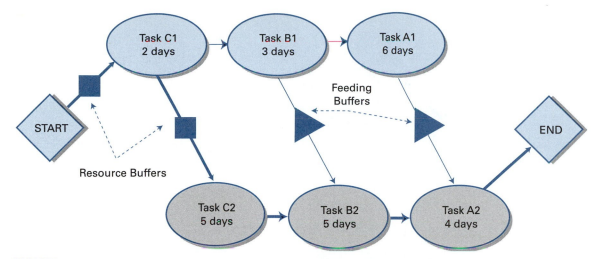

FIGURE 8.16 Modified Precedence Network with Resource and Feeding Buffers

FIGURE 8.17
Evaluation of
Commercial Software
Packages

Commercial Software Package	π_s	Std dev (π_s)
Artemis Schudule Publisher V4.1	4.39	6.04
C.A. Super-Project V3.0C	4.41	6.02
Microsoft Project V4.0	4.49	5.09
Primavera Project Planner V1.0	5.35	6.53
Project Manager Workbench V.1.1.02w	5.43	7.98
Project Scheduler 6.0 V1.02	6.69	8.60
Time Line V6.0.0	9.76	9.82

NONRENEWABLE RESOURCE ALLOCATION PROBLEMS

Nonrenewable resources refer to those resources that have a limit on *total* usage but no limit on utilization rate. For example, the project in Figure 8.5 required a total of 101 worker-weeks; however, there was no way that the manager could allocate more than nine workers *per week* to the project (without hiring more workers, of course). In this section we consider resources that have no limits on the rate at which they can be utilized, although there is a limit on total utilization (consider dollars as an example).

To motivate our discussion, consider the example project in Figure 8.18 with four tasks. Each task needs a specified number of units of some nonrenewable resource; these requirements are summarized in the table in Figure 8.19. We assume that a task cannot be started until all required units of the resource are available; that is, task B cannot be started until twelve resource units are available.

Resources are shipped to the project according to a specified schedule; these schedules are typically negotiated before the start of the project. In this example, we will assume that 4 units of resource are delivered to the project at the beginning of time periods 1, 3, 5, 7, …, 19—representing a total of ten deliveries and forty units. Note that the total resource requirement for the project is thirty-six units.

According to the critical path, the project (ignoring resource constraints) should take 13 weeks to complete (critical path is START-A-B-D-END). However, given the resource delivery schedule and resource requirements, can the project be completed in thirteen weeks? And, if not, what is the minimum time needed to complete the project (that is, minimize project makespan)?

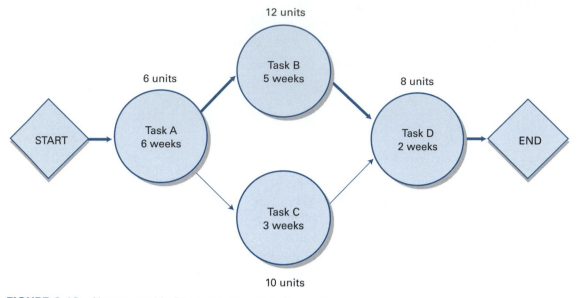

12 units

6 units

8 units

10 units

FIGURE 8.18 Nonrenewable Resource Allocation Example

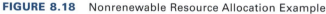

FIGURE 8.19
Summary Information
for Figure 8.16 Example

Task	Duration	No. of Nonrenewable Resources Units Needed	Early Start	Late Start
A	6	6	0	0
B	5	12	6	6
C	3	10	6	8
D	2	8	11	11

Since we are assuming in this case that task durations are deterministic, all tasks can be started at their latest starting times without delaying the project beyond thirteen weeks. In this way, we allow the maximum time for the resources to be delivered before having to start a task. If all tasks are scheduled to start at their latest starting times, the dotted line on the graph in Figure 8.20 indicates the cumulative resource requirements needed to finish the project in thirteen weeks. The other line on this graph indicates the cumulative resource availability (that is, 4 units delivered at times 1, 3, …).

Examining the graphs in Figure 8.20, we see that for the project to be completed in thirteen weeks with no resource delay, the cumulative graph indicating resource supply (continuous line) can never lie below the dotted line indicating resource requirements. This observation comes directly from the assumption that there must be sufficient units of the resource on hand before a task can be started. Thus, it is evident that project/task A cannot be started until the beginning of week 3 at the earliest, since there will not be sufficient resources (six units) until that time.

This observation leads directly to a solution procedure for this problem that can be easily implemented graphically. In this case, we must shift the dotted line indicating resource requirements to the right until all parts of the dotted line lie on or below the line indicating cumulative resources supplied. Shifting the dotted line is equivalent to delaying the start (and completion) of the project. By making the smallest shift needed to move the dotted line on or below the line of cumulative resource supplies, we minimize

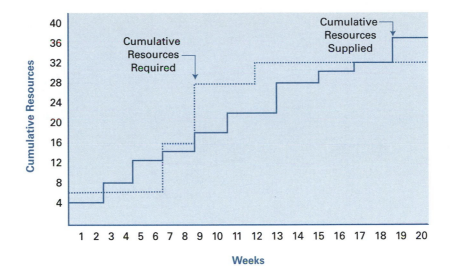

FIGURE 8.20
Cumulative Resource
Availability and
Requirements

the project delay subject to the resource constraints (as proved by Carlier and Rinnooy Kan, 1982). In this example, the minimum project delay is equal to six weeks; this optimal solution is indicated in Figure 8.21.

This example illustrates several points. First, it indicates that many nonrenewable resource allocation problems are relatively easy to solve optimally—compared to renewable resource allocation problems, which are mostly difficult to solve optimally. Second, it implies that if renewable resources are treated as nonrenewable, the solution technique for nonrenewable resources may be used to find a good (but not necessarily optimal) solution to the renewable resource problem, or to better understand a renewable resource allocation problem and possible solutions. (This was the nature of Baker's procedure, described earlier, to find the lower bound on project makespan and/or resource utilization; it effectively treats renewable resources as nonrenewable resources.)

For nonrenewable resources, can the solution process illustrated in Figure 8.21 be extended to handle additional (and more realistic) considerations? For example, what happens if due dates are imposed on some (or all) of the tasks? To illustrate, assume that task B in Figure 8.18 must be completed by the end of week 14. Can the solution procedure be modified to accommodate this constraint and still find an optimal solution efficiently?

If task B must be completed by the end of week 14, it must be started no later than the beginning of week 10 (since the duration of task B is five weeks). The solution process begins in the exact way that we solved the previous problem (with no due dates); that is, we draw the cumulative resource availability curve and the cumulative resource requirement curve and shift the resource requirement curve to the right. If we encounter a due date for some task, we schedule that task so that it will be completed at its due date (in our example, we would start task B at the beginning of week 10). We then remove this task from the problem; that is, we reduce both the supply and demand of resources by twelve units (e.g., the first resource "shipment" now occurs at the beginning of week 7) and continue to solve the problem using the previously described procedure. Assuming a feasible solution exists, this process will find the minimum project makespan.

Carlier and Rinnooy Kan (1982) showed that this process can be modified to efficiently accommodate numerous other extensions (for example, if the manager wants to minimize total task lateness where lateness is defined by the completion time minus the due date). However, if the tasks become available at different release dates or if the tasks produce resource units (instead of consuming resource units), the problem becomes NP-hard for

FIGURE 8.21
Solution for
Nonrenewable
Resource Example

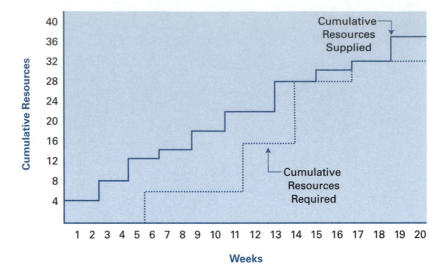

which no known efficient algorithm is known. NP-hard refers to a large class of problems for which a polynomial algorithm is highly unlikely. It is interesting to note that most problems that arise in the context of managing nonrenewable resources in projects fall into the former categories and can be solved quite efficiently.

RESOURCE ALLOCATION PROBLEMS WITH RANDOM TASK DURATIONS

Our discussion to this point has assumed that task durations are known and constant. What happens to resource allocation problems when task times are treated as random variables?

To motivate our discussion, consider the following problem. A manager has a project with four tasks: A, B, C, and D; as indicated in Figure 8.22, task A must precede task B and task C must precede task D. The manager has two workers, Bob and Barb, whom she wishes to assign to these tasks; Bob and Barb are cross-trained so that either worker can perform any task with equal effectiveness. The task durations (for a single worker) are discrete random variables that are described by the information in the table in Figure 8.22.

The manager can assign Bob and Barb to work together as a project team; in this case, they will be able to complete each task in one-half the time that it would take a single worker (since there are two workers). That is, the manager assumes that if Bob and Barb are assigned to task B as a team, the task would take them 9/2 = 4.5 weeks with probability 0.667 or 3 weeks with probability 0.333 (with an expected value of four weeks).

If Bob and Barb are assigned to work on all the tasks as a team, they would perform the tasks sequentially; clearly, the order would not matter as long as the precedence constraints were satisfied. On the other hand, the project manager could assign one worker to each task; for example, she could assign Bob to work on tasks A and C and Barb to work on tasks B and D. While it is likely that each task would take longer (at least the expected durations are greater), Bob and Barb would be able to perform their respective tasks simultaneously. While other assignment configurations are possible (e.g., the worker who finishes their assigned tasks first then assists the other worker), we will consider only these two configurations.

If Bob and Barb work as a team on all four tasks, their expected completion time is merely the sum of the expected task durations. Since the manager has assumed that they can complete the work in half the time needed by an individual worker, their expected completion time is fifteen weeks (30/2 weeks).

FIGURE 8.22

Resource Allocation with Random Task Durations

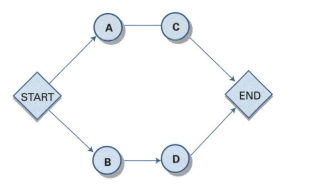

Task A		Task B		Task C		Task D	
Duration	**Prob**	**Duration**	**Prob**	**Duration**	**Prob**	**Duration**	**Prob**
6	0.33	9	0.667	12	0.6	10	0.25
5	0.33	6	0.333	7	0.4	6	0.75
4	0.33						
Expected duration	5.0				10.0		7.0

If Bob performs tasks A and C and Barb performs tasks B and D, however, the manager might think that the expected completion time is also fifteen weeks since the expected duration of both paths (START-A-C-END and START-B-D-END) is both fifteen weeks. Since task durations are described by discrete probability distributions, she can test this assumption by enumerating all possible outcomes. Since the duration of task A can take three values (four, five, or six weeks) and the durations of tasks B, C, and D can take two values, there are a total of $3 \times 2 \times 2 \times 2 = 24$ possible "realizations." These twenty-four realizations are given in Figure 8.23. For each realization, the manager can calculate the duration of each path (START-A-C-END and START-B-D-END) and the duration of the project that is the larger of the two path values. Assuming independence among the tasks, the probability of each realization is the product of the respective probabilities (for example, the probability of realization 1 that A = 6 weeks, B = 9 weeks, C = 12 weeks, and D = 10 weeks is $0.33 \times 0.67 \times 0.60 \times 0.25 = 0.033$).

An examination of the spreadsheet in Figure 8.23 indicates that several realizations result in the same project duration, their values ranging from twelve weeks to nineteen weeks. By combining these realizations (and summing probabilities for realizations with the same project durations), the manager gets the spreadsheet in Figure 8.24.

Given this probability distribution (with seven realizations), let d_i denote the project duration for each i realization, and then calculate the expected project duration E[D] using the usual definition of an expected value for a discrete probability distribution:

$$E[D] = \sum_{i-1}^{7} d_i \Pr(D = d_i) = 12(0.07) + 13(0.03) + \ldots + 19(.17) = 16.42$$

Having Bob and Barb work individually (even though they are working on tasks simultaneously), the expected project duration is increased to over sixteen weeks. Furthermore, the cumulative probability distribution in Figure 8.24 indicates a 50 percent

FIGURE 8.23

Realizations for Bob-Barb Example Problem

Realization #	A	B	C	D	A + C	B + D	max (A + C, B + D)	Prob
1	6	9	12	10	18	19	19	0.03
2	6	9	12	6	18	15	18	0.10
3	6	9	7	10	13	19	19	0.02
4	6	9	7	6	13	15	15	0.07
5	6	6	12	10	18	16	18	0.02
6	6	6	12	6	18	12	18	0.05
7	6	6	7	10	13	16	16	0.01
8	6	6	7	6	13	12	13	0.03
9	5	9	12	10	17	19	19	0.03
10	5	9	12	6	17	15	17	0.10
11	5	9	7	10	12	19	19	0.02
12	5	9	7	6	12	15	15	0.07
13	5	6	12	10	17	16	17	0.02
14	5	6	12	6	17	12	17	0.05
15	5	6	7	10	12	16	16	0.01
16	5	6	7	6	12	12	12	0.03
17	4	9	12	10	16	19	19	0.03
18	4	9	12	6	16	15	16	0.10
19	4	9	7	10	11	19	19	0.02
20	4	9	7	6	11	15	15	0.07
21	4	6	12	10	16	16	16	0.02
22	4	6	12	6	16	12	16	0.05
23	4	6	7	10	11	16	16	0.01
24	4	6	7	6	11	12	12	0.03

FIGURE 8.24

Probability Distribution for Project Durations when Bob and Barb Work Independently

max (A + C, B + D)	Prob	Cumulative Prob
12	0.07	0.07
13	0.03	0.10
15	0.20	0.30
16	0.20	0.50
17	0.17	0.67
18	0.17	0.83
19	0.17	1.00

probability that the project will take as long as sixteen weeks. Why is the expected project duration of this configuration (with Bob and Barb working individually) significantly longer than the configuration when Bob and Barb work as a team, even though they are working at the same speed?

We can use the simple example in Figure 8.25 to explain this phenomenon. In this case there are two tasks A and B that can be done in parallel; the durations of both tasks are described by the same probability distribution (durations of six or ten weeks with equal probabilities). The expected duration of each task is 8.0.

In this example, there are four realizations that are equally likely, as indicated in the spreadsheet in Figure 8.26.

Since the project is not completed until both tasks are finished, the project duration is equal to the *maximum* duration of tasks A and B that is given in the column labeled "Max (A,

FIGURE 8.25
Parallel Tasks with
Random Distributions

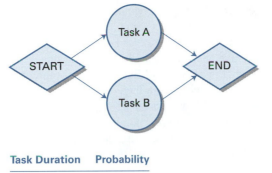

Task Duration	Probability
6	0.5
10	0.5

FIGURE 8.26
Four Realizations of
Simple Example

Realization	Task A Duration	Task B Duration	Max (A, B)	Probability
1	6	6	6	0.25
2	10	6	10	0.25
3	6	10	10	0.25
4	10	10	10	0.25

B).” Although for each task there is an equally likely chance that its duration will be six weeks or ten weeks, for the project there is only a 25 percent chance that the project duration will equal 6 weeks and a 75 percent chance that it will equal 10 weeks. Thus, the expected project duration is 9 weeks—not 8 weeks, which we might think if it were assumed that task durations are deterministic and estimated by their expected values. Stated algebraically,

$$E[Max(A, B)] \geq max \ \{E[A], E[B]\}$$

which implies that a project with parallel tasks and random durations will always have an expected duration that is greater than any task's expected duration (the equality holds only for deterministic task times).

Furthermore, what would happen if there were three tasks (say, tasks A, B, and C) in parallel instead of two? Assuming that all three tasks have the same discrete probability distribution indicated in Figure 8.23 (that is, they can take either six weeks or ten weeks with equal likelihood), what is the new value of $E[Max(A, B, C)]$? We should verify that the expected project duration now increases to 9.50 (by enumerating all eight realizations in this case). In fact, we can show that the expected project duration is monotonically non-decreasing as more tasks are placed in parallel. This is an important factoid: Even though each task has the same distribution and the same expected value, the expected project duration *increases* as more tasks are performed in parallel. This concept was further explored in Chapter 6, "Task Variation and Expected Project Duration."

Returning to the Bob and Barb example, we now understand why having Bob and Barb work individually on simultaneous tasks will, on the average, take longer than having them work as a team—at least as long as we assume that they can complete the work in half the time when working as a team. However, what happens if we relax this assumption?

The manager knows that the project will take an average of 16.42 weeks if Bob and Barb work individually. Now let's say that their efficiency when working as a team is given by variable α; that is, if Bob and Barb work as a team on task j, they can complete the task in time αt_j, where t_j is the time required by an individual to complete the task. (In our previous example, we assumed that α was equal to 0.5.)

The manager can now find the value of α where she would be indifferent between having Bob and Barb work as a team and having them work individually. If they work as a team, they will take $(30\ \alpha)$ expected weeks to complete the project; if they work individually, they will take an average of 16.42 weeks. Thus, letting $30\ \alpha = 16.42$ implies that $\alpha = 54.7$ percent; that is, if Bob and Barb cannot complete a task in less than 55 percent of the time needed by an individual, then they should not be assigned as a team.

The implications of this discussion are critical for resource allocation problems as well as project planning problems. Given a number of tasks that can be performed simultaneously and assuming that a project team can complete a task in time that is proportional to the team size (that is, $\alpha \leq 1/N$, where there are N team members), it would appear prudent to assign these tasks to a project team and have these tasks performed sequentially. Although many other factors must be considered when making resource allocation decisions, a project manager would be wise to remember the effects of parallel paths and statistical variations.

CONCLUSIONS

In this chapter, we explored the issues of resource leveling and resource allocation in both deterministic and stochastic projects. Several major points were emphasized in this chapter:

- The resource allocation problem is one of the fundamental problems faced by project managers and is generally a most difficult problem even when we assume task durations are known and deterministic.

- The resource allocation problem is directly related to the concept of a critical chain that was defined by Goldratt and others.

- The nature of the resource allocation problem changes significantly when we explicitly recognize that task durations are random (for example, the expected duration of a project generally increases as we perform more tasks in parallel).

STUDY PROBLEMS

1. At periodic intervals, the Acme Bank has its lighting and ventilation system thoroughly overhauled. Since this process causes some disruption in bank operations, the bank's managers want the overhaul to proceed in an orderly and efficient manner. To facilitate the project planning, the Acme managers have broken the project into specific tasks. These tasks, along with their immediate predecessors and estimated duration times for fast and slow workers, respectively, are indicated in the following table.

Task	Predecessor	Fast Time (Days)	Slow Time (Days)
A. Check electrical panels and circuits	—	1.5	3
B. Replace all light bulbs	—	4	7
C. Clean and service compressor in air conditioner	A	2	4
D. Test and service heater	A	3	5
E. Refill oil tanks	—	0.5	5
F. Clean and service electro-static filter	C, D	1	3
G. Clean and service blower unit	C, D	2	4

For each task, Acme managers can hire one of two possible contractors to perform the task. For each task, a less expensive contractor can be hired who charges $20 per day but works at the slow rate, or a more expensive contractor can be hired at \$50 per day who works at the fast rate. Because tasks A and B both require the services of an electrical contractor, Acme managers have required that the same contractor perform both tasks A and B. Also, the cost of filling the oil tanks is not a function of the time required; the cost is strictly a function of the number of gallons of oil needed (estimated currently at 15,000 gallons @ \$1.75/gallon). Acme Bank has hired you to manage this project; they have stated that they want the project completed at the lowest possible cost, but that the project must be completed within nine days in order to minimize disruption. Determine which contractors should be hired; what is the estimated total cost for the overhaul? When should each contractor begin work?

2. The managers of the Frigid Midget Widget (FMW) Company, makers of small frozen widgets, have listed the tasks that must be completed to assemble one midget frigid widget (see following table). The managers must decide how large a crew to assign to each task; the size of the crew will determine the duration of the task (generally, there is an inverse relationship between crew size and job duration). Each job can be assigned a crew of minimum size, normal size, or maximum size; no other choices are possible for technological reasons. In addition, union regulations require that an assigned crew cannot be changed for the duration of the task (e.g., they cannot assign a normal size crew for the first two days of a task and then increase the crew size for the remaining duration of the task). Task durations are merely equal to the total number of worker-days divided by the crew size assigned to the task. For example, if a normal crew is assigned to task (1, 2), then that task will require eight days to complete. The FMW Company has a contract to produce one frigid widget every twenty-four days. Assuming that all workers can perform all tasks, determine how the production tasks should be scheduled in order to minimize the workforce needed (hiring and firing costs are very high in this industry).

Task (i, j)	Total Worker-Days	Minimum	Normal	Maximum
(1, 2)	32	2	4	8
(1, 3)	48	4	6	8
(2, 3)	40	4	5	8
(2, 4)	12	2	3	4
(4, 5)	30	3	5	6
(3, 5)	54	3	6	9
(5, 6)	24	3	4	6

3. A print shop has the following jobs available at 7 A.M.:

	Processing Times	
Job	Machine 1	Machine 2
A	3	1
B	4	3
C	1	4

All jobs in the print shop must first be processed on machine 1 and then on machine 2. The shop stays open until all jobs are completed, and no other jobs arrive during the day. Processing times are given in hours.

a. Show how the processing of the three jobs is equivalent to a project by drawing an appropriate precedence network. Calculate the total slack associated with each job.

b. If the print shop manager sequences the jobs using slack (that is, the job with the smallest slack has the highest priority), what is the project duration? Is there another sequence that will reduce the project duration? Is this the minimum project duration? Explain your reasoning.

c. What is the critical resource in this problem? Why?

REFERENCES

Baker, K. *Introduction to Sequencing and Scheduling.* New York: Wiley, 1974.

Bedworth, D. D. *Industrial Systems: Planning, Analysis, Control.* New York: Ronald Press, 1973.

Brucker, P., A. Drexl, R. Mohring, K. Neumann, and E. Pesch, "Resource-Constrained Project Scheduling: Notation, Classification, Models, and Methods." *European Journal of Operational Research* 112, no. 1 (1999): 3–41.

Carlier, J., and A. H. G. Rinnooy Kan. "Scheduling Subject to Nonrenewable Resource Constraints." *Operations Research Letters* 1, no. 2 (April 1982): 52–55.

Davis, E. W. "Resource Allocation in Project Network Models—A Survey." *Journal of Industrial Engineering* 17 (1961): 1,777.

Davis, M., N. Aquilano, and R. B. Chase. *Fundamentals of Operations Management.* Burr Ridge, Ill.: Irwin McGraw-Hill, 1999.

Demeulemeester, E. L., and W. S. Herroelen. "A Branch and Bound Procedure for the Multiple Resource-Constrained Project Scheduling Problem." *Management Science* 38 (1992): 1803–18.

Demeulemeester, E. L., and W. S. Herroelen. *Project Scheduling: A Research Handbook.* Norwell, Mass.: Kluwer Academic Publishers, 2002.

Elsayed, E. A. "Algorithms for Project Scheduling with Resource Constraints." *International Journal of Production Research* 20, no. 1 (1982): 95–103.

Elsayed, E. A. "Heuristics for Resource-Constrained Scheduling." *International Journal of Production Research* 24, no. 2 (1984): 299–310.

Fox, R. E. *The OPTionnaire: Can You Win at Managing the Production Game?* Milford, Conn.: Creative Output, 1990.

Goldratt, E. M. *Critical Chain.* Great Barrington, Mass.: North River Press, 1997.

Goldratt, E. M., and J. Cox. *The Goal: A Process for Ongoing Improvement.* Great Barrington, Mass.: North River Press, 1992.

Herroelen. W. S., B. De Reyck, and E. L. Demeulemeester. "Resource-Constrained Project Scheduling: A Survey of Recent Developments." *Computers and Operations Research* 25 (1998): 279–302.

Johnson, S. M. "Optimal Two and Three Stage Production Schedules with Setup Times Included." *Naval Research Logistics Quarterly* 1 (1954): 61–68.

Kolisch. R. "Resource Allocation Capabilities of Commercial Project Management Software Packages." *Interfaces* 29, no. 4 (July–August 1999): 19–31.

Leach, L. *Critical Chain Project Management.* Norwood, Mass.: Artech House, 2000.

LeBlanc, L., D. Randels, and T. K. Swann. "Herry International's Spreadsheet Optimization Model for Assigning Managers to Construction Projects." *Interfaces* 30, no. 6 (November–December 2000): 95–106.

Nahamias, S. *Production and Operations Analysis.* 3d ed. Chicago: Irwin, 1997.

Newbold, R. C. *Project Management in the Fast Lane: Applying the Theory of Constraints.* Boca Raton, Fla.: St. Lucie Press, 1998.

Ozdamar, L., and G. Ulusoy. "A Survey on the Resource-Constrained Project Scheduling Problem." *IIE Transactions* 27 (1995): 574–86.

Sprecher, A., and A. Drexl. "Note: On Semi-Active Timetabling in Resource-Constrained Project Scheduling." *Management Science* 45, no. 3 (March 1999): 452–54.

Talbot, B. "Resource Constrained Project Scheduling with Time-Resource Trade-offs: The Nonpreemptive Case." *Management Science* 28, no. 10 (1982): 1,197–1,210.

Talbot, B., and J. Patterson. "An Efficient Integer Programming Algorithm with Network Cuts for Solving Resource-Constrained Scheduling Problems." *Management Science* 23, no. 11 (July 1978): 1,163–74.

Whitehouse, G. E., and J. Brown. "GENRES: An Extension of Brooks' Algorithm for Project Scheduling with Resource Constraints." *International Journal of Computers and Industrial Engineering* 3 (1979): 261.

MONITORING AND CONTROL

> It is of the highest importance in the art of detection to be able to recognize, out of a number of acts, which are incidental and which are vital. Otherwise your energy and attention must be dissipated instead of being concentrated.
>
> *Sherlock Holmes*

Once a project has started, project managers must monitor every ongoing project in order to concentrate their energies (in the words of Sherlock Holmes) on identifying those tasks that are truly "out of control" and require corrective actions. To do so, managers must answer four basic questions:

- What is the best method(s) to monitor an ongoing project?
- When is a task "out of control," requiring active managerial intervention?
- If a task is deemed to be out of control, what action(s) should be taken?
- Who should be responsible for the control of a project?

Clearly, there is no single best answer to these questions. As we discussed in the first chapter, all projects are not the same; a monitoring and control system should be appropriate for the complexity and scope of the project. Projects with a high degree of complexity may require more formal review systems while projects with less complexity and scope (e.g., construction projects) may need only informal review systems.

Nevertheless, we will discuss some of the more commonly used monitoring and control systems as well as the trade-offs faced by managers who adopt these systems. In general, we can characterize monitoring and control systems as either **informal** systems or **formal** systems. Informal systems include meetings, e-mail, and just walking around. Formal systems include accounting and other periodic status reports, scheduled milestone meetings, internal audits, client reviews, and external benchmarks. The costs associated with informal systems may be lower than the costs associated with formal systems although significant costs are generally associated with both systems (e.g., considerable time and effort can be spent in meetings, e-mail, etc.). Typically, we use a combination of both informal and formal systems; however, the basic questions with either system are similar: what performance metrics to use, how often reviews should occur, etc. We discuss these issues in more detail in the next section.

DESIGNING AN EFFECTIVE MONITORING SYSTEM

Three basic questions are involved in designing an effective project monitoring and control system:

- How should reviews be conducted?
- How often should reviews occur?
- What performance metrics should be used?

With respect to the issue of appropriate performance metrics, we have the following questions to resolve. What data should be collected? How should these data be collected? From what sources? How often should these data be collected? How should trends in these data be analyzed?

To illustrate these issues further, consider the following example. A project manager has a task that is expected to take four weeks and requires a total of 1,600 worker-hours. At the end of the first week, she finds that 420 worker-hours have been spent on this task. Is this task out of control, needing some corrective action, or should the manager assume the task is proceeding normally and take no action?

Let's assume that she takes no action, and work progresses into the second week. At the end of the second week, the manager finds that a total of 880 worker-hours have been "spent" on this task (that is, 460 worker-hours in the second week). Should she take any actions at this time?

Again, let's assume the project manager decides that the extra worker-hours represent "normal" fluctuations, and the task proceeds into the third week. At the end of the third week, a total of 1,380 worker-hours have been spent. The spreadsheet and graph showing weekly worker-hours used are given in Figure 9.1.

If you are familiar with the concepts of statistical process control (SPC) used in many manufacturing environments, you will recognize that the project control problem is similar to the manufacturing control problem. In both cases it is assumed that the managers know a performance metric as well as the metric's distribution, including the mean and variance. At each review period, the null hypothesis is tested to see if the process has moved to an out-of-control state (in which case some corrective action is needed) or if it remains in control (and no corrective action is needed).

To illustrate how such a process works in our project control example, assume that worker-hours expenditures are constant each week at 400 worker-hours (the project manager's estimate of 1,600 total worker-hours for the task divided by the expected four-week duration). Also assume that weekly expenditures follow a normal distribution. Thus, we would expect that the worker-hour expenditures are normally distributed as indicated for week 3 in Figure 9.1. Knowing the variance of worker-hours, the manager can then compute

FIGURE 9.1
Control System Example

Week	Planned Cost (Worker-Hours)	Actual Cost (Worker-Hours)	Cumulative Cost (Worker-Hours)
1	400	420	420
2	400	460	880
3	400	500	1380

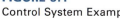

a *z*-score and calculate the likelihood that 500 worker-hours would be used in one week. If this probability is less than some accepted confidence limit, she would accept the null hypothesis and assume that the task has gone into an out-of-control state and take some corrective action(s).

There are several problems with applying this approach to a project control problem. First, it assumes that we know the variance of weekly expenditures. Typically, this information is estimated from a sample of previous performances; however, project tasks are by definition unique, and data on previous performance may not be available. If a manager has sufficient previous experience with similar tasks (such that he can estimate the distribution and parameters associated with resource expenditures), then he may be able to employ SPC methods to test if a task requires some corrective action(s).

Another problem with this approach, however, is our estimate of the expected weekly worker-hours. Recall that the project manager had estimated that this task would take four weeks and require a total of 1,600 worker-hours; her estimate of 400 worker-hours per week is simply based on the assumption that worker-hour expenditures would be equal each week. However, there is no reason why this should be true; in fact, expenditures for many tasks vary during the life of the task in the same way that resource expenditures vary during the course of a project. If tasks are defined with relatively short durations, however, this problem is minimized (another reason for defining more tasks with shorter durations).

The most important problem, however, is that the manager is missing one major piece of the control puzzle; namely, she does not know how much work has been actually accomplished on this task throughout the three-week period. For example, let's assume that only 120 worker-hours are needed in the fourth week to complete the task. In this case, the task is completed on time (in four weeks) with a total expenditure of 1,500 worker-hours—100 worker-hours less than originally estimated.

EARNED VALUE APPROACH

The earned value approach evolved from the earlier PERT/Cost approach that was described in the influential 1962 document, *DoD and NASA Guide, PERT Cost Systems Design*. The PERT/Cost system was based on the principal that costs should be measured and controlled on a project basis rather than according to the functional organization of the firm. The earned value approach is an extension of PERT/Cost.

The earned value approach is based on the observation that three basic building blocks are needed to construct an effective control system. As illustrated by the previous example, we must have values for all three metrics in order to accurately determine the status of all tasks (and the project) at any point in time. At any given point in time, we must know:

- Actual expenditures to date
- Expected expenditures forecast by the project plan
- Amount of work accomplished to date

These three metrics have well-defined terms and acronyms that are generally defined by most commercial project management (PM) software programs. Values for these metrics are usually reported for a defined time period (e.g., weekly) as well as cumulative values since the start of the task or project. These acronyms and terms are defined as follows.

- **Actual cost of work performed (ACWP).** The actual costs or expenditures charged to the task (or project) during a given period. Costs can be measured in monetary units (e.g., dollars, euros, yen), worker-hours, or any other consistent measurement unit. The value of ACWP for week 3 in the example in Figure 9.1

is 500 worker-hours; the cumulative value of ACWP for the three-week period (weeks 1, 2, and 3) is 1,380 worker-hours.

■ **Budgeted cost of work scheduled (BCWS).** The amount that the project manager planned to spend on this task each week, as determined in the project planning process. In the Figure 9.1 example, the manager estimated that the task would require a total of 1,600 worker-hours and four weeks; using a simple assumption that costs will be equal each week, she estimated the value of BCWS to equal 400 worker-hours each week. BCWS is also known as the **planned value.**

■ **Budgeted cost of work performed (BCWP).** The actual value of the work accomplished during the period in question. Clearly, this is the most difficult value to estimate since it requires the manager to estimate the proportion of work completed during each period. BCWP is also known as the **earned value.**

Estimating the percentage of work completed (to calculate BCWP) can be a difficult task itself. To get reasonably reliable estimates, it is usually necessary to have an independent and knowledgeable assessor evaluate the work completed to date; sometimes, estimating BCWP is as simple as counting the number of items produced. However, complex tasks such as programming software can be extremely difficult to estimate (most simple measures, such as the number of lines of code, are inadequate). In this case, project managers sometimes use fixed rules for estimating the values of BCWP.

Fixed rules used to estimate BCWP generally take the form:

X% Completed at the start of a task
$(1 - X)$% Completed at the end of a task

For example, if we set $X = 10$, this implies that we assume that 10 percent of the task is completed immediately after the start of the task; but we don't credit the remaining 90 percent until the task is completely finished. The value of X can vary from zero to one (e.g., a value of $X = 0$ implies that no credit for BCWP is given until the entire task is completed). These rules are easy to apply since no inspection is needed, and they can work well when tasks are clearly defined and relatively short. Typical values of X are 0, 25, and 50 percent; but in theory, any value of X can be used.

Cumulative values for ACWP, BCWS, and BCWP for the example in Figure 9.1 are indicated in Figure 9.2; calculations for BCWP are based on the assumption that it is possible to estimate the percentage of work completed at the end of each week. Note that the values of BCWP are found by multiplying the percentage of work completed times 1,600 worker-hours (the total estimated cost of the task). To find the relative values for each week, the manager simply subtracts the cumulative values from the previous week; for example, in the third week, a total amount of work equal to (1,360 − 800 = 560 worker-hours) was completed.

Examining the table in Figure 9.2 indicates that comparisons among these three metrics can be used to evaluate task progress; for example, a comparison between the work

FIGURE 9.2
Cumulative Performance Metrics for the Example in Figure 9.1

Week	BCWS (Worker-Hours)	ACWP (Worker-Hours)	Percent of Work Completed (Cumulative)	BCWP (Worker-Hours)
1	400	420	23%	368
2	800	880	50%	800
3	1,200	1,380	85%	1,360
4	1,600	1,500	100%	1,600

completed and actual expenditures, or a comparison between the work completed and the amount of planned work. These two comparisons, or variances, define the basis of the earned value system and are defined as follows:

$$\begin{aligned}
\text{Schedule Variance (SV)} &= \text{(Value completed)} - \text{(Value scheduled to be completed)} \\
&= \text{Earned value} - \text{Planned value} \\
&= \text{BCWP} - \text{BCWS}
\end{aligned}$$

$$\begin{aligned}
\text{Cost Variance (CV)} &= \text{(Value completed)} - \text{(Actual expenditures)} \\
&= \text{Earned value} - \text{Actual expenditures} \\
&= \text{BCWP} - \text{ACWP}
\end{aligned}$$

The schedule variance (SV) at the end of week 1 is $368 - 400 = -32$ worker-hours; since the SV is negative, it indicates that the task is behind its planned progress. Likewise, the cost variance, CV (also known as the **spending variance**), at the end of week 1 is negative ($368 - 420 = -52$ worker-hours), indicating that expenditures exceeded work completed (at least during the first week).

The schedule variance and cost variance are absolute measures; that is, the schedule variance at the end of the first week indicates that the task is behind its planned progress by 32 worker-hours. But is 32 worker-hours a significant difference? If the total planned expenditure for the task were, say, 5,000 worker-hours, a variance of 32 worker-hours is most likely insignificant. On the other hand, if the total planned expenditure for the task were 100 worker-hours, a variance of 32 worker-hours would warrant immediate concern.

To avoid this problem, we can use two relative measures, the **schedule index (SI)** and the **cost index (CI),** which are defined as follows:

$$\text{Schedule Index (SI)} = \frac{\text{BCWP}}{\text{BCWS}}$$
$$\text{Cost Index (CI)} = \frac{\text{BCWP}}{\text{ACWP}}$$

The following rules associated with these indices then apply:

If SI = 1, the task is on schedule.
If SI > 1, the task is ahead of schedule.
If SI < 1, the task if behind schedule.

If CI = 1, the task is on budget.
If CI > 1, expenditures are better than expected.
If CI < 1, there are cost overruns.

The values of the schedule variance, cost variance, schedule index, and cost index for the example in Figure 9.2 are given in the table in Figure 9.3.

As indicated in Figure 9.3, all four metrics indicated that the task was proceeding behind schedule and over budget at the end of the first week. By the end of the second week, the work completed equaled the work that had been scheduled; however, the task

FIGURE 9.3
Schedule Variance, Cost Variance, Schedule Index, and Cost Index for Example in Figure 9.1 and 9.2

Week	Schedule Variance (SV)	Cost Variance (CV)	Schedule Index (SI)	Cost Index (CI)
1	−32	−52	0.92	0.88
2	0	−80	1.00	0.91
3	160	−20	1.13	0.99
4	0	100	1.00	1.07

was still over budget. By the end of the fourth week, this task appears to be on schedule and under cost expectations.

Frequently, a graph of the schedule and cost indices is helpful to indicate trends. Note that the example task remained over budget until its completion at the end of week 4. However, a graph of the cost index indicates that the cost performance consistently improved during the four-week course of the task; a graph of the schedule and cost indices is given in Figure 9.4.

Two other variances are sometimes used in addition to the schedule and cost variances: **total variance** and **time variance.** The total variance is defined as the difference between the cost variance and the schedule variance; that is,

$$\text{Total Variance} = \text{Cost Variance} - \text{Schedule Variance}$$
$$= (\text{BCWP} - \text{ACWP}) - (\text{BCWP} - \text{BCWS})$$
$$= \text{BCWS} - \text{ACWP}$$

The total variance is the difference between the planned value and the actual cost. The time variance is best described using the example in Figures 9.1 through 9.4. At the end of week 3, 85 percent of the work on the example task has been completed, which is equivalent to 1,360 worker-hours. Based on the project manager's original plan, at what time did she plan to complete 1,360 worker-hours of work?

Since it was assumed in the planning process that work would proceed uniformly during the four-week life of this task, the manager would expect to complete 85 percent of the work in $(0.85) \times (4 \text{ weeks}) = 3.4 \text{ weeks}$. The time variance is defined as the difference between the planned time (3.4 weeks) and the actual time (3 weeks) to accomplish a given amount of work. Thus, at the end of week 3, the time variance is $3.4 - 3 = 0.4$ weeks. Since the value of the time variance is positive, it indicates that the work is proceeding ahead of schedule in this example.

Earned Value Approach: Example 2

To illustrate the Earned Value approach further, consider the Gantt chart in Figure 9.5. The project represented by this Gantt chart consists of three tasks; note that the planned values for two tasks (A and C) are expected to vary during the course of the tasks. The weekly scheduled worker-hours and cumulative scheduled worker-hours are given in the row at the bottom of the Gantt chart. The total cumulative scheduled worker-hours (128 worker-hours) is known as the **budget at completion (BAC).**

Assume that the project team has now worked on this project for five weeks. At the end of each week, the manager has scheduled a review meeting and estimated the percent-

FIGURE 9.4
Graph of Schedule and Cost Indices over Time

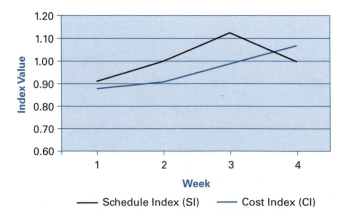

FIGURE 9.5
Earned Value Approach:
Example 2

Week										
1	2	3	4	5	6	7	8	9	10

Task A (36 worker-hours)
| 6 | 6 | 6 | 8 | 10 |

Task B (36 worker-hours)
| 12 | 12 | 12 |

Task C (56 worker-hours)
| 10 | 10 | 12 | 12 | 12 |

	1	2	3	4	5	6	7	8	9	10
Weekly Scheduled Worker-Hours	6	6	6	20	22	22	10	12	12	12
Cumulative Scheduled Worker-Hours (BCWS)	6	12	18	38	60	82	92	104	116	128

age of work completed on each task; these values are given in Figure 9.6. The actual number of worker-hours charged to each task was also reported weekly; these values are given in the table in Figure 9.7.

Based on these reports, the project manager can compute the three performance metrics: BCWS, ACWP, and BCWP. Note that his calculations of BCWP are based on the assumption that resources were used at a uniform rate; that is, he assumes that a 30 percent completion of Task A corresponds to (0.3×36 worker-hours =) 10.8 worker-hours based on his initial plan that Task A would require 36 worker-hours. Conversely, he could assume that the work completed was proportional in time; in this case, he would assume that 30 percent completion of Task A corresponds to (0.3×5 weeks =) 1.5 weeks worth of work.

Based on these progress reports, the manager can find the three performance metrics as well as the schedule variance, cost variance, schedule index, and cost index that are given in Figure 9.8. As indicated, the actual costs exceed the planned values for every week after the first week (the cost variance in week 1 is positive), indicating that the project has exceeded its budget after the first week. Similarly, the schedule variances are negative for the entire five-week period, indicating that the project is falling behind its planned task completion rate. The graph of the three performance metrics, ACWP, BCWS, and BCWP, can help visualize trends. In this example, it appears that the work completed is behind schedule; but this variance is not getting worse, while the cost overruns appear to be increasing over time (although these increases are not monotonic).

FIGURE 9.6
Cumulative Percentage
of Work Completed at
End of Week

Week	1	2	3	4	5
Task A	15%	30%	40%	60%	80%
Task B				25%	65%
Task C		Not started yet			

FIGURE 9.7
Actual Worker-hours
Charged to Project Tasks

Week	1	2	3	4	5
Task A	5	6	8	10	10
Task B				15	10
Task C		Not started yet			

FIGURE 9.8
Performance Metrics and
Control Chart for
Example 2

	Week									
	1	**2**	**3**	**4**	**5**	**6**	**7**	**8**	**9**	**10**
Cumulative Scheduled Worker-Hours (BCWS)	6	12	18	38	60	82	92	104	116	128
Actual Worker-Hours Used (ACWP)	5	11	19	44	64					
Earned Value (BCWP)	5.4	10.8	14.4	30.6	52.2					
Schedule Variance (SV)	−0.6	−1.2	−3.6	−7.4	−7.8					
Cost Variance (CV)	0.4	−0.2	−4.6	−13.4	−11.8					

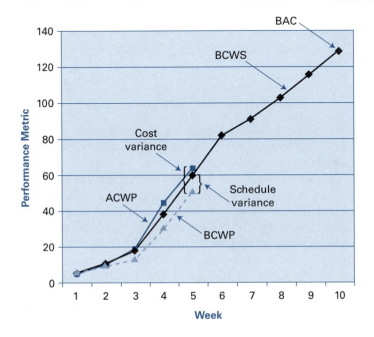

We can use this example to illustrate the difference if the project manager used a fixed rule to calculate BCWP instead of an estimated percentage of work completed. Arbitrarily, let's say that he used a 20/80 rule; that is, he assumes that 20 percent of the work associated with each task is completed at the task's onset but that the remaining 80 percent is not completed until the task is finished. Using the 20/80 rule, (0.20 × 36 worker-hours =) 7.2 worker-hours are completed on Task A by the end of the first week, and an additional (0.20 × 36 worker-hours =) 7.2 worker-hours have been completed on Task B by the end of week 4 (note that no task has been completed by the end of week 5). Using the 20/80 fixed rule, the estimate of BCWP (and ACWP and BCWS) is given in Figure 9.9.

As indicated in Figure 9.9, it appears that the project has more serious problems at the end of week 5 than when the manager estimated the percentage of work completed in Figure 9.8. This is not surprising, since he is now assuming that only 20 percent of the work in Tasks A and B have been completed through five weeks of project work. This example illustrates that managers must be cautious in interpreting the results when these fixed rules are employed. Also note that the same fixed rule does not have to be applied to all tasks. In some cases, different fixed allocation rules are applied to categories of tasks (e.g., a project manager might use a 0/100 rule for critical tasks but a 25/75 rule for non-critical tasks).

FIGURE 9.9
Example 2 Using the
20/80 Fixed Rule to
Estimate BCWP

	Week									
	1	**2**	**3**	**4**	**5**	**6**	**7**	**8**	**9**	**10**
Cumulative Scheduled Worker-Hours (BCWS)	6	12	18	38	60	82	92	104	116	128
Actual Worker-Hours Used (ACWP)	5	11	19	44	64					
Earned Value (BCWP)	7.2	7.2	7.2	14.4	14.4					
Schedule Variance (SV)	1.2	−4.8	−10.8	−23.6	−45.6					
Cost Variance (CV)	2.2	−3.8	−11.8	−29.6	−49.6					

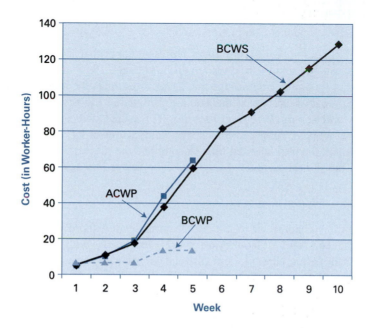

UPDATING COST AND SCHEDULE ESTIMATES

At any point in time, project managers should be able to use available information to update their cost and schedule estimates. Consider the example in Figure 9.8. At the end of week 5, the manager estimates that Task A is 85 percent completed, Task B is 65 percent complete, and Task C has not yet been started. Based on these estimates, work worth 52.2 worker-hours is completed at the end of week 5. Since the manager has forecast a total work content (BAC) of 128 worker-hours, there are $128 - 52.2 = 75.8$ worker-hours remaining on the project.

To date (end of week 5), a total of 64 worker-hours (actual cost) has been used to complete these 52.2 worker-hours worth of work. Thus, the ratio ACWP/BCWP gives the cost per worker-hour completed; that is, the cost per worker-hour completed is $64/52.2 = 1.226$ worker-hours. Since this ratio is greater than one, the manager is paying more per worker-hour than he is getting completed (at least through the first five weeks of this project).

If we assume that this ratio will hold throughout the remainder of the project (a somewhat pessimistic view perhaps), then the manager's forecasted cost of this project must be revised and would be equal to $1.226 \times BAC = 1.226 \times 128$ worker-hours $= 156.9$ worker-hours. This value represents the updated project cost and is known as the **estimate at completion (EAC).** Note that

$$\text{Estimate at Completion (EAC)} = \left(\frac{\text{ACWP}}{\text{BCWP}}\right)\text{BAC} = \left(\frac{1}{\text{CI}}\right)\text{BAC}$$

There are, of course, other assumptions that can be made regarding updated forecasts. For example, the manager can be more optimistic and assume that the problems he has encountered through week 5 will be corrected. In this case, he assumes that the cost overrun that he has encountered through week 5 (that is equal to CV = BCWP – ACWP = –11.8 worker-hours) is a one-time event, and corrections in managing this project will ensure that no further cost overruns will occur. Thus, a second and more optimistic forecast of the EAC is defined by the manager's original cost estimate (BAC) plus the cost overrun experienced to date (CV); in this case,

Estimate at Completion (EAC) = BAC – CV = 128 + 11.8 = 139.8 worker hours

These two EAC estimates represent the probable range of updated completion costs; it is likely that the true value will lie between 139.8 and 156.9 worker-hours.

In similar fashion, the manager can estimate the updated completion time. Under his original assumptions, the manager estimated the project would require a total of 128 worker-hours (BAC) and 10 weeks. This corresponds to 128/10 weeks = 12.8 worker-hours per week. Assume he believes that the final total cost (EAC) will equal 156.9 worker-hours. Then, the total updated time to complete the project would be 156.9/12.8 = 12.26 weeks. Thus, he can expect the project will be delayed by 2.26 weeks over his original estimate.

CONCLUSIONS

In this chapter, we discussed the earned value approach and several related metrics that can be useful for monitoring project progress. As with any metric, managers must use this information carefully and filter all information through their own experience and judgment. For example, there are many reasons why a project might have a negative schedule or cost variance and *not* be "out of control"; some of these reasons include:

- Incorrect estimates in the baseline (planned value)
- Changes in labor rates or charges
- Materials purchased before starting a task(s)
- Changes in the design or scope of the project

In many organizations that use an earned value approach, arbitrary limits are frequently implemented to signal when the status of a task must be carefully reviewed (e.g., a 10 percent cost overrun or schedule delay). In this way, managers know how to focus their energies to keep a project on schedule and budget.

You should also note that the earned value approach is part of a larger system that was originally developed by the U.S. Department of Defense to provide a uniform set of guidelines for primary contractors and subcontractors. The basic idea behind this set of guidelines, known as the Cost/Schedule Control Systems Criteria or C/SCSC, was to give different contractors and subcontractors a common set of thirty-five standards for budgeting, planning, accounting, and controlling projects. In this way, all contractors involved in a project would be able to communicate with each other while retaining individual information systems. For more information about these criteria and guidelines, see Shtub et al., 1994.

While questions have been raised about the applicability and interpretation of these standards since they were issued in 1967 (Fleming and Koppelman, 1994), the earned value approach, as a central part of the C/SCSC, has been implemented and applied successfully in many types of organizations. More information about C/SCSC is available from the Project Management Institute (PMI).

STUDY PROBLEMS

1.   **a.**   Find the schedule variance for a project that has an actual cost at month 22 of $540,000, a scheduled cost of $523,000, and an earned value of $535,000.

    b.   A project at month 5 had an actual cost of $34,000, a planned cost of $42,000, and a value completed of $39,000. Find the schedule and cost variances.

    c.   A project at day 70 exhibits an actual cost of $78,000, a scheduled cost of $84,000, and a value completed of $81,000. Find the schedule and cost indices.

2.   Consider the information about a project plan in the following table.

Task	Immediate Predecessor	Duration	Scheduled Cost/Day
A	—	3	$1,000
B	—	5	$2,000
C	A	4	$4,000
D	B	7	$1,000
E	C	6	$2,000
F	D	8	$3,000

The following table shows the weekly control reports for the first two weeks (assume 5 working days each week).

	End of Week 1		End of Week 2	
Task	Actual % Completed	Cumulative Actual Cost	Actual % Completed	Cumulative Actual Cost
A	60%	$1,500	100%	$ 2,900
B	30%	$3,000	100%	$11,000
C	10%	$2,000	100%	$13,500
D	0%	$ 0	90%	$10,000
E	0%	$ 0	50%	$ 4,000
F	0%	$ 0	0%	$ 0

    a.   Use the earned value approach to calculate BCWP, BCWS, ACWP, SV, CV, SI, and CI for each task and the whole project.

    b.   Calculate the total variance and time variance for the project at the end of week 2.

    c.   Use the original estimate approach and the revised estimate approach to respectively estimate the final cost of this project at the end of week 1.

    d.   Use the original estimate approach and the revised estimate approach to respectively estimate the final cost of this project at the end of week 2.

3.   A manufacturer of communication systems currently overhauls its computerized payroll system. Instead of using LOC (lines of code) to track the effort on developing such a payroll system, the manufacturer adopts a more reliable method, function point analysis, for measuring/monitoring the progress of the project.

    The new payroll system consists of eight modules, each with a certain amount of function points. From the manufacturer's experience, each function point takes one week to develop. The ongoing project is evaluated at the end of the eighth week after its start. The schedule/cost report is provided in the following table. (Assume linearity of cost vs. function point in each module.)

Comment on the status of the project at the end of week 8 based on the calculation of the project BCWP, BCWS, and ACWP. Is the project "in control"?; if not, why not?

Module	Immediate Predecessors	Function Points	Budget (K)	Completed Function Point	Money Spent (K)
A	—	4	$90	4	$110
B	A	3	$65	3	$ 35
C	A	6	$75	2	$ 40
D	B	3	$60	3	$ 75
E	C	8	$55	1	$ 20
F	C	2	$40	1	$ 10
G	D, E	5	$80	0	$ 0
H	F	7	$90	0	$ 0

4. Sandy Point is the project manager of a small project that consists of seven tasks. After careful and extensive planning, Sandy and her project staff agreed on a proposed project schedule that is indicated by the following Gantt chart:

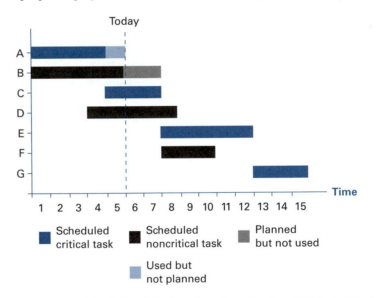

As indicated in their original project plan, Sandy and her staff had estimated the following durations and (total) direct costs for each task:

Task	Duration (weeks)	Planned Value
A	4	$2,000
B	7	$2,800
C	3	$1,150
D	5	$ 625
E	5	$1,350
F	3	$1,050
G	3	$ 270

This morning (beginning of week 6), Sandy received a progress report; as indicated in the Gantt chart, task C could not be started until this week due to the unexpected delay in completing task A. The report also indicates that task B has been completed two weeks earlier than expected. Information from the progress report is summarized in the following table.

Task	Current Status	Actual Expenditures to Date	Percent of Work Completed
A	Completed	$2,000	100%
B	Completed	$2,800	100%
C	Just started	$ 0	0%
D	In progress	$ 330	55%
E	Not started	$ 0	0%
F	Not started	$ 0	0%
G	Not started	$ 0	0%

a. As of today (beginning of week 6), what is the cost variance of the project? What is the schedule variance of the project?

b. Based on information provided to date, what is your assessment of the current status of the project?

5. Consider the information in problem 4. If you use a fixed 30/70 formula to compute the value of the work completed (BCWP) instead of relying on progress reports to estimate the percent of work completed, what is the value of the cost index for the project at the beginning of week 6? What is the schedule index for the project? Does this change your view of the project progress to date?

REFERENCES

Fleming, Q. W., and J. M. Koppelman. "The 'Earned Value' Concept: Back to the Basics." *PM Network,* January 1994.

Shtub, A., J. Bard, and S. Globerson. *Project Management: Engineering, Technology, and Implementation.* Prentice-Hall, Englewood Cliffs, N.J., 1994.

CHAPTER 10

MANAGING MULTIPLE PROJECTS

Few, if any, organizations manage a single project at a time. As we discussed at the beginning of this book, most organizations maintain a portfolio of projects in order to maximize resource utilization and diversify (and minimize) organizational risk. Since resources are typically shared among projects, decision making in a multiproject environment is far more complex than the case when only a single project is being managed. In this chapter, we discuss issues relating to the management of multiple projects and show how some of the complex trade-offs involved can be made.

Most project management (PM) software products are not designed to accommodate multiple projects. Some project managers will use these software products for multiple projects by adding "super-start" and "super-end" nodes that link all projects together into a single giant activity-on-node (AON) precedence network. As we will discuss in this chapter, this naïve approach is rarely helpful.

Managing multiple projects requires that projects be prioritized—by the organization as well as by the individual workers involved. In this chapter, we will discuss how these priorities can be determined as well as the negative impacts when inappropriate priorities are adopted. To illustrate these trade-offs, we look at a simple game (the K&B Clip Game) that can be used to illustrate some important issues relating to managing multiple projects. The K&B Clip Game is described in the following section; PowerPoint slides that correspond to this game are given on the CD-ROM accompanying this text.

Finally, we consider what happens when organizations face multiple projects that arrive at various times. In some cases (e.g., auto repair shops, hair salons), managers can schedule arrivals to reduce some of the arrival variation; but in many other cases, projects arrive randomly at times that are outside direct managerial control (e.g., arrivals to emergency clinics, orders for new cars, etc.).

When projects arrive at random times (whether scheduled or not), managers must decide how long each project will take (when will your car be ready?) in addition to deciding how many resources (e.g., number of hair stylists, auto mechanics, nurses, etc.) to allocate to each project. Clearly, hiring more auto mechanics will reduce the expected project makespan for each auto repair "project" but will also increase the cost of running the shop. In this chapter, we will discuss this trade-off as well as methods for setting due dates and resource levels. Finally, we examine a case study (Pete Moss: Tax Accountant) that illustrates the problems and issues associated with the random arrival of new projects.

MULTITASKING WITH MULTIPLE PROJECTS

To illustrate some of the problems and trade-offs that must be faced when managing multiple projects, we will consider a simple example. Assume that an organization has two projects denote as Project A and Project B; each project requires T time periods to complete. Both projects require the completion of four tasks that have the same expected duration (equal to $0.25T$). Both projects A and B can start at the same time. To simplify our discussion further, we will assume that the same project team must complete all four tasks in each project sequentially.

The project team faces a number of choices, depending on how they prioritize the two projects. In one case, they can weight the projects equally and multitask so that progress on both projects is approximately equal; that is, they would work on tasks A-1, B-1, A-2, B-2, etc. until both projects are completed. This approach is also referred to as a *gated* approach. On the other end of the weighting spectrum, the project team could weight one project (say, Project A) much higher than the other project and work only on that project until it is completed, and then turn their attention to the second project, B. Assuming there is no cost associated with switching between tasks or projects, these two alternative schedules are indicated in Figure 10.1.

Note that the total time needed to complete both projects in Figure 10.1 is approximately the same ($2T$ time periods) whether the project team multitasks or not. When the project team multitasks, project A is completed at time $1.75T$ while project B is completed at time $2T$. When projects are prioritized, however, Project A is completed at time T while Project B is completed at time $2T$.

Assuming that the organization is paid only when a project is completed, one advantage of prioritizing projects is evident—the organization gets paid for Project A at time T (no multitasking) instead of having to wait until time $1.75T$ (multitasking). In both cases, the organization will be paid for Project B at time $2T$. Thus, the firm increases its profits by getting paid sooner while incurring no additional cost.

If there is a changeover cost of switching from one project to the other, the advantage of prioritizing projects is increased. In this case, the firm's profits are even greater when completing Project A before starting work on Project B.

K&B Clip Game

Does the advantage of prioritizing projects still hold when task durations are random? What happens if precedence networks are more realistic (i.e., not all tasks must be performed sequentially)? What are the implications of prioritizing projects when different types of workers must be used? These issues are explored in the K&B Clip Game, which is described in PowerPoint slides in the CD-ROM accompanying this text.

In this game, three projects must be completed: the Red, Blue, and White projects. All three projects are identical; each project requires that three types of clips (standard clips, pretzel clips, and binder clips, which are represented in Figure 10.2) that are mixed in a single bowl be sorted into separate bowls of the same color (that is, the 90 mixed clips in

FIGURE 10.1
Multitasking versus a
Gated (Priority) Approach

FIGURE 10.2
Clip Types Used in
K&B Game

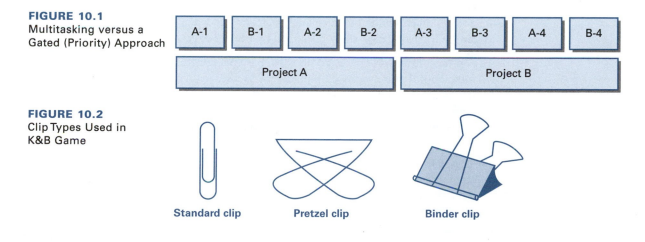

the red bowl must be sorted by type into three separate red bowls, the 90 mixed clips in the blue bowl must be sorted by type into three separate blue bowls, etc.). In this example game there are 30 clips of each type, but any number of clips can be used. The rules for completing each project are as follows:

- One only person (clip specialist) can sort each clip type.
- Only one clip can be sorted at a time (and only one hand can be used).
- The standard clip must be completely sorted before the other two clip types can be sorted.
- A timekeeper tracks the time required to complete each project as well as the total for all three projects.

Two runs are performed as part of this game; they correspond to the multitasking and prioritization strategies indicated in Figure 10.1. In the first (multitasking) run, each worker can sort a maximum of five clips before moving to another project; that is, the standard clip specialist would sort five clips in the Red project and then move to the Blue project. After sorting five standard clips in the Blue project, she can move back to the Red project or move to the White project. Each sorting specialist can perform no more than five clip sorts on a project before moving to another project (unless no other project is available). In this run, each specialist multitasks among the three projects until all three projects are completed.

In the second run, the sorting specialists use a gated or priority approach by focusing on the Red project first and sorting as many clips as possible (the five-clip limit is removed). When the standard clip specialist has completed sorting all standard clips on the Red project, he moves to the Blue project. When he has completed sorting standard clips on the Blue project, he then moves to the White project. The other sorting specialists follow a similar pattern.

In each run, a timing specialist keeps track of the starting and ending times of each project so that project flowtimes can be compared. After completing both runs, you should consider how the two runs differed in their project completion times, project work in process, team member efficiency, and the utilization of team members. Which of these metrics are more important than others in project environments? And what implications does this game have for real-world projects?

PROJECT TEAMS AND INCENTIVES

Should project teams be given special incentives if they achieve certain project goals? Clearly, this is perhaps the most effective way of prioritizing projects in a multiproject environment, but it is controversial in practice since such incentives can cause project teams to cut corners and fail to adequately perform needed tasks. To illustrate these risks, consider the following case study described by Riek (2001):

> A project team was charged with expanding manufacturing capacity and international presence by building a new facility in an offshore site. Because the faculty is capital intensive, the project team was incented to complete construction with capital costs below budget. The project team was comprised of construction and process engineers as this effort was considered to be a straightforward duplication of existing technology.
>
> The plant was constructed with significant capital reduction, and the project team was given hefty incentive awards as promised. However, subsequent plant operations were nothing short of a major disaster. An acidic material was now present throughout the process, and the construction material revisions

were not appropriate. Accordingly, within the first three months of operation, most piping and some major process vessels had significant corrosion. After review of what it would take to remedy the problem, the plant was shut down, written off, and dismantled.

Riek's case study illustrates the trade-offs among the four dimensions given in Figure 1.4 (Chapter 1): cost, budget, design/scope, and quality. When priorities are set so high on a subset of these dimensions (in this case, cost and schedule), the other dimensions are likely to suffer. When incentives are used to set priorities, a good project monitoring and control system is essential to ensure that quality and design goals are not compromised.

A second issue that frequently arises when direct incentives are offered in specific projects relates to project compression (discussed in Chapter 5). If a project team has been offered incentives that relate to specific milestones, it may be difficult to change these incentives and/or due dates if management decides that the project schedule should be changed. Conversely, incentives may make it more difficult to interrupt or terminate a project (for example, when a competitor has brought out a superior product unexpectedly).

ALLOCATING RESOURCES AND SETTING DUE DATES IN A DYNAMIC MULTIPROJECT ENVIRONMENT

In a unique experiment, Dumond and Mabert (1988) investigated a number of scheduling heuristics and due-date-setting rules in a simulated multiproject environment when projects arrive randomly. In their simulated setting, projects contained between 6 and 49 tasks (the mean number of tasks was 24) and arrived randomly during a 2,000-day simulated period. The average project interarrival time was 8 days; the average project critical path was 31.4 days (the range was from 8 to 78 days). The structures (i.e., precedence network) of these randomly generated projects were selected from projects that had been used in prior research studies. Each task could use up to three resource types; resource requirements were set so that the average resource utilization was around 85 percent.

Dumond and Mabert compared the effectiveness of resource allocation and due-date-setting heuristics in two environments:

- **Complete control environment.** When managers can set the due date for all arriving projects.

- **Partial control environment.** When a proportion of projects arrive with a preset due date (e.g., by sales personnel or market requirements).

Dumond and Mabert analyzed five scheduling rules to prioritize the tasks that are available at any given time (by precedence constraints). Priority values were recalculated each time a new project arrived. The five scheduling heuristics considered by Dumond and Mabert were as follows:

1. **First in system, first served.** The task that has been waiting the longest receives the highest priority (ties were broken randomly).

2. **Shortest task from shortest project.** Task priority is calculated by the sum of the task duration plus the project's critical path.

3. **Minimum slack based on the due date.** Task priority is based on the initial due date that is set when the project arrives minus the task's early starting time.

4. **Minimum late finish time based on the due date.** Task priority is the minimum of the latest finish times based on either the initial due date that is set when the project arrives, or the computed latest finish time.

5. **Minimum task duration from the shortest remaining project.** Task priority is the minimum of the priority values computed by rules 2 and 3 (if the priority value from rule 3 is negative).

When projects arrive with no predetermined due dates, Dumond and Mabert studied four heuristics to set due dates. The four heuristics were based on rules that the authors observed in practice as well as rules that had been studied in the job shop scheduling literature. The four heuristics used to set due dates were

1. **Mean flow due-date rule.** The due date is the arrival time of the project plus the historical average time needed to complete a project.

2. **Number of activities rule.** The due date is the arrival time of the project plus some constant (representing the expected task duration) times the number of tasks in the project.

3. **Critical path rule.** The due date is the arrival time of the project plus some constant (representing a delay factor) times the length of the critical path.

4. **Scheduled finish time due-date rule.** The due date is set using one of the scheduling heuristics to schedule the project assuming no new projects arrive and then adjusting this due date by a delay factor.

To compare the effectiveness of resource allocation and due-date-setting heuristics, Dumond and Mabert collected data on four criteria:

■ Mean project completion time

■ Mean project lateness

■ Standard deviation of mean project lateness

■ Total tardiness over all projects and time periods

In the complete control environment (where project managers set the due dates of all arriving projects), the authors found no significant difference across all scheduling heuristics and due-date rules at a 0.05 significance level (using the Scheffe multiple range test) for mean project completion time and mean project lateness. With respect to variance in project lateness, however, the authors found that scheduling rule (2) and due-date rule (1) performed significantly worse than the other rules (at a 0.01 significance level), while due-date rule (4) performed significantly better. With respect to the total tardiness criterion, the authors found that due-date rule (4) also performed better than the other rules.

In the partial control environment, Dumond and Mabert assumed that project managers can set the due dates for "normal" projects but not for high-priority projects (where due dates were set equal to the critical path) and low-priority projects (where due dates were set equal to three times the critical path). The authors tested the cases when 10, 20, 30, 40, 50, and 60 percent of the projects fell into the normal category. As expected, they found that overall performance deteriorated when managers cannot set all due dates. Using due-date-setting rules (3) and (4), Dumond and Mabert found that scheduling rule (4) performed consistently better for all (but one) sizes of normal categories with respect to average completion time. With respect to mean lateness, they found that mean lateness decreased monotonically as the proportion of projects with externally set due dates increased (for either due-date rule).

Another interesting finding in this study was the performance of the combination of scheduling rule (1) and due-date-setting rule (4). The scheduling rule that schedules the task that has been waiting the longest does not consider due dates and therefore avoids (according to Dumond and Mabert) some of the "nervousness" associated with due-date-based heuristics. This combination of heuristics appeared to perform significantly better when the proportion of externally set due dates for "normal" projects was less than 40 percent (at least for total tardiness).

CONCLUSIONS

The structure of an organization has a greater impact on project outcomes in a multiproject environment than in a single-project environment. If project managers are relatively autonomous (e.g., a project matrix organization), projects are more likely to be equally weighted, and workers are likely to multitask as a result. On the other hand, when a single manager controls all projects, projects are more likely to be prioritized and resources are likely to be better utilized.

A portfolio project manager can consider the trade-offs among all active projects and prioritize those that have the largest payoff to the organization. A portfolio manager is also a critical part of monitoring and controlling all ongoing projects, so that the organization can track projects that are delayed as well as those that are completed earlier than expected. As work on projects proceeds and outside factors change, project priorities can be reassessed and project teams reassigned. This increased flexibility can result in an overall improvement to all projects.

REFERENCES

Dumond, J., and V. Mabert. "Evaluating Project Scheduling and Due Date Assignment Procedures: An Experimental Analysis," *Management Science* 343, no. 1 (January 1988): 101–118.
Riek, R. F. "From Experience: Capturing Hard-Won NPD Lessons in Checklists," *Product Innovation Management* 18 (2001): 301–313.

APPENDIX 10A. PETE MOSS: TAX ACCOUNTANT

Peter Moss is a local accountant who specializes in tax preparation for individuals and small businesses. As expected, Pete finds that demand for his services increases significantly after January 1 and continues at a more or less constant rate until April 15 (i.e., the tax preparation season). Being a good accountant and manager, Pete is concerned about his tax preparation process and wonders if he should make some changes in order to increase his profits during the tax preparation season.

Pete has noticed that most of his clients require approximately the same time to prepare their tax returns. Given this observation, Pete charges his clients a fixed fee ($550) for each return. While some returns require more time than others, Pete estimates that his $550 fee represents the price that H&R Block would charge to prepare an average return done by Pete. In addition, he has found that a fixed fee results in more satisfied customers since they know the cost "up front" and are never surprised by any unexpected charges.

Given his billing scheme, Pete knows that he can increase his profits by reducing his costs, assuming that he can still provide quality service to his clients. At this time, Pete has two junior accountants who assist him with clients' tax preparation. Each junior accountant is contracted and paid for forty hours per week (whether they are working on a tax return or sitting idle) at a cost of $20 per hour (fully burdened). Pete can also hire junior accountants on an overtime basis for more than forty hours per week; for overtime, they are paid $30 per hour (although Pete limits the amount of overtime to a maximum of ten hours per week). Overtime decisions, by the way, must be made at the beginning of each week so junior accountants can make appropriate plans.

Pete does not pay himself a salary; instead, he keeps any residual profits as income. In addition, he refuses to work more than forty hours per week due to his busy social life;

however, he is willing to work long days if necessary (that is, Pete does not necessarily work only eight hours per day). While he could perform some (or all) of the tasks normally assigned to a junior accountant, Pete has a policy of never doing any of these tasks.

Most of Pete's tax returns require a similar process that consists of seven individual tasks, which have been labeled as {A, B, C, D, E, F, G}. Some of these tasks cannot be done until predecessors are competed; for example, data cannot be input into the computer until it has been organized and reviewed by a junior accountant. Since clients typically bring their data with them to the initial meeting with Pete, a junior accountant can begin reviewing the client's data as soon as Pete has started the initial client meeting. Three of these tasks must be done by Pete himself (tasks A, D, and G), and he can work on only one task at a time. The list of tasks, task descriptions, estimated task durations, and responsible persons is indicated in Table 10A.1. Since Pete hires only experienced junior accountants, they are able to perform any of the appropriate tasks; however, once a junior accountant has started a task, he is expected to complete the task without interruption or assistance.

During tax preparation season, Pete gets an average of three clients per week, although this number varies considerably (Pete's office is open only five days a week so that Pete can ski on the weekends). Since clients arrive randomly, the office often has more than one tax return in progress at any given time.

To increase his profits (and income), Pete is considering several alternatives. First, he has considered "downsizing" his practice and keeping only one junior accountant (who would work overtime if needed). Pete feels that this would reduce his costs while not significantly increasing the tax return preparation time. Since he charges a fixed rate per completed return, Pete believes that this is one way to increase profits.

Alternatively, Pete is considering an expansion that would increase the number of clients. Specifically, he is considering developing a tax preparation service that would offer services via the Internet (e.g., www.PeteMoss.com). Pete estimates that the cost of developing the Web site for this e-business would be a one-time charge of approximately $2,000. He also estimates that the nature of the tax preparation work would be unchanged from his core business and that he would be able to charge the same amount ($550 per return). However, a marketing research firm hired by Pete estimates that it would increase the average client arrival rate to 3.75 clients per week. (The marketing research firm also discovered that clients arrive according to a Poisson distribution.)

Pete has come to you for assistance and advice. Which strategy would you recommend that Pete adopt? Why? Should Pete start an e-business? If Pete adopts your suggested strategy, what is his expected increase in profits per week? Will Pete be able to offer the same high-quality (e.g., prompt) service to his clients?

FIGURE 10A.1
Tax Preparation
Task Descriptions

Task	Description	Immediate Predecessor(s)	Duration (Hours)	Responsible Person(s)
A	Initial client meeting	—	3.0	Pete
B	Review data from client	(Start of) A	3.0	Jr. Accountant
C	Input data into computer	B	2.0	Jr. Accountant
D	Review initial output	A, C	3.0	Pete
E	Check for missing forms	D	2.0	Jr. Accountant
F	Review relevant tax codes	D	1.5	Jr. Accountant
G	Final review and meeting with client	E, F	2.0	Pete

EPILOGUE

As with all management endeavors, much of project management is based on getting the basic "blocking and tackling" right. Most project managers maintain that effective communication is the most important part of successfully managing projects, and there is considerable evidence to support their claim [as Brooks (1995) notes, construction on the tower of Babel was almost immediately stopped as soon as different languages were introduced].

An examination of numerous projects indicates that four basic elements are critical to the successful completion of any project; projects that lack one or more of these elements are rarely viewed as successful when (and if) completed. These four elements are:

- Effective communication among all stakeholders,
- Strong commitment from top management,
- Well-defined goals and objectives,
- An effective monitoring and control system.

It is difficult to say which, if any, of these elements are more important than the others. Nor are these elements orthogonal. For example, an effective monitoring and control system is an integral part of a good communication system. Well-defined goals and objectives do not mean that changes are never made to a project, but that changes are made within well-defined bounds. With respect to IT projects, the negative impact of imprecise goals and creeping scope is illustrated by the Medicare transaction system case that is described at the end of Chapter 1.

All four factors are directly related to managing project risk and can be considered part of the preventive actions that were discussed in Chapter 7. Furthermore, by reducing project risk, we reduce the expected duration (makespan) of a project as discussed in Chapter 6, and increase the likelihood of meeting the project's deadline.

POST-PROJECT AUDITS

It is rare that any project is viewed as an unqualified success or failure. As noted in Chapter 1, even the movie *Titanic* significantly overran its budget and exceeded its planned schedule even though it is viewed as one of the most successful movie projects ever completed. A post-project audit allows us to learn what worked (and didn't work) in a project and, more important, transfer this knowledge to future projects.

All stakeholders should be involved in a post-project audit, including managers who may not have been a part of the project team itself. It is important to document all findings carefully as results from projects are frequently ignored or forgotten. Participants in the post-project audit should consider many factors, including:

- A review of the project plan and comparison of the plan to actual outcomes,
- Review of risk mitigation actions and actual outcomes,
- Parts of the project that were considered successful (and why),

- ■ Parts of the project that were considered not successful (and why),
- ■ How the project could have been improved.

Following a post-project audit, it is helpful for the project team (or members conducting the audit) to meet with project managers involved with similar projects or anyone who can benefit from the lessons learned. Post-project audits should be viewed as proactive events that can both improve future project management endeavors as well as help to identify new opportunities and markets. Only in this way will an organization and the people associated with that organization continue to expand their knowledge and improve their processes and positions.

COPILOT PORTABLE MARINE RADAR PROJECT

AN INTERACTIVE STUDY DESIGNED TO ILLUSTRATE THE PRINCIPLES INVOLVED IN DEVELOPING, TESTING, AND MARKETING A NEW PRODUCT IN A HIGH-TECH ENVIRONMENT*

BACKGROUND

Dr. Page Turner, a young and ambitious engineer who recently earned a doctorate in electrical engineering at the University of Washington, has been a long-time sailor and boating enthusiast in the Puget Sound area. As such, she has frequently wished for a small, compact, and inexpensive radar unit that she could use at night or in bad weather when it was difficult to identify other vessels and/or navigational aids.

Motivated by her sailing experience, she and several colleagues have, over the past three years, built several prototypes of a small hand-held radar unit, which they have named the Copilot Marine Radar. Two of their designs are indicated in this appendix. They recognize, however, that much work must be done before the design of such a radar can be finalized and the unit is manufactured and sold.

Through the Internet and professional organizations, Dr. Turner has learned that other companies are also developing similar radar units. Thus, she and her colleagues are interested in completing the design work and getting a unit to market as quickly as possible.

To successfully develop the Copilot Marine Radar, Dr. Turner has assembled a project team that includes a number of MBA's from the University of Washington. These MBA's, who have given up promising jobs with local dot-coms in exchange for an equity position in the project, have completed a work breakdown structure (WBS) for the project and identified a series of activities that must be completed in order to successfully market a handheld radar unit. These tasks (which include hiring qualified engineers, programmers, and technicians, acquiring lab space, securing financing, etc.) are listed and described on the "Activities Requirements Sheet"; the precedence relationship among these activities is indicated by the AON network in Figure A.1.

LABOR

Each company must hire technicians, programmers, and senior design engineers to successfully develop the new handheld marine radar unit. The expected time to complete many of these R&D activities is determined by the number of workers on the payroll. After each company has successfully developed a marine radar unit, assembly line workers must be

*Developed with J. Christopher Sandvig.

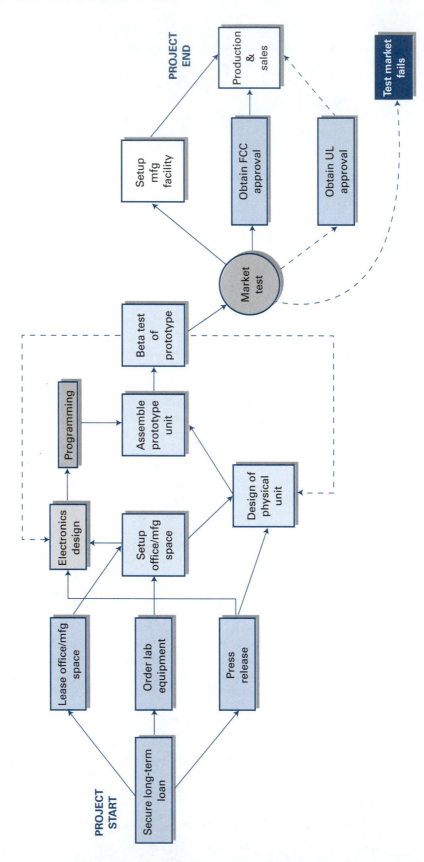

FIGURE A.1   Project Network

hired to produce the units for market. The timeline is shown in Figure A.2. Any number of available employees can be hired at the beginning of any week; technicians, programmers, and assembly line workers can be fired at any time (there are certain critical design phases during which senior design engineers cannot be fired). As soon as they are hired, however, all employees must be paid on a weekly basis.

Technicians

There are an unlimited number of available technicians. Technicians currently earn $2,000 per week; there is a one-time hiring fee of $500 for each technician hired. Technicians can also be hired from another team with their consent at any time; in this case, there is no hiring fee unless such fees are negotiated as part of the employee transfer. If a technician is fired, three weeks of severance pay must be paid.

Programmers

There are an unlimited number of available programmers. There is a one-time fee of $750 for each programmer hired. Programmers can also be hired from another team with their consent at any time; in this case, there is no hiring fee unless such fees are negotiated as part of the employee transfer. Programmers can be fired at any time with four weeks severance pay. Programmers earn $2,000 per week plus benefits (unlimited Pepsi and Twinkies); they can be fired at any time with four weeks severance pay.

Assembly Line Workers

There are an unlimited number of assembly line workers available in the market. Assembly line workers can produce a maximum of fifteen units per week and currently earn $1,000 per week; there is a one-time hiring fee of $500 for each assembly line worker hired and a one-time firing fee of $750 for each fired worker.

Assembly line workers require training for two weeks before they can begin working on the production line.

Senior Design Engineers

Senior design engineers currently earn a minimum of $4,000 per week. There are a total of five senior design engineers available in the local market with the expertise you need.

How can you hire a senior design engineer? If a senior design engineer is currently available (i.e., unemployed), he will accept your offer immediately and join your company for the current market wage (e.g., $4,000 per week). If there are no unemployed senior design engineers, you can still hire an engineer from another company by offering them a higher salary. However, the current company has the option of matching the offer; if his current salary is matched, the senior design engineer remains at his current job at the (new) higher salary. Under no circumstances can a team reduce a senior design engineer's

FIGURE A.2
Copilot Timeline

salary once he is on its payroll. A team can make, at most, one hiring offer for a senior design engineer each week, and each offer incurs a $5,000 fee to an executive search firm. If a senior design engineer is hired from a firm that has more than one design engineer on their payroll, it is assumed that the lowest-paid engineer is transferred to the new company. When a senior design engineer is hired, he is immediately added to the payroll. Once a team begins the "Design of Electronics and Circuits" task, its senior design engineers (up to a maximum of two) cannot be hired away or fired while the circuit design is in process. They can be fired at other times with severance pay equal to four weeks salary.

FINANCE

Each team must maintain a positive cash balance to meet its weekly expenses. You may raise capital by taking out a long-term, relatively low interest rate loan before you begin the project. No interest needs to be paid during development, but the bank demands $1.25 for every dollar borrowed when the loan is repaid at the end of the game.

The project team may also take out **emergency loans** at any time during the game, as cash is needed. These loans have relatively high interest rates (2 percent per week) and interest must be paid weekly, starting the week the loan is taken out. Emergency loans can only be taken in increments of $50,000 with weekly interest payments of $1,000 per $50,000 borrowed. Interest must be paid weekly until the principal is repaid using product revenues (principal can be repaid at any time but interest charges continue to accrue on any unpaid balance).

THE GAME

The Board

The game is played on a precedence network board supplied by the instructor. AON notation is used; that is, each node on the diagram represents an activity. The requirements for completing each activity are described in the *Activity Requirements Sheet.* Following standard project management assumptions, an activity cannot be started until all of its predecessor activities have been completed.

Monitoring Game Play

Each team maintains a *cash balance sheet* to track its cash balance and weekly expenses for salaries, rent, interest, etc. Each team also maintains a *calendar* indicating when future activities will occur (when that information becomes available).

Starting the Game

Before starting the project, each team rolls two dice in order to determine the order that teams will follow in trying to hire senior design engineers. The team with the highest total number always proceeds first, followed by other teams in numerical sequence (e.g., if Team #3 has the highest number on the dice, then—assuming five teams—the progression is Teams #3, 4, 5, 1, 2).

Secure Venture Financing (Long-Term Loan)

Before you start the game, each team may secure a long-term loan from the Warranty Trust Bank. All money borrowed must be repaid at the end of the game along with an interest payment equal to 25 percent of the total amount borrowed. There is also a 1 percent loan fee that is paid "up-front" when the loan is secured.

Playing the Game

A week represents one turn of the game. At the beginning of each week (after negotiating a long-term loan), each team makes hiring and firing decisions (including a senior design engineer), and then proceeds with feasible tasks. At the end of the week, each team reports its current status. A team may start any activity if all of its predecessor activities have been completed. After each team has completed an activity, it marks the activity 'completed' with a colored dot. All relevant information is also entered on each team's calendar and cash balance sheet.

Mergers and Acquisitions

At any time, two or more teams can agree to merge. If they do so, then the new (merged) team acquires the combined debt of both teams up to the time of merger; after that time, they operate as a single team. It is assumed that the new (merged) team has finished all tasks completed by either team.

If one team purchases another team, then the acquiring team assumes both the debt of the purchased team as well as any cost of purchase. With respect to the design characteristics of a team's radar unit, any radar unit that has a different number of features is considered to be a new product—although any remaining time in the development cycle of the *acquired* team is reduced by one-half. For example, assume that a team has successfully completed the development of a radar unit with no features and currently has that unit in production. If they acquire a team that is developing a radar unit with, say, five features, the new (merged) team cannot sell the more advanced radar unit until it has been successfully developed, test-marketed, etc. In this case, however, the time to complete each step in the development process is calculated normally—and then reduced by a factor of one-half.

Licensing Technology

At any time, a team that has successfully developed a marine radar unit can license their developed technology to another team. The team that has bought this technology sells the product in exactly the same way as if they had developed the product themselves. Licensing fees can be in the form of a single (one-time) fee or can be negotiated on a royalty basis (i.e., a part of the selling price goes back to the licensing firm). Specific arrangements are negotiated between individual teams.

Ending the Game

The game ends when all teams have started commercial production of the new radar unit or withdrawn from the market (i.e., filed for bankruptcy) and the last team to enter the market has generated three weeks of sales.

The first team to enter the market receives a bonus of $750,000 from foreign licensing agreements, the second team receives $500,000, and the third team to enter the market receives $250,000. (Other teams receive no foreign licensing payments.)

When the game ends, each team should calculate their average weekly demand during the last three weeks of the game and assume that this demand will continue for one more year (fifty-two weeks). At the end of the one-year period, the effective life of the marine radar unit ends as it is superceded by new technologies. Weekly profits during this 52-week period are calculated as follows:

[(Average demand for last 3 weeks) × (Selling Price)] — [Weekly rents/salaries/expenses]

After all loans and interest have been paid, the team that has earned the highest profit wins the game, the team with the next highest profit takes second place, etc.

ACTIVITY REQUIREMENTS SHEET

Lease Office/Manufacturing Space

As soon as your long-term loan is arranged, you must rent a location for your office, R&D, and manufacturing space. Your real estate agent, Ms. Holly Park, has identified two possible sites. The first location becomes available next week with a rental fee of $2,500/week and requires a $30,000 non-refundable deposit. The second location costs $1,000/week (with no deposit); however, there is some uncertainty when this space will become available since the space is currently occupied. If you select the second space, roll a die once per week until you roll a 3 or less; as soon as you are successful, the space is immediately available.

Order Lab Equipment

You can purchase lab equipment from either of two vendors: Slickquick and Pennycrawl. Pennycrawl offers you a good deal on the equipment, everything you need for only $125,000, but delivery time can be erratic. Slickquick, on the other hand, guarantees on-time delivery, but charges $200,000 for the same equipment. Equipment cannot be delivered until the space is available. Payment is made when equipment is delivered.

If you selected Pennycrawl, roll a die once per turn until you roll a 2 or less (if successful, Pennycrawl will deliver your equipment in one week). If you selected Slickquick, the equipment is delivered in exactly four weeks. Select a vendor and pay the appropriate amount.

If you select Slickquick, it is assumed that the contract with Slickquick cannot be cancelled once it is announced. However, if you select Pennycrawl and do not succeed in rolling a 2 or less in any given week, you have the option of switching vendors in the following week. (For example, if you are unsuccessful in rolling a 2 or less in week #4, then you cannot sign a contract with Slickquick until week #5. Lab equipment will then be delivered at the beginning of week #9.)

Press Release

After securing your long-term loan, you hold a press conference to publicly announce your team's efforts to develop a portable marine radar unit. During the conference some unpleasant questions are raised about past business dealings of your team members. Roll a die to determine if the local paper takes a positive or negative position toward your project. If you roll a 2 or less, the paper prints a negative article and you must hire a public relations firm (at a cost of $20,000) to overcome the bad publicity. If you receive bad publicity, it takes three weeks to conduct a media campaign to overcome this bad publicity. Otherwise, the press release is completed in one week.

Setup Manufacturing/Office Space

Once the manufacturing and office space has been leased and the equipment has been delivered, it takes one week to set up the facilities before design work can begin.

Design of Physical Unit

The mechanical engineers working on the physical design indicate that the design time is very sensitive to the number of technicians on the payroll. Roll one die. If the number on the die is less than or equal to the number of technicians on your payroll, the design task is completed in one week. Technicians must remain on the payroll for the remainder of this task. If the number you roll is greater than the number of technicians on your payroll, you will have to repeat the process the following week; continue trying each week until the design is successful.

Design of Electronics and Circuits

The time needed to complete the electronic design is determined by two factors: the number of senior design engineers on your payroll and the number of features you select for the radar unit.

There are five possible features:

1. 110 VAC built-in adapter
2. GPS (Global Positioning System) interface
3. Variable range option
4. Low power standby option
5. Anchoring (warning) zone alarm

The time needed to complete the electronic design is given by the following equation:

$$\text{Time} = \left\lceil \frac{(D)(F+1)}{N+1} \right\rceil$$

where

D = random number thrown on a die,
F = number of features selected, and
N = number of senior design engineers on your staff $(0 < N \leq 2)$

and $[x]$ indicates the smallest integer greater than or equal to x.

For example, if you select four features (F =4), roll a three on the die (D =3), and have one senior design engineer on your staff (N =1), then

$$\text{Time} = \left\lceil \frac{(3)(4+1)}{1+1} \right\rceil = \left\lceil \frac{(3)(5)}{2} \right\rceil = \lceil 7.5 \rceil = 8 \text{ weeks}$$

Note that this function cannot be completed unless there is at least one senior design engineer on your staff, and having more than one senior engineer results in no additional benefits.

Programming

Programming is a major part of the design of the radar unit since the software will determine how the unit will operate. Once the design of the electronics is completed, programming can begin. The programming instructions, after being written and fully tested, are then placed on ROM (Read-Only Memory) chips that become part of the radar unit. To find out how long this task takes, roll two dice. If the total number on both dice is less than or equal to the number of programmers on your staff, then you have successfully completed the programming task this week. If not, you must roll the dice again next week and continue in this manner until you are successful.

Assembly Prototype Unit

Once the programming and the design of the physical unit are completed, you can assemble a prototype unit. Roll a die, divide the number on the die by 2, and round up to the nearest integer to determine the number of weeks needed to complete this task. The same number of technicians is needed to complete this task as required to design the physical unit.

Beta Test of Prototype

The prototype Copilot Radar is now subjected to both field and laboratory tests in which the unit is tested under various external conditions (e.g., weather, usage, etc.). This task takes three weeks to complete and requires the same number of technicians as was needed to assemble the prototype unit. At the end of the beta test, you will find out if the prototype fails the beta test and if parts of the unit need to be redesigned. To determine if the prototype fails, roll two dice; the total number on both dice is used to determine the following outcomes:

# on Dice	Outcome
2	Failure of both mechanical and electronics; must return to both functions
3	Mechanical failure; must return to "Design of the Physical Unit"
4	Electronics failure; must return to "Design of Electronics and Circuits"
5 or greater	Prototype passes beta tests

Market Test

Once the beta test is successfully completed, the Copilot Radar Unit can be test marketed. This task includes the use of focus groups and limited advertising campaigns in a few selected cities. Roll two dice. If the total number on both dice equals twelve, the market test fails and indicates that there is virtually no demand for the Copilot Marine Radar unit; in this case, the game ends for your team.

The number of weeks needed to complete the market test is determined by the smaller number on the two dice (e.g., if the two dice showed 4 and 6, then the test market task would be completed in 4 weeks).

Set Up Manufacturing Facility

Once the market test is completed, you must set up the manufacturing facility. Production equipment must be purchased, and it is expensive and temperamental. You have a choice: buy the highest quality equipment for $200,000 and proceed with a roll of 4 or less or buy the "Econo-line" equipment for $100,000 and proceed with a roll of 2 or less. Keep trying, one roll per week, until you get the equipment to work. You only need to purchase equipment once.

Obtain FCC Approval

Once the market test is completed, you must hire lawyers to negotiate with the FCC for their approval (you cannot sell a radar unit until you have FCC approval). You can choose experienced lawyers for $25,000 or inexperienced lawyers for $10,000. Experienced lawyers will get you through with a roll of 4 or less, inexperienced lawyers with a roll of 2 or less. If you don't get approval, try again next week. You must pay your lawyers on each try.

Obtain UL (Underwriters Laboratory) Approval

You might want to have UL approval of your Copilot Marine Radar before you put the unit on the market. To determine if you get UL approval, choose a number between zero and six; multiply this number times $5,000 to determine the UL application cost. Roll a die. If the number on the die is equal to or less than your chosen number, you get UL approval. (If you selected the number six, it's not necessary to roll a die as you get automatic approval; if you selected zero, you do not have to roll a die as you have obviously decided to forgo UL approval.) If you don't get UL approval, you must reduce your selling price by $50 per unit.

If you apply for UL approval, the process takes one week. If you decide not to apply for UL approval, there is no time required for this activity and it can be ignored.

Production and Sales

Once you have set up your manufacturing facility, hired assembly line workers, and secured FCC approval (UL approval is optional), you can begin to produce and sell radar units. Remember that each assembly line worker can produce a maximum of fifteen units per week, and it takes two weeks to train a new assembly line worker before she can be used on the production line. Assembly line workers can be hired or fired at the beginning of each week that the game is being played.

Selling Price

The market price for your radar unit is a function of the number of other competitors on the market (regardless of the design of their units) and the number of features built into your unit. The following table determines the selling price:

	Total Number of Companies Selling Portable Marine Radar Units				
No. of Features	1	2	3	4	5
0	$1,000	$ 850	$ 700	$ 550	$ 400
1	1,125	975	825	675	525
2	1,250	1,100	950	800	650
3	1,375	1,225	1,075	925	775
4	1,500	1,350	1,200	1,050	900
5	1,625	1,475	1,325	1,175	1,025

Remember to subtract $50 per unit if you don't have UL approval

Market Demand

To find the weekly market demand, each team rolls two dice and divides the sum of the number on the dice by the total number of companies (including yours) selling portable marine radar units. Take the resulting number and multiply by 20; round up to the nearest integer. (For example, if you roll an "8" and there are three companies on the market, then the market demand is 54 units this week.) In general,

Weekly Sales = Minimum (Market Demand, Production Capacity)

where the production capacity is determined by the number of assembly line workers on your payroll. Multiply weekly sales times the selling price to find the weekly revenue.

INDEX

Free slack, 91–92
Functional matrix, 73

G

Gantt charts, 18, 95–96, 184, 210
    drawing, using MS-Excel, 103
Gated approach, 219
Goes-into chart, 43
Group cohesiveness, balance between group contentiousness and, 66–67
Group contentiousness, balance between group cohesiveness and, 66–67
Group size, relationship between project performance and, 67

H

Health Care Financing Administration, Medicare transactions and, 19–21
Heuristic algorithms for renewable resource allocation problem, 187–89
Heuristics
    parallel, 188–89
    serial, 188
High-tech project, 5
Hurdle rate, 26

I

Impact analysis, 170
Incentives, project teams and, 69, 220–21
Independent slack, 92
Indirect costs, consideration of, in budget, 108, 109
Informal monitoring systems, 205
Information technology (IT) projects, 1
    outcomes, 10–11
    success of, 2
Internal rate of return (IRR), 27
Intraproject coordination, 73
Intra-team communication, relationship between team size and, 67
Inventory costs, 126–28

L

Life-cycle phases, 43
Linear contract, 77
Linear programming (LP) formulations, 93–95
Linear programming (LP) model, 113
    for time-cost trade-offs, 117–21
Linear time-cost trade-offs, 117–21

Loss leader, 107
Low-tech projects, 5

M

Makespan, 87
Manufacturing process change, 6
Mars Climate Orbiter mission, 11
Mars Lander project, 7, 107
Master production schedule (MPS), 128
Material costs, 126–28
    consideration of, in budget, 108
Material requirements planning (MRP) system, 128–29
Mathematical programming formulation for Activity-on-Arc networks, 99–100
Matrix organization, 72–74, 75
    balanced, 73, 76
    functional, 73
    project, 73, 76
Mean flow due-date rule, 222
Medium-tech projects, 5
Microsoft Project, 194
Minimum late finish time based on the due date, 221
Minimum slack based on the due date, 221
Minimum task duration from shortest remaining project, 222
Minimum total cost project plan rule, 107
Money, time value of, 112
Monitoring, earned value approach to, 207–13
Monitoring system, designing effective, 205–7
Monte-Carlo simulation models, 16, 143–49, 168
    with discrete probability distributions, 145–46
MS-Excel, drawing Gantt chart using, 103
Multifunctional project teams, 3–4
Multiple projects, multitasking with, 218–20
Multiproject environment, allocating resources and setting due dates in dynamic, 221
Multitasking with multiple projects, 218–20
Myers-Briggs Type Indicator, 68

N

Net present value (NPV), 25–27, 30, 114
    impact of cash flows on, 112
    relationships between dollar-months and, 133–34
Net present value (NPV)/discounted cash flow (DCF), 24
New product development, 1
    cycling in precedence networks, 146–49
Nonlinear time-cost trade-offs, 121–23
Nonrenewable resources, 181